The Original

Rush
Limbaugh

Missouri Biography Series   William E. Foley, Editor

University of Missouri Press   Columbia and London

The Original

Rush
Limbaugh

Lawyer, Legislator,
and **Civil Libertarian**

Dennis K. **Boman**

Copyright ©2012 by
The Curators of the University of Missouri
University of Missouri Press, Columbia, Missouri 65201
Printed and bound in the United States of America
All rights reserved
5 4 3 2 1   16 15 14 13 12

Cataloging-in-Publication data available from the Library of Congress.
ISBN 978-0-8262-1980-0

∞™ This paper meets the requirements of the
American National Standard for Permanence of Paper
for Printed Library Materials, Z39.48, 1984.

Design and composition: Jennifer Cropp
Printer and binder: Thomson-Shore, Inc.
Typefaces: Minion and Abadi

Cartoon page vi, by Daniel Fitzpatrick, reproduced
courtesy of the State Historical Society of Missouri

For Jillon

THE STORK THAT FAILED.

Contents

Preface

Rush Hudson Limbaugh Sr. was in Kansas City, Missouri for the 1991 annual meeting of the Missouri Bar. He had served a term as president of the bar some thirty-five years before. Although now advanced in years, he still practiced law in the Cape Girardeau firm he had founded in the 1920s. With him in Kansas City were a number of family members, including his grandson and namesake, radio talk show host Rush H. Limbaugh III. The family was there to mark the occasion of Rush Sr.'s one hundredth birthday. He and several family members were driven from the Hyatt Regency Crown Center to KMVZ Radio where Rush interviewed the centenarian on his syndicated radio show. The radio station, which had fired Rush in 1983, pulled out all the stops to give his grandfather "the red carpet treatment," sending a limousine and having a large birthday cake prepared. Always "impeccably dressed" in suit and tie, the patriarch sat in the studio with his grandson awaiting the interview. For him this was a rare occasion in the national spotlight. Only once before, in 1935, when he had presided over a sensational kidnapping trial in St. Louis, had he been the focus of the national media. Surprised by the fame and attention, he had held the hearings with care and courage despite receiving a number of anonymous death threats. Now, fifty-six years later, his grandson proudly introduced "Pop" to the country.[1]

In the interview, Rush first extolled his grandfather's virtues and mentioned some of his accomplishments. These included winning the highest awards in college debate and oration, appointment as editor-in-chief of a student newspaper, election as state legislator, author of scholarly books and articles, appointments as special commissioner by the St. Louis Court of Appeals and the Supreme Court of Missouri, representative of the United States to India as a goodwill ambassador, and service upon civil rights commissions to establish equal rights for African Americans. To his grandson's praise, however, he replied with unfeigned modesty that "I am just a country boy." Later, when he remained reluctant to speak of his accomplishments, Rush admonished him not to be modest. Nevertheless, to this his grandfather responded simply that he "was never much of a man to strut." During the interview he discussed growing up on a farm, being educated in a one-room schoolhouse, and his decision at the age of sixteen to become a lawyer. To him the Constitution of the United States was almost a sacred document, for upon it order, the rule of law, and important protections of individual liberties were founded. For this reason he considered it a great privilege to serve his community as a lawyer. His conservatism developed naturally from the conviction that the United States' constitutional system must be preserved and interpreted as it was understood by the generation which had ratified it.[2]

As the program progressed, Rush noticed that his grandfather, who sat relaxed during the commercials and was the "same old Pop just as you knew him at Thanksgiving or Christmas," was somewhat transformed when the interview resumed. Then his "head jerked, the shoulders squared, and he assumed the posture of statesman-diplomat." Moreover, Rush was amazed that at one hundred years of age his grandfather spoke fluently without "los[ing] his train of thought." To fill a short segment of the show, Rush asked his grandfather about the controversy surrounding the nomination of Judge Clarence Thomas to the Supreme Court of the United States. The centenarian registered his surprise at the opposition, noting that Thomas was clearly a fine and intelligent lawyer and a good man. Moreover, he expressed surprise that some members of the black community opposed him. Finally, both discussed the ramifications of the United States' development into a great world power. During this discussion, Rush Sr. extemporaneously expounded upon late nineteenth- and much of twentieth-century history, often providing dates and names of the major actors of various important events. In particular, he credited President Theodore Roosevelt with having strengthened the country by expanding and modernizing the Navy, thereby enabling the United States to project power beyond its shores. This expansion of power was possible, he believed, because of the United States' unique constitutional and economic system.[3]

Before the interview of his grandfather had begun, Rush had noted that some of the personnel of KMVZ Radio had seemed worried about interviewing a centenarian live on the air. As the program progressed, however, "the crowd in the production room on the other side of the glass had grown and grown and grown." By the end, "everybody in the radio station" was there watching and were "enthralled," for the elderly man possessed "a dramatic way of making a point; a dramatic way of telling a story." Afterward Rush related that his grandfather "went in and had some birthday cake and thanked [the radio personnel] profusely."[4]

While Rush finished his three-hour show, his grandfather and the rest of the family traveled back to the Hyatt Regency Crown Center to attend a luncheon of the Missouri Bar. Because of the radio interview they arrived late and sought to make their way unobtrusively to the front of the banquet hall where a table was reserved for the family. As soon as Rush Sr. entered, however, murmurs were heard throughout the crowd of 600 or 700 people, who spontaneously rose to their feet and gave him a standing ovation. This expression of appreciation overwhelmed him and he didn't know how to respond. Doreen Dodson, who was then serving as president of the Missouri Bar, having learned that the conference coincided with the centennial birthday of Missouri's oldest practicing lawyer, had made special preparations to commemorate this milestone during the evening banquet which concluded the annual meeting. Unknown to him, Dodson had a birthday cake prepared which was brought out to the singing of "Happy Birthday." Despite believing that no such fuss should be made over him, for, as he put it, "all I did was survive," it was apparent to her that he enjoyed the attention, smiling and speaking to those nearby. Dodson remembered him as a funny and witty man. "Everybody loved him; he was Missouri law."[5]

This biography tells the story of Limbaugh's rise from the farm to preeminence as a lawyer, philanthropist, and civil libertarian. Born only twenty-six years after the American Civil War ended, Limbaugh's life spanned a period of remarkable change. During this time, horses and mules were replaced by automobiles, while aircraft quickened and revolutionized travel. When he was still on the farm, communications were slow and one could not expect to learn about most events, even those happening nearby, until several days after their occurrence. By the end of his life, however, the advent of radio, television, telephone, and satellite communications made possible the instantaneous broadcast of events occurring thousands of miles away. Limbaugh lived through two economic depressions, two world wars, observed the use of atomic weapons, the Apollo moon walks, and the rise and fall of the Soviet Union. Throughout all of this, he demonstrated a remarkable zest for life and interest in his family, community, country, and the world. Indeed, his famous namesake believed that perhaps his defining characteristic was intellectual curiosity. "Life to him was a learning experience." Not content simply to observe the world about him, Rush Sr. helped to shape events through the practice of law, participation in politics, and the promotion of philanthropic causes and civil rights. His professional conduct personified that of the "lawyer-statesman," providing wise counsel and representation to his clients and many pro bono services to charities and society throughout his life. Among his descendants he is remembered affectionately as "Pop"; a caring, generous, and thoughtful father, grandfather, and great-grandfather, who exemplified the devoted husband and family man. Moreover, he was the very embodiment of the Christian gentleman, a believer who lived his faith and sought to make himself of service to God and others.[6]

Acknowledgments

Without the help of many people this biography would not have been possible. Foremost of these was former Federal Judge Stephen N. Limbaugh Sr., who made available his father's papers and graciously submitted to several hours of taped interviews. He also answered many queries by phone and email. His son, Federal Judge Stephen N. Limbaugh Jr., who is now the sitting judge at the federal courthouse named for his grandfather, introduced me to family members and others who had known his grandfather, and answered questions as well.

I am grateful to Manley and Mary Limbaugh, the son and daughter-in-law of Rush H. Limbaugh Sr. They willingly and candidly answered my questions, adding invaluable insights into Limbaugh's character and activities. Their son Daniel B. Limbaugh provided the vast majority of the early correspondence between his paternal grandparents during their courtship and also helped me better to understand his grandfather's attitudes toward the Vietnam War. I especially enjoyed going with him and his father Manley to the Limbaugh farm to see the old family homestead where Rush Limbaugh Sr. was born and raised and where several family members were buried. I am also indebted to Mike Kasten, who leases the Limbaugh farm and showed us where various buildings, cisterns, and other features were located. His insights about the agricultural operations were particularly helpful.

A number of other family members agreed to interviews and provided a great deal of insight into Limbaugh's life and character. His grandson David Limbaugh was especially helpful in better understanding his grandfather's last years and the details of the final illness of his father Rush H. Limbaugh Jr. The interview of Rush H. Limbaugh III also added important information, in particular concerning the interview of his grandfather on the occasion of his centennial birthday on his radio program. Doreen Dodson, then president of the Missouri Bar, added other details otherwise unknown concerning Limbaugh's activities at the professional conference coinciding with his one hundredth birthday. Another family member, Helen Gillespie, the niece of Rush Limbaugh Sr., recalled for me her time living with the Limbaughs as a college student during World War Two.

Very important to learning and comprehending many of the details of Rush Limbaugh Sr.'s activities as a member of the Missouri Commission on Human Rights were the recollections of Lewis A. Akenhead, who in the 1960s worked as a field representative of the commission under Limbaugh's supervision. Larry Carp, Limbaugh's fellow commissioner, provided his unique perspective and memories during this time as well. Sherwood and Robert Wise helped in understanding Limbaugh's activities on the Special Commission on Civil Rights and Racial Unrest upon which their father Sherwood W. Wise was a fellow member. Amy Nickless, then a student at Southeast Missouri State University, made an important contribution to understanding Limbaugh's intellectual life when she found, catalogued, and made available for reading in the Honors House that part of his library donated to the Honors Program after his death.

Finally, I would be remiss if I did not mention others I interviewed, each contributing important information and insights. They are Harold Whitfield, Lloyd Smith, Glenda Wunderlich, and Congresswoman Jo Ann Emerson.

The Original

Rush
Limbaugh

Chapter One

Farm Boy

During the nineteenth century, many advancements in technology, energy, and communications revolutionized the production of goods and transportation. These innovations, however, scarcely affected the lives of Americans living in isolated rural communities throughout the country. During the last decade of the 1800s, the georgic rhythms and methods of cultivation continued very much as they had when Thomas Jefferson was president. To break the soil one still guided a plow behind draft animals and planted seed by hand. Most travel was on foot or horseback, although longer distances could be traversed by railroad or boat. Into this world, on a small farm in southeastern Missouri, Rush Hudson Limbaugh was born on September 27, 1891 to Joseph and Susan Limbaugh. While the particulars of his birth are unknown, without a hospital nearby and with only a few doctors in the region, a local woman probably assisted Susan when her time came. Whatever the circumstances of his birth, the boy was the last of the couple's children. While by today's standard the family was large, Rush being the seventh surviving child, the size of their family was not unusual for the era. The boy was named in part to please his maternal grandmother, whose maiden name was Hudson, and in part because his father Joseph liked the sound of Rush Hudson, a name borne by a distant relative.[1]

The family, although poor, was well-respected and hardworking, maintaining a farm of just over 400 acres. While half the land was arable, the bottom land was the most fertile and was situated "in parcels along the creek" amounting to a little more than 30 acres in all. On this and other less productive land, "row crops" such as beans, wheat, and corn, were cultivated. The rest of the farm was composed of "ridge land," which was used as pasture to graze stock, and of timber along the Little Muddy Creek. This small waterway, which sometimes flooded the bottom land, cut through the middle of the farm in a northwesterly to a southeasterly direction. At different times it had been called Anthony or Limbaugh Creek as well. Rush lived his first fifteen years upon this farm learning to cultivate crops, tend livestock, and to accomplish many other tasks necessary for the family's livelihood. His father, Joseph, had bought out his brothers' stakes in the farm, and while still a bachelor lived with his mother in the log cabin constructed by Rush's paternal grandfather, Daniel R. Limbaugh.[2]

Apparently, until two generations before Rush's birth, the line of the Limbaugh clan from which he descended had filled important judicial, political, and military positions in Pennsylvania, North Carolina, and Missouri. The first of the clan to journey to North America was Johannes Michael Limbaugh—who originally spelled his surname *Limbach*. Born in Germany in 1708, Johannes was the great-great-great grandfather of Rush. Johannes had immigrated with his wife Maria Margaret and their son Frederick, arriving in Philadelphia on the ship *Brothers* probably in 1752. Unfortunately, little is known about Johannes, who settled in Pennsylvania and died in 1769 at Upper Milford and was followed in death five years later by his wife. More, however, is known about Frederick, who had been born in Baden-Baden, Germany in 1737. He became a prominent member of his community, serving as a justice of the peace, a major in the second battalion of the Northampton County Militia, was elected to the state assembly, and was a judge in the county court. In the late 1780s he moved to Mecklinburg County, North Carolina. Later Frederick with his son Michael, at the urging of Frederick Bollinger, moved west crossing the Mississippi River into Missouri, then part of French territory, on January 1, 1800. Other family members followed them settling nearby in the Whitewater region of southeastern Missouri. At the town of Cape Girardeau, situated on the Mississippi River, Frederick served as one of the territorial judges with Louis Lorimier, the town's founder. Thus in Frederick began a family tradition of employment in the law in different capacities, which was resumed by Rush and is continued by some of his descendants to this day. Frederick died in 1815.[3]

Frederick's son Henry, born in 1775, remained in North Carolina until 1811 when he followed his father to southeastern Missouri. Little is known about Henry's circumstances in North Carolina and why he had not relocated with his father and brother eleven years earlier. As his great-grandson Rush later noted, Henry and his wife were "evidently very poor" and traveled "in an ox-drawn covered wagon with their five children . . . establishing their residence on a tract of land where I was born." According to family lore, they arrived a short time before the New Madrid fault earthquakes and aftershocks, which began on December 16, 1811, and continued for several months afterward. This unusual seismic activity manifested in a series of powerful quakes, three of which exceeded an 8.0 magnitude, with aftershocks that numbered in the thousands. From the epicenter, located in southeastern Missouri and northeastern Arkansas, the most violent quakes were felt as far away as Québec City, Canada, a distance of over 1,300 miles. According to eyewitness accounts, the first of the three most powerful earthquakes began around two o'clock in the morning, awakening the inhabitants in the region with a tremendous boom and violent shaking, a nightmare which was followed by a number of lesser aftershocks that morning.[4]

In 1973 a seismologist estimated this first earthquake at 8.6 on the Richter scale—a magnitude of great power. The next severe earthquake on January 23, 1812, was 8.4, and the most powerful of all was an 8.7 on February 7. According to eyewitnesses along the Mississippi River, many of its vertical banks collapsed, water levels rose and fell dramatically, and the channels were altered. The most dramatic effect, however, was the temporary reversal of the river's current for a few hours on February 7. This event was probably caused by the violent upheaval of the riverbed, creating a back current which swept away "whole groves of cottonwood trees" and left behind two sets of falls, one a mile above the town of New Madrid and the other eight miles below. In a few days these falls disappeared as erosion quickly leveled the riverbed. Moreover, land in the epicenter collapsed in some places and was lifted in others forming ponds and lakes. In some regions rich agricultural land was turned into marsh, leading Congress to pass legislation allowing its owners to apply for New Madrid land grants to swap their ruined farms for unsettled public lands. Considering the trauma these events must have caused the family, it is not surprising that stories of their experiences were passed down through the generations and are vaguely remembered today by some members of the family two hundred years later. After such an experience, Henry and his family no doubt questioned the wisdom of settling in such a place, although perhaps other inhabitants assured them that nothing like this had happened before. In the end they remained and were the first of the family to settle upon the homestead where Rush was born and raised.[5]

Henry and his wife Maria raised five children, four of whom were boys. All of them settled nearby while the second oldest, Daniel R., Rush's paternal grandfather, took over his father Henry's place. After his first wife had died, Daniel married Delilah Shell, the "daughter of Michael Shell, a soldier of the Revolution, who was in the Battle of Lookout Mountain." Rush remembered his paternal grandmother well, for when he was a boy she lived in a log cabin located a short distance from their home. Before her death, which occurred when Rush was only five years old, his grandmother left behind stories of her father's Revolutionary War adventures and hardships, which Rush remembered the details of many years later. Moreover, Rush and the rest of the family were told of the sad details of his paternal grandfather's death on their farm in September 1862. Different versions of this tragedy have come down through the family. These all agree, however, that Daniel had become embroiled in a dispute with another man, either a local teacher who boarded at their home or a rejected suitor to one of his daughters, and that he had been killed in the fight that ensued.[6]

Joseph took over his father's farm and apparently remained in the log cabin with his mother until at some unknown time, perhaps before his first marriage, when he built the home in which Rush and his siblings were born. Joseph's first wife died from smallpox only four months after their marriage and Joseph, who also contracted the deadly disease, almost succumbed to it as well. The two-story home was rectangular in shape and had no running water, plumbing, electricity, or any of the other conveniences often taken for granted today. A large fireplace in the west room on the first floor provided the Limbaughs with their primary source of heat and was the main gathering place of the family in the evenings. At night when the weather was cool, this fire supplied the chief source of light as well. While lamps were also available, the expense of coal oil probably limited their use given the Limbaughs' modest income. A smaller fireplace was located on the east end of the house. No fireplaces or stoves were available on the second floor of their home. The kitchen was joined to the west end of the house where heat from its stove would not intensify their discomfort during the hot summer months. Rush remembered sleeping with his parents until he was three and then joining his brothers, Roscoe and Burette, who were closest to him in age, in the trundle bed which was stored under their parents' bed during the day. Later this trio removed to the upstairs and joined their older brother Arthur who slept in one room and where in another the three girls Jennie, Hattie, and Lillie stayed.[7]

The front porch looked out upon the yard where fruit and nut trees provided welcome variety to the Limbaughs' diet during the summer. From the west end of the house a foot path led some 200 feet to the log cabin where "Granny" remained until she could no longer take care of herself and moved the short distance to her son's home. This path also led to a cistern, where the family's water supply was located. Other outbuildings and structures near the house included a chicken house, goose nests, a smokehouse, a wheat house, and a barn surrounded by a horse lot. Draft animals and the milk cows were stabled in the barn where hay and corn were stored. In the surrounding fields and woods roamed cattle, pigs, and sheep. When it was time to feed the hogs, Rush remembered his father calling them with "a deep voice that carried far." These animals provided meat and homemade sausage for the family, a good portion of which was preserved in the smokehouse where the kraut and sorghum barrels were kept as well. In the cellar beneath their home was stored the milk, the hand-churned butter, and canned fruits and vegetables which came from the family garden.[8]

Although he died when Rush was only seven years old, Joseph had a profound impact upon his youngest son. His first memory of his father was of a tall man "nearly 6 feet, [who] had thick dark hair, gray eyes, and wore a mustache. He [had] . . . a stern countenance, stood erectly as a soldier, and walked rapidly. He was slim in figure, agile in movement, and determined in purpose." Many years later, Rush remembered how he had felt as "a boy, small, walking in his shadow, subject to his will, dependent upon his guidance." Because he was too small to labor on the farm and could not attend school until he was six, Rush spent a great deal of time with his father as soon as he was old enough to accompany him around the farm. As was the custom of the time, and out of necessity, all the members of a farm family worked long days in all kinds of weather. Rush remembered that everyone worked at an early age and "the large part of our time for both men and women was spent on the outside, in the garden, in the fields, sowing, cultivating and harvesting the things that provided for our existence."[9]

Rush's father usually arose around four o'clock in the morning to start the fire and feed the livestock, and then awakened the oldest children first, who attended to their morning tasks. As the youngest, Rush remembered waiting until the last possible moment, especially on very cold mornings, to leave his warm bed to begin the day. Everyone was up early to eat "a hearty breakfast," and was expected to be in the field before the sun had risen, "for my father never let the sun beat him to the field." While together, which was most of the day, Rush's father taught him "how to count, the names of the domestic animals, the names and purposes of tools and utensils," and much other useful information. Rush also learned by observing his father and the others as they plowed the fields; planted, tended, and harvested crops; built fences; sawed lumber; broke horses and mules; and accomplished other tasks around the farm. While everyone worked hard, they also shared camaraderie and a sense of fun, sometimes playing jokes on other members of the family. Of course, Rush was not exempt from this, even at the age of three. Inquisitive at that age, Rush remembered walking alone to a field where his father and brother Arthur were plowing straw into the soil to prevent erosion. As a joke, and probably to see how he would react, Joseph tossed some straw in the direction of the curious lad, who beat a quick retreat to avoid the straw from falling on him. The two laughed, enjoying the young boy's reaction, a welcome momentary break from their work.[10]

Not long after this incident, Rush learned of just one of the many dangers which might befall a small boy on the farm when, while playing near a hot pot of soup, he lost his balance and placed his foot directly into it, scalding himself severely. Fortunately, Rush's mother Susan was "an expert in home remedies." She made a poultice of baking soda but the pain of the burn was too great for Rush to tolerate it. She then sprinkled baking soda directly on his injured foot, along with some sorghum molasses, which soon relieved the pain.[11]

Other memories from this period, however, were happier, and Rush recalled them many years later with nostalgia, for as the youngest he was often indulged by his parents and siblings and encouraged in his desire to make contributions to the family. Thus, when young Rush desired to gather a goose egg for breakfast one morning, his oldest brother Arthur kindly agreed to accompany him to the goose nests. Because they would need to steal the prize before breakfast,

Rush gained the privilege of sleeping with his brother upstairs, which he re-membered made him feel "unusually important as [he] cuddled next to him in the warm bed." The anticipation and thrill of this adventure caused Rush to awaken early and to begin fidgeting until Arthur awoke also. Anxious to discover whether the goose had laid an egg, Rush suggested that they go im-mediately. Although it was before his regular time to rise, Arthur indulgently helped his youngest sibling to dress, readied himself, and then quietly escorted Rush out of the house to the goose nest. When he attempted to reach under the goose, she clucked a warning, causing him to withdraw his hand. However, Ar-thur reassured him and directed that he try again. In the end, Rush was able to remove the egg and return home with it in triumph to show his parents, who were then just rising for the day. Reflecting upon this incident ninety years lat-er, Rush was impressed that his fourteen-year-old brother "had gone through this night and early morning venture to please me and during the time had not scolded or shown impatience or spoken other than in brotherly happiness to help me attain one of my early childhood joys."[12]

As he grew older, Rush was expected to do what he could around the farm and at first was given simple tasks to perform which, nevertheless, were im-portant and beneficial to the family. At the age of five, his mother directed him to carry a bucket of water to his brother Roscoe, who, while only ten himself, was plowing alone in a field a half mile away. The field could not be seen from the house and Roscoe had been working there all morning in the summer heat without a drink of water. Already physically strong and inured to long hours of labor, Roscoe was doing the work of a man, although it seems probable that his progress would have been slower than that of most adults. Rush followed a path from the house to the field, and because he never wore shoes in the summer, felt the heat radiating from the ground as he moved swiftly along. Unfortunately, he encountered "a sleek blue racer," a variety of non-venomous but aggressive snake. Despite his shouts, the blue racer refused to abandon the path to Rush, who out of desperation went into the grass to avoid it. Imagining that the snake was after him, and that indeed the field was full of them, he be-gan to run and stumbled losing most of the water he was carrying. Crying and screaming as he made his way to the field, Roscoe abandoned his work and ran to the frightened boy. While "still crying and sobbing," Rush explained what had happened and requested that his brother save some water for him as he "was utterly starved for drink." Although still of a tender age and very thirsty himself, Roscoe demonstrated much maturity and kindness in reassuring Rush and drank but a little of that which remained in the bucket, leaving the rest for his younger sibling.[13]

Later that fall in 1896, while the other children attended school, Rush ac-companied his father to the town of Jackson, a trip of some fourteen or fifteen miles from their home. They traveled by wagon behind a team of mules with sacks of wheat to sell to the mill located on the west side of the town. While in Jackson, Joseph, a staunch Republican and supporter of William McKinley for president, attended a gathering and flag raising with other Republicans at a park. Several men together raised a pole with its flag around which everyone gathered. Then speakers harangued the crowd, a band played, and the crowd sang. On the return home, Joseph spoke to Rush about what had happened and his desire to see McKinley elected president.[14]

In the decades following the Civil War, falling prices of agricultural goods had caused economic distress, but the collapse of 1893 made circumstances especially difficult for farmers, who struggled to eke out a living from the soil and to preserve their independence. Out of desperation, many farmers joined a social and political movement called the Populists, who sought to promote agriculture as the primary economic pursuit in the United States. This group harkened back to the ideal of agrarian republicanism, an ideology most closely associated with Thomas Jefferson, who had wanted to prevent the country from becoming industrialized and sought to limit its commerce, and thus its contact, with the rest of the world. Jefferson believed that the conversion of the populace from yeoman farmers to economically dependent laborers in factories would undermine the people's virtue and independence, without which republican government could not be preserved. The Populists, who closely associated the nation's economic and political ills with industry and commerce, sought to reverse this trend, or at least to stop its continued progress, and gain the adoption of an economic program they believed would benefit both farmers and factory workers. Their motto was: Wealth should go to those who produce it.[15]

Despite the efforts of Jefferson and his successors, by the end of the nineteenth century industry and commerce had supplanted agriculture as the primary pursuits of Americans and were responsible for a phenomenal increase in national wealth. Thus, although reluctant to leave the farm, more and more people found themselves compelled by economic forces to abandon the land and move to the cities in search of employment. This transformation of the economy did not occur smoothly, however, and in 1893 an economic downturn rapidly developed into a full-blown depression. Because of this, the Populists found many more Americans receptive than before to their critique of the moneyed class and their message of fundamental economic reform. The popularity of their message resulted from the social and economic disruption in which "knots of idle men clustered murmuring around plant or store entrances, whiling away time at home, or tramping the countryside." While estimates of the extent of unemployment for this period are based upon inadequate information, the ratio of the workforce without a job may have been as high as one-fifth. More than 800 bank failures occurred during the period of 1893 to 1897, businesses failed at an astonishing rate of 20 to 50 percent, "and by mid-1894 156 railroad companies with about $2.5 billion capitalization . . . were in receivership." One estimate believed that the "economy [was] operating perhaps at 20 to 25 percent capacity through 1894."[16]

More importantly for farmers like the Limbaughs, the value of agricultural goods plunged precipitously, greatly diminishing their incomes. In 1893 the United States Department of Agriculture concluded that for the past decade "the cost of production" exceeded the return in price of wheat, corn, and other crops. This circumstance alarmed farmers throughout the country, causing many more to join the Populists, who sought to establish a subtreasury system to allow farmers to store their produce and obtain low-interest, federal loans upon much of its value. These loans would enable farmers to pay their bills while waiting for the price of grain to rise. The scheme was never adopted by the federal government, although farmers eventually implemented many of these measures themselves through cooperatives, or co-ops, which still exist today. In the presidential election year of 1896, the Populists fused with the Democratic Party, whose leaders were desperate to fend off electoral disaster by avoiding blame for the depression. However, this temporary alliance was to no avail, for a strong majority of Americans like Rush's father voted for the Republican candidate William McKinley, who campaigned on a platform of higher tariffs to protect the domestic market for American goods and to maintain the gold standard. After the election of 1896 the Populist Party, like other third parties before it and since, soon dissolved.[17] After McKinley's victory, despite the region being "predominately Democratic," Rush's father and a number of other Republicans held a parade and rally in Sedgewickville to celebrate. One of the most important issues of the campaign had concerned currency and the gold standard, which the Republicans wished to preserve at a ratio of one part gold to sixteen parts silver. Thus the phrase "sixteen to one" had become a watchword and motto of the campaign. To illustrate this in the parade, the organizers arranged for sixteen girls to dress in white to represent silver and another girl to wear "a rich yellow color" to represent gold. "The golden girl" was Rush's sister Elizabeth Virginia, or Jennie as she was generally called. The following Fourth of July, the Republicans again celebrated McKinley's election with a picnic, but this celebration was marred by a thunderstorm which forced the festivities to end prematurely.[18]

In the fall of 1897 Rush began school. As the youngest, he had often observed the departure and return of his older siblings along "the old school road" and yearned to accompany them. The one-room schoolhouse was a little more than a mile away from their home and all seven of the Limbaugh children made the journey together. As they trekked along this trail Rush and the others sometimes chased rabbits from their hiding places, traversed the Little Muddy Creek at different points, and played pranks upon one another. Still, various hazards and dangers required vigilance, especially when the creek rose making parts of the path impassable.[19]

During the first weeks of school the Limbaugh children and many of their classmates did not wear shoes. Later, after the temperature cooled, the school children donned footwear. Unfortunately for Rush, after wearing his shoes for only a day, blisters formed on his feet and on his return home he could only limp along slowly. Fearing that he could not keep up with his older siblings on the road, Rush left before them but was soon overtaken a short distance from school. Not wishing to be left behind and in pain, he began to cry, gaining the sympathy of Arthur, who lifted Rush upon his back "with remarkable ease" and proceeded along the path. After covering a good bit of distance, he remembered how Arthur stopped to rest for a minute and inquire about his welfare.

> I remember that minute distinctly. It dawned on me there somehow how much I was indebted to my brother for that kind act. By such acts of help and willing self sacrifice we as brothers and sisters of each family are bound together by that indefinable love and loyalty which is preserved even when the old home is abandoned and each goes out into a separate corner of the world to fight the battle of life. That minute of rest was not only a revelation of helpfulness but of sympathy. As we stood there together in the old path Arthur asked me if my feet still hurt and other simple questions . . . which showed in his voice, manner, and words that he sympathized with me in my littleness and delicateness. And it was worth a world to me that I could have the sympathies and the help of a brother so big and strong.[20]

As the school year progressed, their teacher, George Conrad, a well-educated local man, proved incapable of maintaining order and discipline among the students. This task was not easy, for the school building provided too little space for the seventy-five students under his charge, whose ages ranged from six to twenty-one years. As Rush later described the situation, "we became a restless, seething, surging society that soon got out of the control of the teacher." Unfortunately, Conrad was not large or strong enough to punish some of the older boys. This led to a complete breakdown in discipline as the other children also disregarded their hapless teacher's instructions and orders. Soon the oldest of the students "had become disgusted and quit school." To address this situation, the school board directors decided to meet, one of whom was Rush's father. Because of his ill-health, the other directors came to the Limbaughs' home to discuss what could be done. In one instance, some of the students had locked Conrad out of the school building until he promised to "treat them with a box of candy on the last day of school." Learning of this, Rush remembered his father stating emphatically that "if he can't keep order, he can't teach school!" Nevertheless, because another teacher could not be hired that late in the school year to replace Conrad, the directors decided to make the best of the situation. But they also vowed that next year's teacher would be someone capable of maintaining order.[21]

The disorder in the schoolhouse not only made learning difficult, but it may have had another serious ramification, for under the influence of some of his classmates, Arthur, who was still a boy of seventeen years, determined to leave home. Apparently he had found his responsibilities increasingly burdensome as the oldest son of a very ill man, for in the early morning of Monday, February 14, 1898, he ran away. In a note he left for his family, Arthur indicated his intention never to return. At school that day the students and teacher soon learned of Arthur's departure and through them the entire community was soon informed of it. Out of sympathy, neighbors and friends visited the Limbaughs to offer their condolences. Despite his sadness, Rush's father, Joseph, who was by then bedridden and weakened by tuberculosis, made provision for Arthur's absence by hiring a young man in the neighborhood to work for him that summer. However, this became unnecessary when Arthur returned to the family the following Sunday. Everyone, including Joseph, was elated and accepted Arthur's apology for having behaved so irresponsibly. It is unknown where he had gone, but perhaps while traveling he had time for reflection and concluded that he had made a terrible mistake in listening to his peers. If so, this might explain Arthur's request of his father "to quit school and spend his entire time on the farm." Joseph agreed to this, perhaps recognizing as well that Arthur's decision to leave was made under the bad influence of classmates in an environment of disorder.[22]

During the last year of his life, Joseph was unable to do any strenuous physical labor and increasingly found other activities difficult. This decline was the result of an accumulation of maladies and misfortunes which apparently weakened him and rendered him vulnerable to disease. After surviving smallpox, which was unexpected and almost "miraculous," while still in his twenties Joseph developed a chronic intolerance for many foods. He also developed a fistula and traveled to St. Louis for an operation. This procedure was largely unsuccessful for he continued to suffer from this malady for the rest of his life. Just before Rush's birth, he also was bitten by a copperhead snake. Susan, who had heard that whiskey could cure venomous snake bites, administered the remedy to her husband, although she later doubted that it had cured him. Another farming mishap befell Joseph while unloading hay in the barn, when one of his fingers was caught in the mechanism of a hayfork. Fortunately, his finger was saved, but Joseph contracted tuberculosis soon afterward.[23]

From the early part of the summer of 1898, Joseph was largely bedridden and suffered from the severe heat. To gain some relief, he sometimes went to the cellar, which was constructed under the house, where the temperature was "a little cooler" than elsewhere. Being only six years of age and still unable to participate much in the farm work, Rush became his father's constant companion, providing him with some relief from the heat by fanning him with a palm leaf and doing whatever else might be helpful. This experience profoundly affected Rush, for during this time while the rest of the family attended to their duties, he "could not escape the feeling of want and suffering [his] father endured." He also regretted that as a young boy he had not been better able to aid his father more in his final illness.[24]

As the summer progressed, Joseph evidently concluded that he would soon die, for he decided to make out his will. He therefore requested that a neighbor, Dean B. Hill, who had become "a legal adviser" in the community, come and help him write it. Hill took notes and on July 5, 1898, he returned with a draft of the will, accompanied by two men, Elisha Masters and Jefferson Cook, to witness its signing. Privately, Hill consulted with Rush's father to ensure that it reflected exactly his wishes for the division of his estate. In it, he bequeathed all of his personal property to Susan, which included full possession of his real estate with the right to lease or sell it according to her own judgment. However, desiring to leave his children a small patrimony, Joseph designated that his "money and notes . . . be equally divided" between them. Later, his portion of this money helped Rush finance his college education. Moreover, even as a small boy, the experience of witnessing his dying father sign his will in such a "grave and sober manner" left a lasting impression upon Rush.[25]

Through the remainder of the summer and the beginning of fall, Joseph suffered very much and became increasingly exhausted. As the end of his life neared, various family members and neighbors visited and offered advice hoping to relieve his suffering. One of the visitors urged Rush's father to seek the help of a faith healer. After some resistance to the idea, Joseph finally consented to meet with him. The man ordered fruit jars to be filled with water and placed in a closet. Moreover, he gave specific directions concerning the order in which each jar was to be drunk by Joseph, warning that the remedy would not work if his instructions were not followed exactly. When the faith healer returned later and was informed that Joseph had not improved, he first accused Rush's mother, and then Rush, of not having followed his instructions properly. Joseph, however, who had been skeptical from the start, bluntly told him that "what you are pretending to do is nothing but humbug." Sometime after this, Joseph's condition became more serious and on a Sunday evening in October he gathered his children around him and told them that he knew his life was almost over. Indeed, it was clear to everyone that his death was imminent.

To everyone's surprise, he rallied for a short time lingering until November 2, when at about nine o'clock in the morning, with the family gathered around him, he died. Rush remembered how he and his siblings wept and clung to one another for comfort. Rush's mother, despite her personal grief, explained to her children the importance of striving and working together well and the desire of their father that they always cherish one another. Rush described himself as "utterly heartbroken" and for some time thereafter found it difficult to accept that he would never again see his father. Members of the Masonic Lodge in Millersville, to which Joseph had belonged for many years, conducted his funeral. He was buried in the family graveyard on the farm, where a monument was erected to mark his final resting place. In his dreams, Rush continued to remember his father decades later as a "large, bold, helpful [presence] leading [him] through dangerous and difficult places." During times of stress, he often visited his father's grave to reconnect to his heritage and beginnings.[26]

Unfortunately, this was not to be the end of the family's sorrows, for Rush's two oldest sisters, Jennie and Hattie, twelve and nine years his senior, respectively, began to exhibit the symptoms of tuberculosis in the winter of 1900–1901. At eighteen years of age, both young women had quit school and expected to marry soon and raise families of their own. Indeed, as they matured, several young men courted them and groups of young people sometimes visited the Limbaugh home to hear Jennie play a wind organ and sing folk songs popular at the time. Eventually, Jennie became engaged to Turner Smith, but because their families were poor, they had postponed marriage. Likewise, Hattie became engaged to a local man, Walker Statler, but her illness prevented their marriage. Throughout the illness of Jennie and Hattie, both Smith and Statler stood by them, hoping for their recovery.[27]

Jennie, unlike her father and sister, contracted pulmonary tuberculosis and suffered from periodic hemorrhages in her lungs. These spells left her exhausted but were followed by interludes of improvement. Hattie's symptoms, like her father's, included chills and fevers, the gradual loss of weight, and eventually complete exhaustion. She became bedridden in early 1902 and developed soreness on the left side of her lower back. Her maternal uncle and physician, Dr. Charles E. Presnell, visited their home and diagnosed an abscess on her kidney and believed that surgery was necessary to save her life. However, before taking such a dangerous step, he consulted two other doctors practicing nearby. Doctors A. A. Mayfield and Chandler concurred with Presnell's diagnosis and treatment. By this time Hattie had become desperately ill and, unable to climb the stairs to her bedroom, remained in the living room. Presnell, assisted by the other doctors and Rush's mother, removed the abscess. This provided temporary relief, but by June 1902 her condition became very grave. Presnell continued to attend to both girls, but it became evident that Hattie could not survive long. She died on July 8 and was buried in the family graveyard near her father.[28]

Jennie's condition was also very serious. Hoping to improve her health, it was decided that Arthur should take Jennie to California. Before departing, Limbaugh remembered, on a Sunday "a large number of young people ... came to our home to bid Jennie and Arthur" farewell and to communicate their wish that she would soon return to them cured. Arthur and Jennie traveled to Pasadena by train and the family was hopeful of her recovery. For a time she rallied, but Jennie soon suffered setbacks which led to her death on December 4. Her body was returned to Missouri and she was buried next to her sister. Thus, at the age of ten, Rush had already experienced the passing of his paternal grandmother, his father, and two sisters. In particular, because of their youth and good characters, the death of his sisters affected him and many family members and friends most deeply. Many could not help but ask why such fine young women were taken from them and searched for some explanation for the tragedy. His sadness in losing his sisters remained with Rush all his life. Almost seventy years later, while on a trip to England, he recorded his visit to the graveyard where Thomas Gray had written his famous elegy on the fleeting nature of life. As he stood there and recited the poem, Rush could not help but think of his sisters, who had died when they were so young and seemingly had the fair prospect of long lives yet before them.

> Let not Ambition mock their useful toil,
> Their homely joys, and destiny obscure;
> Nor Grandeur hear with a disdainful smile
> The short and simple annals of the Poor.
>
> The boast of heraldry, the pomp of power,
> And all that beauty, all that wealth e'er gave,
> Awaits alike th' inevitable hour:-
> The paths of glory lead but to the grave.[29]

Chapter Two

Intellectual Development and Courtship

By the end of 1902, the Limbaugh family had been reduced by death from nine to six members. Despite the loss of her two oldest daughters, Jennie and Hattie, within a few months of each other, Rush's mother Susan had little time to grieve. The continuing struggle of holding her family together and meeting the challenges of managing the farm, even with the help of her oldest son Arthur, was an all-consuming task and required the immediate return to her labors. Many years later Rush recalled how hard his mother worked to feed and clothe him and his siblings. Working from early in the morning to late at night, Susan maintained "a happy disposition and a feeling of triumphant grace and achievement." Perhaps these labors would have been too much for her if not for the help of her eighteen-year-old daughter, Lillie, who helped with the spinning, cooking, cleaning, and other tasks.[1]

After his father Joseph's death, Arthur accompanied his mother to Marble Hill to begin the administration of the estate and arranged to have his maternal uncle, Dr. Charles E. Presnell, appointed as guardian over his minor siblings, who upon reaching the age of majority would receive their share of the life insurance policy money as provided in the will. Arthur also began directing the farm work, determining what crops to grow and how many cattle to raise. Moreover, he made improvements upon the farm such as building a wheat house, clearing a large thicket near the graveyard, and preparing other fields for cultivation. Probably, Joseph had intended to begin many of these projects himself.[2]

When Rush reached the age of ten, it was decided that he would learn how to plow. His brothers Roscoe and Burette had both begun plowing at eight, but Rush, being small for his age, did not attain the requisite size and strength necessary for such work until he had lived a full decade. Although tardy to the plow, Rush should not have experienced any embarrassment, or considered himself a failure, for Ulysses S. Grant, also small for his age, did not begin to till the fields until he was eleven. Apparently, a slow start in the race of life does not preclude later success. On Thanksgiving Day of 1901, Rush and his brother Roscoe arose early and with their plow teams made their way to the field some three miles away. A certain urgency was felt to accomplish as much as possible, for the weather had been unusually cold and soon no more plowing could be done. Roscoe, who was then fifteen years old, provided Rush with the easier team to handle and went to work plowing in the same field. He soon discovered, however, that plowing a field behind horses was not an easy task to master. As he related later, "one bad thing followed another. The lead horse was always getting her foot over the traces in turning around, the plow was striking a rock and coming out of the ground, a single tree clip was coming off, a line was pulling in two, the off horse coming disconnected with the other or some other perplexing misfortune. Finally things had grown so bad with me that Roscoe, who was going along without any trouble, had to come and straighten out my outfit and put me on the right track again." However, Rush's struggles were soon rewarded and by noon he was doing better. Having finished the seven-acre field they had been working, Rush and Roscoe next began plowing another field, despite the sky growing darker. By mid-afternoon it began to rain, slowly at first, but in a short time a downpour forced them to abandon their labors. Despite hurrying to escape the worsening conditions, by the time they arrived home the two boys were soaking wet and their slickers were covered with ice. Many years later, reflecting upon these boyhood travails and others, Rush believed that as he matured these types of adversities gave him self-confidence.[3]

From the start, Rush enjoyed and excelled at school work and reading. Fortunately, the teacher employed, while a compassionate and patient man, was able to keep order better than his predecessor. Alex Seabaugh used competition, positive reinforcement, and repetition to help his pupils learn. Moreover, Rush remembered his teacher's encouragement of reading, a skill which he was thankful to acquire. Seabaugh took special pains with the slower students and awarded headmarks to those who did best in their class for spelling and "from his own meager salary he gave small cash prizes for those who had the most headmarks and those who were not absent or tardy." These spelling bees fired within Rush a strong competitive spirit, which, when coupled with his fine memory, ensured that he quickly mastered his lessons.[4]

Of course, Rush's life was not all labor on the farm and schoolwork. Perhaps the most memorable event from this period was his attendance of the 1904 World's Fair in St. Louis. Many people from Sedgewickville and the surrounding community had already attended—including Lillie, Roscoe, and Burette—and had related the great wonders they had seen and experienced. All insisted that Rush and his mother also make the trip. Taking the St. Louis Iron Mountain and Southern Railway from Marquand to St. Louis, Rush remembered that from the trip's beginning to its end, "everything . . . was breathtaking and prolonged excitement." He marveled at the speeds they traveled and the electric lights illuminating the towns through which they passed. Having never before been more than twenty miles from home, Rush saw the Mississippi River for the first time. At Union Station in St. Louis, he and his mother saw many locomotives and large numbers of people arriving and departing.[5]

The next morning Rush and his mother attended the fair where they saw many exhibits displaying people from all parts of the world wearing their traditional dress. Rush remembered particularly a reenactment of a battle of the Boer War in South Africa, and the boat ride called "Creation" in which they "traveled around in a circle looking at various scenes of the world." He also enjoyed seeing the Cascade, "a waterfall with different colored lights." Another highlight of the visit was his ride upon the giant Ferris wheel with thirty-six cars, each of which was "almost as large as a street car." Perhaps his favorite experience, however, was eating hot dogs and ice cream cones for the first time, a delight that he never forgot. This trip, Rush believed, was an important event in his life, for it introduced him to the wider world, and along with his education and reading made him hungry to learn more and be a part of it all.[6]

In school, Rush soon advanced through the grades more quickly than his classmates and was encouraged in particular by his sister Lillie to read literature and develop his public speaking and debating talents. At the age of twelve, Rush memorized the Gettysburg Address and Lincoln's Second Inaugural Address, and committed other speeches, poetry, and literature to memory. Lillie also bought for her precocious brother a book on public speaking, which provided excerpts of speeches made by the nation's founders and other statesmen. Some of Rush's favorites were orations by George Washington, Daniel Webster, Patrick Henry, and Abraham Lincoln. By September 1905, he had already worked through all of the textbooks available at "the home school," and thus began a review of his lessons. This led Rush to make the momentous decision to leave the farm and pursue his education elsewhere. Fortunately, his sister Lillie had recently married and was living in Millersville, where a two-year high school was located. She and her husband, a young physician who had just finished medical school in St. Louis, opened their home to Rush so he could attend high school. With his mother's consent, Rush moved to Millersville, which was seven miles from their home. Despite his strong desire for an education, the prospect of leaving home was frightening to the fourteen-year-old boy. Fortunately, he was able to spend each weekend on the farm and usually returned to his sister's home on Sunday afternoon or Monday morning where he remained until Friday.[7]

In January 1906, Rush took courses in early American literature, ancient and American history, and arithmetic. For the first time, because the school had a modest library, Rush was able to read a number of literary classics and history books. He soon became an avid reader and as he later remarked, he "found in the new books . . . sources of genuine delight." One of the courses he found especially interesting and rewarding was a class on the works of the great playwright William Shakespeare. Of these, Rush liked *Julius Caesar* and *Othello* best. Later, this literary interest paid an unexpected dividend when on a date he recited for a young woman a passage from *Othello*, which impressed her very much. He also participated in a debate for the first time, representing Millersville on the question of who was the greatest statesman, Benjamin Franklin or George Washington. Rush argued for Franklin but lost. While at Millersville High School he found both the coursework and extracurricular activities very exciting and determined to attend college if possible, although he was unsure how he could afford it. The prospective college student credited one of his instructors with having influenced and encouraged him and his classmates to consider the educational opportunities available to them. By the end of his second year, Rush had begun making preparations to attend college.[8]

In September 1907, Rush enrolled in the Normal School, a teachers' college in Cape Girardeau. His mother, desiring to help Rush, gave him sixty-five dollars. Regretting that she could do no more, she hoped that it would be enough to hold him over until he found work sufficient to cover his tuition and living costs. Soon after classes began, Rush attended a meeting held outside of Academic Hall at which the faculty and students became acquainted with one another. While there, two students approached him and asked if he was Rush Limbaugh. This question surprised him, for he could not imagine how they knew him. They explained that they had heard about his debating for Millersville and invited him to join the Benton Literary Society, a student club whose members participated in oratory and debate contests.[9]

After his first year of college, Rush took a year off to save money for his education. In addition to his classes in English, Latin, ancient history, and physical geography, he had also taken a course in teaching in which he learned about planning lessons and establishing learning goals. During the summer of 1908, Rush passed the teacher's examination, and with the recommendation of Dr. W. S. Dearmont, the president of the Normal School, gained an appointment to teach the Lone Grove School, a one-room schoolhouse set in a rural community.[10]

While teaching Rush boarded with his maternal aunt, Marcelly Bridges, her husband Francis, and their six children during the week. On the weekends, as he had done while at Millersville, Rush went home to the farm. Two of Aunt Marcelly's sons were teaching also and in the evening during dinner they and Rush often discussed their days; undoubtedly each benefitting from the experiences of the others. In the evening Rush usually read in his bedroom, which he shared with his fellow teachers Lyman and Linus, where they all gathered around a kerosene lamp. Rush, who apparently needed less sleep than most, sometimes stayed up after his roommates had gone to sleep and "read far into the night." Although living with his aunt required him to walk three miles to school, Rush did not mind for he enjoyed the exercise and having the time to think and plan for the future. The schoolhouse was a rectangular frame building and was located on high ground above Hog Creek. The enrollment of the school was fifty-five students ranging in ages from six to seventeen. Classes were from eight o'clock in the morning to four o'clock in the afternoon, Monday through Friday, with only two ten-minute recesses and a break for lunch.[11]

At sixteen years of age, Rush was still small for his age and some of his students were older and larger than him. Nevertheless, he had little in the way of discipline problems beyond the occasional prank which students played upon a fellow student or him. These pranks, Rush remembered, "were never of a serious nature and they occurred largely for frolic and fun and rarely for the purpose of showing a willful disregard of the rules." He was also fortunate for there was little absenteeism, indicating that parents were serious about their children's educations. Rush began each day by devoting the first ten minutes to the evening exercises assigned the day before. These assignments included lessons about nature and "other things of common interest in which all could participate." He also assigned what were called "memory gems," which were probably passages selected from literature and speeches for memorization. At the end of the school day Rush gave special instruction to a small number of students and reminded everyone how they were to conduct themselves on their way home. Years later, Rush considered this "one of the happiest periods" of his life and met the end of his tenure there with conflicting emotions. He "felt both the exhilaration of being released from responsibility but a sadness in parting with my pupils," feelings shared by many teachers today at the end of a semester or a school year. However, having determined to become a lawyer, he knew that he must continue his own education to achieve that goal.[12]

At the end of his first year at the Normal School, Rush had finally gained the courage to approach a young woman he had been interested in for a date. Bee Seabaugh had grown up in Sedgewickville, only four miles from the Limbaugh farm, but nevertheless their first meeting did not occur until they were nine years old. At the age of five, Rush had learned about Bee from his mother who had returned from a funeral and described tearfully how Bee and her three-year-old brother Bland had followed the coffin of their father, Emerson Seabaugh, to the grave. He had contracted tuberculosis and died in 1898, the same year in which Rush's father Joseph succumbed to the disease. Later, Rush learned from his sister Lillie of Bee's popularity in the community and her reputation for being a dedicated student and a fun-loving and "vivacious" girl. When ten years old, Rush had briefly seen Bee when she attended the funeral of his sister Hattie and again a year later when she performed at a church Christmas program in 1903. Bee's presence and performance profoundly affected Rush and he began to admire her from afar.[13]

As was the custom then, Rush sent Bee "a colored postcard," beginning a correspondence that led to their meeting during commencement in May 1908 at the Normal School in Cape Girardeau. Bee was there with her mother to bring home her older sister Myrtle, who was then teaching at one of the schools in town. At the time, Bee dated a number of young men, but much to Rush's relief, "she declined to give repeated dates to anyone." After their brief meeting in Cape Girardeau, Rush ventured to ask Bee out on a date, to which she agreed. On a Sunday afternoon in September 1908, when he was still teaching at the Lone Grove School, Rush visited Bee at her home in Sedgewickville. Afterward he took her by buggy to the home where she boarded while teaching school outside of town. On the way, Bee had taken the reins and had mischievously slapped them, causing the horse to jump forward into a gallop, and thus slinging mud upon them. Apparently Bee enjoyed her time with Rush, for she agreed to another date. Later, through an exchange of letters, Bee agreed to allow Rush to visit her again at her home on October 25.[14]

On the appointed day, Rush, who was at home on the farm that weekend, rose early to do his chores and prepare for his date that afternoon. Sharing in her son's happiness and enthusiasm, Susan helped Rush by readying his clothes. Rush drove his buggy the four miles to Sedgewickville and met Bee in the parlor of her home. At first they discussed literature and Bee played the piano. In an attempt to demonstrate his affection for her, Rush offered to place a rose in Bee's hair, which she refused. He then handed it to her while praising "her beauty and sweetness." Apparently unwilling to allow things to turn serious between them, Bee plucked the rose apart petal by petal, thereby ending Rush's praises of her. At the end of their time together, Rush asked Bee for another date, but she declined. Although she had enjoyed their time together and "would like to," she "insisted that it was not best" for young people of their age, (they were both seventeen years old), to date steadily. In the months ahead, Rush learned that Bee had dated others, and although he "occasionally wrote her," she did not respond.[15]

During his final months of teaching in 1909, Rush wrote to a number of university presidents about entering law school. His application, however, was rejected by all but that to Dr. George H. Denny, president of Washington and Lee University. He explained to Rush that before admittance into law school he needed to take pre-law courses for a year and a half before beginning work on his law degree. Depending upon his progress, Denny estimated that Rush might finish within four years altogether, or perhaps within three or three and a half. He also promised to help the young Missourian find a job to fund his education. Rush was impressed with the interest in and direction of Denny's reply and determined to attend Washington and Lee University that fall. Thus he saved as much of his teaching salary as possible, as well as other earnings that summer from working on the farm.[16]

During the summer of 1909, while still in the midst of his preparations to leave for Virginia, Rush learned that the former presidential candidate William Jennings Bryan was to give a lecture in Cape Girardeau. Bee and her older sister Myrtle happened then to be there taking courses at the Normal School. Wishing to attend the speech and to gain another opportunity to be with Bee, Rush offered to take a friend by horse and buggy in return for free room and board while they were there. Once they had arrived in town, Rush gave his friend a note in which he asked Bee to attend the speech with him that evening. Bee agreed to accompany him and they walked from the house where she was staying to the auditorium in Academic Hall on the Normal School's campus. While Bryan's speech that night was excellent, Rush was much more thrilled with the opportunity of spending time with Bee. After the lecture, Rush learned that Bee would soon be taking the teacher's examination at Jackson and he offered to give her a ride from there back to Cape Girardeau. Bee agreed to this proposal. Upon this occasion, Rush sought to tell Bee that he had missed her, but she refused to allow him "to open [his] heart to her." Nevertheless, he offered to drive Bee home from Jackson in August after the summer term was over. On this journey, Rush again sought to express his feelings for Bee and asked her to correspond with him while he was in Virginia and to see him whenever he returned. This she declined to do. As they neared her home in Sedgewickville, Rush even pressed her hand to his lips and told Bee he loved her. This breach of etiquette angered her very much and she told him that she regretted allowing him to drive her home. For the rest of the journey, Bee remained silent, breaking her silence only to refuse to see him again before he left Missouri. Thus matters stood for some time thereafter.[17]

On September 6 Rush caught a train to St. Louis and from there to Washington, DC, to Virginia. He quickly found a place to board with a family living near campus and accidently met Dr. Denny on the street. In his office, the university president made the young Missourian welcome and Rush looked forward to getting started in his studies. Within a day or two, after acquainting himself with his roommate and the university, he suddenly came down with a fever. The physician examining Rush found his temperature to be 104 degrees and diagnosed his malady as typhoid, probably because Rush had told him his brother Arthur had contracted the disease that summer. This diagnosis scared Rush a good deal, for he had observed the terrible suffering his brother had endured. The doctor believed that Rush was going to be very sick for a long time and advised that if he intended to return home he should do so immediately. That afternoon he was on a train returning to Missouri. At one point he became very ill but the chills subsided by the time he arrived in Cape Girardeau, where his brother-in-law Dr. Dayton L. Seabaugh and brother Burette awaited him. Bundling Rush into a surrey, they brought him to Millersville. After examining him, however, his brother-in-law concluded that Rush was suffering from malaria rather than typhoid. After regular doses of quinine for six weeks, the severity of the chills diminished considerably, leaving him "very weak, thin, and pale." Over the next two years, occasional recurrences of these chills, less severe than before, sometimes weakened him for short periods of time. Eventually, these symptoms completely disappeared.[18]

Hoping to salvage the fall 1909 semester, Rush returned to the Normal School and enrolled late in five courses, completing all but one of them that semester and the fifth during the next. To meet his educational and living expenses, he took a job working on a forty-acre farm owned by L. R. Johnson, one of his professors. In return for taking care of the livestock, milking the cow, cutting wood, and doing other farm work, Rush received free room and board. Most of this work was accomplished after school and on weekends, enabling him to attend to his coursework and extracurricular activities. Wishing to develop his natural speaking abilities, he took courses in argumentation and debate and became deeply involved in the activities of the Benton Literary Society. During the spring semester of 1910, Rush was chosen to represent the society against the Webster Literary Society on Washington's birthday in the annual intersociety debate. The topic was whether "bank deposits should be guaranteed." Rush and his teammates argued that they should. Unlike today, college debates then were very important events, drawing large crowds of students and townspeople. The debate was held in the auditorium of Academic Hall and a silver cup was presented to Rush's team. Participation in the debate alone was prestigious, but being on the winning team enhanced his status on campus and in the community.[19]

At the end of each school year during commencement week, an "annual declamation contest for the Regents' medal" was held. Rush entered the contest and secured one of the five places reserved for the finalists. Again, the contest was held in the auditorium of Academic Hall and large numbers of students and townspeople attended. More importantly to Rush, his mother Susan and sister Lillie were present to witness his performance of McCartney's speech, "National Apostasy." Their presence was especially gratifying because Rush won. Many of the newspapers, including the *Marble Hill Press*, the newspaper read by Rush's friends and neighbors, reported on the event and his victory.[20]

Before returning home for the summer to work on the family farm, Rush agreed to remain in Cape Girardeau to help the Johnsons with the strawberry harvest, and could not arrange for his return home until the work was finished. Thus, when he was ready, Rush called long distance to his home. This required a connection through the switchboard in Sedgewickville, which was then operated by Bee's mother and sometimes by Bee herself. Almost a year had passed since she had firmly reprimanded Rush for behaving in a manner she considered too forward and presumptuous. During this period he had written her once from Lexington, Virginia, but had received no reply, and after his return from Washington and Lee University Rush feared that Bee considered him to be nothing more than "a boastful fraud." For this reason, he had made no attempt to contact her and was surprised to hear her voice answer as the switchboard operator. At first she did not recognize his voice and asked for his number to make the connection. However, when Bee realized who he was, much to his surprise she complimented him on his winning the Regents' medal and other academic accomplishments that year. Seizing upon this opportunity, Rush asked Bee how she had been, and learning that she would be remaining in Sedgewickville asked if he could see her that summer. To his great relief and joy, half expecting another "stern rebuke," Bee agreed to resume dating. They attended picnics and other social functions together and got along well, although she would not permit Rush to compliment her beauty and physical contact of any kind was strictly forbidden. Nevertheless, Rush was very happy and in September 1910, just before his departure for Cape Girardeau, he requested that she give him a picture of herself. This she was reluctant to do, but eventually consented, although she made it clear that it was for his viewing alone. This Rush promised and the photograph became an ornament upon his desk for sometime thereafter.[21]

When he returned to the Normal School for the fall semester of 1910, Rush was just a few days shy of his nineteenth birthday and had achieved considerable success academically and in debate and public speaking. He again returned to board with the Johnsons and to work on their farm. As a pre-law student he took courses in history, English, government, economics, and speech. He continued as an active member of the Benton Literary Society and participated in the debates they held during regular meetings. Moreover, to strengthen his writing and analytical skills, Rush sought opportunities to write papers on special assignments for classes and to record his thoughts on a number of topics. By struggling with important issues and learning the art of effective composition and argument, he hoped to prepare himself for the professional and public roles he intended to fill once he had completed his education. In one of these papers, Rush indicated a deep concern about the corrupting influence of machine politics. Just months before, in March 1910, a group of Republican representatives in the United States House of Representatives had combined with Democrats to remove Speaker Joseph G. Cannon's power to appoint members to the rules committee. This insurgency was hailed in many newspapers throughout the country as a progressive revolt against the speaker who personified corrupt machine politics. Many then believed that this machine benefitted Big Business to the detriment of the peoples' interests. To this time Rush had considered himself a Republican, undoubtedly in large part out of loyalty to his father who had strongly supported the GOP. However, Rush soon abandoned the Republican Party, not to join the Democrats, whom he considered to be equally corrupt, but to support the Progressive Party, through which he hoped American politics might be transformed.[22]

The Christmas holiday did not bring a cessation to Rush's labors, for he was then writing a speech for an oratorical contest. He was also preparing for the next intersociety debate at which he hoped again to represent the Bentons against the Websters. These activities delayed his return home, leaving him only four days for the Christmas holiday. Quite significantly, Rush and Bee spent all of Christmas day together. After the morning church service and a drive with some other couples, they returned to Bee's home for their Christmas supper. To this time, Bee had discouraged Rush from making any plans regarding their future together, but during this visit he sensed a thawing of much of her former reserve and a greater friendliness to his overtures.[23]

Perhaps one of the reasons Bee's attitude had changed towards Rush resulted from his emerging interest in Christian activities and Bible study. In the early part of the fall semester of 1910, he had joined the Centenary Methodist Church in Cape Girardeau, which began his association with it to the end of his life. He also taught a Sunday school class for boys from ten to twelve years of age. As he later explained, his interest in the Christian faith was awakened through Bee, who obviously gained joy and solace from it. Rush also became involved in activities sponsored by the Young Men's Christian Association, or YMCA, which at that time took a prominent role in college life. Often throwing himself wholeheartedly into endeavors he judged to be worthwhile, Rush organized four Bible study classes, one of which he taught, and actively recruited his fellow students to attend.[24]

All of these activities filled Rush's days and he found it necessary to budget his time strictly to accomplish everything, often working to midnight or later, leaving less time for sleep. This hard work, however, enabled him to fund his education, maintain good grades, and participate in the various extracurricular activities he found so rewarding.[25]

At this time, Rush also prepared to vie for the right to represent his college in the internormal oratorical contest. On January 30, he presented his oration, "The Perils of American Politics," in which for the first time he expressed his views on current events. Political parties were essential institutions to democratic societies, he believed, for through them the peoples' representatives were chosen and their opinions were implemented in the development of principles and policies. So long as parties were the servants of the people they performed their proper function, but when a small group of party bosses, what amounted to an "oligarchy," insisted that all voters and politicians adhere to a party platform, then the system was turned upside down and parties became tyrannical. Rush also noted that both parties were guilty of this type of political corruption. Having noted the corrupting influence of money and unscrupulous politicians, he nevertheless warned reformers against concluding that the American constitutional system was flawed. One should not, he believed, become too taken with "the dreams of the reformer," or listen to the promises of socialism. Moreover, while certain progressive reforms such as "Direct Primaries, the Initiative, the Referendum, and the Recall may all have remedial value if applied wisely," Rush asserted that these could not substitute for true representative government exercised under the constitutional system "expounded by Marshall, defended by Webster, and preserved by Lincoln. These are the principles on which depend the stability of our institutions. In them lies our hope and in them we must confide."[26]

In the contest, Rush came in second to Clyde C. Harbison, who was also editor-in-chief of the student newspaper, the *Capaha Arrow*. Harbison's oration was entitled, "The Conflict," and addressed "the struggle between capital and labor, and the disadvantages to both elements arising from differences." By coming in first and second, both Harbison and Rush won the right to represent their college at the internormal oratorical contest in Warrensburg on March 17. Once again Rush came in second to Harbison, who by his victory gained the privilege to represent Missouri at the interstate contest which would be held in May at Cape Girardeau. Rush's performance was described as "so aggressive in the way he went after his audience that just as he swung into the peroration, he actually walked into the footlights." Despite this mishap, he quickly recovered and "raised his voice a little and shot out his right hand in a gesture that commanded attention." Upon their return to campus, both Harbison and Limbaugh were given a reception by the four literary societies at which many students were present.[27]

Despite his competitive fire and strong dislike of losing, Rush had little time to ponder his loss for he and Edward Roberts were chosen to represent the Cape Girardeau Normal School in a debate at Marvin College on April 17. This required intensive study of the topic and strategy sessions between the two debaters. The debate question was whether the United States should fortify the Panama Canal. Rush and Edwards were assigned the task of arguing against fortification. After the debate, a judge noted that their deliveries "were more convincing in style" than that of their opponents. For this victory, they received gold medals.[28]

As the semester came to a close, despite his disappointment in losing the oratorical contests to Harbison, Rush had achieved a good deal and had become one of the notable and popular students on campus. Due to this, he was elected by student subscribers to the *Capaha Arrow*'s board, upon which sat other students, faculty, and alumni of the school. Rush was also selected as a delegate to a YMCA conference which was held in June at Lake Geneva, Wisconsin. Having achieved so much, Rush was content and looked confidently to the future with satisfaction and ambition.[29]

In the midst of his triumphs, Rush's contentment and confidence was shaken, albeit only for a brief time. After returning from the oratorical contest at Warrensburg in mid-March, Professor Vaughan arranged matters so that Rush, who had been working a bit too hard, could have a weekend at home. While there, he spent all day Sunday with Bee. Unbeknownst to him, during his absence Bee had been dating others and had canceled a date she had with another young man on that day. In April, after the school where she was teaching had closed for the summer, Bee took a trip to Sikeston and arranged to stay overnight at Cape Girardeau where she had boarded during the past summer. Rush met her at the train and they spent the remainder of the evening together until her train for Sikeston arrived. Returning two or three days later, Rush again met Bee at the station. At this time, Bee confessed that she had been dating other men during his absence. This news "jolted" his confidence and bruised his "pride." He had intended to propose marriage that summer and now he felt unsure about their relationship. Bee asked him if he did not date other girls. This prompted him to deny even wanting to date another and expressed "as fervently and positively as" possible his love and desire only to be with her. Perhaps feeling defeated and resigned to losing her, Rush acknowledged that he had no right to insist that she only date him. To this Bee replied that she would do what he wanted, implying that she would make a deeper commitment to him if he asked her. The next morning, Rush again escorted Bee to the train station and bid her farewell. Somehow Bee's demeanor was different, "more gracious and subdued" than before. Tacitly the two had come to an understanding of devotion to the other and both looked forward to Rush's return home that summer.[30]

The summer of 1911 was indeed momentous for Rush and Bee. In addition to spending every Sunday together, the couple spent as much time together as possible. In early June, they shared their first kiss. Rush explained that he would be unable to finish his education for some time yet. He was, he admitted, nothing more than "a penniless student." In this frank assessment of his circumstances, Rush was stating implicitly that Bee could not expect marriage anytime soon. Bee, however, expressed her continued optimism about their prospects, which encouraged Rush to propose marriage. Bee accepted immediately.[31]

In September, Rush reluctantly returned to college in Cape Girardeau. Soon after this a faculty committee in charge of overseeing the publication of the biweekly *Capaha Arrow* met and elected Rush to be the next editor-in-chief. Also, a faculty member involved with the work of the YMCA on campus informed Rush that he had been chosen as the organization's local "executive secretary," which included taking charge of campus activities that year. Some of these were Bible study classes, morning prayer meetings, a regular Thursday meeting, and classes like "The Challenge of the City" that sought to inspire young men to take "a deeper interest in those persons who labor in the sweat shop and the pit." Moreover, part of his responsibilities included counseling troubled students. Because these new activities took up a good deal of his time, Rush renegotiated his duties on the Johnson farm, assuming primarily a supervisory role over another student. With his earnings from these positions, combined with the money he made during the summer, Rush was able to finance his education for another year.[32]

For the fall semester, Rush enrolled in English, economics, sociology, English history, and government. After his classes, his duties as editor-in-chief of the *Capaha Arrow* probably consumed the greatest part of his time. His staff was composed of six students, four of whom were editors of different sections of the newspaper, and a business and advertising manager. The first issue published under his leadership was dated September 27, 1911—his twentieth birthday—and covered a variety of academic, sporting, and social events, which included an interesting literary section and helpful advice to new students. Most of the columns did not have a byline, but some of the items certainly contained all the hallmarks of Rush's philosophy of life, work ethic, and ambition. One of these in particular encouraged students to work hard to achieve great things.

> The things which we desire, the things worth while, are only attained through sacrifice and through service. . . . And as we go about our work we need not forget the old home–nay, we must not. But instead let us remember with tender sympathy those whom we left behind, those who have not the opportunities which we enjoy and those who help to make it possible for us to be here. Let us not forget the duty we owe to them. But let us strive to meet this duty by getting the most out of life at school. The way we meet our school duties will largely determine the way we meet the duties of life.[33]

During work on this first issue, Rush and his staff struggled to learn their new duties under the added pressure of doing the work of the news editor who had resigned. As was explained later: "With much confusion and many hard-spent moments, we succeeded in filling up the columns at the last moment." Moreover, it was conceded that "all of us were rather 'fresh' in knowing how much news it took to fill a paper like the Arrow." However, this was not the end of their difficulties, for the printing of the first issue was further delayed because the staff of the printer had taken time off from their work "to see the aeroplane flights at the fairgrounds." After these initial difficulties, Rush and the staff apparently settled into a routine and successfully published a fine student newspaper.[34]

During the fall semester of 1911, Rush and Bee corresponded extensively with one another. Returning home during the Thanksgiving and Christmas holidays, Rush spent as much time with Bee as possible. Because he was making extra income that semester, he was able to save $100 and purchased an engagement ring, which he gave to Bee sometime after the spring semester of 1912 had begun. Like many young women, Bee could not resist wearing her ring. When her friends saw it, they immediately understood its meaning and soon the couple's secret was common knowledge in Sedgewickville and the surrounding community.[35]

On New Year's Day of 1912, Rush composed a resolution for the coming year. In it he expressed his wish to improve himself by embodying characteristics he considered most desirable. First of all, he sought "to strive to make proportional development physically, mentally, and morally." He also wished to use his time and money economically, to become a good citizen, and "to meet manfully–with careful reasoning and reliable foresight–all the problems that life brings about, to strive to live and be a <u>Man</u>." This resolution demonstrates well the idealism which motivated and drove Rush to strive to do and learn so much. Having overcome his hardscrabble beginnings to gain an education, he sought to take full advantage of his opportunities and to prove to others, especially to Bee, that he could be successful.[36]

In the midst of everything else, Rush continued his participation in the Benton Literary Society, whose members elected him to the office of critic. Moreover, Rush composed a speech for the upcoming intersociety oratorical competition to be held on February 3. On a Saturday evening the contest was held and the judges determined that Rush was the winner. When published later, the scores of the judges showed that Rush had won the contest quite easily, receiving a perfect score for his ideas and a near perfect score for his delivery.[37]

In his winning discourse, "Political Ideals and Industrial Progress," Rush charged an "industrial autocracy" with corrupting and controlling politics through the leadership of party machines. Thus politicians, instead of representing the people, worked for the plutocrats passing legislation that protected their monopolies and guaranteed the maximization of their profits to the detriment of workers. Moreover, as long as great numbers of immigrants were allowed into the United States every year, the wages of workers were kept artificially low. This unfavorable environment for workers, Rush believed, could not change without the implementation of government reforms, which would break the hold of business upon state and federal government. To ensure that the people rather than plutocrats were in charge, certain progressive reforms had already been effective in breaking the political machines' hold upon city government. The introduction of commission government and more direct democratic processes had enabled the people to overturn legislation through the referendum, to fire elected officials by recall elections, and to expose the influence of money upon government through the publication of campaign donations. At the national level, Rush argued that the direct election of United States senators would help break the hold of business upon that body and the nomination of candidates through primaries would guarantee that the voters determined their party's nominees. Later that year, these policies became the major planks of Theodore Roosevelt's presidential candidacy, leading to Rush's support of the Progressive Party.[38]

As the internormal contest neared, preparations were made to host the event in Cape Girardeau. Tickets were distributed among students and townspeople, providing Rush and Allison Reppy, who had taken second in the intersociety contest, with much support. Contestants from each of the Normal schools at Warrensburg and Springfield soon arrived to participate in the contest as well. In addition to Rush's speech on political economy, the other orations covered the Spanish-American War, civil liberties, the Irish fight for independence, child labor, and "the power of the will." Rush spoke fourth on the program and his speech took first in both content and delivery and was described as "a forceful, convincing and eloquent presentation of the great dependence of political freedom on industrial freedom, and a stirring plea for interest and attention to the needs of our country." It was noted also that he rose to the occasion speaking with "convincing earnestness . . . [and] magnetism, a powerful and musical voice, and the power without which all else is in vain, to weld sentences and paragraphs into a consistent whole and make on an audience one vivid, lasting impression." In the categories of content and delivery, the judges awarded Rush the victory in content, despite a low mark from one of the three judges on the thought panel, and a quite easy victory in the performance judging. Of a possible 600 points, Rush received 579. Undoubtedly, his victory was all the sweeter because two of his brothers, Arthur and Roscoe, were present for the contest. After the competition, a raucous mass meeting was held in which the performances of both Rush and Reppy were celebrated.[39]

As the winner of the internormal contest, Rush won the privilege of representing Missouri in the interstate competition to be held on May 3 in Emporia, Kansas. Despite his success, Rush could not shake the feeling that he would lose the competition in Kansas. In the end, he finished fourth in a field of five orators from Kansas, Iowa, Illinois, Wisconsin, and Missouri. According to an account of the contest in the Emporia, Kansas, *State Normal Bulletin*, all of the participants were polished, able speakers and the contest was very close.[40]

Once the contest was over the audience was almost at sea as to first choice–a better indication of the closeness there could not be. Seatmates ranked the same man first and fifth and even the judges failed to approach much nearer agreement, for Iowa and Kansas both received firsts–and both fifths. In fact, the outcome of the contest was seemingly determined by individual preference as to oratorical style and content. Yet, despite the wide variation little unfavorable comment followed the decision. The only general dissatisfaction to be noticed was regarding the place accorded Limbaugh of Missouri, a great number in the audience feeling he fell far below his just deserts in the final ranking.[41]

Rush "was deeply disappointed" and probably dreaded facing his fellow students to whom he had hoped to bring home a victory or, at the very worst, a good showing. After returning to Cape Girardeau, Rush soon returned to his coursework, his work, and various other activities. During this difficult period, Bee offered her support and encouragement in letters indicating her concern that he not overwork himself and her confidence in his abilities and determination to succeed. It is clear from her letters that Rush had quickly recovered from his disappointment and that more than anything he wished to move forward with his education as quickly as possible and "get into the real fight," by which he probably meant taking his place in the community as a lawyer and involving himself in politics.[42]

As he prepared to return home again to work on the Limbaugh farm that summer, Rush, in a moment of nostalgia, probably penned the valedictory of his tenure as editor-in-chief of the *Capaha Arrow*. In "The Last Word of the Staff," he apologized to anyone who might have felt wronged by anything published in the paper and wished the next staff great success. He also recognized the great debt he owed to the Normal School and spoke for the rest of the staff in bidding "farewell to our dear old home, the school we love so well, and depart with hearts full of hope that she may ever live to impart to others as she has to us the things most dear." With these words Rush looked forward to new challenges as a student at the University of Missouri in Columbia as he drew nearer to his goal of attending law school and becoming a lawyer.[43]

Student at the University of Missouri

Rush H. Limbaugh spent the summer of 1912 working on the family farm and assisting his mother and brothers as needed. On Sundays, holidays, and whenever he could get away, Rush spent time with his fiancée, Bee Seabaugh, as they began making plans for their life together. With the summer's end, however, he again prepared to leave for college, this time to the University of Missouri in Columbia. Before his departure, through the help of one of his professors, Arthur W. Vaughan, Rush was hired for the following school year to serve as student secretary of the Young Men's Christian Association (YMCA) in close association with the Methodist churches in Columbia. He was to work twenty hours a week for which he received $500 for the school year.[1]

Rush arrived in Columbia sometime in September 1912. A short time after his arrival he acquainted himself with his new duties for the YMCA and enrolled in classes. On September 27 he turned twenty-one years old, and received his part of the inheritance from his father Joseph's life insurance policy, which amounted to a little more than $400. This and the salary from his position with the YMCA provided enough money to pay his college tuition and living expenses, and to save a portion to pay for classes the following year.[2]

Drawing from his experience working for the YMCA in Cape Girardeau, Rush worked closely with Reverends C. W. Tadlock and A. C. Johnson and a special subcommittee established to expand student participation in the Broadway Methodist Church in Columbia. During his first semester at the University of Missouri, Rush made sixty-seven visits to students, organized student Sunday school classes for men and women, and attended the meetings of the church committees and organizations to learn about "the different phases of church work" to coordinate his efforts with that of others. He also worked with the local Epworth League, a Methodist service organization for young people who wished to make a difference in their communities. By the end of the fall 1912 semester the league had 121 members, but regularly 200 students attended its meetings and participated in activities such as "visit[ing] . . . either the County jail, the county infirmary, the Negro settlement, or a suberb [sic] mission for the purpose of doing special work there, or conducting devotional services." Moreover, members of the league raised money to support missionary work in Korea and Cuba.[3]

In addition to his work and classes, Rush participated in meetings of the Athenaean Literary Society, a club dedicated to debate and speech, to which he was elected in September. The Athenaeans met each Saturday and debated a variety of topics including the establishment of state taxes, home rule in Kansas City and St. Louis, and old-age insurance. At the meeting following his election to the organization, Rush presented a five-minute talk on illegitimacy, reflecting his concern about the legal disabilities suffered by children born outside of marriage, an issue he would revisit later as a law student and as a lawyer. He also spoke on the failure of the German old-age insurance system and participated in the tryout for a place on the debate team. However, perhaps because he was a newcomer, he failed in this first effort.[4]

As already noted, Rush was deeply interested in politics from an early age and was strongly opposed to monopolies and corruption in government. This perspective probably developed through the influence of some of his professors and newspaper accounts exposing the malfeasance and cronyism of the political machines of the era. Thus, when former president Theodore Roosevelt emerged from the Republican convention in Chicago accusing party leaders of having stolen the nomination and characterizing his third-party candidacy as a battle "against bossism, against privilege social and industrial; we are warring for the elemental virtues of honesty and decency, of fair dealing between man and man," such rhetoric appealed strongly to Rush's idealism and support for progressive reforms of government. Bolting from the Republican convention, Roosevelt accepted the nomination of the Progressive convention and began a remarkable tour of the country, traveling through thirty-four states and covering some ten thousand miles. As president, Roosevelt could point to his support of many reforms including the passage of the Pure Food and Drug Act, arbitration of labor disputes, protection of the country's natural resources, and the buster of trusts. During the campaign Roosevelt advocated a minimum wage for workers, the prohibition of child labor, shorter working hours for women, and insurance for workers against illness, on-the-job injuries, and old age.[5]

Another aspect of Roosevelt's appeal to Rush derived in part from the great fire and incredible zeal of the former president's speeches with which he campaigned more like a crusading evangelist than a politician seeking office. As a young man aspiring to influence his community and generation through public speaking, "get[ting] into the real fight" as he once expressed it, the opportunity to support Roosevelt must have strongly appealed to Rush, especially since this was the first presidential election in which he was eligible to vote. Seeking to find some way to help, Rush wrote to Missouri's headquarters of

the Progressive Party in St. Louis offering his services to the campaign. This
led to his returning home to give six speeches in Bollinger County during the
last three days of the campaign. These rallies were hastily organized by Roosevelt's supporters, the chairman of the Progressive Party being Rush's former
teacher George E. Conrad. One of these speeches was made on November 2 in
Sedgewickville, where for the first time Bee heard her intended give a public
speech. Some years later, in a speech at one of the communities where he had
spoken in the 1912 campaign, Rush remembered himself during this period as
an earnest, naive young man, perhaps too credulous in his belief that progressive solutions would improve politics and society. He also expressed his desire
to apologize "for the boyishness of that effort and for what may have appeared
to you to have been an excess of enthusiasm for a short-lived cause." Moreover,
he noted how kindly he had been received by the community, especially those
Republicans who tolerated his speaking

> against the election of the candidate of the party to which my father had claimed
> unbroken allegiance during the whole period of his voting age. To many of you, I
> know that act appeared ungrateful, if not disloyal. My father was the kind of Re-
> publican who never scratched his ticket. But I had acquired the notion that his
> strict partisanship, together with that of millions of others in this country, was
> responsible for party bossdom, which was at that time revealing itself as one of
> the greatest evils of politics. It was not with a feeling of disrespect that I spoke
> against the party of my father's choice. I persuaded myself to believe that, had he
> been living, he would have done likewise. To you who heard my efforts that day,
> I owe grateful thanks, for I recall that you received me kindly and considerately,
> and your presence and courtesy was an inspiration that I have never forgotten.[6]

After the disappointment of Roosevelt's loss and his return to Columbia,
Rush resumed his classes, work with the Methodist church, and debate activities. By the end of his first year at the University of Missouri, he decided to take
summer classes at the Normal School in Cape Girardeau where he took Latin,
comparative government and English constitutional history, and Greek history.
Without the extra courses he would be unable to graduate in May 1914 and begin law school that fall. Bee also attended classes at Cape Girardeau, enabling
them to spend every day together and have a measure of autonomy and privacy
they could not enjoy at home. In a letter written just before their reunion, she
joked that she "might even promise to be up at five oclock [sic], just to play ten-
nis with you before breakfast, but if you manage to keep me from sleeping a lot
this summer you will be the first somebody that ever did." In preparation for
their marriage and Rush's work as a lawyer, Bee took classes in shorthand and
learned to type so she could do secretarial work for him.[7]

During the 1913–1914 school year, Rush returned to the University of Missouri and resumed his classes and extracurricular activities. Having resigned his position with the YMCA, he took a full load of courses and had more time for participation in debate. To support himself and pay for college he worked a number of odd jobs such as tending a horse for a lady in Columbia, waiting upon tables in a boarding house, and construction work. During the fall, the Athenaean Literary Society prepared for the upcoming intercollegiate season, holding tryouts for its varsity team, of which Rush was chosen as one of its members. Later, Rush and James P. Smith were chosen to debate the issue of immigration in April of 1914 in Austin, Texas, against the University of Texas debate squad. Despite the efforts of Rush and Smith, the decision went two to one against them. During the spring semester of 1914, Rush entered two oration contests, taking second place in one supporting international cooperation. Apparently Rush was popular among the society's members, for they elected him president for the coming semi-semester. His duties required him to preside over meetings and serve as "toastmaster" for a banquet held for members and alumni on May 8. During commencement week, Rush also competed for the prestigious Stephens Medal, winning with his speech, "Daniel Webster, Orator."[8]

During the summer of 1914, Rush returned to the family farm near Sedgewickville, where he worked with his brothers and mother while Bee remained at home helping her mother attend to the telephone switchboard and teaching piano lessons. After their engagement, Rush and Bee prudently postponed marriage, recognizing that their educations required most of their time and money. However, after Rush's absence for a year at Columbia, Bee, while conceding the difficulties, expressed her impatience to begin their lives together. "I do not see why we need to be so afraid. If we should decide to be married, and if we determined to get through we would succeed in spite of everything. It would be hard of course, but it is hard too the way things are with us now. Besides if we waited until everything was finished, and you had done it all alone, I would feel that I had missed a big part of you that I should have had. If I were somewhere else and had a chance to grow it would be a different matter altogether." Apparently the logic of Bee's argument and their yearning to start their lives together overcame Rush's fear about his possible inability to support them while at the University of Missouri, for they decided to marry before the fall semester of 1914. Rush and Bee decided to marry on August 29. Because of their financial circumstances, a church wedding was impossible, leading them to arrange for Dr. Ivan Lee Holt, pastor of the Centenary Methodist Church in Cape Girardeau, to conduct the ceremony at his home. To save money, Bee and her mother made her wedding dress. On the morning of their wedding, Rush worked with his brother Roscoe plowing a field until noon when he left behind the plow and farm work forever. After readying himself and traveling to Sedgewickville, he met Bee and her siblings Myrtle and Bland for their trip to Cape Girardeau in a hired car. Without anyone else available to operate the switchboard, Bee's mother was unable to attend the ceremony. Short on funds, the newlyweds had no honeymoon and within ten days began their journey to Columbia.[9]

Traveling by train, Rush and Bee arrived in Columbia after a series of derailments made it impossible for them to catch their connection in Perryville, where they stayed the night. Having intended to enroll and purchase his books the next morning, Rush was angry that his timetable had been upset and that he must unexpectedly pay for a hotel room. Bee, however, through her enthusiasm and optimism, was able to infect Rush with the same spirit of adventure with which she confronted their difficulties. From the train station in Columbia, Bee and Rush walked to their new home. Although they leased only one room in a two-story house, as part of the arrangement with the owner they were given the privilege of using the rest of the house. Soon after settling in, Rush discovered that Bee would not tolerate his haphazard ways. Instead of eating irregular meals or skipping them altogether, she insisted upon having three meals a day at specific times. Because they had no other means of transportation, like most students of that era they walked everywhere they needed to go. Thus, they made frequent visits to the grocery store to purchase and carry home their food. Bee also imposed order upon their living quarters, establishing a place for their belongings. In the mornings Rush attended classes and walked home for lunch and then with Bee returned to the university in the afternoon. While he prepared for the next day's classes at the law school library, Bee spent her time reading in the university library. After completing his work, they returned home. Because of the distance from their apartment to the university, they later moved closer to campus.[10]

On Sundays, Rush and Bee attended services at the Broadway Methodist Church where he had developed friendships with many of its members when he served as the YMCA's student secretary. Bee joined the Women's Missionary Society and developed friendships "with some of the most active women of the church." They also attended social gatherings with fellow students and "played rook" with other couples on Saturday nights. Moreover, the Limbaughs attended various student functions and lectures at the university.[11]

When Rush entered law school there were sixty-six students in his class. Some of his classmates were not interested in becoming lawyers, only wanting to gain some familiarity with the law before beginning their business careers. The faculty did their best to force these and other unsuitable students out of the program. Knowing this, the students strived for excellence to prove their ability and worthiness for the profession. At this time, students did not evaluate their professors, who ruled the classroom autocratically, failing those unwilling or unable to meet their standards. The law school was headquartered in the Law Department Building, which the students referred to as the law barn.[12]

During his first semester, Rush took courses in contracts, torts, and criminal law. In his second semester he learned about bailments, personal property, common law procedure, partnership, and criminal procedure. At that time there were no electives and students spent ten hours a week in class. While such a load appears light, the preparation for each class required a good deal of time. By then the school had largely converted over to "the case method of instruction," in which students were assigned court opinions provided in casebooks. The professor demanded that students fully understand the court's decision, be able to summarize it, and answer questions and engage in a dialogue about it. Of course, this required more preparation by the student than simply memorizing the details of a case. This method had the advantage of developing students' critical thinking skills and ability to argue the details and merits of legal issues in the same manner as lawyers do in the courtroom. By 1914, most law schools had adopted this method as superior to "the text and lecture method," in which the professor followed the textbook's presentation of the law with examples from cases.[13]

Rush's favorite professor, Manley O. Hudson, used the case method and was known for challenging his students intellectually and showing little patience with those who could not support their ideas and arguments. As one of his intimates related many years later, Hudson's "greatest joy [was] to cross intellectual swords with an antagonist," although this "was a technique at which some sensitive souls quailed." Rush, who had become accustomed to the rough-and-tumble of college debate, enjoyed the challenge of Hudson's classes in which he could develop the skills he would need to become a successful lawyer. Many years later Rush remembered him as "a very extraordinary man. He had a very unusual intellect, and he had a way of expressing himself that was always intriguing and interesting." Moreover, Rush enthusiastically supported Hudson's ideas concerning the need to establish international cooperation among nations to avert war.[14]

As before, Rush was active in the Athenaean Literary Society. Some of his duties included serving as sergeant-at-arms and critic and representing the society on the debating board. Rush also continued to participate in debate contests. To this time, Rush's grades at the University of Missouri were superior despite working his way through school and participating in a number of extracurricular activities. For the first time, however, at the end of his first semester of law school he received disappointing grades. The grading system, like that used today in many schools and universities, was based upon a five-grade scale and was calculated to determine an overall percentage of the student's performance during the semester. The highest grade was an E (95–100 percent), next was an S (85–95 percent), then an M (70–85 percent), an I (50–70 percent), and finally an F (below 50 percent). Moreover, the law school had a policy that dictated to the instructors that fifty percent of their grades be Ms, twenty-five percent be below Ms, twenty-five percent above Ms, and only two percent be Es. Rush received three Ms and two Is, a result which surprised him. As he related many years later, these grades were "a blow to my pride and spirit from which I never recovered." Fortunately, during this period of despair, Bee, with strong loyalty to and belief in her husband, refused to consider these lackluster grades to be an indication that Rush "would not make a successful lawyer." Instead, she concluded that too much of his time was consumed in social activities and determined to curtail these to allow him more time to study.[15]

Not long after the spring 1915 semester had begun, Dean Eldon R. James called Rush into his office after learning that he was chosen to represent the university in a debate in Boulder, Colorado, later that semester. James confronted him with his poor academic performance the previous semester and, according to Rush's account many years later, demonstrated a "very unfriendly and antagonistic attitude." Successful law students, he asserted, applied themselves exclusively to their coursework. James conceded that he could not forbid Rush from going to Colorado, but he promised him that if he "persisted in going on with the debate" he would again make poor grades that semester. If James believed that his warning would be heeded, he was mistaken. Rush resented the dean's threat and became more determined than ever to go. Later that day when he related to Bee what had happened he was surprised that she was even more outraged about the matter than he had been. Indeed, she urged her husband to attend the debate and prove to James and the faculty that he could do both. In retrospect, Rush admitted that this decision was probably "a mistake," made more in a spirit of impetuosity than in careful deliberation. However, although his grades were not spectacular for the spring 1915 semester, he did improve, receiving one S and the rest Ms.[16]

In addition to taking his law courses and pursuing his debate and Athenaean activities, Rush continued his work as a reader for the English department, for which he was paid $50 a month, and graded papers for Dr. Frederick H. Tisdel, head of the speech department, for $75 a month. In March he entered the Peace Oratorical Contest held in Columbia. His speech, "Is there a Substitute for Force in International Relations?," reflected Professor Hudson's influence upon Rush's thought concerning the conduct of international affairs. Presented at a time when the great slaughter of the First World War had just begun, he argued that "the art of government" should be extended to "exercise social control over nations," and establish a world not "based upon physical force." International affairs, he believed, must be conducted under a system of law through an international organization where disputes could be debated peacefully. He also supported establishing a world court where violations of peace and international law could be prosecuted. Moreover, while Rush conceded that in extreme circumstances preparation for war might be necessary, he asserted that military force alone could not provide security. For this effort, Rush won first honors.[17]

After participating in the debate against the University of Colorado at Boulder, Rush wound up his participation in Athenaean activities by attending their banquet, the final event of the 1915 school year. More than fifty members and alumni attended and Rush, as the society's former president, spoke along with six alumni, who gave "interesting accounts" of what the Athenaean Society had meant to the earlier students in the university. The main speaker was United States Senator Thomas B. Catron, who had attended the university before the Civil War and had been a member of the Athenaean Literary Society, graduating in 1860. The senator, much to Rush's surprise, had accepted his invitation to attend the banquet on his return from Washington, DC to New Mexico where he had settled after the war. At the meeting, Catron, who had served in the Confederate Army, gave a stirring speech about the siege of Vicksburg and the Union soldiers' magnanimity in sharing their rations with him and the rest of the surrendered soldiers. Another man, Colonel R. B. Price, also an alumnus of the society, replied that he also was one of the soldiers inside the citadel, confirming Catron's story. Afterward, the two men embraced.[18]

Because of the European conflict and the influence of Professor Hudson, Rush became increasingly interested in foreign affairs. Sometime during the 1914–1915 school year he had joined the International Polity Club and been elected president of its local chapter. This organization's purpose was to promote peace and interest in international affairs. Of special interest to its members, most of whom were college students, was to keep the United States out of the war. Firmly opposed to militarism and imperialism, Rush believed that international negotiation and the establishment of a world parliament and court could prevent most wars.[19]

Thus, to better understand world events, during the summer of 1915 Rush took two classes in European and American diplomatic history. During this time, his mentor Professor Hudson gave him William Leighton Grane's book, *The Passing of War*. Published in 1914, when the great conflict in Europe was just beginning, Grane argued that arbitration must replace an almost reflexive resort to arms and that collective security was best preserved through "the comity of nations." Thus, by creating this association, no nation would ever again "brave the penalties involved in the ostracism of other nations and the condemnation of the world" through an aggressive act of war against another. That Rush took Grane's ideas seriously is evident from his later opposition to the

United States' entrance into the war, demonstrating an independence of mind and a willingness to stand for his ideals despite their unpopularity. In particular, Rush abhorred war, agreeing with Grane that it was not an "ennobling and beneficent" enterprise, as many argued, but instead was "a barbarous anachronism of which the civilised world ought to be utterly ashamed."[20]

Undoubtedly, these issues took on a greater importance to Rush when Bee revealed that she was then carrying their first child. Fortunately, she had become friends with several of the ladies in their neighborhood, who provided assistance in Marguerite's birth on July 28, 1915. For the next week, these women took care of mother and child and attended to the couple's household needs. One of these women, "Mrs. Pegg, wife of a university professor, took the place of Bee's absent mother and expressed delight in joining her neighbors in doing everything possible to make Bee and the baby comfortable." On the day of their daughter's birth, Rush was scheduled to make a presentation on United States diplomacy during the Napoleonic period in Dr. E. F. Stephens' class. Bee had gone into labor only an hour before Rush was to give his talk and he called Professor Stephens to explain his predicament. The professor's wife answered the phone and after learning that Bee had gone into labor she ordered him to "take care of [his] darling wife," adding that Dr. Stephens could "take care of his class" just fine without him.[21]

Between the summer and fall semesters, Rush worked temporary jobs to earn extra money. At first he found a job driving a team of draft animals and operating a scraper to excavate basements for a building contractor. After this he worked for the university farm clearing land and erecting fence, work with which he had much experience on the family farm. In late August while Rush was doing this very strenuous work, for "several days in succession" Bee cooked a hot meal and brought Marguerite by baby carriage to spend the noon hour with him. This walk was over a mile, much of it through a field, and Rush protested that it was too soon after their daughter's birth for her to make such a strenuous trip each day. However, after Bee disagreed, noting that she felt "strong and healthy," Rush first acquiesced and later looked forward to her visits and the meals she brought.[22]

With the beginning of the fall semester of 1915, Rush redoubled his efforts to do well in law school. Bee assisted him not only by taking care of Marguerite and their home, but also by typing up his class notes and papers. Perhaps finally recognizing the wisdom of Dean James' advice to focus exclusively upon his law studies, Rush significantly curtailed his participation in Athenaean Literary Society activities. This did not please some of his fellow Athenaeans, especially since he continued to be active in the International Polity Club; one member even went so far as to write that "grades even in law school do not mark the successful lawyers." More important than an E or an S, his friend Harry Poindexter asserted, was the reputation a student made while in college. Moreover, he warned Rush not to "let old Manley O. [Hudson] flatter you in that peace pro[pa]ganda."[23]

Despite his friend's advice, Rush did not renew his debate and speech activities, although Poindexter's counsel may have influenced him in another more important decision later that semester. In the afternoon while studying at home, Rush received a phone call from Professor Hudson summoning him to his office. As he made his way over to the law school, Rush feared that he was again to be reprimanded about his grades. It turned out, however, that Hudson had just received a telegram from the great automotive industrialist Henry Ford requesting that he choose a student at the University of Missouri to travel with a delegation "to the scene of the war then raging in Europe for the purpose, as he expressed it, of getting the armies out of the trenches by Christmas." Hudson offered the opportunity to Rush, adding that Ford would be paying his expenses. Surprised, Rush explained that he had a wife and child and was only with difficulty able to pay for law school. Before giving him an answer, he requested that he be given a short time to return home and talk the matter over with Bee after which he promised to return. Hudson thought this a good suggestion. Bee, who shared Rush's views about the war and the need for greater international cooperation, urged him to go, adding that she could return to Sedgewickville to stay with her mother during his absence. Despite her willingness to make this sacrifice, Rush concluded that he could not leave her and Marguerite alone for two or three months and thus delay finishing law school for another year. Although he must have been disappointed at missing the opportunity to travel to Europe and work to end the war, this did not dampen his enthusiasm to learn more about international relations, participate in the International Polity Club's meetings, and to advocate a pacifist policy in which war was to be only a last resort.[24]

Toward the end of the fall 1915 semester, Rush and Bee together considered the possibility of his taking the bar examination the next summer and starting his law career without completing his law degree. Thus he wrote to a number of friends requesting information about where it might be best for a young lawyer to begin his career. Not limiting himself to Missouri, he investigated opportunities in Wyoming and Colorado, gathering a good deal of information about different communities where lawyers were needed. He also investigated completing law school in Chicago. Just how seriously he contemplated spending his final year of law studies in Chicago is unclear, but financial concerns probably influenced his decision not to go there.[25]

One of the first people to whom Rush had written about beginning his law career after completing his second year of law school was Benson C. Hardesty. Rush had become well acquainted with him while attending the Normal

School in Cape Girardeau through his debate activities and his membership at the Centenary Methodist Church. Hardesty replied that he could give no definite answer then, although later he would write and make "such suggestions as I can, as I have always been interested in your career and wish you the best in the world." While awaiting Hardesty's promised letter, Rush wrote to one of his former professors, Robert S. Douglass, inquiring about the prospects in Cape Girardeau for a young lawyer. Douglass replied that although the town was "crowded with lawyers" there was always room for those who were "<u>intelligent, honest, industrious</u> and a <u>judge of human</u> nature. Such a man will succeed anywhere there is business. The business is here and I think you have the essential requisites of success. I shall be glad to see you established here if you decide to come." In April 1916, Hardesty wrote to invite Rush to work in his law office during the summer. If nothing else, Rush could gain some experience and possibly make a little money. As far as going into partnership with him, Hardesty made no promises. Nevertheless, Rush concluded that beginning his career in an established firm was better than striking off on his own and he accepted the proposal. Both understood that there was a strong possibility Rush would return to Columbia for his final year of law school. Rush's course would be dictated by circumstances.[26]

In May 1916, the lease on the house in which the Limbaughs were staying expired two weeks before the end of the spring semester. For this reason, it was decided that Bee and Marguerite would stay with her mother in Sedgewickville while Rush remained to finish the school year. During that time he roomed with a fellow student and stayed another two weeks to prepare for the bar examination he would take in June. Immediately after taking the exam in Jefferson City, Rush traveled by train to Cape Girardeau, arriving on June 22. As soon as they opened, Rush visited the offices of Davis and Hardesty, located in the First National Bank building. His friend and mentor Hardesty greeted Rush cordially and invited him to stay in his home until he could find a place of his own. He had already set aside some collections work for his young protégé and thought that in time Rush might help him with some cases. In a few days, Bee and Marguerite traveled to Cape Girardeau for a visit, although they could not stay for long because Rush had no money. It was decided that she would continue to stay with her mother, where she remained until the end of the summer.[27]

Rush began to make collections, walking from place to place throughout Cape Girardeau, work which he described as an "exceedingly unprofitable business." Fortunately, on July 4 he learned that he had passed the bar exam and soon procured some legal work of his own. In his first case, brought before a justice of the peace, Rush prosecuted a claim against a debtor, winning a judgment of $35 for his client. These courts, before which the majority of his early practice was conducted, handled civil actions which amounted to no more than $250. These cases exposed him to a great variety of civil law, giving Rush important experience in many facets of litigation including "landlord and tenant actions, cases in tort, in contract, and on account." He also learned about criminal law by handling misdemeanor cases and "preliminary hearings in felony cases." Apparently, Rush's diligence and hard work impressed both Benjamin F. Davis and Hardesty, for they urged him not to return to law school. After discussing this with Bee, they concluded that attending law school for another year was impractical, especially since Rush had developed valuable contacts and was then engaged in cases with the potential to make money. Their first home together in Cape Girardeau consisted of two upstairs rooms they leased, where they would remain for a year and a half. While this was at best a very modest beginning, they were very thankful nevertheless, for most important of all they were together.[28]

During the fall of 1916, while Rush struggled to establish himself as a lawyer, Bee maintained their home and cared for Marguerite. Whenever possible, she helped Rush in his work and made extra money typing documents such as a long abstract for which she received $50. With this money she purchased a sewing machine, enabling her to economize by making the family's clothes. In this way, despite their making little money that fall and the following winter, Rush and Bee managed to eke out a living. Thus were the modest beginnings of a long and happy marriage, and an even longer and prosperous law career. In the coming years, Rush slowly built up his clientele and increasingly handled cases before the state and federal district courts. Moreover, from the start he donated a considerable amount of his time to various community organizations and gave public addresses supporting political candidates, and perhaps most surprisingly, the Great War.[29]

Chapter Four

The Great War and Growing Law Practice

As he pursued his legal career in southeast Missouri, Rush H. Limbaugh also kept himself informed about political and international affairs and occasionally addressed the public. During the presidential campaign of 1916, Limbaugh spoke at Republican rallies and undoubtedly was disappointed when the party's presidential candidate, Charles Evans Hughes, narrowly lost to President Woodrow Wilson. In conversations with friends, Limbaugh found himself increasingly alone in opinion concerning the United States' policy toward the European war, especially after Germany declared unrestricted submarine warfare upon American shipping in early 1917. Even after the publication of German Foreign Secretary Arthur Zimmermann's telegram seeking an alliance with Mexico on March 1, Limbaugh still resisted abandoning his hope that the United States might avoid war. In Cape Girardeau almost no one else shared this view, believing that the time for talk had ended. Nevertheless, he sought to learn more about the issues and tried to persuade others—and increasingly himself—that the United States should remain neutral. At the end of March, Limbaugh turned to his former law professor, Manley O. Hudson, for help in strengthening his arguments against war.

> Enthusiasm over the prospects of war is boundless here and men are enlisting in the army very rapidly. I can find no one here with any conception of how we are to perform our international duty in any other way than by entering the war. I wish you would please send me some of the arguments that you have been using against our going to war with Germany. I cannot maintain my position of refusing to support the President and Congress as against the bitter attacks made by those who see no other way except war. The arguments we have used are not enough to convince those who are crazed by the war talk or at least, I lack the 'punch' to make them convincing. If you have anything prepared at all that you can conveniently part with, I will be very grateful to you if you will forward the same to me at once. Of course, I want your own arguments for I owe my conversion to you, and I know your arguments have that element of 'punch' which I need just now. I am disgusted with the attitude of the 'New Republic.'[1]

A week later, however, the hope for peace vanished when the president sought a congressional declaration of war against Germany. As required by law, Limbaugh was one of the first to register for the draft and soon made public addresses supporting the war "on numerous occasions." Undoubtedly, his *volte-face* would not have occurred without the German military's decision to unleash its submarines in unrestricted attacks upon American shipping in the Atlantic Ocean. This destruction of American lives and property made opposition to the war impossible except for only the most ardent pacifists, or "peace-at-any-price men," as William Jennings Bryan had expressed it in a speech Limbaugh had attended in Columbia, Missouri. Nevertheless, Limbaugh's support for the war, it should be noted, did not end his opposition to militarism and imperialism. He still believed that the competition among European nations for colonial acquisitions around the world had led to the buildup of their military forces to unprecedented levels and to the conclusion of military alliances, some of them secret, which in the end had made them less secure. Because of these alliances, only a minor incident was required to touch off a calamitous conflict leading to the deaths of millions of soldiers and civilians in Europe. During the war and after, Limbaugh supported the League of Nations, an institution in which he hoped disputes between nations could be negotiated peacefully. He also sought the establishment of courts to enforce international law.[2]

On June 19, 1917, Limbaugh spoke at a Red Cross meeting in Cape Girardeau, urging his fellow citizens to donate what they could to provide medical aid to both civilians and soldiers in Europe. He noted "the inhuman practices" of the German military in its ruthless and cruel suppression of opposition. In August he delivered a speech to Company L of the Missouri National Guard on the occasion of their departure. By the following March, in a speech delivered at a mass meeting in Morehouse, Missouri, Limbaugh noted that the conflict in France had reached a critical point as there was some danger that Germany might break through the Allied lines. If that happened, he feared, the war might continue for many more years and there was the danger that Germany would be "master of Europe and in a position to vanquish the entire world." Then "democratic nations and liberty loving people will be compelled to fight her as long as breath lasts." German success might also embolden some of her supporters in the United States, presenting a possible threat at home. Moreover, Limbaugh criticized those farmers, laborers, and consumers, who apparently were unwilling to make wartime sacrifices and were then agitating for economic benefits while many thousands of American men were leaving their jobs and homes to serve in the military. In other addresses, Limbaugh explained to students at the Normal School and to the general public the reasons why the United States went to war.[3]

While some might criticize him for not volunteering, as a husband and father of a growing family, Limbaugh probably felt he had an obligation to his family not to expose himself unnecessarily to danger. This consideration for men with families had caused the United States Congress to organize the draft so that single young men would enter the service first. However, because they believed that their induction into the military was only a matter of time, Limbaugh and others who had not yet been drafted prepared themselves for military service by meeting once or twice a week to drill in a home guard unit. These men were also subject to call up "for duties connected with the war effort." These duties included four-hour marches, maneuvers, and drills. Concerning one of these call ups, which was particularly exhausting, Captain Allen L. Oliver sarcastically promised "the men [that] they will be thoroughly enthused by the time they get back." In addition to these activities, Limbaugh served a day each week on the draft board in Jackson and assisted in the sale of liberty bonds, sometimes traveling out of town to help raise money for the war effort. After the war had ended, he learned that he would have been in the next group called for military service. On November 11, 1918, when it was learned that the war was over, the inhabitants of Cape Girardeau were awakened at five o'clock in the morning by whistles and bells sounding throughout the city, bringing men, women, and children from their homes into the streets in a spontaneous celebration of the end of the carnage and the return of their loved ones.[4]

With the war's end, Limbaugh felt great relief, not only to escape military service and war, but also to be freed from his many wartime activities to pursue his profession unfettered and without further interruption. Serving on the draft board in Jackson had made the war very real to him, for part of his duty was to help the newly drafted men prepare for their imminent departures from loved ones. In this capacity he had observed "the heartaches" of the wives, parents, and children of these men and he undoubtedly learned of the wounding and the death of some of these same men later. Now that the war was over he and Bee "rejoiced" that the threat of separation or worse no longer existed. Feeling the enthusiasm of a reprieved man, Limbaugh left home "before daybreak" and walked to his office, making his way through the celebrating crowds.[5]

During the war, Limbaugh made very little money and he and Bee maintained frugal habits to make ends meet. Nevertheless, he was forced to borrow money from his brother Arthur. On February 26, 1918, a son was born to the Limbaughs and was named Rush H. Limbaugh Jr. Only days after this, Limbaugh was surprised to learn that a group of businessmen in Cape Girardeau had chosen him to run for mayor. Because the position involved much work and little pay, others had refused to run and they had finally decided upon Limbaugh, whom they regarded as an energetic young man with much promise. Another factor contributing to their decision may have been Limbaugh's strong support for establishing a commission form of government in which "he had taken a leading part in the campaign for the adoption of the new system," which had recently been adopted by Cape Girardeau. His candidacy was announced in the *Southeast Missourian* on March 2, with the businessmen noting that "he is a fine young man who can afford for a few years to sell his time and ability at a low price because of the prestige of the future a successful administration as mayor would give him." Bee, however, did not share this opinion about their financial situation and was not a little displeased that her husband had agreed to run for office. She doubted that he could make as much money as mayor as he had made practicing law and knew that a family of four was more expensive than a family of three. Nevertheless, she eventually "acquiesced" in the decision, although without enthusiasm.[6]

During the campaign, supporters presented Limbaugh as the person best suited to serve as mayor, for he understood the commission form of government well and would be able to devote all of his time to city business, unlike his opponent, H. H. Haas, who was the local druggist. This was important, for Limbaugh's supporters believed that making the new commission government work properly would require a mayor to work full time at city hall for two years. In his own communication to the voters, Limbaugh promised to work solely for "the common interest and welfare of all the people." In conducting the office, he intended to make himself available to everyone and to have all city business transacted in public to ensure transparency. "The city's business should be an open book to every citizen. No matter of public importance should be hidden from the public eye." In this manner, he expected to give everyone and every point of view "a square deal." Limbaugh also believed that the new commission form of government would provide a simpler and more efficient means of conducting the city's business, and to make it work he promised "to be on the job all the time" and to "have regular office hours." Another matter of great importance was to economize. He would not raise taxes, although he would insist that everyone pay their proper obligations. To achieve this, a budget would be established and the money apportioned to each department. As mayor he would insist that the city spend no more than it received in revenues. As he put it, "there will be no patronage to hand out; no political pie of any kind to distribute." For himself he would ask for "nothing but a living wage. And I shall earn what I receive."[7]

One of the major issues in the country at the time concerned prohibition. State legislatures were then voting upon a constitutional amendment to ban the "the manufacture, sale, [and] transportation of intoxicating liquors." Of course, "the liquor element" opposed the supporters of prohibition and were very active in protecting their interests. Thus, "a prominent liquor dealer" referred to the businessmen who supported Limbaugh's candidacy for mayor as "a bunch of cranks" and said other unflattering things, some of which a reporter for the *Southeast Missourian* intimated to his readers he could not repeat verbatim for decency's sake. If elected mayor, Limbaugh promised to raise the cost of a liquor license, noting that "the saloon men and liquor interests of this city are not bearing their share of the burden of taxation. . . . I reiterate my former statement that I stand for a square deal for all. If any man or interest in this city looks to me for more I shall have nothing pleasing to offer him." While if elected mayor he did not have the authority to close the saloons, some of which doubled as prostitution and gambling houses, he certainly supported the constitutional amendment then in the process of ratification. As an active member of the Centenary Methodist Church and a public speaker, Limbaugh also supported other reforms intended to improve society through the application of "the social gospel"—a set of Christian principles meant to help achieve "social and industrial justice." Thus, Limbaugh wholeheartedly advocated emancipating women and giving them the right to vote, the passage of laws prohibiting the employment of children in factories, and changing the laws restricting the rights of illegitimate children.[8]

Although not running against one another, but unopposed for the nomination of their respective parties, some concern probably existed among Limbaugh's supporters when his opponent, Haas, received almost twice as many votes. Perhaps, because they were fighting for their livelihood, Haas' supporters were more motivated, but for whatever reason this result indicated that Limbaugh could win only with difficulty and must find a way to change minds and increase the enthusiasm of those inclined to vote for him. After the primary, Haas' supporters were confident of victory in the general election. This group also opposed the commission form of government.[9]

Soon Limbaugh's opponents accused him of being disloyal, perhaps remembering his opposition to the United States entering the war and questioning whether he supported the government and was "doing his part to win the war." This accusation angered him and ignored the active role he had taken in supporting the Red Cross and selling liberty bonds, his work on the draft board, and the public speeches he had given urging his listeners to support various measures undertaken to aid the troops. Moreover, at a time when dissent was punishable by a stiff fine and long imprisonment, such accusations sometimes led to arrest and prosecution under federal law, a circumstance that many people across the country, including a young man from nearby Charleston, had discovered that week. To rebut the accusations of disloyalty and other "lies and various statements made against" him, Limbaugh announced that he would give a speech in downtown Cape Girardeau from an automobile on March 23. Speaking before a large crowd on a street corner, the newspaper account described his speech as "a typical Limbaugh address–patriotic, frank, clear, and honest. There was no mincing or hedging." In it Limbaugh promised to support the troops as mayor and addressed other local issues and questions that the voters might wish answered. At the end of his speech he withdrew from the race, explaining that it had been discovered that a recent state law required that candidates be at least thirty years of age to serve as mayor in Cape Girardeau. Such circumstances undoubtedly embarrassed and disappointed him, although he noted many years later that "Bee was happy with this turn of events."[10]

After working out of the offices of Davis & Hardesty during the summer of 1916, Limbaugh moved to another office, probably to reduce his professional expenses. Nevertheless, he and Benson C. Hardesty still occasionally tried cases together, a relationship which would continue for a number of years. One of these cases concerned a contested will in which Limbaugh participated in two trials of the suit, the first of which ended in a hung jury. In the second trial they secured a judgment upholding the will. In another estate case, Hardesty provided Limbaugh with employment by appointing him as "inheritance tax appraiser," work which provided him with a modest but welcome fee. In *Caler v. Caler*, Hardesty brought Limbaugh into a contested divorce case. While doing this and other work he picked up on his own, in August 1917 Limbaugh was appointed city attorney for Cape Girardeau, replacing a lawyer who was entering the military service. The position was not lucrative and did not even provide a salary. Instead, his compensation came through securing the conviction of persons accused of violating city ordinances, earning $3.00 for every successful prosecution in court. While the pay was meager, through this and his other work he gained experience and became more generally known to fellow lawyers and the community.[11]

Much of Limbaugh's early legal work was before justice of the peace courts where it was not unusual for him to spend an entire day litigating a case in which he might receive only $15.00. Of course the time he spent on such a case was not limited to the trial, for it was necessary to expend a significant amount of time in research and other preparation beforehand. His remaining legal work involved writing deeds and wills. To help him with the drafting of these legal documents, Hardesty provided Limbaugh with "boilerplate" forms from which to begin. Fortunately, in addition to the work he received through Hardesty, his prosecutions as city attorney, and suits before the justice of the peace courts, Limbaugh increasingly gained the opportunity to try cases in the Cape Girardeau Common Pleas Court and circuit courts in several counties.[12]

Perhaps the most sensational trial in which Limbaugh and Hardesty were involved was a case defending Reverend W. L. Halberstadt, minister of the Centenary Methodist Church, of which Limbaugh and Hardesty were members. During the summer of 1919, Halberstadt and other concerned citizens, including Limbaugh and Hardesty, had established the Law Enforcement League to gather evidence of liquor sales and the operation of prostitution and gambling houses. It had become evident to them that the city authorities and the candidates favored by "the liquor interests" during the 1918 city election, were not enforcing prohibition and the other anti-vice laws. For this reason, the league hired detectives W. O. McDonald and Earl Craft to investigate and gather evidence of criminal activity and present it to the authorities for prosecution. During the detectives' investigation, they purchased liquor from a number of persons, found evidence of gambling operations, and also discovered prostitutes working out of a house owned by Charles Stebbins. The league presented its evidence against Stebbins to the prosecuting attorney, James A. Bark, for action. After reviewing the evidence, Bark agreed with the league that Stebbins was likely to be convicted upon it. Later, however, Stebbins was not convicted when he was tried before a justice of the peace. Stebbins then sued Halberstadt for damages, for personal humiliation and harm to his reputation, and for lawyer's fees expended to defend himself against the charges.[13]

At trial, Craft testified that he had posed as a prospective buyer of Stebbins' house and the services of the prostitutes there. Stebbins told the detective that he was assured by Mayor Haas and Police Chief Segraves that the operations of his house would not be interfered with and noted that the girls, Nell Jones and Frances Watson, were good earners and claimed that between the prostitution and gambling activities he made from $40 to $50 a night. After he was told of the detectives' activities, Halberstadt testified that the mayor "had threatened to kill the detectives on sight." Police Chief Segraves told the minister "that they would not 'look good' when he got through with them." Stebbins, who took the stand, denied all the charges brought against him, claiming that the women were maids and honest women, but that he had decided he could not afford to keep them on and had dismissed them. This testimony was contradicted by Craft who related that when he had concluded the contract to buy the house Nell Jones read the contract and turning to Stebbins said "'it looks like you sold us (meaning herself and Frances Watson) with the house.' Nell Jones then turned to him, Craft said, and pointing at him said, 'there is our new daddy.'" Hardesty, who took the lead in Halberstadt's defense, offered four affidavits in court from the detectives relating to their purchase contract for Stebbins' house, a list of policemen "patronizing the house and associating with a certain girl," and details of a gambling operation there. Called by Stebbins' lawyer, Mayor Haas took the stand to deny "that he approved of immoral houses or immoral women, but on the contrary had always taken a stand against such places and persons. He denied vehemently that he had told Craft in his drug store that he would not interfere with him in operating immoral houses."

Similarly, Police Chief Segraves, while admitting that he had spoken with him, denied that Craft had even mentioned that he was purchasing the Stebbins' house to run an illegal prostitution and gambling operation. Moreover, the police chief asserted that he certainly had never promised not to interfere with it.[14]

During the trial, the patience of Judge John A. Snider of the Court of Common Pleas was tested when during Mayor Haas' testimony the attorneys on both sides objected several times. This contentiousness, the sometimes rowdiness of the spectators who packed the courtroom, and the testimony caused the judge to exclaim that he would "never sit upon the bench long enough to again be called on to hear such a case as it is the most revolting he has ever presided over." At the end of the testimony both sides were given an hour to make their closing arguments to the jury. The attorney for Stebbins used his time to attack Halberstadt, opposing counsel, the Law Enforcement League, and the detectives. Hardesty and Limbaugh, according to a journalist's account, "confined themselves strictly to the evidence." As was noted in an editorial about the trial, no question existed in the mind of the jurors concerning who was telling the truth, for they returned with a verdict in Halberstadt's favor in only eight minutes. Thus, the editorialist concluded, "decency has won a victory that will establish the fact that vice can be suppressed if strong enough efforts are made by those who are vitally interested in cleaner conditions."[15]

Another important early case on which Limbaugh worked involved his maternal uncle, Charles E. Presnell, in a case before the Circuit Court of Bollinger County. As he related many years later, Limbaugh found the experience rewarding, as the caliber of the lawyers involved in it was very high, from whom he learned a good deal. His uncle had gotten into a dispute with Oscar Fuller, the owner of a lumber enterprise, over a deal to sell lumber cut from his property. According to Presnell, he learned that the terms under which he had agreed to deliver the timber to Fuller were unfair to him. He also claimed that Fuller's agent, W. F. Wells, had misrepresented the terms of the contract regarding the type of lumber to be delivered. Thus Presnell renegotiated with Fuller personally and prepared the lumber, making it available for inspection and sale according to the terms of their verbal agreement. Nevertheless, after preparing the lumber and offering it for inspection and delivery on "frequent" occasions, Presnell asserted that Fuller had refused to inspect and receive the timber. Thus after repeated attempts to sell it to Fuller, Presnell then sold the lumber to another dealer.[16]

Claiming breach of contract, Fuller sued Presnell for damages. At the same time Fuller sued another landowner, Jacob M. Taylor, under similar circumstances, leading the men to combine their resources in hiring lawyers to fight their suits against Fuller. Taylor, who was a prominent merchant in Marble Hill, also happened to be friends with Charles G. Revelle, a noted attorney and former judge of the Supreme Court of Missouri. After hiring Revelle, Presnell suggested that they employ Limbaugh in the case so his nephew could gain the experience. Once they had consulted together, both Judge Revelle and Limbaugh concluded that as outsiders to the community of Marble Hill, they needed to bring in a local lawyer to help them prepare for trial. Thus they hired "the Dean of the Bar at Marble Hill," William M. Morgan, to act mostly as an adviser in the case. The opposing counsel was headed by Robert H. Davis, who "was cunning and skillful before country juries" and from whom Limbaugh believed he learned a good deal during the course of the trial. While Judge Revelle took the lead in the case, Limbaugh cross-examined some of the witnesses and made the closing argument before the jury, who decided against Presnell, awarding Fuller $1,710.[17]

From this judgment, Limbaugh, Revelle, and Morgan appealed to the Springfield Court of Appeals. Their case came before the court during the March 1920 term. They argued that the jury's verdict was contrary to the evidence presented in court. First of all, no evidence was presented to contradict Presnell's testimony that Fuller's agent, W. F. Wells, had misled Presnell concerning what constituted No. 2 grade lumber in the contract. Moreover, Fuller never proved in court that he had suffered damages resulting from Presnell's "alleged breach of contract." And finally, Fuller's own evidence demonstrated that he was unable to fulfill his part of the agreement. Another aspect of the trial to which Limbaugh and his fellow counsel objected was the judge's decisions on evidence and some of the remarks he made in court, which tended to prejudice the jury against Presnell's case. Particularly prejudicial was the judge's seeming agreement with the statements of Fuller's lawyer, Robert H. Davis, who sarcastically accused Presnell of seeking to escape the contract after the price of lumber had increased significantly. These arguments presented on appeal were rejected by the court, although it did rule that the jury's award was excessive and that Fuller must remit that part of the judgment exceeding $1,215. This amount was the difference in the increase of the price for lumber which accrued from February 9 to March 1, 1920, the court ruling that the former date was the proper one at which to fix the compensation of damages to Fuller. This decision was appealed to the Supreme Court of Missouri during the October 1921 term, seeking a rehearing of their case on the grounds that the court of appeals had wrongly applied the law and precedent in the case. The supreme court's decision against them ended their litigation. While he only collected a small fee for his trouble in preparing and trying the case and then appealing it to the court of appeals and the supreme court, Limbaugh noted that he had "gained invaluable experience in being associated with a profound lawyer in his senior years, a most distinguished lawyer and judge, between whom [he] sat during the trials at the counsel table, and having as an adversary a popular trial lawyer at the peak of his career with both natural and cultivated skills in winning verdicts before country juries."[18]

During this early period of his professional career, the most important case in which Limbaugh became involved was *Dewey Robison v. Floesch Construction Company*. The case was the first major suit on which he took the lead. This occurred largely because the case of his client, Dewey Robison, a minor, and his parents was considered hopeless by those lawyers with whom the family had consulted before offering it to Limbaugh. The boy's father, J. C. Robison, after failing to find a lawyer to take the case, remembered that he had heard Limbaugh speak two years before at a political rally in Zalma, Missouri, and decided to consult with him. Robison explained that his son had been injured while working on a construction crew, had suffered a severe fracture of his left leg, and had been hospitalized. In October 1918, four weeks after the accident, Louis W. Mees, an attorney for Floesch Construction, came to Dewey's hospital room and offered to pay his hospital bills and $250 as compensation for his injury. The young man, who was only seventeen years old at the time, wanted to consult with his father before making any agreement, but the attorney insisted that his offer was a one-time deal: either accept the money or get nothing. When Dewey suggested that he receive $350, the attorney stated that he was only authorized to go as high as $250. The real reason Mees did not want to pay more was that no case valued over $250 could be adjudicated before a justice of the peace. Moreover, if taken before a higher court, the agreement could not have been concluded so quickly or without greater scrutiny upon its terms. In haste then, the attorney left the boy's hospital room and requested Samuel M. Carter, secretary of the Southeast Missouri Trust Company, to serve as Robison's "next friend" in a "friendly suit." All that was required, the attorney explained, was for Carter to sign the papers in which Robison agreed to surrender all of his legal rights in return for the compensation provided. Carter's involvement as next friend was necessary because as a minor Robison could not legally make any binding agreements himself. Remarkably, Carter never inquired into the facts of the boy's case, accepting the word of the attorney for Floesch Construction. The attorney then gained the cooperation of Justice of the Peace F. A. Kage, who went to Robison's hospital room, where an informal hearing was conducted and a judgment of $250 in Robison's favor was recorded.[19]

When he had learned of this afterward, the boy's father considered the payment woefully inadequate and sought to rescind the agreement with Floesch Construction. Later, the boy's leg became infected and it was necessary to amputate it, further punctuating the inadequacy of the settlement. In all, Dewey spent seven months in the hospital and his leg required further medical treatment for some time afterward. While unsure he could help the family, Limbaugh was outraged by the manner in which the matter had been handled and believed that an injustice had been done to this very poor family. Therefore, he advised Robison not to cash the check and promised to research the law and determine if anything could be done. First, Limbaugh turned to experienced members of the bar to gain their advice. His friend and mentor Hardesty believed that nothing could be done to overturn the judgment, but thought that Limbaugh should consult his partner Davis, who "had served as a judge of the Common Pleas Court" and was known as a man of integrity and good judgment. The judge agreed with Hardesty. Limbaugh, however, found it difficult to accept "that such an injustice was invulnerable" to legal action and spoke to other experienced lawyers, who all agreed with Davis and Hardesty. Nevertheless, believing that the way in which the matter had been handled "was grotesquely wrong," Limbaugh advised Robison not to accept the settlement for his son's injury and promised to continue his research. Finally, one morning just before he was to leave to try a case in Millersville, he came across a decision that appeared to be very similar to the Robison case. Unfortunately, Limbaugh could not read the opinion until after he returned from court. And so, after concluding his legal business that day, he arrived at his office in the late afternoon and immediately turned to the decision, for he "had been in suspense all day to know the significance of the case." To his great delight and satisfaction, Limbaugh found that the Supreme Court of Kansas had ruled in *Missouri Pacific Railroad Company v. Lasca* "that a judgment regularly entered and satisfied could be set aside by a court of equity if it appeared that the judgment had been entered only after a perfunctory instead of a real hearing, especially where a grave injustice had been perpetrated." It was upon this decision that he believed he could build his entire case.[20]

To prepare for the upcoming trial, Limbaugh wrote to the Robisons that he would travel to Greenbrier, where the family lived, to investigate the facts of the case. Father and son met him at the train station and together they went to the site of the accident and the two explained all the particulars of it. For the next two days, Limbaugh gathered the information he would need to try the case. At the end of this time, he was convinced that "the boy had been clearly injured because of the negligence in the operation" of the dragline excavator, a large machine operating on tracks used to construct ditches for the Little River Drainage District project. Two counts became the basis of his case. The first was to set aside the justice of the peace judgment in equity, a legal procedure which allowed the removal of an injustice when no other means under the law was available to a litigant. The second count was to institute a suit against Floesch Construction to gain $10,000 in "damages for the loss of Dewey's leg."[21]

The case came before Judge John A. Snider of the Cape Girardeau Court of Common Pleas in December of 1919. Limbaugh had received help from Hardesty in preparing for trial, who sat with him for a part of the proceedings, although he did not participate in its conduct. The opposing counsel was State Senator Arthur L. Oliver and his son Allen L. Oliver. The first count of the case to set aside the justice of the peace judgment was concluded in Robison's favor by noon of that first day. The second part of the trial began as soon as a jury was empanelled and continued to midafternoon of the next day. A journalist covering the trial wrote that "the plea made by Limbaugh was one of the best ever heard in Common Pleas court and the jurors followed every word closely. The spectators in the room were also greatly affected by Limbaugh's and young Robinson [sic], the plaintiff, and his father occasionally wiped away tears as the young lawyer referred to the young man going through life crippled. Persons about the courtroom were confident that damages would be in the full amount, $10,000." In less than an hour after hearing the lawyers' summations and receiving Judge Snider's charge, the jury returned with a verdict of $10,000 for the Robisons. At this outcome of the case, Limbaugh's colleagues heartily congratulated him in winning such a large award for a poor and deserving family. However, this was not the end of the case, for Floesch Construction promptly appealed the case to the Supreme Court of Missouri.[22]

In their appeal, the Olivers argued that the original proceeding before the justice of the peace had been properly conducted and therefore could not be overturned. They also claimed that Limbaugh had not proven fraud in the proceeding, which they claimed was at the heart of his case. Moreover, the Olivers asserted that because Robison had failed to surrender the $250 check to Floesch Construction before filing his suit, he had forfeited his right to sue and, in effect, had accepted the settlement. For all these reasons the original consent decree should have been upheld by Judge Snider. Concerning the jury's damage award to Dewey Robison for the loss of his leg, the Olivers stated that Floesch Construction could not be held responsible, for the accident resulted from the boy's own bad judgment.[23]

In his reply to the Olivers' brief, Limbaugh noted that they claimed he had sought to set aside the justice of the peace settlement "upon the ground of fraud." This, Limbaugh asserted, was incorrect. Instead, he had proved before the lower court that the consent judgment had been "entered without the hearing of any evidence [and] without any judicial determination of [Robison's] rights." Moreover, Carter, who had served as Robison's "next friend," an office intended to be exercised intelligently and with a full knowledge of the facts in the protection of a minor's rights, did nothing to ascertain the boy's circumstances and legal options. Indeed, Carter had never even met Robison until more than a year after becoming "his next friend," and then only to give testimony in the suit before the Court of Common Pleas of Cape Girardeau. Judge Snider set aside the judgment both because Robison had refused the payment, having returned the check uncashed upon filing his suit, and because it was "grossly inadequate to compensate him for his injury and bars him from seeking further recovery until such judgment is set aside." Thus, unlike the other legal officers involved in the matter, Judge Snider fulfilled his duty as a "minister of the law to watch with jealous care the rights of infants [that is, minors]."[24]

In their appellant's brief, the Olivers provided an extensive discussion of the ditch-digging operation in which Robison had been involved, describing the dragline excavator, the crew and their responsibilities, and its operation. This information was given to establish that Robison "was guilty of contributory negligence." As a pit hand, the Olivers claimed that he should never under any circumstances have been in the cab of the excavator. When Robison was directed by the operator, who happened also to be his older brother, to leave the cab and go down to "tighten up the jacks," he did so while the excavator was in operation, thus placing himself in danger. The boy further contributed to this danger by taking an unsafe route down from the cab, and when the boom threatened to crush him, he unwisely sought to escape on the inside of the excavator's frame. He took this route, the Olivers' asserted, despite being able to avoid the danger by simply dropping off or using a ladder. The injury was thus not the fault of Floesch Construction and should not be compelled to compensate the young man for injuries resulting from his own folly.[25]

In reply to this argument, Limbaugh noted a number of factors which demonstrated the unsafe conditions under which the crew worked. A major contributing factor to the danger was the pressure placed upon the operator not to stop operating the boom, even when he thought it unsafe. Contrary to the opposing counsels' assertion, members of the pit crew were sometimes sent up to the cab to retrieve oil, where it was kept, or to bring it back up after its use. As an inexperienced crew member—this was only his second night on the job—Robison could not be expected to understand all the dangers of the job and those in charge should have done more to protect him. Moreover, contrary to the assertion of Floesch Construction's attorneys, the ladder on the outside of the excavator was not in a fixed location, but was moved about to where it was needed. Because the machine was almost without any lighting on the frame where Robison was descending from the cab, he could not see the ladder and was delayed in attempting to use it. Because it was nighttime and the ground could not be seen, he could not jump the ten or twelve feet below, especially with the added danger of possibly landing upon uninsulated and "highly charged electric wires" which supplied power to the excavator. Thus "the facts failed absolutely to show that there was a safe method for getting down off the machine."[26]

After arguing the case on April 25, 1921, before the Supreme Court of Missouri, Limbaugh and his clients waited for a decision almost until Christmas. Not only was a large legal fee at stake and an important legal principle, but Limbaugh also truly believed that Dewey Robison deserved compensation for his disability. And so it was with great relief and joy that he learned of the court's ruling in his client's favor. In his opinion, Judge William T. Ragland held that "a judgment in favor of an infant for compensation for personal injuries is not binding on him, where it is entered by a justice of the peace, upon papers prepared by defendant's attorney; the justice being taken to the sick room of the plaintiff for the purpose, and acting without any judicial hearing or determination." The justice of the peace proceeding conducted in Robison's hospital room was nothing more than "a screen" to prevent a damages suit from being brought against Floesch Construction. Thus, Judge Ragland considered the so-called "friendly suit" to be anything but friendly in its intent and declared it to be "fraudulent," as it had been instituted solely "to take advantage of the incompetency of an infant to protect his own interests . . . and as the alleged proceeding before the justice of the peace was designed for no other purpose, it should be so treated." Receiving one-third of the judgment of $10,000, Limbaugh shared it equally with Hardesty out of recognition for his help through the years. Later, Limbaugh represented Dewey Robison's parents to gain compensation for the loss of his services resulting from his disability. In this case he won a judgment of $1,000. From these fees, Limbaugh paid his bills, bought furnishings for his home, and bought his first automobile, a used Dodge, for $500.[27]

Prior to arguing the Robison case before the supreme court, Limbaugh traveled to Texas to prepare for a trial in the representation of Dr. John D. Porterfield, a physician and surgeon in Cape Girardeau. Porterfield had taken over his father's "wide practice" and seemed destined to financial success. However, despite having become a more skilled surgeon than his father, he was unfortunately gruff in manner and tended to drink to excess, leading to a number of financial difficulties. Eventually the Sturdivant Bank required Porterfield to sell some of his assets, including a damages suit against some railroads in the destruction of a printing press purchased in Texas. Through his investigation, Limbaugh learned that four different railroads had handled the shipment, that the damage had occurred on the second carrier due to a train accident, and that according to a decision by the Supreme Court of the United States, *Blish Milling Company v. One or More Railroad Companies*, the initial carrier was liable for the damages. Thus, Limbaugh traveled to Texas, hired a lawyer there to serve as fellow counsel, and prepared for trial by interviewing witnesses. On the morning of the trial the opposing lawyer offered to settle for $3,500, an amount which Porterfield accepted. During Limbaugh's absence in Texas on March 18, 1921, Bee bore him a third child. Naming him Manley O. after his favorite law professor, Manley O. Hudson, who was then a professor of law at Harvard University, Limbaugh later wrote to inform him that he had a namesake. Hudson replied humorously that "it gratifies my vanity that you should have taken the risk of giving your son such a handicap as to bear my name. . . . I shall at once begin to look forward to the day when the young gentleman presents himself in the class in Torts in the Harvard Law School and I get a crack at him. I feel quite sure already that he is going to discuss Davis v. Munn with both lucidity and passion, and when he comes to Dairy v. Peak, I am expecting him to be a genius. So please remember this in deciding what you will feed him."[28]

After winning the Robison case, Limbaugh's reputation as a lawyer had grown and more business came to him. During this period he also formed a partnership with Hardesty in the building where he had worked when he first began practicing law in 1916. Judge Benjamin F. Davis, Hardesty's partner, had drowned in 1921 and for a time Hardesty had carried on alone. The lawyers decided to share the expenses of the office and the salary of a secretary. Davis' old office was converted into a reception room. According to their arrangement, whenever they worked together on a case, the fee would be divided according to the amount of time each devoted to it. Although this arrangement "could scarcely be called a partnership," they decided to formalize the agreement by giving their firm the name Hardesty & Limbaugh, under which they operated for several years.[29]

In the fall of 1922, the mayor and city council of Cape Girardeau hired Limbaugh as special counsel and Judge James A. Finch to assist him "to condemn a right of way for an outlet for sewer district number 5." One of the property owners, Herminia Hunze, through whose land the city proposed to excavate the line, sued to prevent sewer pipe from being laid on her property. Her main objection to the city's plan was having the outlet ditch, which was designed to take away overflow during times of heavy rainfalls, feed into the Painter Spring Branch, which flowed directly into the Cape LaCroix Creek. During normal operations the sewer pipe would empty directly into the Mississippi River. To compensate her for the use of a ten and a half feet wide strip of land through her property, where the twenty-one inch pipe was to be laid, a special commission appointed by Judge Snider had offered $1,500. Hunze, who was represented by the firm of Spradling & Dalton, sought $25,000 in compensation for damages to her property, especially for polluting the creek and "render[ing] it unfit for use."[30]

In preparation for trial before the Court of Common Pleas in March 1923, Limbaugh spent several weeks researching the law, taking depositions of witnesses, and gaining technical information and insight about the science of hydraulics from his key witnesses, the engineers who designed the sewerage system, Chris E. Stiver, city engineer of Cape Girardeau, and W. W. Horner, chief engineer of sewerage and paving for St. Louis. It would turn out, however, that the information, and especially the testimony in trial, provided by C. E. Smith, a consulting engineer for St. Louis and other cities, was very important to Cape Girardeau's case. On the stand for three hours, Smith provided so lucid and clear an explanation of the technical aspects of the science of hydraulics to the jury that afterward, once the jury had left the courtroom, Judge Snider declared Smith's testimony "more interesting" than any other he had ever heard in court. Writing about the case many years later, Limbaugh remembered it as "the most spectacular trial in which I ever engaged."[31]

In trial, Limbaugh presented evidence that a very dangerous health hazard in sewer district five had led to the city's decision to build a new system. The city contended that three sources fouled the Cape LaCroix Creek. The first of these were "numerous privies and outhouses located near the banks of the creek . . . above the Hunze farm." Another was a series of slaughterhouses located along the creek, which was used to dispose of the refuse from those operations. And the last "source of pollution . . . was overflowing cess pools." Much of this pollution drained into the creek from the surrounding area. Chemical analysis of the creek's water demonstrated that much "organic matter" and "B. Coli" was found, which was dangerous to all "warm-blooded animals, including humans," and was known to cause typhoid. This finding was not challenged by opposing counsel. Thus, all that remained in trial to determine was the proper means of removing the public health hazard and an equitable compensation for the use of the Hunzes' land.[32]

The sewerage system proposed by Cape Girardeau's engineers was called "a combined sanitary and storm water system." It was designed to collect "sanitary sewage" and rain runoff into pipes coming from homes and other collection areas. These pipes drained into larger pipes through which the flow collected into concrete basins called interceptors, of which there were two provided. These were constructed to "collect all sand, gravel, and other substances flowing into the system" and prevent it from clogging the twenty-one inch pipe through which the drainage traveled into the Mississippi River. Periodically, these interceptors would be cleaned by sanitation workers. Moreover, in their testimony the engineers emphasized that the system was designed to accommodate a significantly larger population of the district than was expected to settle there. This sewerage system had the advantage of diluting the sewage so that its concentration was so low that it could do no harm to the public health. Indeed, instead of fouling the Cape LaCroix Creek, during normal operations no sewage would enter it and even during periods of rain overflow the sewage dumping into it through the outlet ditch would be diluted to levels far below what was considered safe. The acceptable rate of dilution was 30 to 1, but the new system would create a rate of 1,600 to 1 during periods of runoff.[33]

To counter Limbaugh's case, opposing counsel presented four expert witnesses. G. N. Jacobs, an engineer from St. Louis, testified that he was experienced in drainage work, but when cross examined by Limbaugh did not know basic information about the project such as "the carrying capacity of the 21 inch pipe as compared with the volume of sewage which would be used by the people in the district when fully populated." When informed of the particulars,

Jacobs admitted "that the dilution would be immense." During the course of his examination, Limbaugh also gained Jacobs' admission that he did not know what had been determined to be a safe dilution ratio of sewage to water in "the Chicago sanitary sewage case and generally accepted in the engineering world." Another engineer, W. A. Thompson, also admitted that before he could give an opinion about the proposed sewerage system that he would need "to make a complete study of the whole system."[34]

The final two expert witnesses for Hunze were medical doctors, who gave testimony explaining the ill effects the new sewerage system would have upon the public health. One of these men was Dr. John D. Porterfield, who only two years before had been a client of Limbaugh. Both Porterfield's and Dr. A. L. Fuerth's testimony was premised upon the false notion that the Cape LaCroix Creek would be transformed into an open sewer. In fact, it was clear that with the new system the creek would have far less sewage running into it than before and as a result would become cleaner. In considering what should be paid in damages to Hunze, the main consideration, Limbaugh contended, should be the use value of the ten and a half foot strip of land for the period of time needed to install the pipe. As this comprised only "six-tenths of an acre" over land "subject to overflow," it was clear that this was not rich agricultural land or any other of high value. Moreover, city workers would need periodic access to this property to allow for the cleaning of the pipe, for which some compensation should be made. The amount of $1,500 which the city commission had decided upon, Limbaugh believed, was more than fair given the rental rates for agricultural land like that of the Hunzes' farm, which typically ran from $4.00 to $5.00 per acre annually. Apparently, in the end the jury agreed with him, for it awarded the Hunzes that very amount. The case was appealed to the Supreme Court of Missouri, but the verdict and damages were upheld.[35]

For some time, Rush and Bee had talked of taking a vacation, but because of the press of business, the responsibilities associated with raising young children, and a lack of funds the opportunity had not presented itself. In the spring of 1923, however, Limbaugh had learned that the American Bar Association (ABA) was holding its annual meeting in Minneapolis, Minnesota, that year. He and Bee decided that this was a fine opportunity for them to get away for an extended vacation, see some interesting places, and escape the Missouri summer for a time. Planning to travel by car and to take Marguerite, who was then seven years old, and Rush Jr., who was five, they began their preparations several months before their departure. Young Manley, who was two and a half when his parents and siblings departed, would remain at home with his maternal grandmother and aunt. At a time when few paved roads existed, and many of these were only partly paved and often poorly marked, the traveler inevitably encountered great difficulties on the road. For this reason, Limbaugh joined an auto club which provided necessary services such as reports about road conditions, the best routes to take, hazards to avoid, and what services were available along the way.[36]

On August 17, the Limbaughs departed Cape Girardeau after arranging to have "chains spliced" to travel the muddy roads, some of which were so bad that they were rendered almost impassable, and in some places hazardous, especially when meeting oncoming traffic. Nevertheless, they were able to make it to St. Louis, arriving at "a tourist camp" in Forest Park at eight o'clock in the evening, sleeping in a tent that first night. The next day they temporarily traveled upon the wrong road and later had to turn around to retrieve a sweater "Junior," that is Rush Jr., had left behind at a restaurant. However, once they came to the state highway on their way to Springfield, Illinois, they found the road well paved and marked, with signs warning the traveler of curves, railroad crossings, and other hazards. The next morning, after enjoying a sound rest in a hotel room, the Limbaughs visited the capitol building, Lincoln's grave site, and the Lincoln home. They left Springfield after lunch and began their journey to Chicago, stopping overnight and arriving there in the afternoon of August 20.[37]

While in Chicago over the next three days, the Limbaughs went to Marshall Field's department store, Lincoln and Grant parks, took a steamer on Lake Michigan, visited the public library and the University of Chicago before leaving town for Madison, Wisconsin. There they visited the state capitol, museums, and the university, occupying the better part of a day. On August 25, the Limbaughs began their journey to Minneapolis, arriving there in the evening of August 27. On their way up, they had spent over $100, about one-quarter of this being various expenses associated with traveling by automobile.[38]

While in Minneapolis for the ABA meeting, the Limbaughs stayed at the West Hotel for $6.00 a night. On August 28, Limbaugh traveled to the headquarters of West Publishing, a law book publisher, visiting the factory where the books were made and the on-site library where he did some research. That night the Limbaughs attended a vaudeville show. They enjoyed this entertainment a good deal, Marguerite and Rush Jr. agreeing that the clowns were their favorites. The next morning Limbaugh went alone to the first session of the conference while Bee, Marguerite, and Rush Jr. ventured out to see the sights around Minneapolis. Many legal and political luminaries attended the day's proceedings, including former president and current Chief Justice of the Supreme Court of the United States, William H. Taft, and Secretary of State Charles Evans Hughes. For the afternoon session, Bee accompanied Limbaugh, having hired a lady to take care of the children in their absence. As a knowledgeable practitioner and critic of public speaking, Limbaugh found some of the speeches to be wanting in substance and originality and their presentation poor. Some notable exceptions, however, were that of the president of the

ABA, John W. Davis, and Lord Birkenhead's speech comparing the British and American constitutional systems. Limbaugh found Lord Birkenhead the very model of the practiced orator who spoke in "a good voice, rather strong, and usually closed his sentences with a rising inflection." The substance of his remarks were just as appealing for their frank and terse discussion of the two constitutional systems and thoughtful consideration of some of the challenges which the United States must overcome as it grew economically and became increasingly involved in world affairs.[39]

On August 30, during the penultimate session of the conference, a number of reports were made to the members by committees tasked with formulating policies on various legal issues such as criminal law, bankruptcy, and international law. This last was of particular interest to Limbaugh and he followed the debate closely. The Committee on International Law was unable to agree on a report and the chair, George W. Wickersham, former attorney general under President Taft, offered "a resolution favoring participation of the United States in the World Court" with certain conditions. After some debate, the matter was sent to the executive committee. That evening the main speaker was Secretary of State Hughes, who, in his address on American foreign policy, placed the United States' policies in the context of the Monroe Doctrine. Limbaugh believed Hughes to be a very good speaker with a strong voice and pleasing manner and judged his account of the historical facts to be concise and accurate. However, Limbaugh disagreed with Hughes' interpretation of "the present meaning of the Monroe Doctrine." In his estimation, Hughes' formulation was a "narrow, nationalistic doctrine." Hughes declared the United States' position was "one of independence, not of isolation." Limbaugh feared the consequences of such a policy and thought it out of step with recent trends.

> Let every nation pursue this policy and international cooperation toward any purpose is impossible. He said in effect that America reserves the right of deciding on every contingency as it arises as to what course she will take. This is not only independence. It is anti-international, ultra-nationalistic. Such policy points directly toward imperialism. If followed, it will surely lead to war. And this is the latest interpretation of the Monroe Doctrine. This is the last official pronouncement of our attitude on a policy a hundred years old. It is a representation of the nation's position on a question involving twentieth century internationalism as opposed to nineteenth century nationalism. It shows that the two terms as applied to actual conditions mean the same thing. We have caught the word internationalism but we have yet to catch the spirit. If the attitude of Mr. Hughes as was expressed in that speech is representative of the attitude of the nation then the aim and purpose of the Allies in the late war have been wholly misunderstood and lost sight of in America.

Limbaugh's tough analysis and disagreement with Hughes' approach to international affairs under President Calvin Coolidge demonstrated that he still maintained considerable faith in international institutions as a panacea to the world's problems and as a means of avoiding war. Not long after this, however, his attitude changed and his confidence waned.[40]

On September 2, the Limbaughs began their long journey home over roads made almost impassable by rain, necessitating a number of detours from the route provided by their automobile club. In particular, they were warned to avoid driving through Iowa, where the condition of the roads was particularly bad. After a number of difficulties, however, they arrived in Cape Girardeau on September 6 in the early evening. As they approached their home after an absence of almost three weeks, their two-and-a-half-year-old son Manley, who was then outside, saw them and "ran home with unusual delight." Their relief at again finding themselves in familiar surroundings with friends and family was great. As Limbaugh noted in his final journal entry for the trip: "We had just travelled 1902 miles and would not have taken a million dollars for our experiences but would have been unwilling to have given ten cents to have gone through with them again." In the end, the entire journey had cost $254.86, not an insignificant sum in 1923.[41]

After returning from law school, Limbaugh became an active member of the Cape Girardeau community, supporting a variety of local organizations and educational initiatives. From 1916 to 1920, he served as commissioner of the Boy Scouts "superintending three troops in Cape Girardeau." In 1930, under Limbaugh's leadership, the scouts of southeast Missouri in thirteen counties applied for a charter for local council with him as president. This organization, he believed, was very useful for it helped boys develop "initiative and self help. . . . A scout learns through perseverance to carry his own load; to explore his own territory, to build his own fires, to swim and row, to hike and run; to build his own shelter with his own hands, to capture his own meat, to cook his own food. He knows how to help himself." From 1916 to 1918, Limbaugh taught an intermediate boy's Sunday school class at Centenary Methodist Church, and a high school and college boy's class from 1925 to 1930. Moreover, Limbaugh became a member of the Advisory Board of the Salvation Army in Cape Girardeau, beginning an association which would continue for more than fifty years. During this period and after, he also made a number of public addresses before various organizations, at high school commencement exercises, and Fourth of July celebrations. These speeches covered a wide range of topics including the commission form of city government, political trends, the lives and work of different presidents, the American Revolution and the Constitution of the United States, the Russian Revolution, international affairs, and the establishment of world organizations and courts.[42]

As noted already, one of Limbaugh's particular interests from his time as a student at the University of Missouri was international affairs. Observing from afar the carnage of world war, he had placed much hope in the establishment of the League of Nations and international courts to mediate controversies between nations peacefully. For this reason, he had been greatly disappointed in the speech of Secretary of State Hughes, who had called for the United States to stand aloof from full membership in international organizations. Of primary concern to Hughes and President Coolidge was to prevent the surrender of American sovereignty to such institutions. Initially, Limbaugh had reacted negatively to this policy, but over time his ideas evolved and he became far less sanguine concerning the effectiveness of international organizations to avert war and conflict. It is unclear what event or events transformed his thinking, but only a few months after attending the ABA meeting in Minneapolis he noted in a public speech the inadequacy of international organizations to prevent war and revolutionize the manner in which nations interacted. This realization did not cause him to abandon the ideal of international cooperation altogether, but apparently led him to adjust his expectations for what could be accomplished through such institutions. Moreover, having seen the failure, or at best the lackluster performance of both domestic and international reforms, his faith in "progressive" ideas began to wane and he soon returned to Republican policies.[43]

On January 23, 1925, Rush, Bee, Marguerite, and Rush Jr. welcomed Daniel Francis into their family. From the beginning the infant had respiratory problems, but otherwise seemed to be healthy, and he grew normally. However, in early June he developed bronchial pneumonia and despite the efforts of a pediatrician, Dr. Paul R. Williams, Daniel Francis died on June 8, a few short months after his birth. This tragedy "cast a shadow on our home," but especially upon Marguerite, who had taken "delight in helping her mother care for him." Limbaugh was particularly impressed with his wife's strength during the crisis, for she never succumbed to her grief and helped her husband and children cope as she dealt with her own sadness.[44]

Unfortunately, this loss was not the family's last. The next was such that it shook Bee's strength and faith for a time. During the following spring, Cape Girardeau readied itself for the arrival of the great evangelist Billy Sunday. Members of the various denominations in town pooled their resources and built a temporary pine building with a sawdust floor to hold the thousands expected to attend. Sunday's appeal was great and only those arriving early for the meetings were able to attend. Overflow crowds were so large that one of Sunday's colleagues was recruited to preach to them. Limbaugh took an active interest in the revival, promoting it to friends and neighbors. He wrote to his brothers, offering to bring them to a Sunday meeting for men. He also gave a speech at an African American meeting to which Sunday had agreed to preach. At this time American society was segregated and the civil and political liberties of African Americans were severely restricted. In his speech Limbaugh noted the important contributions that African Americans made to the community. He thanked them for their attendance and praised their efforts to improve and contribute to the city.

> When Mr. Sunday agreed to preach to you today, therefore, he consented to meet and carry the influences of his campaign to a valuable part of the life, population, and activities of this city. We are glad for this meeting. We are glad of his presence here. We are glad to welcome you in this Tabernacle. . . . Through your coming here this morning, you have indicated that you are interested in that very thing, and we rejoice in this opportunity you will have to learn of how to make it easier to do right and harder to do wrong. The people of your race in this city have a good record in trying to do that very thing. By and large you have been substantial citizens, interested in movements that have promoted progress and better living conditions. You have and are maintaining good schools for the education of your people. You have maintained good churches for the promotion of religious influence in the community. In every enterprise that is launched for the good of this city, we have always found you friendly, enthusiastic and ready to serve.[45]

In the midst of this exciting time, the Limbaugh's only daughter and oldest child, Marguerite, became very ill. At the age of ten, she had already shown a good deal of promise intellectually and spiritually. She enjoyed her academic studies and loved to read books and memorize poems. Because she was dependable and exhibited good judgment, her parents attended one of the revival meetings, leaving her home in charge of her brothers Rush Jr., who was then eight years old, and Manley, who was five. When Limbaugh and Bee returned home that night they found the boys in bed asleep and Marguerite reading James Fenimore Cooper's book, *The Spy*, which she managed to finish despite feeling unwell and restless because of an infected pimple upon her face. In the early morning of March 18, 1926, Marguerite awakened her parents, suffering from chills caused by the infection. Fearing that the illness was serious, they called in a relative and physician, Dr. Dayton L. Seabaugh, who recommended a new drug which had been found effective in fighting infections. Awakening a local druggist, Limbaugh persuaded him to make a special trip over to his store to purchase the drug. However, the drug apparently had little, if any, effect upon the infection and Marguerite's condition quickly worsened and soon became critical. By this time, two other physicians were there to alleviate the young girl's suffering and save her, all to no avail. For the next few days she suffered from chills and a high temperature, once reaching as high as 106 degrees. On March 23, Marguerite died from sepsis and a strep infection. Her funeral was held at the Centenary Methodist Church on March 25. All of her schoolmates and members of her Sunday school class attended. Men from the Sunday school class Limbaugh taught served as pallbearers. Hundreds of people attended the service.[46]

Marguerite's death left her parents devastated, who found it impossible "to subdue [their] grief in the presence of Rush and Manley." Bee struggled for some time with the meaning of her daughter's death and apparently went through a time of crisis in her faith. In July she attended "a training school" sponsored by the Methodist church for its lay teachers at a retreat near Fayetteville, Arkansas. During this time she took courses on the New Testament and comparative religions taught by liberal ministers, one of whom she described as "a liberal among the liberals," but nonetheless found his and the others' teaching more helpful than Billy Sunday's "fundamentalist" sermons which "rather upset" her. Sunday's preaching and the death of their daughter had caused her to "doubt things too much." However, with time to reflect and learn, she concluded that death did not seem "so terrible" any more, and found it "beautiful to think that Marguerite may still be among us although we cannot see her." In this manner, Bee slowly adjusted to her loss and renewed her faith. By his own account, Limbaugh found solace in his work, which served as a distraction from his pain.[47]

Chapter Five

State Legislator

In the months following Marguerite's death, Rush H. Limbaugh and Bee struggled with their sorrow and comforted their surviving sons, Rush Jr. and Manley. Apparently, the family found solace in various activities including evening readings of literature such as *The Swiss Family Robinson*. This book, Limbaugh believed, had provided the family with relief from their loss in the distraction of "following the adventures of this shipwrecked family until they became our intimate friends." From this story, they had all gained an "increased interest in nature and outdoor life, kindness toward animals, [and] greater love and loyalty in our family group." While Bee continued to struggle with her loss, she may have derived some pleasure from the simple activities of daily life and from looking after the needs of her family. Because of her husband's very busy professional life and in keeping with the values of the time, she was the boys' primary caregiver, seeing to their daily needs and guiding them through many of life's ups and downs. She oversaw their educations, made sure they made it to school and to other activities punctually, and knew where they were and what they were doing after school. Musically talented herself, Bee encouraged Rush Jr. in his efforts to master playing the violin, who later became proficient enough to achieve the position of lead violinist for the orchestra at Central High School in Cape Girardeau. Manley practiced the piano but found the cello more to his liking. Bee encouraged both boys to develop their singing voices as well. In addition to everything else, she often attended sporting events, picnics, and Boy Scout activities, encouraging the boys to remain active and to grow both intellectually and socially.[1]

A year and a half after Marguerite's death, the Limbaughs' last child, Stephen N., was born on November 17, 1927, at St. Francis Hospital in Cape Girardeau. Perhaps to lessen the burden of caring for a newborn and the rest of the family, they decided to hire a college girl to help Bee with her many domestic duties. Over the years, the Limbaughs hired a number of young women, who stayed with them while they attended Southeast Missouri State University. During this time, the Limbaughs also opened their home to nieces and nephews who desired to obtain an education, making the household a place "of intense activity."[2]

In 1928, Limbaugh was elected chairman of the Cape Girardeau County Republican Committee, a position he held until 1938. As a leader of the Republican Party in southeastern Missouri, he supported the candidacy of Herbert Hoover, who in 1928 was running for the presidency against New York Governor Al Smith. In speeches supporting Hoover, Limbaugh noted that Smith had long ties to the Tammany Hall political machine in New York City, which "was steeped in vice," supporting criminals, saloons, gambling houses, and prostitution rings. These criminal enterprises all paid the political bosses of Tammany Hall for protection and supported their candidates for office. In this way, the machine gained political power and grew rich. Limbaugh also reminded his listeners that in 1924 Smith had eulogized Tammany boss Charles F. Murphy as "a noble, clean, wholesome, right-living man." Thus the Democratic presidential nominee, apparently without reservation, heaped praise "upon one of the most notorious and corrupt political bosses that has ever left a record in the history of American politics."[3]

In contrast to Smith's political career, Limbaugh noted how Hoover, who was orphaned when still a boy, had struggled to gain an engineering degree and had been very successful in his chosen profession traveling throughout the world. When the First World War began, Hoover helped United States citizens stranded in England to return home. After his return, President Woodrow Wilson appointed Hoover to oversee wartime food rationing. After the war, Hoover worked to help those suffering in Germany and Austria. When Wilson protested these efforts, Hoover replied that "while we are strictly speaking at war with the German and Austrian governments, we have never been at war with the German and Austrian women and children." Because of these efforts, Hoover was remembered by many in Europe as a great humanitarian. Moreover, Limbaugh, who was himself a strong supporter of prohibition, touted Hoover's promise to uphold the eighteenth amendment to the Constitution and to prosecute vigorously anyone violating it.[4]

During this period, Limbaugh became involved in a case he considered one of the most interesting of his career. An elderly man came to his office to have documents notarized. Morven R. Fakes brought an old photograph of "a long, lost brother" and an affidavit, which he was sending to the probate court in Houston to determine, if possible, whether a recently deceased man was his brother. Because he had not seen or heard from him for forty years, Fakes did not believe the man in Houston was his brother but was curious enough to send the information requested by the probate court. Many years before, the family "had made an exhaustive search for him," but not finding him had concluded that he was dead. Limbaugh, after reading the affidavit and talking to Fakes, became convinced that the man in Texas was his brother, for he thought it highly unlikely that more than one person had the same unusual name of Ossian Fakes. After further investigation, Limbaugh learned that the man's estate was substantial, that he had no known relatives, and had left behind no will. It was decided that Limbaugh would travel to Houston with Judge Thomas B. Dudley to investigate the matter.[5]

Limbaugh and Dudley investigated the extent of Ossian Fakes' estate, first in Houston and then in San Antonio. While in Houston, they also learned "that a pretended will that was unsigned and lacking in witnesses had been presented to the court for probate by two different firms of lawyers in Houston." Upon their return to Missouri, Dudley believed that there was no use in pursuing the matter any further, for inevitably the cost of litigation would consume the value of the estate. Limbaugh disagreed and persuaded Fakes to allow him to continue his investigation. Limbaugh agreed to "handle the case . . . on a contingent basis" if Fakes would pay his expenses. Because proceedings in the case had already begun, Limbaugh traveled again to Houston where he met with the judge, the lawyers, and the beneficiary of the contested will. After speaking with the beneficiary, who claimed to be a friend of Ossian Fakes, Limbaugh became convinced that the man knew very little about the deceased. After consulting with his client by phone, Limbaugh traveled to Tampico, Mexico. He obtained a passport and left by train, crossing the Rio Grande River at Laredo, Texas. From there they passed through Monterey to Tampico.[6]

At Tampico, Limbaugh stayed in a hotel near the United States embassy, and felt fortunate to gain the very helpful assistance of a young American in charge there. The embassy held some of Ossian Fakes' belongings and correspondence, providing new clues to different periods of his life, and further evidence that he was indeed the brother of Limbaugh's client. While there, because his client had requested it, Limbaugh also visited Ossian Fakes' grave, which was located in a very well-kept cemetery located "on a hillside sloping gently down toward the waters of the Gulf." In following up the leads he had developed in Tampico, Limbaugh eventually traveled to Washington, DC, and Savannah and Murphysboro, Illinois, where he spoke to Fakes' friends and pieced together various aspects of his career. It became clear beyond any doubt that he was Morven Fakes' brother. At eighteen years of age, Ossian had impregnated a young girl and had left home when the girl's brothers threatened his life. He first moved to Iowa, working the harvest, and then lived in Savannah, Illinois. After this he settled in Louisiana, Texas, and eventually Mexico.[7]

Having gathered this information and believing that he had a strong case, Limbaugh returned to Houston, where he engaged a lawyer at the firm of Baker, Botts, Parker, & Garwood. He first met with the managing partner, Walter Walne, a native Missourian. Limbaugh proposed that the firm take the case on a contingent basis as he had done. Walne explained that they did not accept cases on that basis, instead working only for a set daily fee. Depending upon the lawyer employed, the rate ranged from $50 to $350 per day. Limbaugh, perhaps a bit shell shocked by the fees, requested Homer Bruce, one of their bottom-rate lawyers. Bruce suggested that they meet with their adversaries. Telephoning them, he arranged for a meeting with the lawyers and their client. One of the lawyers dominated the interview, making outlandish statements, claiming to be a friend of Missouri Congressman Champ Clark, and telling stories of great victories in the courtroom. However, it became clear that the man "was the very crudest kind of imposter. . . . [and] it did not require much intelligence to conclude that he was a gigantic fraud." When an attempt was made to talk about the case, Limbaugh and Bruce were told that they should drop the matter as they would only succeed in spending their client's money "needlessly." The other lawyer was the son of the probate judge and for this reason apparently suffered from overconfidence, for he allowed Limbaugh to depose witnesses without arranging for opposing counsel to be present and ask questions. After this meeting, Limbaugh returned to the firm and made use of their extensive law library, researching Texas law "about proof of an unexecuted will," the issue upon which the case would be decided.[8]

A hearing for the case was set for July 1928 in Houston. Upon arriving, Limbaugh spent much of the first day working with Bruce to prepare for the hearing and trial. Soon they received a call from their adversaries asking for a conference. For the next couple of days, Limbaugh and Bruce negotiated with the other side, who apparently had dropped their false bravado and sought to salvage something for their client while avoiding going to trial. In the end, Limbaugh and Bruce secured for their client the vast majority of his brother's estate, which turned out to be worth $25,000. In addition to the substantial fee he earned, Limbaugh believed that the case was very beneficial to him because of his association with the Houston law firm. This experience convinced him of the importance of having available "a great library," maintaining an "orderly and efficient" law office, and keeping an accurate record concerning the time spent on each case. Moreover, it is clear that Limbaugh made a strong and favorable impression upon members of the firm, for during the Second World War one of them recommended him to serve "as regional counsel for [the] War Emergency Pipelines [in southeast Missouri] and later as counsel for Texas Eastern Transmission Corporation."[9]

The period of 1923 to 1929 was a time "of unparalleled plenty" in the United States. New conveniences, the mass production of goods, the extension of credit to consumers, and the surge of the stock market brought with it a new materialism and caused many to seek the quick acquisition of wealth. In Missouri this new prosperity was less than in many other parts of the country, although southeast Missouri boomed from the reclamation of swamp and other lands through flood-control projects. Upon these new lands farmers expanded their operations, some finding that cotton, then a profitable crop, grew well there. Because of this, during the 1920s Cape Girardeau increased in population by 38 percent; Sikeston, its neighbor to the south, increased by 57 percent. This all changed, however, with the slowdown of the economy and the eventual crash of the stock market. At the time, Limbaugh and Bee happened to be in Memphis, Tennessee, attending the 1929 annual meeting of the American Bar Association. One morning the newspapers were filled with headlines and stories about the crash of the stock market. To them, the event seemed inconsequential, for they owned no stock and did not understand the impact this would have upon the nation and themselves. Unfortunately, Limbaugh was affected directly with the failure of the Cape Exchange Bank, Cape Girardeau's newest and smallest bank, upon whose board he served. The bank failed and the board negotiated the sale of its assets to the Sturdivant Bank. These were sold at a loss and it fell upon the board members to pay the balance of the bank's debt. Limbaugh, who had some savings, although it was "meager" by his own account, was reduced to borrowing against the value of his home to pay his part.[10]

Despite this setback, Limbaugh continued to support various associations and groups, devoting much of his free time to promoting the betterment of his community and profession. During this period he remained a member of the board of the Salvation Army in Cape Girardeau. In 1930, Limbaugh was elected president of the Cape Girardeau County Bar Association. At his invitation, for the first time the Missouri Bar held its annual meeting in Cape Girardeau. Thus, he and Bee shouldered many of the responsibilities of organizing the entertainment, and held many preliminary committee meetings in their home. Of course, this meant that Bee provided refreshments and made other preparations to welcome the committee members. Limbaugh also continued his affiliation with the Boy Scouts as a scoutmaster and in 1931 served as the first president of the Southeast Missouri Area Council after its organization. Whenever he could, Limbaugh helped others seeking employment, writing letters of recommendation and showing a genuine interest in their welfare. Moreover, he was a popular choice to make commencement speeches for local high schools, in which he encouraged the graduates to pursue their ambitions, but always for a higher purpose. Other talks were given before service organizations like the Rotary Club at which he often spoke on subjects such as the US Constitution, sketches of the lives of former presidents, and current events.[11]

Very much interested in public policy and finding solutions to problems, Limbaugh followed the work of the survey commission, which the state legislature had created in 1929 to make "a careful and detailed study of the state's needs, its revenues, and the present distribution of funds." Appointed by Governor Henry S. Caulfield, the committee members were commissioned to find more revenue for the state and "to more nearly equalize the tax burden on all the people in all sections of the state." This effort had become necessary with the coming of increasingly hard times, especially for farmers, who paid disproportionately more taxes than did the rest of the populace. One of Limbaugh's friends, Fred Naeter, editor of the *Southeast Missourian*, was on the survey commission and devoted a good deal of his time to this effort. The commission eventually published an extensive report presenting their findings and recommendations. Because of Limbaugh's support, Naeter and fellow commission member Langdon Jones urged him to run for state representative to help implement the commission's recommendations. At first, Limbaugh declined, pleading that his financial situation could not sustain the loss of his income as a lawyer for several months. The pay and stipend for state representatives was only five dollars a day plus minimal expenses and would not even cover the added expenses of living in Jefferson City. Eventually, however, he relented, agreeing to serve if Jones and Naeter took care of the details of getting him elected. This they did, filing Limbaugh's name as a Republican candidate, and seeing to it that he ran unopposed. Nevertheless, much of his free time was spent during the campaign attending various political events and meetings.[12]

On January 5, 1931, Limbaugh gained a continuance of a case in the Jackson Circuit Court and left by train for Jefferson City. Because there was no direct line from Cape Girardeau to the state capitol, he took the train north to St. Louis, where at Union Station he boarded another train for Jefferson City. During the trip he discussed with friends various legislative matters, read, and wrote. After getting a room in the Missouri Hotel, Limbaugh spent his first evening in the capitol discussing policy issues with commissioners, legislators, and judges. The representative from Cape Girardeau County spent the next six months, excepting occasional weekends at home, in Jefferson City, devoting all of his time and industry to his duties as a legislator.[13]

The next morning Limbaugh went to the House of Representatives and obtained the key to his desk, number sixty-eight, on the floor. He then looked at a room for rent where he could stay while in Jefferson City. His next stop was Governor Caulfield's office, where Lewis Ellis, the governor's personal secretary, greeted him and stated that for several days the governor had wished to see him. Ellis escorted the new Republican representative into the governor's office ahead of a long line of people waiting there. The primary reason the governor wanted to see Limbaugh concerned State Treasurer Larry Brunk, a fellow Republican. The governor had suspended Brunk from office upon learning about and investigating accusations of malfeasance and other corrupt practices against him. However, the Supreme Court of Missouri had reinstated Brunk after ruling unconstitutional a statute which had given the governor the power to remove state officers. The court found that elected state officers could only be removed by impeachment. This decision had embarrassed the governor, pleasing some Democratic legislators, who were content to let the matter stand there in the hope that it would harm Caulfield's chances if, as expected, he ran for the United States Senate after his gubernatorial term expired in two years. Moreover, the Democrats may have further reasoned that allowing Brunk to remain in office provided them with their best opportunity to gain the election of a Democrat as state treasurer against a wounded Republican incumbent. Among Republicans, the governor had few supporters for his decision to remove Brunk and was grateful to Limbaugh for publicly approving his action. The governor also needed a reliable Republican to head the investigation, if there were to be any chance of passing articles of impeachment against Brunk in the House. Thus, when in their meeting Limbaugh reiterated his strong support for his action, the governor must have been relieved to have found a needed Republican ally. In addition, Limbaugh's reputation for pragmatic action and willingness to work with Democrats to solve problems made him the ideal person to help push through the governor's agenda.[14]

Later that evening after his meeting with the governor, Limbaugh attended a caucus of the Republican members of the House. As the minority, the Republicans met in the House lounge, where they chose their leadership for the upcoming session. Jones Parker, former speaker of the House, was elected as the permanent caucus chairman and his supporters filled most of the other caucus positions. The next morning, Limbaugh found at his desk on the floor the journals of the last House and Senate sessions, the survey commission report, writing materials, and the daily Kansas City and St. Louis newspapers. On the floor he met lobbyists; other members of the House; and George Cross, who had been Cape Girardeau County's representative in the previous session. Instead of offering a word of encouragement to his successor, Cross emphasized that as a freshman representative Limbaugh "was a nonentity" and would achieve little without help. Moreover, Cross claimed that the real leader of the Republican caucus was not Parker but Ed Duensing, and "that what was done on the floor of the House amounted to little, and that liquor and parties in the late hours determined legislative questions." Limbaugh listened skeptically to this lecture and later learned from other members of the House that Cross was unpopular and considered to be a very poor legislator, with one representative going so far as to say that "he wasn't worth a damn." Limbaugh was also told that Cross and Duensing had kept liquor in an office provided for a committee of which both were members and had used it as a place to meet "lewd women."[15]

The House elected Democrat Eugene Nelson to be speaker. Limbaugh was favorably impressed with him and the rest of the Democratic leadership. Another important organizational matter to be decided was committee assignments. Each representative provided a list from which the leadership decided the appointments. Limbaugh requested service on the "judiciary, roads and highways, municipal corporations, wills and probate, [and] swamp lands, drainage, and levees" committees. His list reflected a deep interest in legal issues and the importance of swamp land recovery to southeast Missouri's economy. His appointment to the survey, judiciary, swamp lands, municipal corporations, Teachers Colleges, and Brunk investigative committees was very unusual for a freshman legislator, for three of these committees were given a top priority by both parties and the governor. Without the governor's influence, it seems unlikely that Limbaugh would have been appointed to them. This unusual circumstance was noticed by a number of legislators including Democratic Floor Leader James Blair, who commented to Limbaugh after the appointments were announced that "somebody up here must think you are an h–of a fellow." He also observed that the Brunk investigative committee would have "one of the most difficult tasks of any committee . . . during the session."[16]

One of the first matters brought before the House was the lynching of a black man in northwestern Missouri for the rape and murder of a young white woman. According to newspaper accounts, Raymond Gunn, who had served four years in the state penitentiary for assault and may have suffered from mental illness, assaulted Velma Colter, a nineteen-year-old schoolteacher and member of a prominent family in Maryville, Missouri. The incident occurred in the one-room schoolhouse where she taught. After his arrest, fearing mob action, Gunn was moved to St. Joseph, where an attempt to kill him was unsuccessful. Hoping to thwart vigilante violence, Governor Caulfield mobilized fifty members of the National Guard with orders to assist the local police authorities if they requested it. Despite ample warning that a mob planned on lynching Gunn, Sheriff Harve England and the mayor of Maryville, William O. Garrett, did nothing to stop Gunn's seizure. Sheriff England, with a handful of deputies, drove Gunn into a mob of 2,000 angry people gathered at the courthouse awaiting the arrival of the defendant. Prior to this the sheriff had refused help from the National Guard and offered little resistance when the mob seized Gunn and marched him the three miles to the schoolhouse where the murder had occurred. After a short interrogation by leaders of the mob Gunn admitted to the crime. He was then made to ascend a ladder and lay on the roof where he was chained, and the school set on fire. Among the large crowd witnessing this atrocity were a number of women and children. Afterward many of the spectators rummaged among the charred remains for souvenirs of the ghastly murder.[17]

In response to these events, Democratic Representative Gil P. Bourk from Kansas City introduced a resolution "condemning the lynching and calling upon the governor and attorney general to conduct 'a searching investigation'" of the lynching. Only Republican and former Speaker Jones Parker spoke in favor of the resolution to which William Job, representative from Nodaway

County where the lynching occurred, replied vigorously and "was loudly applauded" for stating that the people of his county could handle the matter without outside interference. Democrat Nick M. Bradley, representative of Johnson County, spoke out against the resolution, stating that "he thought the Negro 'got just what he deserved.'" Limbaugh, who supported the resolution and hated this type of lawlessness and racist cruelty, observed that a majority of Republicans supported the measure and that the debate threatened to turn partisan. In the end, a Democratic representative moved that the resolution "be indefinitely postponed," thus tabling the controversial issue. Nevertheless, Governor Caulfield ordered Attorney General Stratton Shartel to investigate the lynching of Gunn, calling it "a defiance of the law, an outrage upon justice, and a disgrace to the state." The governor's statement elicited a reply from Job, who provided to the public some of the details of the crime and the lynching which, he argued, tended to prove that Gunn was guilty and that the mob was responding more out of outrage to the heinous nature of the crime than out of racism. Later in the session, a bill was passed to punish "officers failing to protect prisoners from mob violence" and establishing a "$10,000 indemnity to families of lynched prisoners payable by the county in which the lynching occured [sic]." Governor Caulfield, however, vetoed the measure. In his message to the state senate, he explained that the bill failed to allow a change of venue in the prosecution of persons accused of lynching to another county where a conviction might be possible. Moreover, the bill exempted the county sheriff from punishment for failing to protect defendants from being lynched. Caulfield asked the General Assembly to pass a bill providing to the supreme court or the governor the power to fire "summarily" any officer "derelict" in preventing mob violence.[18]

Much of Limbaugh's time at first was consumed in committee meetings and House sessions, which during the early part of the session were usually brief. Interested in educational matters and a member of the teachers college committee, he collected circulars and statements from teachers' groups, educators, school board members, and others opposing and supporting bills before the committee or otherwise relating to education. He also collected newspaper clippings from the daily newspapers concerning a controversial proposal to change the system of hiring and retaining primary and secondary education teachers in St. Louis. Apparently, teachers received life tenure after meeting an established set of time and performance standards. Supported by the St. Louis school board, the proposed bill would remove protections for new teachers and establish an annual hiring system. Teachers' associations mounted an effective campaign against this proposal in the newspapers, held rallies, and lobbied legislators. The teachers argued that the bill would open up the hiring process to politics and favoritism and end the careful selection of teachers according to their qualifications. Apparently these arguments prevailed, for even the bill's sponsor, Representative Louis C. Hehl, announced in the *St. Louis Globe-Democrat* his willingness to allow it to die.[19]

One of the issues before the teachers college committee was legislation affecting the operations of the several colleges in Missouri established chiefly to train primary and secondary school teachers. As a former student of Southeast Missouri State University in Cape Girardeau, formerly called the Normal School, it was natural for university president Joseph A. Serena to seek Limbaugh's help in gaining appropriations and intervening with Governor Caulfield on various matters. When the tax commission failed to provide adequate funding for repairs to an auditorium, for the payment of tax bills, and for a deficit in salaries, Serena wrote to Limbaugh explaining the situation and requesting his help in gaining a supplemental appropriation for these expenditures through the subcommittee of the House appropriations committee. Eventually, Limbaugh appeared before this subcommittee. Moreover, he arranged for Serena to meet with the governor after questions arose concerning Serena's use of incidental funds to pay for the repairs to the auditorium and the purchase of materials from Regent W. C. Bahn. Eventually, although displeased with these irregular business practices, Caulfield faulted the president's judgment, rather than his ethics, and allowed the matter to drop.[20]

During this controversy, Limbaugh also found himself vouching for Serena's character with the governor. This became necessary after a report surfaced in early 1931 that the president had used university employees and equipment to construct "a tourist camp and a filling station on property owned by" him. Later, a state investigator found that the president had already "reimbursed" the university, or at the very least had submitted a report to the board to determine how much he owed. While Caulfield again concluded that Serena had not acted unethically, he also believed that the president was guilty of acting imprudently and had made himself unnecessarily vulnerable to accusations of impropriety. Seeing an opportunity, the editor of the *Cash-Book*, a Democratic newspaper in Jackson, Missouri, called upon Caulfield to oust Serena and to appoint two Democrats to fill the positions of regents whose terms had expired. Because the Board of Regents had the power to install a new university president, there was some concern among Republicans that the governor, although a member of the GOP himself, might appoint anti-Serena regents. Thus, Caulfield found himself importuned by both Democrats and Republicans over the appointments. The governor quickly grew tired of the partisan bickering and believed strongly that his primary responsibility was to choose the best appointee, not to strengthen Republican dominance over the institution. Limbaugh, who was a friend of the Republican lobbyists, advised them to moderate their efforts as aggressive lobbying could backfire. Several times the governor discussed this matter over

with Limbaugh, whom he considered to have the best interests of the university at heart. Thus, when he had made his decision, the governor again consulted
Cape Girardeau County's representative for his opinion. Although one of the
appointees was a Democrat, Limbaugh considered him to be "very satisfactory," for "he was an alumnus of the school, a civic worker in the community, and
a man of good reputation and influence all over the section of the state which
the college served."[21]

Not all educational controversies concerned partisan and budgetary issues.
One of the more interesting questions arising concerned the teaching of communism and pacifism in Missouri's colleges and universities. According to information provided to the House appropriations committee, in late 1930 the
Springfield Teachers' College paid Victor Yakhontoff, a former major-general
of the Soviet Army, and Paul Harris, southern secretary of the National Council
for the Prevention of War, fifty dollars each to speak at a forum where "approximately 1,000 students" gathered. Soon the committee received information of
other speakers and professors presenting communist and radical ideas to their
students, including accusations of a covert effort to promulgate "anti-American
ideas among our teachers." Always seeking the perspective of others before
forming his own opinion, Limbaugh first discussed this issue with Representative George Willson and "President Williams," perhaps referring to C. H. Williams of the University of Missouri-Columbia, who thought the alarm of some
regarding these incidents was unwarranted. He said that "he was glad that colleges help young people to become tolerant of the ideas and ideals of the other nations of the world." A few days later, Limbaugh asked the governor for
his views. With a son in college, Caulfield noted that there was a "tendency
. . . to encourage liberalism" and that "his own son was now wrought up about
Russian conditions and was making an intensive study of Russia." Nevertheless, he thought that this should not be a matter of deep concern, for opinions developed in college often become "tempered with experience and revised
with age." Given his own college experience and dalliance with progressivism,
this observation made a lot of sense to Limbaugh. And yet, Caulfield opposed
teachers imposing their political views upon students and thought educational
institutions should be encouraged not to advocate ideologies and take partisan
positions in the classroom. This opinion explains Caulfield's decision to send
correspondence concerning such activities to the appropriations committee,
where funding for schools was decided. The governor's balanced and objective
analysis of the situation impressed Limbaugh very much.[22]

While never one to react precipitously to issues, Limbaugh nevertheless held
strong convictions he had developed through the years. The major influences
upon his personal philosophy and ethical standards were his Christian faith
and his reading of history and Western literature. Not inclined to impose his

views upon others, or even to share them unsolicited, Limbaugh demonstrated his faith and convictions through example—a most powerful form of witness. These beliefs necessarily informed his decision making as a legislator and led him to oppose a bill seeking to legalize gambling at horse races and measures intended to undermine the prosecution of prohibition. Believing that gambling and drinking damaged families and society, he was not swayed by arguments claiming that laws governing such activities did more harm than good. In his correspondence with constituents and lobbyists, Limbaugh made clear his opposition to legalizing these twin vices and recorded his private judgments about the character of those supporting such measures. Thus during the debate on the bill to legalize racetrack gambling, he criticized the remarks of Jones Parker, who "took the usual position of riding two horses going in opposite directions at the same time." Limbaugh considered George B. Calvin's arguments to have demonstrated "the lowest kind of moral principles and ideals." Concerning another, he noted with some satisfaction that after the bill's defeat, Duensing, who was thoroughly ashamed of his sponsorship of the bill, sheepishly apologized, claiming that he was a churchgoing man.[23]

Limbaugh also strongly disapproved of efforts to prevent the enforcement of prohibition. As a lawyer and a firm believer in the rule of law, he thought that the efforts of the "Wets," apart from the propriety or impropriety of the law, were especially pernicious, for in pursuing them the opponents of prohibition sought to undermine the implementation of an amendment to the Constitution. Early in the session after Congress failed to pass a resolution asking for the repeal of the eighteenth amendment, Representatives Calvin and A. A. Wolff announced their intention to submit a referendum to the people of Missouri in the 1932 election for the repeal or modification of the state prohibition law. On March 3, Limbaugh was the lone member of the judiciary committee to vote against a bill repealing the enforcement of prohibition. However, two days later when the bill was brought before the House it was defeated 78–51. Perhaps out of frustration and gathering confidence that the repeal of prohibition was not distant, the Wets scoffed at their opponents and stated that prohibition was a farce, for anyone could get "all the hooch [they] want." In a letter to a supporter of the bill, Limbaugh explained that he was against it for he believed that "the proposed resolution attempted to do something by an illegal and unconstitutional method, and, in the second place, I am of the opinion that a prohibition referendum at this time would be unduly expensive and unnecessary, since we had an expression of the people on this proposition just a short time ago." Moreover, he thought that "an earnest effort" to enforce prohibition had not yet been made and until then he wished to continue the experiment. He also noted that he would not want to return to the days when almost no restrictions were placed upon the consumption of alcohol.[24]

Much of the legislation before the House during the 1931 session, while of a more mundane character, was nevertheless important. Certainly, the efforts to construct a road and highway system to make travel and transport easy and safe was greatly needed and had the added benefit of providing much needed jobs to Missourians. For this reason, Governor Caulfield pushed the legislature to appropriate enough money to keep laborers employed. The state was then in the midst of a long-term construction project which had begun in 1922 and was expected to be completed in 1937. If construction continued as planned, when completed, Missouri would have over 15,000 miles of paved roads. Perhaps even more important than the construction of new roads was the need for new regulations on buses and trucks, a driver's license requirement, and new rules of the road. During his 1923 trip from Cape Girardeau to Minneapolis, Minnesota, Limbaugh had gained firsthand experience concerning many of the inconveniences and dangers of poor roads and few signs, an inadequate infrastructure, and no or little enforcement of the few rules of the road. Limbaugh concluded that much was required to lower the number of deadly accidents and to reduce the hardships and time involved in travel. For these reasons, he supported many of the measures before the House, especially regulations on buses and trucks to make their operation safer. One of these statutes, for instance, reduced the maximum length of vehicles and trailers, an important measure leading to fewer accidents on the road.[25]

Another important measure concerned the establishment of a state highway patrol. This legislation was sponsored by the Automobile Club of Missouri, the governor, and the attorney general. The House roads and highways committee reported the bill out favorably, although their amended version of it provided for less patrolmen, 115 instead of 144, and other changes to the original proposal in salary and qualification requirements. In the Senate, opposition to the bill was less formidable than in the House, and while some amendments to the original bill were passed, none of these were of a nature to change the character of the highway patrol significantly. In the House, the struggle against the bill continued into late February, during which several days were consumed in debate, and opponents argued among other things that the patrolmen "would become a 'group of prohibition snoopers.'" These arguments reflected the strong desire of many, especially in rural areas, to maintain local autonomy over policing and a suspicion of all centralizing efforts to give authority to a state institution. The opponents also offered a number of amendments to make the patrol less effective or to revise it into a form unacceptable to its sponsors and kill it. One of these amendments, making patrolmen subordinate to county sheriffs, was adopted to the great discouragement of the bill's supporters. Efforts to remove the amendment failed. Concerning this debate, Limbaugh noted that those opposed argued "that the patrolmen would stop innocent people, search their cars, and if they found a bottle would arrest them and subject them to fines and humiliation." Democratic Floor Leader Blair argued that "he did not propose to do anything in Missouri that would give any prohibition officials any further right to search his car." Moreover, Minority Floor Leader William Elmer made a series of remarks which "represented the point of view of the criminal [trial] lawyer and made remarks in the course of his speech that were vicious and incomprehensible coming from a man of leadership and experience in legislative matters."[26]

After these setbacks to the establishment of a highway patrol, Limbaugh and other supporters did not abandon the effort. As he explained in a letter, because the House bill "has been so mutilated," supporters of the highway patrol had decided to abandon it and try to pass the Senate version later. In the meantime, the governor and other supporters spoke out, explaining the great advantages to having patrolmen help and protect motorists and enforce reasonable laws to prevent accidents and identify those problem motorists who caused the greatest part of the property damage, injuries, and fatalities due to reckless driving. On April 17, the Senate bill was brought to the floor of the House. Again opponents to the highway patrol sought to pass amendments to make its passage and reconciliation with the Senate version difficult. Limbaugh spoke in favor of the Senate bill and against two amendments in which the first sought to reduce the number of patrolmen from 115 to 40, and another to increase their number to 140. He talked "for more than the allotted time and refused interrogation by a number who rose to interrogate me during my remarks." Only after he had finished his prepared remarks did Limbaugh then yield the floor and answer questions "from Heege, Snyder of Lewis, Rebo, Spearman and Elmer, [who] were all on their feet to interrogate" him. While the poisoned-pill amendments to the bill were defeated, so was the bill itself. After the session, Limbaugh and the bill's other supporters decided to telegram those in favor of it who were absent, appealing for their return to Jefferson City when the House convened on Monday, April 20. Apparently these absent legislators had left early to enjoy an extended weekend. The story on Monday was very different. With Speaker Nelson's help, the bill was passed by a large majority.[27]

As already noted, Limbaugh's friend and fellow Republican Fred Naeter and Democrat Langdon Jones had urged him to run for state representative to support efforts to translate the survey commission's report into legislation and to shepherd it to passage. The commission held extensive hearings around the state, employed experts to determine the needs of "state-supported institutions," and made recommendations to reform the manner in which Missouri collected taxes. To understand systems of taxation better, how their collection affected the economy, and its ethical ramifications, Limbaugh considered the subject in light of the colonial and revolutionary periods of American history, the history of Missouri, and at least one scholarly treatise, *Essays in Taxation*, written by progressive professor of political economy and finance at Columbia University, Edwin R. A. Seligman. Instead of viewing taxation as payment for "goods and services provided by government," Seligman and other progressives argued that this was the wrong perspective and that all members of society should "contribute to the common welfare of the state based on his taxpaying capacity." Under this system the emphasis was to tax annual income instead of a tax based solely upon a person's holdings of land and real estate, or *tangible* property. In 1931, Missouri predominately taxed tangible property, but this system, in particular, placed a disproportionate burden upon farmers, who were then hit hardest by the Depression and had begun to protest this inequity. To address this problem, members of the survey commission proposed instituting a state income tax as a fairer method of collecting revenue from Missouri's residents to include a tax upon profits realized from *intangible* property such as stocks, bonds, and interest from loans. Because his brothers Arthur, Roscoe, and Burette still farmed, Limbaugh was well aware of the farmer's economic plight and favored the commission's proposals to relieve their tax burden.[28]

On January 22, Jones, who was chair of the House survey committee, "was jubilant" that the committee's members favored the legislation he had drafted "and that things now looked like his proposed program would go through the House without serious opposition." This expectation, however, turned out to be overly optimistic, for business leaders soon organized and lobbied the House vigorously against the state income tax. On February 11, when the tax bills were debated in the House "as a special order of business," opponents argued that the burden to business would drive industry from the state. Limbaugh countered this argument by noting that the Marquette Cement Company had threatened to leave Cape Girardeau in 1925 when it was about to be annexed and thus faced the additional burden of paying city taxes. Nevertheless, after its annexation the company had remained and prospered despite its increased tax burden. That evening, the Senate survey committee held a hearing at which some 500 businessmen from Kansas City and St. Louis came to Jefferson City to protest. Their main spokesperson was Walter Weisenburger, president of the St. Louis Chamber of Commerce, who, apparently buoyed by the "enthusiastic" support from the gallery, gave an able speech. During questioning, Weisenburger "responded each time with a witty remark," bringing cheers from his supporters. Wishing to counter this, Limbaugh asked Weisenburger about a *St. Louis Star* article which reported that a number of industries were then "rapidly coming into St. Louis." Did this not demonstrate, Limbaugh inquired, that despite the proposed tax increase upon business it would not drive industry from the state as he claimed? Weisenburger deflected this question by claiming to know that these incoming industries "were those who did not attempt to anticipate what a legislature would do." How he knew this, however, he did not explain. Others interrogated the St. Louis businessman, but he handled each of the questions ably and escaped the hearing unscathed. At a later hearing, Limbaugh noted that Weisenburger's performance before a less friendly audience was not nearly as impressive.[29]

Despite the overwhelming support in the House for a redistribution of the tax burden, little enthusiasm existed for this legislation in the Senate. Much of the opposition came from senators from Kansas City and St. Louis and other municipal areas where the change would be felt most heavily. As early as February 27, the Senate "substantially" amended the House tax bill "reducing the graduated schedules" recommended by the survey commission. At the same time, the Senate doubled the corporate franchise tax, which would have shifted more of the tax burden upon business. On March 15, the Senate again modified the tax bill by eliminating the increase in the corporate franchise tax. Still some, like the editorial page of the St. Louis Post-Dispatch, argued that the tax bill was long overdue to begin the process of funding the consolidation of Missouri's rural school districts. While this need was recognized by many, others thought it foolish to increase the tax burden upon Missourians during a time of economic hardship. Senator Russell Dearmont, Limbaugh's friend and former classmate, led the effort to bring the House tax bill through Missouri's highest legislative body, where senators were able to filibuster, causing a long deadlock; indeed the longest experienced on any bill in Missouri to that time. During these fourteen days of debate, no other business came before the Senate. This deadlock ended, however, on March 25 with passage of a bill increasing state revenue substantially, although not as much as the legislation passed in the House. Personal income was taxed on "a graduated basis," from one to four percent, based upon one's income, although some deductions were allowed for those in the higher brackets. Corporation taxes were set at a flat rate of two percent. Thus Missouri joined the ranks of those states with a personal income tax.[30]

As the legislative session of the House wound down the representatives experienced various emotions, some of goodwill and others of animosity and impatience. During debate over an appropriation for the Commission for the Blind, Democratic Floor Leader Blair and former Speaker and Republican Parker almost came to blows. In Limbaugh's account of this dispute, Parker showed disrespect for the commission and for the governor. Blair accused Parker of nursing a grudge against the governor for refusing to appoint his brother as secretary of the commission. Parker claimed that this was untrue, for his brother "would not want that kind of job." Blair refused to retract his statement and as Limbaugh reported it, Parker stated "any man who made that charge was a

____ ____ liar. As he did this he advanced toward Blair in a threatening manner. A number of members present stepped between the two men, whereupon Parker returned to his seat." While it cannot certainly be known, Blair's accusation may have been true, for early in the legislative session Parker had strongly criticized Caulfield for his handling of the Brunk matter. For a legislative leader to direct such criticism at the governor of his own party was very unusual to say the least. At the time, in private conversation with Limbaugh, Caulfield had noted Parker's animus toward him and attributed it to his refusal "to appoint Parker's brother as a physician for the police board in St. Louis," adding that he believed his brother was incompetent.[31]

According to custom, a number of gifts were exchanged at the end of the legislative session to demonstrate the members' appreciation for one another despite their disagreements. Thus all of the members donated money to purchase watches, which were presented to Speaker Nelson and to H. O. Maxey, the Speaker *pro tem*. Minority Floor Leader Elmer received a fishing rod and a fountain pen was given to Reading Clerk Robert McClanahan, affectionately known as "Uncle Bob." Having served in the House for fifty-two years, McClanahan was deeply touched by this recognition and wept. While all of this was happening, Limbaugh was approached by the pages—the teenage boys serving as messengers on the House floor—who requested that he present their gift, "an emblem of the Democratic mule," to the speaker. Exactly why he was chosen to make this presentation is unknown, although it probably resulted from Limbaugh's genuine interest in young people and friendly and approachable manner. Whatever the reason, Limbaugh carried out his commission "approach[ing] the speaker's desk and announc[ing] that this simple gift was the expression of esteem the pages had for the speaker." Wiping away tears, the Speaker responded "that he had not been touched quite so much by anything before because he had not expected that even the pages would remember him." After this, the House adjourned and the members lingered to visit with one another.[32]

The 1931 legislative session proved to be long and difficult. Much legislation was considered and passed, perhaps the most important of which was that establishing a highway patrol and other bills making Missouri's roads safer. The survey commission legislation, seeking to impose a state income tax and distribute the burden of taxation more fairly, was the most controversial of that considered. This and the education bill touched off debates that crossed party lines with rural legislators often at odds with members from urban areas. Here constituent interests trumped party affiliations, although when considering the overall picture it is clear that even independent-minded members seldom broke ranks with their caucus. Certainly this can be said about Limbaugh as well. Nevertheless, he pursued his own course more than most and certainly broke with his party leadership on one of the most important issues of the session—the decision to investigate charges made against the state treasurer, Republican Larry Brunk. Because of the governor's confidence in his integrity and independence, the speaker appointed Limbaugh to the special committee to investigate Brunk. As will be seen, Cape Girardeau County's representative was soon immersed in the taking of depositions, witness testimony before the committee, and studying impeachment law and proceedings. Believing as he did in the importance of transparency in government and the protection of state revenues, Limbaugh did not allow partisan considerations to influence his work on the Brunk Investigative Committee, even after some Republicans expressed concern that the impeachment of Brunk might have an adverse impact upon the GOP in Missouri.

Left to right, Stephen N. Limbaugh Jr., Rush
H. Limbaugh Sr., Stephen N. Limbaugh Sr.

(Above left) Rush H. Limbaugh Sr., World War Two era

(Above right) Bee Limbaugh, wife of Rush H. Limbaugh Sr., World War Two era

(Opposite left) Rush H. Limbaugh Sr., 1916, age 25

(Opposite right) Rush H. Limbaugh Sr., 1950s

Joseph H. Limbaugh, father of Rush H. Limbaugh Sr., circa 1875

Susan Presnell Limbaugh, mother of Rush H. Limbaugh Sr.

Bee Limbaugh, wife of Rush H. Limbaugh Sr., early twenties

Rush H. Limbaugh Sr., age 17

Left to right, THE LIMBAUGH LAWYERS (back row) Stephen
N. Limbaugh Sr., Rush H. Limbaugh Jr., Pierre Dominique, Rush
H. Limbaugh Sr., (seated) Stephen N. Limbaugh Jr., Daniel B.
Limbaugh, John M. Limbaugh, David Limbaugh

Left to right, Willie and Arthur Limbaugh, Cora and Burette Limbaugh, Dr. Dayton L. and Lillie Seabaugh, Roscoe and Josie Limbaugh, Bee and Rush H. Limbaugh Sr.

Left to right, Justice Clarence Thomas, Stephen N. Limbaugh
Jr., Rush H. Limbaugh Sr., Stephen N. Limbaugh Sr.

Bee and Rush H. Limbaugh Sr., circa 1970

Rush H. Limbaugh Sr., delegate at the 1936 National
Republican Convention, Cleveland, Ohio

Left to right, Rush H. Limbaugh Jr., Marguerite
Limbaugh, Manley O. Limbaugh, circa 1925

Rush H. Limbaugh Sr. in his library at home, 1947

Rush H. Limbaugh Sr., circa 1930

Rush H. Limbaugh III, Rush H. Limbaugh
Sr., and Rush H. Limbaugh Jr.

Rush Hudson Limbaugh Sr. United States Courthouse

Chapter Six

The Brunk Impeachment

While serving in the Missouri House of Representatives in 1931, Rush H. Limbaugh was chosen to serve on the special committee to investigate State Treasurer Larry Brunk's conduct in office. Soon after his appointment, Limbaugh met with other members of the committee composed of four Democrats, Stanley P. Clay, Nick B. Bradley, Willis H. Meredith, and Don C. Carter; and two Republicans, George F. Heeges and Edward L. Britain, (Limbaugh being the third Republican). The committee first decided to obtain copies of the Supreme Court of Missouri's opinion overturning Governor Henry S. Caulfield's ouster of the state treasurer and to request information concerning the matter from him. Perhaps because he was well acquainted with Caulfield and a fellow Republican, Limbaugh became the committee's liaison to the governor's office and to others within the administration involved in or knowledgeable about the Brunk matter. The following morning Limbaugh spoke with Bank Examiner Jessie L. Mulligan, who was then putting together materials for the committee, and Attorney General Stratton Shartel. Both explained the allegations and evidence of corruption and malfeasance against Brunk and the testimony of two former secretaries who claimed that he had sexually harassed them. The state treasurer was also accused of improperly accepting favors from bond salesmen, who in one instance threw a party for him "where women and liquor . . . [were] in abundance." Moreover, Limbaugh spoke with the governor, who stated his intention to withdraw from the Brunk matter after providing the committee with the materials sought by the House. Understanding the political nature of impeachment proceedings, the governor suggested that before making any public statements the committee wait until it had collected evidence and testimony about Brunk's conduct in office and had decided what to do.[1]

From an early age Limbaugh had developed a deep interest in public affairs, believing strongly that elected officials should be held accountable to the public for their actions in office. Thus, as a member of the committee, Limbaugh took his responsibilities very seriously and spent the vast majority of his time, when not attending to his legislative and constituent responsibilities, working on the impeachment investigation in one capacity or another. Because the impeachment of officers was an unusual proceeding, he began to educate himself concerning the process and precedent by obtaining from the library of the Supreme Court of Missouri a transcript of the impeachment trial of President Andrew Johnson. This reading would intensify and be extensive, especially as he prepared for key debates on the floor of the House and the trial later. Limbaugh also talked to a number of people, including others on the committee and journalists, to gain their perspectives about the Brunk matter. But probably most important, Limbaugh personally took an active role in making committee decisions, collecting evidence, and questioning witnesses throughout the investigation.[2]

On January 20, the committee made some very important decisions with serious ramifications for the investigation and impeachment later. Mulligan presented bank records to the committee in which he believed was proof of Brunk's involvement in a scheme to defraud Missouri of bank interest payments from which he profited personally. Confronted with the complexity of the evidence and the difficulty of understanding its significance, someone on the committee suggested that Mulligan and a member of the attorney general's office participate more actively in the investigation and questioning of witnesses. The four Democrats on the committee supported this idea, but Limbaugh thought "it would be improper for the committee to accept the assistance of a representative of the governor and the attorney-general in making the investigation." His Republican colleagues agreed with Limbaugh, and after some discussion the Democrats, finally acquiesced in their judgment. Judge Bradley, who had no doubt about Brunk's guilt, sought to limit the investigation, believing that it was unnecessary. Again, Limbaugh disagreed, noting "that it would be poor policy for us to make a report until we had done everything in our power to get at the actual facts." Bradley resented that his fellow Democrats did not support him, and "seemed to think that the Republican members were getting by with too much in shaping the policy of the committee."[3]

Perhaps the committee's most controversial decision was to meet in secret. The controversy arose largely because some journalists wanted access to report on the testimony and evidence as the story developed. Asa Hutson, reporter for the *St. Louis Globe-Democrat*, threatened "to write up the activities of the committee unfavorably" if its hearings remained closed, later making good on his threat. However, not all journalists agreed with Hutson. *St. Louis Post-Dispatch* reporter Boyd Carroll told Limbaugh that although holding open hearings would make his job easier, "from the standpoint of public service he knew it was best for the committee to exclude all persons except the witnesses testifying." Within a couple of days, Representative Elmer Jones presented a resolution to force the Brunk investigative committee to hold open hearings. While few details of this debate are known, Jones' resolution was debated "spiritedly . . . for more than an hour and a half" and was defeated by an un-recorded vote. As unidentified members of the committee participated in the debate, it is probable that their argument was similar to the one presented in the committee's report to the House on February 17. In this report, the committee noted that they were operating like a grand jury and that closed hearings were necessary, for citizens would "testify much more willingly and freely" if the proceedings were not public. The committee also was aware that some of the testimony "might be given affecting the solvency of some bank in the state." Later, Brunk claimed that the secret hearings were unfair, for his attorney did not have a chance to challenge the witnesses and evidence pre-sented before the committee. While this allegation appeared serious, the in-vestigation was not a trial, but only an effort to discover and weigh evidence to determine whether a basis existed for presenting an indictment in the form of articles of impeachment.[4]

The investigation entailed many hours of gathering evidence, questioning witnesses, and writing and revising the committee's report. Often in prepa-ration for the questioning, Limbaugh consulted with Mulligan, others in the attorney general's office, and the governor. During this stage of the investi-gation, Governor Caulfield advised Limbaugh never to allow his focus to be averted from the primary fact "that Brunk had been stealing state funds." The evidence strongly indicated that the state treasurer had conspired with offi-cers of the Bank of Aurora in his hometown to profit from the shorting of the state in its interest payments on state deposits. After its failure in 1930, an au-dit of the bank's accounts uncovered these irregularities and demonstrated that Brunk had personally profited from them. When this was discovered, the governor ordered a more thorough investigation of Brunk's conduct and soon learned of another scheme in which the state treasurer profited from the use of public funds.[5]

The committee called witnesses to gather evidence on both conspiracies. Some of the witnesses were hostile or uncooperative and it was necessary to subpoena them. Typically, these witnesses were either fellow conspirators or one of Brunk's friends. The testimony of D. W. Tudor, chief clerk in the state treasurer's office, was particularly combative and was "so unbelievable that members of the committee cross-examined him rather severely. Carter, in par-ticular, was severe in his remarks to Tudor, which remarks were not all record-ed." Another witness, Ed Zuendt, vice president of the First National Bank of Jefferson City, however, was helpful pointing the committee to some of Brunk's personal banking transactions, which he considered suspicious and worthy of further investigation. Ed R. Adams, president of the Bank of Aurora, appeared before the committee with his lawyer, Sam Wear, for he and Magnus T. Easley, another bank officer, were under indictment for alleged illegal banking practices. Because their testimony was considered crucial to the investigation, Attorney General Shartel explored making a deal with Brunk's fellow conspirators. Governor Caulfield, a former judge of the St. Louis Court of Appeals, opposed this but apparently changed his mind, for in the end Adams received a deal in return for his testimony. One of the most important witnesses interviewed by the committee during this early period of the investigation was William H. Norwine, vice president of the Provident State Securities Company, whom Brunk improperly aided in his sale of bonds to state banks. Norwine, who may have been unwilling to perjure himself to protect Brunk, admitted that the state treasurer had aided him in the sale of bonds to fund the construction of the Pierre Chouteau apartments in St. Louis. During this testimony, however, it was also clear that Norwine wished to entangle both the governor and attorney general in the bond scheme if possible. Norwine may have been inspired to do this after the newspapers reported recent criticism in the House of the governor's handling of the Brunk affair.[6]

On the evening of January 26, after a brief session of the House and a hearing of the Brunk investigative committee, Limbaugh stopped by the Central Hotel where he learned from newspaper reporters that Britain, a Republican member of the committee, had been arrested on charges of bribery. *St. Louis Globe-Democrat* reporter Hutson, apparently enjoying his predicament, told Limbaugh that "you are on a hell of a committee. One of your members is in jail and two others are likely to be dismissed from the House any time because they have members of their family on the payroll." According to the reporters, Britain had sought a bribe of $2,000 from Brunk in return for a favorable committee report. Brunk contacted Cole County prosecutor Nike G. Sevier and arranged to pay Britain with a down payment of $400 in marked bills, after which he was arrested. This information came to Limbaugh "like a thunderbolt." Earlier that day while in executive session of the committee, Britain had complained that they were spending more time than he liked on the investigation. He claimed to need Thursdays and Fridays to work in his office and had to get away early. Even before the committee had begun to hold hearings, Britain had told Limbaugh that he thought the impeachment was partisan and suggested that they might file a minority report. He also believed that "the movement against Brunk [was] to the disadvantage of the party."[7]

After speaking with reporters, Limbaugh walked over to the committee room in the capitol building and met other members of the committee who had gathered there along with Democratic Floor Leader James Blair and Speaker Eugene Nelson. It was apparent to them "that Brunk was seeking to discredit the committee and that it should be our purpose to go on with our work." They also discussed a rumor circulating that Britain had told Brunk that Clay, Carter, and Heege could all "be bought" and that Limbaugh "could be influenced on the ground of partisanship." Finally, the committee released a statement that they had no knowledge of the facts in Britain's arrest and could not comment on it. However, they also expressed the hope that Britain be dealt with according to the law if he was guilty. The next morning, Limbaugh carefully read the newspapers, which "were full of the Britain bribery story," and then went to the speaker's office where he learned from Nelson that Gray Snider had been sent to the Cole County jail where Britain had spent the night. There Snider secured his resignation from the committee. Floor Leader Blair offered a resolution before the House, proclaiming the members' confidence in the Brunk investigative committee and urging their investigation to continue. Both Britain's resignation and the resolution passed unanimously without debate. Later in the session, however, a resolution to oust Britain as a member of the House failed.[8]

On February 1, the committee invited Brunk to testify before the committee, but after three days he refused through his lawyer, who asserted that the state treasurer's testimony would be meaningless, for "the committee has already reached a decision in the matter without hearing Mr. Brunk or any evidence on his behalf." By February 9 the committee had drafted a report. Limbaugh's wife, Bee, and his secretary, Lucille Feurth, traveled to Jefferson City to spend the next several days helping Limbaugh improve and revise it. Limbaugh attended to this work whenever the House was not in session and he did not have committee work to do. As the report was being readied and the work of the committee appeared to be almost finished, the members decided to play a practical joke upon Bradley, representative from Johnson County, who had argued at the start of their investigation that given Brunk's obvious guilt only the most cursory inquiry was necessary. A fake minority report was drafted in which it was stated that the minority regretted the necessity of reporting "that one member of the committee had from the beginning been unjust and intolerant of Mr. Brunk." When Bradley came into the committee room the practical jokers pretended to be arguing about this matter. Surprised by this unforeseen turn of events, Bradley was handed the fake report. According to Limbaugh, he "read a few lines and stopped to swear. He demanded that we tell him . . . [who] proposed to sign such a report. Clay insisted that he read on. After reading a few more lines he again stopped to swear. By this time he was in a rage." It was only then that the others broke into laughter and informed Bradley of the joke. Fortunately, he was a good sport and joined the others in appreciating the humor at his expense.[9]

By the evening of February 16, the printer had completed the 431-page report and it was released to the press. In it, the committee accused Brunk of being "a party to two well defined conspiracies, the object of both being to enrich Larry Brunk and his fellow conspirators at the expense of the State Treasury." These conspiracies involved the underpayment of interest to the state treasury for state deposits in the Bank of Aurora and in aiding the Provident State Securities Company to sell the Chouteau bonds to secure state deposits. The report provided details of the conspiracies and the transcripts of testimony and evidence gathered in the committee's investigation. The next morning it was distributed to members of the House. Articles appeared in the morning newspapers with a statement from Brunk in which he declared the investigation unfair because the committee had not held open hearings and had not permitted his attorney to cross-examine the witnesses. He also demanded an opportunity to answer the charges before the House. Brunk's complaint was repeated on the floor of the House by supporters of the survey legislation. Their concern was not primarily to ensure fairness to the state treasurer, but to prevent the impeachment proceedings from derailing the survey legislation then before the Senate where opposition to it was more formidable than in the House. Despite these efforts, the House voted to consider the report in one week as "a special order of business."[10]

Prior to presenting the report to the House on February 24, Limbaugh joined fellow committee members Clay and Carter in the speaker's office to decide how best to answer Brunk's demand in the newspapers for time to defend himself before the House. After some deliberation, they agreed "to pass a resolution expressing a willingness to hear Brunk." Perhaps not satisfied with this decision, Limbaugh consulted with Mulligan who argued that it would be unwise to allow Brunk to defend himself in the House, for Mulligan feared that the state treasurer would tell "a pitiful story" and thereby gain the sympathy of enough representatives to defeat the impeachment vote. Limbaugh then went to the governor's office to gain his counsel. The governor also thought it unwise to allow Brunk a forum in the House, although his reason was completely different from Mulligan's, believing that such action could be construed as a repudiation of the Brunk investigative committee's work. Moreover, the committee had offered Brunk the opportunity to appear before the committee but he had declined. Limbaugh reported Mulligan's and the governor's arguments to Speaker Nelson, who tended to agree but said they "would watch developments" and act accordingly.[11]

When recognized on the floor of the House, Clay moved that the Brunk report be adopted. Immediately, Representative O. B. Whitaker, a Republican and strong supporter of the survey bills, rose and objected. Known as an effective parliamentarian, he was a formidable opponent and proved persistent in his efforts to kill or slow the impeachment process. Throughout Clay's presentation, Whitaker repeatedly interrupted him, even after the speaker ruled his interruptions out of order. Whitaker and his allies in the House argued that the Brunk investigative committee had acted improperly and unfairly to Brunk and therefore its report was invalid. They sought to refer the entire matter and report to the judiciary committee where a new investigation could be conducted. This motion, which incidentally would not have included the powers to subpoena witnesses and take testimony under oath, was defeated easily.[12]

At the very end of this debate, Limbaugh was given the privilege of having the last word on the floor of the House before its members voted. He first summarized the arguments already made against Whitaker's motion and provided three primary reasons why it should be rejected. First, Limbaugh noted that a complete investigation had already been made "at great expense," and despite all the claims to the contrary the committee had treated Brunk fairly. Instead of testifying when given the opportunity, Brunk refused, preferring to make his case in the press where he would not be under oath and could not be cross-examined. Second, Limbaugh asserted that the judiciary committee would inevitably come to the same conclusions set forth in their report, for the documentary evidence, he argued, demonstrated that "Brunk's guilt could not be disputed or explained." And third, Limbaugh stated that Brunk's conduct constituted a serious breach of the public trust and a danger to the state treasury. Therefore, "in the interest of good government, the legislature could not afford to delay positive and aggressive action in the face of circumstances so flagrant and so challenging." Afterwards, several people, including two judges of the Springfield Court of Appeals, congratulated Limbaugh for his speech.[13]

After Whitaker's motion was defeated, the Brunk investigative committee's report was approved, 116 to 5. However, the resolution to impeach was defeated, "owing to an improper wording." Limbaugh—along with Clay, Carter, and Meredith—redrafted the resolution, which was presented before the House the next day. This provoked "a sharp" but brief debate, after which the resolution was approved when it was understood that its adoption did not constitute the actual impeachment of Brunk. In the months that followed, in the midst of all their work and difficulties, Carter often asked Clay in jest, "Why did you introduce that resolution in the first place?" Remembering this on a chance meeting some twenty-six years later, Limbaugh humorously repeated the question to Clay as they parted. Following this, the committee next began drafting the articles of impeachment. During this time, Limbaugh heard from supporters of the survey bills, like his friend and political ally Fred Naeter, expressing their concern that the impeachment proceedings against Brunk could prevent passage of the survey legislation in the Senate. Limbaugh also spoke with Governor Caulfield, who believed that the House should proceed with the impeachment, for "if the senate intended to kill the survey program they would do it whether the Brunk case was referred to them or not." Committee members Bradley and Clay also wanted to move forward immediately with impeachment. Limbaugh disagreed and wished to delay passage of the articles of impeachment, although he thought it wise to be prepared when the right time arrived to deliberate on the matter.[14]

On March 4, the committee adopted articles of impeachment, which, after consultation with the speaker, were printed. Nevertheless, over the next few days more revisions were necessary, including one suggested by the governor. In committee, on March 10 Clay, Bradley, and Heege all "insisted" that the articles be reported to the House soon. Limbaugh argued successfully for a short delay to give Carter, who was absent, an opportunity to participate in the decision. By this time, however, it was clear that the committee's patience, especially Chairman Clay's, was almost expended, and was anxious to move forward.[15]

Seeking a schedule agreeable to all parties, Limbaugh discussed the matter with the speaker, who asked the investigative and survey committees to meet. Earlier on his own, Limbaugh had spoken with Langdon Jones, the chair of the survey committee, gaining his agreement not to "insist on further delay." On March 13, Clay presented the articles of impeachment on the floor of the House and asked that the matter be debated on March 17 as a special order of business. No opposition was made to this proposal. In preparation for this debate, Limbaugh had visited the law library at the University of Missouri-Columbia and borrowed a number of volumes on impeachment, which he studied over a long three-day weekend at home in Cape Girardeau. Previously, he had already studied the records of the Andrew Johnson and Warren Hastings impeachment trials to inform himself concerning the charges against them, the methods used in investigating their alleged misdeeds, and how the trials were conducted. The day before the debate, Limbaugh dictated a brief on the law of impeachment. The next morning he left by train at 3:45 a.m. and spent his time studying until he arrived in Jefferson City by noon.[16]

On the floor of the House, Meredith informed Limbaugh that he thought an agreement had been made "to vote the Brunk impeachment that afternoon." At 1:30, when Clay introduced the resolution to impeach Brunk, a large number of people were in the galleries to observe the debate. Among these were newspaper reporters, members of the Public Service Commission, the entire staff from the governor's office, and "officials and representatives from practically every office in the Capitol." Introduction of Clay's resolution led to immediate debate for the rest of the afternoon. Again, leading the fight to delay impeachment was Representative Whitaker, who sought to have each of the nine articles of impeachment debated and voted upon separately. Proponents of the survey legislation, chief among them Representative Langdon Jones, and Republican minority leaders supported Whitaker's motion, "while members of the Brunk committee and other majority members declared [that Jones] and other survey leaders were merely seeking further delay." To Limbaugh, the House seemed to be "in an uproar" and "sentiment for impeachment of Brunk had subsided." Opponents of Clay's motion argued that the articles of impeach-ment were poorly drafted and that no crime by Brunk was alleged in them. In the midst of the debate, Limbaugh went to Jones and requested that he stop trying to pass the resolution to vote on the articles of impeachment separately, but he refused.[17]

At approximately 5:00 p.m. Limbaugh rose and was recognized to speak. As he later related, he found it necessary to "break away from the arguments propounded by the leadership of my own party in the House, which was not easy for me as a freshman member to do." For this, some treated him thereaf-ter "with friendly indifference and some with unrestrained hostility." First, he argued that the articles of impeachment should be voted upon as a unit, for "it took the nine articles to make out a complete case." Next, Limbaugh noted that in the Warren Hastings impeachment and proceedings against others often criminal charges were unnecessary for their conviction. To those who warned the House that it was unfair to "stigmatize Brunk by voting articles against him . . . [Limbaugh] answered that Brunk had already stigmatized himself by his conduct in office, and that [they] would stigmatize [them]selves by failing to vote his impeachment." Finally, Speaker Nelson addressed the House in fa-vor of Clay's motion, which was the first time during the entire session that he had taken the floor to speak on any resolution or bill. The House voted upon Whitaker's motion to have the articles of impeachment voted upon sep-arately, defeating it easily. Then all of the articles were voted upon together and were passed overwhelmingly on a vote of 118 to 7; some representatives, including Jones, refused to vote. All seven votes against Clay's motion were cast by Republicans.[18]

After Limbaugh's speech, a number of spectators and members of the House came and congratulated him for ably defending the committee's work. After ad-journment of the House, Jones approached him and claimed that in supporting Whitaker's motion he had only wished to support the committee. Limbaugh was unconvinced, although he apparently said nothing in reply. However, Rep-resentative Walter C. Ploeser, who was among those who had praised Lim-baugh, answered Jones, observing that Limbaugh's speech "was the best that had been given in the House during the session." Upon hearing this, Jones de-parted "abruptly." The following day, Jones sought to have Clay announce on the floor that he had not "double-crossed the Brunk Committee." When it was clear that Clay was reluctant to do this, Jones appealed to Limbaugh for sup-port. Although somewhat sympathetic, he replied that he had not heard any-one say that Jones had double-crossed the Brunk investigative committee, although he had heard a number of persons say that Jones "had made a mistake in coming to the House that day, since he had been away from every other ses-sion except when survey bills had been considered." This was not the consensus of Republicans, but of Democrats, Jones' own party. Limbaugh also told Jones that he was willing to help him, but making an announcement on the floor that he had not double-crossed the committee was counterproductive to his interests, for this accusation had not occurred to most members and that such a statement would only "raise suspicions" among many. During this conversation, Jones was especially angry with Carter, claiming that if he had not been so favorably disposed to the work of the Brunk investigative committee he could have destroyed Carter's arguments in debate. In response, Limbaugh sought to reconcile the two Democrats, noting to "Jones that he and Carter were both too useful to permit small matters of that kind to come between them." Limbaugh then offered to arrange a meeting for the two "whereby they could meet and agree to lay their differences aside." Jones, who was unenthusiastic about reconciling with Carter, finally agreed to Limbaugh's proposal, who then immediately went to Carter and asked him to patch things up with Jones. Unfortunately, Jones, who apparently had a serious drinking problem, spent the next few days intoxicated until his family came to Jefferson City and brought him home. A few days later he returned to Jefferson City but did not again exercise the influence and leadership in the House that he had exerted formerly.[19]

On March 18, Clay presented a resolution to appoint the Brunk investigative committee to serve as House managers to prosecute the state treasurer before the Senate. Before this, at least two representatives not on the committee had approached the Speaker expressing an interest in becoming House managers and others, tired of Clay's impatience to bring the impeachment resolution before the House, wished to replace him. Apparently, Clay viewed his chairmanship as a stepping stone to political advancement and his behavior, degraded by ambition, had offended some in the House. Nevertheless, without debate the members passed Clay's resolution, although two days later some members threatened to have him removed as a manager after he angrily walked out of the House during a dispute over redistricting legislation.[20]

On March 19, Limbaugh and the House managers met a Senate committee in the Speaker's office to begin the process of coordinating their arrangements for Brunk's trial. The senators thought an appropriation of $40,000 would be necessary and proposed that the managers receive $15 a day and $10 for the senators. Two of the senators thought that this was unconstitutional, however, for the state constitution dictated that legislators were to be paid $5 a day during the scheduled session of the General Assembly and afterwards only $1 a day. Consulting the governor about this, Limbaugh found that Caulfield had concluded that the managers must settle for $1 a day compensation. When on April 1 the managers discussed the matter among themselves, despite his own very difficult financial circumstance at the time, Limbaugh argued that it was unconstitutional for them to accept $15 a day. When the matter was debated on the House floor two days later, Limbaugh again opposed their receiving increased compensation, which "displeased" the other managers very much. In the end, they received $1 a day plus their expenses.[21]

After receiving the articles of impeachment, on March 23 the Senate communicated their readiness to admit the House managers into the Senate chambers the following day. After learning this, the managers worked out a procedure to follow. The next morning the House clerk escorted them into the front of the Senate chambers to "chairs arranged in a semi-circle in front." Upon taking their seats, the House clerk read the resolution of impeachment, Clay announced to the Senate that Brunk had been impeached, and Carter read the articles of impeachment. The managers then rose and left the Senate. Following this, the Senate voted to serve Brunk with a subpoena charging him with high crimes and misdemeanors. Upon receipt of the subpoena, by law Brunk was automatically suspended from office and the governor appointed his personal secretary, Lewis Ellis, as state treasurer, but only after Limbaugh and a member of the governor's staff had investigated Missouri's statutes and determined the proper interpretation of the law bearing upon the executive's responsibility. Apparently, the governor wished to avoid the embarrassment of having the Supreme Court of Missouri again overturn his action in the Brunk matter.[22]

On April 2, the Senate summoned Brunk and the House managers to appear before them and to hear the defendant's answer to the charges. Brunk, through his attorney John G. Madden, declared his innocence and filed a motion declaring "the insufficiency in law" of the articles and "denying to the House of Representatives or its purported managers the right to alter, amend, modify, supplement or withdraw any part, portion, section, or sections" of the articles. Madden also sought thirty days to prepare an answer to the articles, noting that he would need the time to examine witnesses and documents and draft his reply. Clay answered that the managers had no objection to this, although he also noted their desire for the trial to begin as soon as possible. After a good deal of debate among the senators, Madden was granted his request. Later that day, Limbaugh discussed this development with Governor Caulfield who expressed his agreement with this decision, for "it would give the senators a chance to adjourn, go home, forget their differences and return refreshed for taking up the trial, and that it would also give the managers an opportunity to make their preparations."[23]

As noted earlier, when it became increasingly likely that Brunk would be impeached, Limbaugh had begun a very intensive study of impeachment law and the proceedings employed in various trials. His intention was to "make [him]self as familiar with the whole remedy of impeachment as anyone else in the House or Senate." He had already studied the records of the trials of President Andrew Johnson and Warren Hastings. Not content with this, Limbaugh also enlisted help to acquire more material from the governor, the attorney general, journalist Boyd Carroll of the *St. Louis Post-Dispatch*, and Floyd C. Shoemaker, longtime director of the State Historical Society of Missouri. The governor's office contacted the St. Louis Public Library, which sent to Limbaugh "the official proceedings in the Sulzer, Johnson, Archbald, and English impeachment cases." Attorney General Shartel wired his counterparts in Oklahoma and Texas to acquire the records of the impeachment trials against Governors John C. Walton and James E. Ferguson. At the University of Missouri law school, Limbaugh gained permission to check out "a large number of volumes on impeachment." Carroll of the *Post-Dispatch* provided newspaper clippings on the Brunk scandal from its beginning. Moreover, Limbaugh studied the journal of the 1875 state constitutional convention pertaining to impeachment. The governor also made available a stenographer to whom Limbaugh dictated a brief on procedure, which, along with copies of the rules of impeachment for Missouri and the United States, were made available to Senator Ralph Wammack, who promised "to draft a new set of rules to govern proceedings in the Brunk case." These briefs and notes from his investigations were important, for Chairman Clay, apparently aware of the great amount of information he had amassed on impeachment law and proceedings, asked Limbaugh to prepare a brief for the managers on the entire case. When finished, this brief was 111 pages, and provided his fellow managers with much information useful to their trial preparations.[24]

Even after the Senate had decided to try Brunk, the House managers continued to interview witnesses. On April 21 both sides met and the managers agreed to provide Brunk's attorney, Madden, with the managers' witness list five days before trial, and the managers agreed to inform him immediately if any witnesses were added. In return, Madden agreed to allow "the Chicago testimony" to be used in trial without taking depositions. This testimony probably was developed when Clay and Carter had traveled to Chicago in early February to investigate the source of a $10,000 loan Brunk had received. Later that day, Limbaugh met with Brunk, Mulligan, and Madden to arrange a procedure for introducing documents into the record of the trial. It was decided that the originals, mostly financial and bank records and letters, should be presented as exhibits and that photostatic copies would be provided to Madden. On May 2, just a little over two weeks before the impeachment trial began, Madden filed a motion "to quash and dismiss the articles of impeachment." In this document, it was asserted that none of the charges were "impeachable" offenses and that no crime had been committed. Moreover, he claimed that the legal and constitutional provisions against the state treasurer profiting from state money "do not apply to State funds or moneys other than those thus in the State treasury."[25]

The impeachment trial of Brunk began on May 18. The Senate's first order of business was to rule upon Madden's motion to quash and dismiss the articles of impeachment against his client. Clay argued that the senators should hear the evidence and testimony against Brunk, for it was their duty to protect the state from the misconduct of its officers. Madden replied that the charges were insufficient to impeach Brunk and to hear the evidence would only waste the state's time and money. After considering these arguments, the senators voted 21 to 12 to continue with the trial. Because the Senate was composed of nineteen Democrats and fifteen Republicans, at least two members of Brunk's own party—one Republican senator being absent—had voted to set aside Madden's motion and to begin the impeachment proceedings without further delay. Despite the decision in their favor, the House managers recognized that Brunk's prosecution would be very difficult, in part, because Madden was an able and experienced criminal trial lawyer. The managers also knew that the state treasurer had served in the Senate with several of its current members and had many friends there. Moreover, unlike a regular trial over which a judge presided and whose decisions would be bound by a fixed procedure and precedent, the senators were the final arbiters of all questions of law and fact and could be as arbitrary or biased in their decisions as they pleased.[26]

Once Madden's motion to dismiss was denied, the Senate was transformed into a courtroom, providing a witness stand and tables for opposing counsel and newspaper reporters. The Senate chambers were packed with senators, their guests, and representatives of the House. The galleries were also filled—mostly with spectators and newspaper photographers—who throughout the opening statements of both Limbaugh and Madden, snapped photographs, illuminating each during their speeches with the flash of their bulbs. Limbaugh, described in the *Kansas City Star* as the "youthful representative from Cape Girardeau," spoke without notes for an hour and a half "in a ringing voice exclaiming with forceful gestures." In the first part of his presentation, he explained the history and nature of impeachment proceedings, noting that they were a special procedure developed for the purpose of removing from office public officials. Those sections of the 1820 Constitution of Missouri pertaining to impeachment were still operative in 1931 and made certain executive and judicial officials "liable to impeachment for any misdemeanor in office." In establishing this procedure, which is much misunderstood, Limbaugh noted that fundamentally it was political in nature. For this reason, despite Madden's argument in his motion to quash to the contrary, Limbaugh explained that impeachments were founded and determined in legislative bodies where the rules of criminal and civil law did not apply. It is immaterial, therefore, "whether these articles state a criminal offense. It is not necessary for them to do that." That this is true, Limbaugh added, is demonstrated when one carefully exam-

ines the records of other impeachment trials in which convictions were secured, for in the majority of these cases the officeholder was removed "because
of offenses other than crime." Moreover, Limbaugh might have added that the
framers of Missouri's Constitution adopted the same prohibition as the United
States Constitution in stating that any official convicted will suffer no punishment beyond "removal from office, and disqualification to hold any office of
honor." Nevertheless, a defendant, despite being acquitted before the Senate,
could later be criminally prosecuted for the same charges. That the framers did
not consider this to be double jeopardy demonstrates the exceptional and limited nature of impeachment proceedings.[27]

After explaining the history and nature of impeachment proceedings, Limbaugh next "dramatically . . . traced the activities of the accused from the time
he sought the Republican nomination for state treasurer in 1928 through his
successful election up to the time of the failure of the Bank of Aurora in June
1930. Several times Brunk's attorney Madden objected to his remarks, but the
chair overruled the protests." Limbaugh also presented evidence of Brunk's improper arrangement with William H. Norwine to help him sell the Chouteau
bonds for the Provident State Securities Company to state banks as security for
state deposits. In return for this, Brunk received $10,000. In the conclusion of
his remarks, Limbaugh noted that

> the impeachment process has been likened to the sword of Goliath that is kept
> in the temple and brought out only on great occasions. You have never been
> asked before to use this process against another state official, but we ask that it
> be used now, in the interest of protecting the integrity of the funds of Missouri,
> in the interest of protecting the integrity of the office of state treasurer, in the in-
> terest of protecting good government in Missouri, in these interests we ask you
> in the name of the House of Representatives which voted these articles of im-
> peachment, in the name of the people of the state of Missouri, we ask you, if we
> produce these facts before you, to record your judgment against this accused,
> of guilty.[28]

At the end of Limbaugh's remarks, Madden requested that the Senate recess
until after lunch so that he might present his remarks without interruption in
the afternoon. This request was granted and for three hours Madden read from
a prepared manuscript. The defense attorney first complained of the secret and
ex parte nature of the House investigation into the charges against Brunk. The
House managers, he asserted, instead of seeking the truth, were interested only
in discovering information to prosecute the state treasurer. Thus "no hearsay
testimony was too remote to be accepted; no conclusion was too speculative
to be received." According to Madden, Brunk was "a victim of circumstances,"

being the beneficiary of "improper transactions" of which he was completely ignorant. This defense was the only available, for the evidence developed in the investigation by the House managers had demonstrated that the Bank of Aurora had underpaid its interest payments to the state and that part of this money went into "a Brunk rent account." Regarding the $10,000 his client had received from the president of the Provident State Securities Company, which had benefitted from the state treasurer's help in selling the Chouteau bonds, Madden contended that this was a loan, not a bribe. In his conclusion, he asserted "that this prosecution is the product of ancient and personal political animosities."[29]

The following day, the prosecution began its case against Brunk. Limbaugh questioned J. E. Cahill, special deputy commissioner of finance, and Edward G. Robison, assistant attorney general, who helped in the investigation of the Bank of Aurora and Brunk's relationship to Magnus T. Easley and Ed R. Adams, the bank's top officers. Limbaugh first introduced into evidence seventy pages of bank records and then questioned Cahill about them. From this, Limbaugh was able to establish that at the time of the bank's closing in 1930 Brunk owed it over $25,000, that the bank had withheld $4,903 in interest payments to the state, and that someone in the bank had placed $2,750 of this underpayment into an account called the "Brunk rent account." In testimony by another witness, it was established that Easley was responsible for the transfer of money into the Brunk rent account. Madden objected to referring to the account in this manner but was overruled. Cahill testified that after the bank's closure Brunk requested the examiners to compare his account records to that of the bank's to determine if they agreed. The audit demonstrated that his records corresponded exactly to the bank's in the amount he owed, and even to the exact amounts of debits and credits on his account, including those "taken from the 'Brunk rent account.'" Both Cahill and Robison testified that when Governor Caulfield confronted him about the account, Brunk "became excited, pale, and flushed." They also said that Brunk denied any knowledge of the account. During his cross-examination, in an effort to exonerate his client, Madden emphasized Brunk's ignorance of the shortfall in the interest payments and the Brunk rent account from which payments were made upon the state treasurer's debt to the bank, his city property taxes, and even his Shriners' dues. At the end of the trial, during his cross-examination of Brunk, Limbaugh was able to gain Brunk's admission that he had never inquired about these obligations, that he had made no payments on the interest or the principal of his loans from the Bank of Aurora for two years, and that the accrued interest alone for this period was $4,000. Of course, such behavior indicated that Brunk had indeed known about the payments from the rent account or, much less probably, that he had ignored these obligations completely, despite visiting Adams and Easley about once every two weeks while in office.[30]

As the trial proceeded, the six House managers divided the responsibility of interrogating witnesses. After Limbaugh's questioning of the bank examiners, different employees of the Bank of Aurora testified, providing more detail concerning the payment of interest to the state and demonstrating that these were lower than the contracted amount, paying 2.75 percent rather than 2.98 percent. According to Catherine Gardner, bookkeeper at the bank, Easley had directed her each month to place sums of $100 to $250 from the calculated interest into the Brunk rent account. Moreover, a letter showing that Brunk had requested financial help from Easley during his campaign for state treasurer was introduced as evidence. In it Brunk warned that he was contemplating quitting the race but stated that "if I could have gone on and be elected, I realize I would be in a position to do you boys some real favors for four years, and of course you know I would do it."[31]

As the trial progressed, it became evident that the House managers were having difficulty gaining the cooperation of key witnesses. Both Adams and Easley were under indictment for accepting deposits to the bank after it was insolvent and refused to testify, citing their constitutional right not to incriminate themselves. Because of this, the House managers hesitated to call them but later decided to bring them before the Senate. Despite the managers' direction to Adams and Easley to remain in Jefferson City, the managers discovered that both men were no longer there. Under the rules adopted for the trial, witnesses could only be excused upon agreement of counsel of both sides or by the Senate. Upon learning of the two men's departure, Limbaugh stated his intention to seek from the Senate "an attachment for the two bankers" and that they be punished "for being out of reach of the Senate." Another important witness unavailable for the prosecution was Norwine, a salesman whose testimony was critical in presenting the facts concerning the Chouteau bond sales. Despite repeated attempts, the Senate's sergeant-at-arms was unable to deliver a subpoena to Norwine.[32]

Without the testimony of Adams and Easley, the managers were forced to move forward with other aspects of the trial which they had intended to present later. Thus, the managers called William E. Zuendt, president of the First National Bank in Jefferson City, to question him concerning Brunk's private financial transactions. Limbaugh introduced into evidence "the ledger sheets of the Brunk account . . . [and] the original deposit slips" showing that most of the money the state treasurer deposited was in currency. The transactions demonstrated that Brunk had deposited far more money into the bank than the salary he received from the state. The bank ledger sheets documented that Brunk had deposited approximately $29,000 in the Jefferson City bank, and later it was discovered that he had deposited $13,000 more in a Kansas City bank, the Commerce Trust Company, during a period when his salary was less than $10,000. Nevertheless, Zuendt also noted that Brunk never kept a substantial amount of money in his account. Moreover, a register from the New Bismarck Hotel in Chicago showed that Brunk was registered there on June 4, 1929, the same day the state treasurer's expense account claimed reimbursement for a trip to St. Louis. Brunk was also there in April 1930 with Norwine and Otto J. Busch, cashier of the Cole County Bank, who purchased Chouteau bonds from Norwine. According to the records, during this period Brunk had received over $3,000 in reimbursements for expenses—a remarkable sum at a time when many earned less than that amount each year.[33]

Limbaugh next turned his attention to Zuendt's experience in the matter concerning Norwine's sale of the Chouteau bonds. This testimony supported the charge against Brunk that he had entered into a conspiracy with Norwine to aid him in his sales by providing "Norwine with confidential information from the treasurer's office. Zuendt testified that Norwine had a list of securities owned by the First National Bank." According to Zuendt, Norwine, who had somehow gained this list, told him that his bank had far too much in government bonds and that the Chouteau bonds would yield significantly more in interest. When Zuendt objected to Norwine having this list, he refused to disclose who had provided it to him. When asked by Limbaugh where such information could be obtained, Zuendt answered that only the bank and the state treasurer's office held it. Moreover, Zuendt was confident that the information had not come from the bank. Other testimony about this corroborated Zuendt's testimony that Norwine held insider information about other banks' securities. In the testimony of J. M. Bohanan, cashier of the failed Farmers' Exchange Bank in Marshfield, he "time and again" claimed not to recall details of his transactions with Norwine. Some of the senators were incredulous that Bohanan was that forgetful and intervened, asking the witness a number of pointed questions, demonstrating their strong doubts about his testimony. On the other hand, S. A. Killian, the president of the Marshfield bank, remembered that Norwine had a list of the bank's securities. Moreover, Busch in his testimony not only stated that Norwine had a list of the Cole County Bank's securities, but that he claimed to "have influence with Treasurer Brunk and had arranged acceptance of the [Chouteau] bonds as collateral for state deposits, and that deposits secured by them would not be drawn upon." Unfortunately for their case, the House managers could not use the testimony that Norwine had given before the trial in which he admitted that Brunk had provided him with "the lists of securities which the various state depositories had up with the state treasurer."[34]

Other testimony demonstrated that as state treasurer, Brunk was improperly associated with officers of the Provident State Securities Company, especially in his acceptance of $10,000 from its president, J. Kenneth Edlin. Brunk's defense that the money was a loan and not a bribe only shielded him from criminal prosecution later, but necessarily conceded that he had imprudently and improperly benefitted from his office as state treasurer. During Limbaugh's questioning Attorney General Shartel testified that Brunk seemed unusually solicitous for the success of Norwine's efforts to sell the Chouteau bonds. However, after learning that they were ineligible "as security for state loans," Shartel refused Norwine's request to approve the bonds and recommended to Governor Caulfield that they be refused. According to law, the matter was brought before the governor, attorney general, and state treasurer, meeting as members of the Fund Commission at which both Caulfield and Shartel voted to require banks to substitute approved securities for the Chouteau bonds. Brunk argued that the bonds were good and that some of the banks might be harmed in being forced to substitute them with other securities. Moreover, as further evidence of Brunk's determination to help the Provident State Securities Company, Limbaugh had learned that Brunk had gone to the governor's office with Norwine to convince Caulfield that the bonds were acceptable. The governor, nevertheless, denied their request, forcefully making clear his strong conviction that the bonds were unacceptable.[35]

Finally, as the House managers were finishing the presentation of their case, they were able to work out an agreement with Adams to testify concerning the Brunk rent account and his debts to the Bank of Aurora. Adams stated that Easley was responsible for shortchanging the state in the bank's interest payments and had created the rent account to benefit Brunk and pay some of his debts. Adams asserted that he had personally told Brunk about the account and at least some of the payments on his debts from it. When he met with the governor at Brunk's urging, Adams told Caulfield that he believed Brunk knew about the rent account, which led Missouri's chief executive to suspend Brunk as state treasurer. Brunk's attorney, Madden, sought to undermine the credibility of Adams' testimony by reading into the record the agreement made between Adams' attorney and the House managers in which the managers, along with the prosecuting attorney, agreed to a continuance in the prosecution of Adams' case in return for his giving satisfactory testimony. While this information undoubtedly tended to create a doubt in the minds of some senators, the testimony of another bank employee, Robert J. Mitchell, a former state senator, corroborated key parts of Adams' testimony concerning the rent account and Brunk's debts to the bank. When Mitchell asked Easley about the rent account and what should be done to collect the debts, Easley had replied that this was unnecessary for "we have a little arrangement with Larry (Brunk) by which we are going to take care of that." Moreover, Mitchell stated that Brunk visited the bank every two or three weeks and that often he met secretly with Easley and Adams when there.[36]

On May 29, 1931, the House managers rested their case. In response, Brunk's attorney filed a demurrer—a motion to dismiss the case—on the grounds that the testimony of several witnesses was hearsay, and therefore insufficient proof existed to prove the charges. Madden also sought the suppression of the testimony of these witnesses, a strategy he had pursued throughout the trial, in a last-ditch effort to end the trial without putting Brunk on the stand. Previously, the defense attorney had won some of his challenges, but to this point most of the testimony excluded was not essential to the House managers' case. To determine these questions, the Senate decided to hear both sides' arguments concerning the demurrer on Monday, June 1, after recessing for the weekend. After returning, in a surprise move probably suggested by Limbaugh, Carter, who was an experienced prosecutor, moved "to strike demurrer from the files," arguing that in the entire history of impeachment trials never had a demurrer been "permitted in an impeachment trial, and no precedent for such procedure can be found in the law, and for the further reason that such procedure is against public policy." Carter argued that Madden's demurrer motion was nothing more than an attempt by him to discover whether he had the necessary twelve of thirty-four votes to win his client's acquittal. If he gained these votes Madden then would not put his client on the stand. Moreover, Carter asserted that the managers had investigated every impeachment trial in the country— undoubtedly here referring to Limbaugh's labors—and found none "wherein a demurrer has ever been filed, much less sustained; and I now challenge counsel on the opposing side to cite you any law or any decision in any impeachment trial that has ever been heard in the upper house of the national Congress, or any state in this Union, wherein a demurrer has been filed." In response, Madden accused the managers of purposely having introduced their motion to strike the demurrer without prior notice and complained that it was unfair. He denied that he was seeking to determine whether he had twelve votes and accused the managers of being "afraid" the motion would get seventeen. Madden, however, did not challenge Carter's assertion that a demurrer motion had never been used in an impeachment trial. The Senate voted to strike it, 17 to 16, one senator being absent. The trial continued.[37]

For the defense Madden first called J. Kenneth Edlin, president of the Providence State Securities Company, to testify concerning loans to Brunk of $10,000 and $1,000. The former loan had been repaid but the second was accumulating interest and Brunk had been unable to make his regular payments upon it. Edlin claimed he had made the loans because he was fond of Brunk, with whom he had become acquainted in the past year. Edlin denied that any improper deal or relationship had been arranged between him or any of his employees. However, he admitted that Brunk had been helping him to find banks in Missouri to purchase as an investment, one of which was the Bank of Aurora. Edlin regarded this to be within the realm of acceptable business practices. In his cross-examination, Carter questioned the witness about the arrangement between Brunk and Norwine to sell the Chouteau bonds to Missouri's banks. Edlin claimed to have no knowledge of any conspiracy between them and stated that Norwine was just one of many salesmen employed by his firm. Madden introduced into evidence documents showing that Edlin had secured his $10,000 loan to Brunk and letters in which Edlin prodded him to pay upon the obligation. While this tended to demonstrate that the money was a loan, it was also evidence that Edlin possessed significant financial leverage over the state treasurer.[38]

Much of the remaining testimony was from the townspeople of Aurora—friends and neighbors who vouched for the good character and integrity of Brunk. Other testimony sought to prove that Brunk was not responsible for the shortchanged interest payments of the Bank of Aurora and other state banks. One of these was M. T. Davis, a member of the depositors committee for the Bank of Aurora and a strong Brunk supporter, who claimed that Adams had told him after the bank failed that Brunk did not know about the rent account. Another was Frank McNew, a bookkeeper in the state treasurer's office, who testified that as far as he knew no one attempted to determine whether or not the banks were paying the proper amounts of interest on deposits. Moreover, he disclosed that Brunk directed his office to keep a record of the banks' payments, something which had not been done before. This account, it turned out, merely recorded the amount of interest paid and the interest rate for each bank. Apparently, no calculations from the deposit balances of the banks were made. Nevertheless, McNew admitted that despite Madden's attempt to demonstrate that Brunk could not have possibly known how much the banks should pay, the necessary records were available to the state treasurer if he had wanted to investigate. McNew also claimed that Brunk frequently made loans to many employees which were repaid to him. This information was offered to account for the deposits Brunk had made in his private account far in excess of his salary and expenses during a two-year period. Cross-examination by one of the House managers, however, elicited from McNew the names of only two employees who had borrowed money from Brunk in this way.[39]

The testimony of another defense witness, Joseph B. Thompson, state insurance superintendent, tended to undermine the narrative Madden sought to establish regarding the eligibility of the Chouteau bonds as security for state deposits, which he contended were acceptable. The defense had subpoenaed a letter written by J. O. Rathbun, deputy state insurance superintendent, to Norwine on July 9, 1929, stating the department's approval of the bonds. Of course, this only proved their suitability as security for insurance policies, the rules for which were not as strict as for state bank deposits. During cross-examination, however, Thompson testified that Norwine had requested that he write him such a letter, but that he had refused, regarding it to be improper. Undaunted, Norwine apparently waited until Thompson was out of his office and gained the letter from Rathbun, who knew "he was to be removed from his position" in four days anyway. Moreover, testimony showed that before checking his department's files, Thompson had no knowledge of the letter. According to the press, some senators concluded from this that Norwine had told Brunk about the letter, pointing to a closer relationship between them than Brunk wanted to admit. Furthermore, the letter corroborated the managers' contention that Norwine sought letters to help him sell his bonds.[40]

Finally, it was time for Brunk to testify. Under the friendly questioning of his attorney, he first told of his early career. His father had died when he was only nine and being poor, Brunk had been forced to quit school and begin working at the age of twelve. Despite this, he was able to rise economically and gain election as mayor of Aurora three times, and eventually to the offices of state senator and state treasurer. He was the hometown boy made good. Brunk denied any knowledge of the rent account or any bank, including the Bank of Aurora, underpaying interest due to the state. He asserted that he had never treated his hometown bank differently from any other, but could provide no satisfactory explanation concerning why its officers never pressed him for two years to pay the interest and principal on the substantial debt he owed. Brunk denied that he had provided any unusual help to Norwine and others selling the Chouteau bonds, and claimed that his association with Norwine and Edlin was superficial and professional and did not indicate a conspiracy to profit from his position as state treasurer. Brunk also attempted to explain the $42,000 he had deposited into his private accounts, which was substantially in excess of the $14,000 he had received from the state in salary and payments for expenses. He stated that the deposits were from several sources, including money returned to him by employees to whom he had loaned money and revenues he had received from investments and property he owned. Nevertheless, these revenues, when tallied, did not come close to accounting for the amounts he had deposited.[41]

The cross-examination of Brunk presented a number of challenges. For it to be effective, a great deal of information and many significant details from the evidence and witnesses must be remembered and used appropriately in the interrogation to elicit admissions tending to undermine his testimony. Throughout his questioning of the state treasurer, Limbaugh's complete mastery of the facts in the case and understanding of their significance was evident. This was the result of much hard work and the gift of a remarkably retentive memory. During his cross-examination of Brunk, Limbaugh demonstrated an unerring ability to find the weaknesses in Brunk's testimony, which he exploited through close and pointed questioning. First, Limbaugh focused on issues relating to the Bank of Aurora. He asked Brunk about ledgers showing that the bank had paid interest to the state. Brunk denied that the ledgers had been received but "could not explain how they had been stamped" by his office. Later, however, he claimed that the responsibility for monitoring the state banks' interest payments was not his at all but that of his Chief Clerk, D. W. Tudor, although he was forced to admit that Tudor had never told him that "he was figuring the interest on all these depositories." Moreover, Brunk admitted that he had no idea whether any of the banks were paying the proper amounts of interest to the state and had only assumed that they were and had never inquired into the matter. In the end, after some prodding, Brunk reluctantly conceded that ultimately he was responsible for oversight of the treasurer's office and thus responsible to protect state revenues. More questioning revealed that until the governor had informed him, Brunk had not known about the Bank of Aurora's underpayment of interest, that the Bank of Aurora had received state deposits without having a contract and without securities, and that the treasurer's office had never checked the abstracts of real estate securities for any of the state banks. This information led an incredulous Limbaugh to ask the state treasurer if he had ever bothered to read the statutes, or at the very least to employ a lawyer to interpret them so he would be clear about his responsibilities. Incredibly, Brunk admitted to having done neither.[42]

Related to the Bank of Aurora's underpayment of interest was the issue of the Brunk rent account, for into it was placed a part of the interest fraudulently retained. In his questioning, Limbaugh developed the facts in the case and confronted Brunk with what appeared to be an arrangement to benefit the bank and himself at the expense of the state. Again the state treasurer pleaded ignorance. As already noted, Easley had used a part of these funds to pay Brunk's city property taxes, interest on loans, and Shriners' dues. When Limbaugh asked Brunk why he had not checked into the payment of these obligations during the period when Easley was paying them, the state treasurer could provide no explanation. Moreover, "during the time that these credits were being entered," Brunk admitted that he had paid no interest or principal on his notes. Limbaugh also questioned Brunk about his relationship with Adams and Easley. According to Brunk they were just two of many friends and associates in Aurora with whom he met whenever he visited his hometown. He acknowledged, however, that he had requested substantial loans from Adams and Easley and that they had bankrolled his campaign, providing from $4,500 to $5,000. Apparently, they had tendered these funds to Brunk upon his assurance in a letter to Easley that as state treasurer he could "be in a position to do you boys some real favors for four years, and of course you know I would do it." When Limbaugh pressed him about what he meant by favors, "Brunk finally said: 'Oh, such favors as getting state fair passes for Easley.' 'But,' Limbaugh said, 'you could get state fair passes as a state senator, couldn't you?' Brunk admitted that he could." Whatever these favors were, according to Brunk, they did not include the falsification of records later. The state treasurer claimed to have received a letter in which Adams, who had given damaging testimony against him, had requested that Brunk "falsify the state records to deceive the bank examiners." Limbaugh wanted to know why the defense had not offered the letter into evidence, a question to which Brunk had no good answer, only stating that he was unsure if he had the letter but that he would look for it. In his questioning Limbaugh made clear that it was strange that the defense, who had submitted many other letters as evidence, some of which were hardly relevant to the case, had not thought to produce Adams' letter.[43]

Next, Limbaugh questioned Brunk about his relationship with Norwine and Edlin concerning the Chouteau bonds, Edlin's loans to Brunk, and other business arrangements with them. In this questioning, Limbaugh again sought to establish that Brunk had used his office to gain connections beneficial to himself and harmful to the state. Limbaugh walked Brunk through the documentary evidence and testimony, which showed that the state treasurer had more than a strictly professional association with Norwine, with whom he had met every couple of weeks in his office, for dinner, to attend the theater in Jefferson City, and on several occasions in both St. Louis and Chicago, staying at the same hotels while there and even taking a pleasure boat trip on Lake Michigan together. Despite the evidence showing that he was registered at the New Bismarck Hotel in Chicago in June 1930, Brunk denied being there, for otherwise he would have been admitting to having submitted a false expense account for a trip to St. Louis at the same time. He did not attempt to deny that he had met with Norwine in most of the other instances, including for dinner and the theater. Concerning his attending the theater with Norwine, Limbaugh pointedly asked Brunk if Norwine had lied about paying for Brunk's theater tickets. Brunk's attorney Madden objected to this as "cross-examination not designed to elicit facts, [but instead an] insulting, abusive, argumentative type of question." In his answer, Brunk claimed that he had largely paid for his own tickets and dinner. Moreover, on some of the occasions when he was registered at the same hotel where Norwine was staying, Brunk asserted that either this had occurred accidentally or that he had not even been aware that Norwine was there. Regarding the boat trip, the state treasurer maintained that he had paid his way and that it was a coincidence that Norwine happened to be on the same cruise. Brunk denied that he had ever provided a list of different banks' securities to Norwine or had done anything else improper to aid him in the sale of the Chouteau bonds, although he conceded that recently he had traveled with him to Kansas City about a job. Finally, Brunk admitted that just two weeks before the trial he had met with Norwine in Chicago, but had failed to discuss the trial or the need for the bond salesman to testify.[44]

In his cross-examination, Limbaugh turned to another important issue, the association of Brunk with Edlin, the president of the Providence State Securities Company. In his own testimony, Edlin had stated that the only reason he had sought to help Brunk in his financial difficulties was out of fondness for his new friend. He asserted that he had never requested or gained any advantages for himself or his company through his relationship with the state treasurer. Concerning Edlin's possible investment in state banks, including the Bank of Aurora, Brunk maintained that this was not his idea and he had only put him in contact with Adams and Easley. Concerning the $11,000 he had received, Brunk explained that Edlin had provided him with the money unsolicited out of friendship and that it was a loan, certainly not a gift. Limbaugh further developed that Brunk had gained another loan of $2,500 from his best friend Albert Newman, who, unlike Edlin, had not required security or a contract. After Brunk had responded to a number of questions maintaining that he did not recall, Limbaugh noted sarcastically that "that is another thing you don't know anything about." This comment provoked Madden to say: "I move that be stricken out as an improper comment." Apparently irritated by testimony he considered dishonest and misleading, Limbaugh asked Brunk's attorney "What are you mad about?" to which Madden retorted, "Your business is to ask questions, and not make comments." Limbaugh replied, "I am asking them." Madden persisted in his demand to have the comment stricken to which Limbaugh said, "You made arguments all day, Mr. Madden, yesterday. I am surprised that you would take offense." This elicited from Brunk's attorney the point that Limbaugh had been "free to object" and insisted on his objection being ruled upon but was not sustained.[45]

The impeachment trial was concluded by the closing arguments of House Manager Meredith and Madden for the defense. In his summary of the evidence against Brunk, Meredith noted the responsibility of the state treasurer to ensure that the full amount of interest was paid to the state, that the state's assets were properly protected, and that he showed no favoritism to anyone in conducting the public's business. Moreover, the state treasurer was not to profit personally from his position beyond his salary and expenses. Meredith asserted that the evidence demonstrated at best, even according to the defendant himself, an incompetent and imbecilic performance of his duties. By his own testimony, Brunk admitted that he had failed to oversee and insure that the state banks had paid the proper amount of interest owed to the state, had formed improper associations with bank officials, salesmen, and company officials conducting business with his office, and had profited financially from these associations. Meredith noted that despite his protestations, it was clear

Brunk had conspired with the officers of the Bank of Aurora and had shared insider information with bond salesmen for profit. Thus Brunk's pleas of ignorance and incompetence and his attempts to make others responsible, or at least to share responsibility, for these misdeeds were unconvincing and implausible. Regarding the state treasurer's performance in office, Meredith told the Senate that "you are the board of directors for the state of Missouri and are not called upon to convict Brunk of any crime, but to pass on his competency. The question is whether such misconduct and incompetency in the treasurer's office shall continue."[46]

Brunk's attorney, Madden, spoke for three hours. He claimed his client was "a victim of a conspiracy and of relentless investigation for eight months in which he said 'evidence was not sought to establish facts, but to establish guilt.'" Madden asserted that to convict Brunk the Senate "must find that he was actuated by corrupt motives and intent, asserting that a court of impeachment could not act as a court of recall for public officials because of errors in judgment." Madden also declared it unfair to convict Brunk for the failures of subordinates, noting that the responsibility for supervising the payment of interest by the state banks was Chief Clerk Tudor's. The defense attorney also "assailed" those whose testimony was most damaging to the state treasurer, particularly that of Bank Examiner Cahill, Mulligan, and Adams. Moreover, Madden argued that the Chouteau bonds were good securities and that the question of whether Brunk had provided Norwine and others with lists of banks' securities was irrelevant. He characterized Edlin's loans to Brunk as legal "made in an open and frank manner." Having addressed the main charges against his client, Madden finally turned to excoriate the House managers for conducting their investigation in secrecy, for attempting to prejudice the Senate against his client by providing a transcript of their hearings, and characterizing the prosecution as partisan.[47]

Instead of debating the charges and evidence before voting as originally intended, immediately after the closing arguments the Senate voted on the nine articles. Nineteen senators were Democrats and fifteen were Republicans. Under the state constitution a two-thirds vote, or twenty-three of the thirty-four senators, was required to convict and remove Brunk from office. This meant that a conviction on any of the articles would require at least four Republican votes. On most of the articles, the House managers were unable to muster even a majority, three receiving guilty votes only in the single digits, and one of the articles accusing Brunk of depositing large sums into his personal banking accounts received only one vote in all. On two of the articles, however, a majority of senators voted guilty, although in the end the votes were insufficient for a conviction. These articles charged Brunk with conspiring with the officers of the Bank of Aurora to underpay interest and for being negligent in ensuring that the correct interest amounts were paid. The former of these obtained eighteen votes for conviction, two of which were from Republicans. The last charge garnered nineteen of the twenty-three votes needed for conviction, gaining the support of three Republicans. After the roll call, which took approximately half an hour, Brunk's supporters in the gallery and on the floor "broke into cheers and applause"—many of these being senators who had served with the state treasurer.[48]

Limbaugh and the other House managers, despite expecting Brunk's acquittal, "were very much disappointed" in the result. In the end, Limbaugh believed that some of the charges were not proven by the evidence he and the other prosecutors had presented, although he also thought that the two charges for which they received a majority vote should have resulted in Brunk's conviction. Nevertheless, Limbaugh did not regard his and his colleagues' labors as wasted, for afterward measures were taken to prevent Brunk and his successors from ever again denying to the state the proper payment of interest to the state.[49]

Throughout the investigation and trial of Brunk, the newspaper scrutiny was intense. Four newspapers devoted substantial resources to reporting upon the 1931 legislative session: the *Kansas City Star*, the *St. Louis Globe-Democrat*, the *St. Louis Post-Dispatch*, and the *Jefferson City Capital News*. During a period when partisan biases were more transparent than they are today, almost from the start the reporting of the *Globe-Democrat* and the *Capital News* was negative in their stories about the investigation and trial. In his reporting, Asa Hutson of the *Globe-Democrat*, a Republican paper, apparently sought to color his stories to the detriment of the prosecution. As noted earlier, Hutson had promised to embarrass the House investigators if they persisted in their decision to hold secret hearings. In this he kept his word, often interjecting judgments into his stories about the trial noting how that the testimony of a witness had "materially weaken[ed] the case built by the House managers," or as he stated concerning the testimony of Edlin about the $10,000 loan to Brunk, that it "largely blasts the Pierre Chouteau bond charge against" the state treasurer. Moreover, Hutson sometimes characterized the prosecution's evidence as circumstantial and after the vote on Madden's demurrer motion claimed that this "disclosed the impossibility of convicting Brunk of the charges." However, Hutson's decisions about what to include or omit in his stories probably influenced his readers' views more than anything else. Thus for instance, when reporting on the testimony of Catherine Gardner, a bookkeeper at the Bank of Aurora, Hutson provided none of her testimony under the questioning of the House managers, only writing about those parts of her testimony favorable to Brunk under Madden's cross-examination. In this manner, Hutson presented a very one-sided and negative view of the prosecution to his readers.[50]

Immediately after the case, the *St. Louis Post-Dispatch*, whose coverage of the trial had presented both sides' evidence without commenting on its value or meaning, published an editorial condemning the Senate's decision. Noting the difficulty of proving conspiracy charges with "100 per cent proof that Brunk was guilty," the writer believed that the senators had adhered to certain "picayunish distinctions and hair-splitting technicalities" to provide themselves with plausible cover to acquit a guilty man. While such technicalities were appropriate in a criminal case, in an impeachment trial the senators should "have taken a larger view of the evidence and the arguments" and removed Brunk. This was especially true given the state treasurer's "very sorry showing" in the evidence and testimony presented by the House managers. Indeed, it was difficult to imagine what evidence could have convinced the Senate to convict. The Senate's verdict brought shame upon it and undermined "the ideal that public office is a public trust and that occupants of important posts should be above the breath of suspicion." Moreover, when one analyzed the votes on the articles, it was difficult not to conclude that the votes were partisan and that the Republicans in particular had refused to weigh the evidence impartially.[51]

Very soon after the trial, Limbaugh penned a short article on the history and law of impeachment for the July 1931 issue of the *Missouri Bar Journal*. In it, he traced the evolution of impeachment from its first use in England to its adaptation to the circumstances in the American colonies and later as an independent country. The article demonstrated the extraordinary amount of knowledge Limbaugh had acquired through his exhaustive study of impeachments, which he presented objectively for the education of his fellow lawyers on a much misunderstood topic. He also explained the features of impeachment in Missouri, delving into certain constitutional and legal aspects of it. Limbaugh also provided them with a brief history and the results of impeachment trials in England; the United States; and individual states, including Missouri. In noting the results of Missouri's impeachment trials, he included the acquittal of Brunk. While not directly referring to it, in his concluding paragraphs Limbaugh, perhaps indirectly, referenced certain criticisms to the Brunk impeachment by noting that some regard impeachments to be obsolete, too subject to partisan influences, and too expensive. Therefore, it is argued "that the impeachment remedy should be abandoned or a substitute devised." While a new and improved process for the removal of government officials might be devised, Limbaugh believed that the impeachment process should not be abandoned before a workable substitute was found, especially given the difficult economic circumstances then existing in which the temptation among public servants was strong to "yield to corruption and faithlessness in office."[52]

In 1943 Missouri convened a constitutional convention at which the impeachment process was changed. One of the delegates elected to the convention was former House manager George F. Heege, who may have influenced the convention to revise the process. Instead of trying impeachment cases before the Senate, the state supreme court was designated as the venue where these trials would be held, the only exception being when the governor or a judge of the court was impeached. A special commission would substitute for the supreme court in those exceptional cases. While it cannot be known with absolute certainty, it appears that this reform resulted from a consensus that the Senate had acquitted Brunk because of their reluctance to convict a former colleague. This revision of the constitution changed the character of the impeachment process, transforming it from a political to a judicial process. As the Supreme Court of Missouri observed, every state but Missouri and Nebraska decided whether to remove an officeholder in the Senate. Under this process the state House of Representatives must first approve charges presented as articles of impeachment stating "that an officer of the state has committed acts such that, were an election held, the people would not permit the impeached officeholder to remain in office." The Senate's judgment to convict or acquit simply "affirms or rejects the judgment of the House." With the new system, however, the supreme court must focus upon the evidence to determine if the charges under the articles are proven without considering the politics of the matter.[53]

Fifty years after the constitution was changed, the first impeachment of a state official was instituted against Secretary of State Judith K. Moriarty. The House of Representatives had voted to approve three articles of impeachment against her after she was convicted in a circuit court for the misdemeanor of "issuing a false certificate" in her son Timothy Moriarty's filing his declaration of candidacy. Her son had improperly filed the papers and after the deadline. As secretary of state she certified these papers as correct. After her impeachment Moriarty was suspended with pay and ordered to answer the charges by November 7. While awaiting trial, a reporter called Limbaugh as the only surviving member of the House managers in the Brunk trial to gain his perspective. More than sixty-three years had passed since the trial and he was then 103 years of age. Asked about the acquittal of Brunk, Limbaugh believed that "cronyism" explained the verdict. His advice to the Supreme Court of Missouri was for "them to use the impeachment process, as we have it and as the law governs it, rigidly. Make sure it's by the law." While he admitted to following the Moriarty case, Limbaugh declined to say whether she should be removed from office. To have given any other answer would have been inappropriate, for his grandson Stephen N. Limbaugh Jr. was one of the seven judges whose responsibility it was to decide the case.[54]

In December 1994, the case against Moriarty was heard. The secretary of state's defense was that Barbara Campbell, an administrative aid in her office, had "botched the paperwork" of her son's filing of intent to run for office. Moriarty's attorney, Stuart K. Berkowitz, attempted to discredit Campbell and was partially successful. Still, fellow workers corroborated key parts of Campbell's testimony. In its opinion, the court observed that Moriarty's office was run in such a haphazard way that conformity to the law was "as much by accident as by design." Moreover, contrary to the defense's claim that the filings of Moriarty's son had only been changed to correct Campbell's mistake, the court determined that "the time and date" on Timothy Moriarty's filing "are false. [These errors] are not the product of a clerical error; they are outright fiction." Finally, the court concluded that regardless of how one viewed the evidence and testimony it was "beyond dispute that the Secretary of State discovered the absence of the signatures . . . on her son's declaration of candidacy to meet the requirements of the law, she nevertheless certified him or permitted her staff to certify him over her signature as a properly filed candidate." Limbaugh's grandson Stephen, summing up his impressions from the evidence and testimony in the trial, observed concerning Moriarty's behavior that the fact she had backdated election documents to help her son was "an aggravating factor, in addition to being illegal." Apparently the rest of the court agreed, for the judges unanimously found her guilty of the charges.[55]

Chapter Seven

The Muench Kidnapping Trial

After serving as a state representative for the first six months of 1931, during which his compensation did not cover his expenses, Rush H. Limbaugh returned to Cape Girardeau and redoubled his efforts to provide for his family. Even before his service in the legislature, the Limbaughs' financial circumstances were poor because of the failure of the Cape Exchange Bank. Indeed, during this period his income was so inadequate that he fell weeks and even months behind in the payment of bills. In May 1932, E. G. Gramling, president of the Cape Girardeau Building and Loan Association, offered Limbaugh a position as attorney. With the economy worsening and few professional opportunities available, this was a very appealing offer, for the position provided a steady income and professional advancement. Before accepting, however, Limbaugh discussed the matter with his partner, Benson C. Hardesty. In previous years, Limbaugh had already received a number of offers to form partnerships with other firms or individuals, including from Russell L. Dearmont, his former classmate at the Normal School, from Albert M. Spradling, and from the firm of Oliver & Oliver. Limbaugh probably had declined all of these offers out of loyalty to his friend and mentor Hardesty. Nevertheless, because of his appointment in 1924 as city counselor for Cape Girardeau, which occupied most of his time, Limbaugh seldom worked on cases with Hardesty during the last half of the 1920s and the beginning of the 1930s. Thus, as Limbaugh explained years later, the "partnership had been largely one in name instead of reality." Despite his disappointment, his friend Hardesty graciously agreed to dissolve their partnership, encouraging Limbaugh to accept the offer. Because the association had a significant amount of legal work to handle, Limbaugh agreed to move his office into the building of the association to be more readily available to the firm for consultation. Most of his time was spent in examining abstracts of title, studying law questions, drafting contracts, providing legal advice to Gramling and the board of directors, and representing the association and other clients in various courts. Moreover, this arrangement with the association left him free to develop his private practice in which he handled the cases of other clients thus achieving a fair amount of "professional freedom" as well.[1]

While his stint in the legislature caused a temporary economic hardship, Limbaugh believed that his service as one of the House managers in the Larry Brunk impeachment trial made his name more generally known among the public and led to new professional business. Moreover, in recognition of Limbaugh's sacrifices and his integrity, Governor Henry S. Caulfield appointed him special deputy commissioner of finance in charge of the property of the Sturdivant Bank, which had been seized by the state in late 1932. This work as liquidating officer for the closed bank was lucrative and helped to improve his financial circumstances.[2]

In addition to the financial problems, Rush and Bee's sons Rush Jr., Manley, and Stephen experienced various health maladies, both minor and major, which undoubtedly caused their parents considerable consternation. Just a year after Marguerite's death in 1926, Manley developed pneumonia, as did Stephen two years later. In the 1930s, Rush Jr. experienced asthma attacks, the severity of which were not diminished until a medical physician specializing in allergies discovered that he was sensitive to certain foods and house dust. These maladies, however, were inconsequential in comparison to Stephen's health problems.[3]

In the fall of 1931, just a few months after the Brunk impeachment trial, Limbaugh traveled to Ironton, Missouri, on business. Because Stephen, who was not quite four years old, had not seen the Arcadia Valley, Bee decided to accompany her husband so that their youngest child could experience the beautiful scenery. While driving through the region, Stephen appeared unwell and developed a fever. During lunch, he "appeared chilly and unusually nervous" and thereafter listless. After this episode, he fell asleep but at different times "his body suddenly jerked," apparently leaving him exhausted. After returning home, he experienced chills and a nervous state again, leading his parents to call a doctor who examined Stephen and concluded that he had influenza. After "three or four days in bed," it became evident that he had lost his ability to walk. Greatly alarmed, they consulted a "young physician" from the state department of health, who diagnosed Stephen's ailment as polio and recommended that he be taken to St. Louis where experienced physicians could give him the best treatment available. For the next several weeks, Bee remained in St. Louis while Stephen was treated. Whenever possible, Limbaugh traveled from Cape Girardeau to see his wife and son, who eventually recuperated fully and was soon back on his feet, although for a short time he walked with a limp. This outcome was very fortunate, for polio sufferers sometimes died, were left partially paralyzed, or wheelchair bound.[4]

Because he was often busy with his profession, speaking engagements, and intellectual and political activities, Limbaugh spent the majority of his day away from home Monday through Saturday. Often he worked late in his office or at home when he was not attending meetings of various organizations elsewhere. Nevertheless, he found time to attend various school functions such as debates in which Rush Jr. participated, the prom with Bee at Central High School in Cape Girardeau (presumably serving as chaperones), and sometimes met with friends to eat and converse in the evenings. Occasionally on the weekends, he and his family took leisure drives to locations such as the Black River to swim or to Wickliffe, Kentucky, to see the mounds where the remains of a pre-Columbian, Native American village was located. On Sundays, Limbaugh continued to teach Sunday school classes and attend the regular church service. Afterwards, he and his family often went out to eat for lunch and then for walks or drives. Sundays were also a time for visiting his mother and siblings, and for reading books, especially biographies and history, magazines and newspapers.[5]

In the early 1930s, Limbaugh's paternal Uncle Hunter died "a childless widower." As administrator of his estate, it became his duty to find and contact the descendants of Hunter's siblings. Of course, the branch of his father Joseph's family was easy to locate, but many others were scattered around the country as far away as California. This work, however, had the benefit of providing him with the opportunity to reconnect with family, and led to visits and correspondence with various members, including his cousin Minnie Smith, who traveled from California to Cape Girardeau, staying with the Limbaughs in their home for several days. Moreover, in 1937 the Limbaughs combined a business trip to Santa Fe and Denver with a stop to see his cousin Bertha V. Maddox who lived in Colorado Springs. Limbaugh had not seen his cousin since he was a young boy. Years later his cousin and her husband returned the visit by traveling to Cape Girardeau and staying with the Limbaughs.[6]

The late 1920s and 1930s was the period of Limbaugh's life when he was most active in politics. Before running for the state legislature in 1930, he was already serving as Republican committee chairman in southeast Missouri. His responsibilities included working with the party's leadership; holding meetings; finding candidates to run for office, including for the tenth congressional district; introducing statewide candidates to persons in the region; organizing campaigns and developing strategy; and speaking at various Republican meetings. Moreover, Limbaugh took a special interest in fostering support for the Republican party among African Americans, speaking to groups at their churches and helping to establish a "Lincoln Rep[ublican] Club for Colored People," even drafting a constitution for the organization.[7]

While willing to expend much time and labor in promoting the agenda of the Republican party and its candidates for office, Limbaugh was very reluctant to seek office himself. The primary reason for this was probably his unsuccessful run for mayor in 1918. This failure, his own natural modesty, and the manner in which his effort had ended had left him strongly disinclined to run for office again. Indeed, he only ran for the state legislature in 1930 after his friend Fred Naeter, editor of the *Southeast Missourian*, and Democrat Langdon Jones, had appealed to his strong sense of public service and further promised Limbaugh to arrange matters so that he could run for the legislature unopposed. Moreover, he preferred the practice of law to politics and believed strongly in the ideal that lawyers were the administrators "of ultimate justice" through the rule of law. Thus, when his good friend and fellow lawyer Albert M. Spradling asked him in the spring of 1931 to run for mayor he replied "emphatically that [he] would not do so." Nevertheless, a group of citizens began circulating a petition to draft Limbaugh as a mayoral candidate. After resisting for some time, Limbaugh finally relented and announced on February 15, 1932, that in response to "persistent requests over a period of many weeks" he was entering the mayoral race. By March 11 a total of five candidates, including the incumbent Edward L. Drum, were on the ballot.[8]

On March 2, Limbaugh issued a detailed policy statement. First, he promised that if elected he would be under no obligations to anyone and would not favor any person or any group in his administration. Recognizing the exceptionally difficult economic times, he promised to reduce city expenses, and to lower the taxes of property owners, especially those of modest means. Finally, he pledged to provide aid to unemployed persons through city improvement projects. Through these policies, Limbaugh believed that he could restore the confidence of the people in their community and foster cooperation between its citizens and those of other communities. On March 5, a campaign committee was organized and its headquarters was established in downtown Cape Girardeau.[9]

From March 15 to 21, the eve of the primary, Limbaugh gave four talks on radio station KFVS and made a series of campaign speeches at a variety of venues. On March 14, he spoke at the African American Antioch Church in Smelterville, part of his continued outreach to African American voters as chair of the Cape Girardeau County Republican Committee. On March 16, he spoke on "Finances of the City Government and Problems of Unemployment," and the following evening on the radio addressed the problem of "Taxation and Economy in City Government." Presumably, most of Limbaugh's time and efforts involved meeting as many voters as possible in each of Cape Girardeau's ten wards. Unfortunately, just four days before the primary, Limbaugh and his sons became ill, making it impossible for him to canvass during the home stretch of the primary campaign. However, the Limbaugh organization was strong and continued without the help of its candidate, even providing voters with rides to polling stations. These efforts paid off when Limbaugh gained enough votes to qualify as one of two finalists for the election two weeks later on April 5. The primary vote, which brought out a total of 4,964 voters, was the largest in the city's history to that time. Of these, Limbaugh won 1,789 votes, coming in a distant second to Mayor Drum's total of 2,895 votes.[10]

On March 28, 29, and 30, Limbaugh placed advertisements in the *Southeast Missourian* to explain more fully his earlier policy statements. In these he reiterated his commitment to reducing government expenses, the lowering of taxes and property tax valuations, and providing jobs to the unemployed. He again promised to eliminate the city counselor position by taking over those responsibilities himself as mayor. In perhaps his most controversial statement of the campaign, Limbaugh raised the issue of the city's relationship with the Missouri Utilities Company. He was against granting a long-term franchise with any company and stated his determination to require all parties to fulfill their contractual obligations. Although he wanted it understood that he intended to treat the utility fairly, Limbaugh accused the mayor and city council of having ignored the peoples' will in concluding a contract with the company in April 1931, just a few months after the public had voted by a large majority in December 1930 to reject granting a franchise to the utility. Limbaugh had opposed granting the franchise because for twenty years the Missouri Utilities Company had failed to fulfill its contract to provide pure water to Cape Girardeau under the franchise that was then expiring. In the meantime, the utilities company had built a new waterworks and distribution system and had gained the authority to construct and improve other utilities such as street lighting. Finally, Limbaugh promised not to allow a reduction in city employee wages, noting that they, like everyone else, had mortgages and other bills to pay.[11]

A March 29, 1932, editorial responding to Limbaugh's campaign platform was published in the *Southeast Missourian*. Published by his good friends and fellow Republicans Fred and George Naeter, one might have expected their full endorsement of his policies. However, concerning Limbaugh's opposition to granting any new franchises, they interpreted this to mean that he would not honor the city's promise to the Missouri Utilities Company to "call an election to pass on a franchise as soon as the new water plant had been accepted." This, the editorialist believed, would be unfair, for the company had built a better treatment facility than was promised and the Public Service Commission and the State Board of Health had both approved it with the highest possible rating. As it turned out, the editorialist's interpretation of Limbaugh's statement was incorrect, for as he clarified in a subsequent policy statement, he did not think that Cape Girardeau could legally or by any other means escape the contract which the mayor and council had concluded with it. Therefore, Limbaugh stated that he would not oppose the contract, although he made clear his belief that the peoples' will had been thwarted. Having expressed concern about this issue, the editorialist endorsed the rest of Limbaugh's policies, in particular supporting his idea of eliminating the office of city counselor. Noting that the duties of the mayor, city counselor, and city attorney only required at most a few hours of labor each week on average, the writer believed that their duties could be accomplished by one person, saving the city $3,300 a year—then a substantial sum.[12]

Just a few days before the election on April 5, Limbaugh made appearances around town, meeting with various groups and supporters of his campaign. Bee also did her part by opening up their home to supporters and participating in the planning and organizing of the political operation. On the eve of the election, Limbaugh and his supporters made their final canvass for votes and prepared for their get-out-the-vote effort. Again the vote was large, setting another record with more than 5,200 votes cast. In the end, incumbent Mayor Drum won the election with almost 56 percent of the vote, winning nine out of ten wards. Defeated, Limbaugh was very disappointed, considering it a humiliation for himself and his family and very much lessening his enthusiasm for the pursuit of political office.[13]

After the mayoral election, Limbaugh returned to his law practice and his many community-oriented activities. During this period he apparently considered himself underemployed, despite his position as a lawyer for the Cape Girardeau Exchange Bank, and therefore in 1933 he contracted with the Thomas Law Book Company to write a series of books to serve as practical guides and references on the practice of law. While the research and writing of these volumes was congenial to his scholarly inclinations and his love for the law, Limbaugh regretted that the work reduced greatly the amount of time he had available to spend with his family. Nevertheless, despite the pressure from the publisher to meet deadlines, he refused to "permit a line to be published in either volume that would be questioned for authoritativeness and that no case or statute would be cited that was not applicable or accurate." Usually he worked on his books before and after his regular duties as a lawyer. Moreover, he sought the advice of lawyers and judges and consulted with the publisher throughout the process. Over time this grind wore him down and, he believed, caused him to suffer more frequently from minor ailments such as colds. Despite all of the obstacles he encountered, in the autumn of 1935 Limbaugh neared completion of the first volume of his project. This work, however, was unexpectedly delayed, interrupted by one of the most interesting episodes of his life.[14]

On the afternoon of October 4, 1935, Limbaugh was busily working on a complicated legal brief when he was interrupted by a telephone call. In addition to his law practice, he had received a letter that day from A. S. Robinson, president of the Thomas Law Book Company, again prodding him to finish the final portion of his manuscript. As he recalled many years later, when he heard the ring indicating that it was long distance, Limbaugh somehow knew that "something ominous and compelling" was about to happen. His intuition was correct, for on the line was Judge William D. Becker of the St. Louis Court of Appeals. He and his fellow judges Jefferson D. Hostetter and Edward J. Mc-Cullen were calling to inform Limbaugh that they had decided to appoint him as a special commissioner to preside over hearings in an important case determining the custody of an infant. Because some of the parties involved were well known in St. Louis, and the case was generating a great deal of public interest, the judges believed it best to appoint someone from outside the city, and that they had unanimously decided upon Limbaugh. Despite protests of judicial inexperience and responsibility to his clients, the judges, having anticipated these objections, promised personally to reschedule Limbaugh's cases and to aid and support him in his temporary duties. As one who took obligations seriously, and the lawyer's duty to serve as an officer of the court was one of the most important, Limbaugh believed that he had no choice but to accept this unusual responsibility.[15]

Just a few days before Limbaugh was notified, Judge Becker had conducted a preliminary hearing in the case on an appeal from the St. Louis County Circuit Court. Anna Ware, a young woman of nineteen years, had filed a writ of habeas corpus to recover the child to whom she had recently given birth, claiming that the infant was then in the custody of Nelle Tipton Muench and her husband Dr. Ludwig O. Muench. The petition named as fellow respondents Wilfred Jones, Helen Berroyer, Rebecca Winner, and Carl M. Dubinsky. During the hearing, it became clear to Judge Becker that the litigants disagreed strongly on the facts of the case and that the court must appoint a special commissioner to take testimony and recommend what action the court should take. It was then that the judges appointed Limbaugh, with whose abilities and temperament they were well acquainted, for frequently through the years he had represented clients before them. Moreover, in making their decision the judges probably consulted with Commissioner Walter E. Bennick, who had been a fellow student with Limbaugh at the Normal School in Cape Girardeau in 1911 and 1912. Bennick had worked on the staff of the *Capaha Arrow* when Limbaugh had served as editor-in-chief, knew him quite well, and could vouch for his good character and judgment.[16]

On October 8, Limbaugh traveled by automobile to St. Louis and was in court when Judge Becker heard motions from the lawyers on both sides of the dispute. After ruling on these motions, the judge announced that Limbaugh had been appointed to preside over the case and called him forward to take his oath of office. In the court's order he was given judicial authority to preside over the hearing, providing him with the power to subpoena witnesses, compel testimony, hold persons in contempt, force the production of evidence, and decide all motions presented by the lawyers in the cause. This ended the hearing and afterward Limbaugh met the lawyers and then unexpectedly found himself surrounded by newspaper reporters and photographers. To this point, he had only the sketchiest idea what the case was about and was astonished that there was so much public interest in it. That evening on the front page the three major daily newspapers in St. Louis provided a personal and professional profile of his career, including a picture of him. Limbaugh disliked the photograph, considering it a bad one. Later, a friend who distributed newspapers and magazines ribbed him for not smiling, claiming that the photograph had made it more difficult to sell newspapers. Noting Limbaugh's appearance in some of the photographs, Judge Becker, also in the spirit of well-intentioned fun, in the presence of the other judges of the court stated that "we may not have selected the most handsome lawyer to act for the court in this case, but we got one well equipped with jaw bone and even I am the only one who can boast of a longer face."[17]

Making his way through the reporters and crowd, Limbaugh met the three judges and two commissioners of the St. Louis Court of Appeals in the chambers of Judge Becker, who took the lead in most matters of the court. Wishing to reassure Limbaugh after his encounter with the press and the public, Becker explained that he and the other judges and commissioners were there to help him and that he should not hesitate to bring his problems to them. While serving as special commissioner, Limbaugh was provided an office and the clerk of the court was directed to take telephone and other messages and to collect his mail, which soon arrived in bagfuls. Becker warned him that the public's interest in the case was intense, and that many persons would try to offer advice, and others might attempt to intimidate or coerce him in some fashion. After collecting from the clerk's office the file containing the motions and transcripts of the proceedings in the case to that point, Limbaugh became increasingly curious to learn why "every mother in St. Louis knows about this case," as Stella Barker, the clerk of the court, had told him. However, unable to satisfy his curiosity at that time, Limbaugh made the journey home to Cape Girardeau, giving him some time to reflect upon the events of the day, consider what had happened, and the possible repercussions of it all. As he recalled twenty-seven years later, he worried about the financial losses he might suffer and how the case might affect his family. Moreover, he regretted that the hearing of some of his clients' cases would be delayed and that others might be forced to take their legal problems to other lawyers. And finally, Limbaugh was unsure how he would perform as a judge, for the first time ruling "without deliberation and reflection," upon the admission of evidence and other legal issues. However, having reflected upon these matters, he suddenly felt self-confident, and determined to perform his task in a manner which would bring credit to himself and justice in the case.[18]

During the week before his return to St. Louis, Limbaugh was busy arranging his personal and professional affairs in preparation for his extended absence. For this reason, he found it necessary to explain to his clients, opposing counsel, and judges the necessity for the postponement of cases. He also accomplished a good deal of his most pressing legal work, which left him with less time than he liked to review the St. Louis case. Instead of plunging into the court records provided to him, he decided to research two legal questions before considering anything else in the case. The first question concerned the court of appeals' authority and jurisdiction to hear a writ of habeas corpus case as the original court of record. As a lawyer he found this an intriguing issue, for it seemed odd for an appellate court to function in this manner. In a short time, however, he discovered that Missouri's courts of appeals did indeed have this power. The next question he researched concerned the appropriateness of using a writ of habeas corpus to demand the return of Ware's infant. As he understood it, this "writ was used solely for the purpose of compelling the sheriff or other officers of the law to surrender the custody of one whom he was illegally holding." However, his research soon demonstrated, contrary to his expectation again, that the writ could be "used to free any person from the custody of another who had no right" to hold them. Having determined these questions, he then turned to the records of the case. Again, Limbaugh did not find what he had expected in his examination of "the huge collection of papers in the court file," but instead discovered that the case concerned whether the Muenches unlawfully held the infant of Ware—a young, unwed mother. That this matter concerned "every mother in St. Louis" was perhaps the most surprising aspect of the case to him.[19]

Before leaving Cape Girardeau, Limbaugh agreed to meet with an elderly lady who insisted upon him handling a legal matter for her, for she had known his father Joseph. While waiting, she saw Limbaugh conferring with another client and involuntarily exclaimed, "Oh, Joe." Hearing this caused "strange and sobering sensations" to run through Limbaugh, for the elderly woman had mistaken him for his father who had been dead then for thirty-seven years. Afterwards, reflecting upon the past few weeks, Limbaugh realized that he had not thought of his father and "to a large extent [he] had lost [his] identity with the past." This realization disturbed him, and he determined to visit the graveyard upon the family farm before returning to St. Louis. There he reconnected to his beginnings, remembering many incidents of his youth and recognizing the familiar paths and places where he had grown to manhood. At his father's gravesite, he remembered the man who still appeared to him in dreams and never failed to lead him "through dangerous and difficult places." As he stood there he remembered that his father

> had lived through the crisis of Civil War, the disasters of small pox epidemic, the plague of cholera and the scourge of consumption. I knew that he had endured

the rigors of primitive life where law and order often depended upon the courage and the physical prowess of those who were determined to maintain them. I recalled that as I grew to manhood men of the community who had known him told me that he never retreated from a position of principle or honor, not even to avoid personal combat. I had seen him in the presence of danger from fire and flood and storm and threat, but I had never seen him wince or cower or appear afraid.

Remembering his father's example of courage and steadfastness during great peril inspired Limbaugh to face his own challenges and reminded him of those ancestral values of duty and honor which he cherished and sought to uphold. This heritage and his strong idealistic belief in the necessity of maintaining the rule of law through the fair adjudication of causes guided him in his service as a judge under the white-hot scrutiny of the press, the public, and most importantly to him, the legal profession.[20]

On October 14, the day before the hearing was to begin, Limbaugh traveled to St. Louis and settled into a room at the Mark Twain Hotel, where he stayed during the trial. That evening he reviewed his notes and the case file in preparation for the next day's proceedings. In the morning, he traveled to the Civil Courts Building where he happened to meet Judge Becker, who had just arrived also. Taking the elevator together to the twelfth floor, they were surprised when the door opened into a hallway filled with people. To control the crowd and to prevent any disturbances or disruptions, Becker called the police to detail officers there as soon as possible. At a little before ten o'clock that morning, Limbaugh met the court's judges in the conference room, which was adjacent to the courtroom, where they waited until ten o'clock, and then entered and took their seats on the judge's bench. Limbaugh was surprised to discover that the elevation of the bench enabled him easily to observe everyone and everything happening in the courtroom. Before him was the counsel's podium, from where the lawyers addressed the court, the counsel table where they sat, and behind them in the rectangular courtroom were chairs to accommodate some eighty members of the public. To the judges' left sat the court reporter, Herman DaCosta, and to their right sat Joseph E. McDermott, marshal of the court. The witness chair was situated to the left of the court reporter and near to the defendant side of the counsel's table. As Limbaugh and the judges entered, everyone in the crowded courtroom rose and then were seated.[21]

Judge Becker first introduced the lawyers to Limbaugh. Becker reminded them that they were to observe "appellate procedure," and that Limbaugh represented the court and held the same powers as them in the adjudication of the case. Indeed, they should "understand that he is the court," and that the judges would not hear any motions or petitions during the trial. With that, the judges rose and left the courtroom, turning the matter over to their special commissioner. Immediately upon their departure, Edgar J. Keating, a Kansas City lawyer representing the Muenches, sought to have the record show that Julius Klein, a reporter for the *St. Louis Star-Times*, was seated at the side of Harry C. Barker, the St. Louis lawyer representing Anna Ware. Barker stood and explained that Klein had helped in the preparation of their case and was there to assist him. Paul Dillon, also representing the Muenches, excitedly and vehemently argued that Klein had no right to sit at the counsel's table, for "he is no party to the suit . . . he is not a member of the bar . . . [and] this is not a trial for the benefit of the newspapers." On the grounds that the case was frivolous and concocted to profit the newspapers, Dillon moved for a dismissal. Over the next several weeks, the counsel of the Muenches and their fellow respondents complained repeatedly about the newspapers' role in bringing and funding the suit against their clients. To this Barker explained that the petitioner, Ware, was "a poor girl," and that the *St. Louis Star-Times* was paying his salary to help her. Recognizing that the lawyers were becoming increasingly argumentative and that he might lose control of the courtroom if he did not intercede, Limbaugh ignored Dillon's motion to dismiss and overruled his objection to Klein's presence at the counsel's table. Nevertheless, the lawyers continued to jockey for advantage, especially during the first days of the trial, frequently objecting to questions or testimony offered in the hearing.[22]

Having temporarily quieted the courtroom, Limbaugh then proceeded to announce the schedule of the hearings, and turning to Barker, asked if he was "ready to proceed," to which he replied in the affirmative, calling as his first witness Nelle Tipton Muench. After overruling the respondents' further motions "to enter judgment . . . on the pleadings" and to dismiss the case, Barker asked Muench a few preliminary questions before Dillon interrupted him again with an objection to the first substantive question asked: Had she given birth to any children? Objecting to this question as irrelevant and immaterial, Dillon advised his client "to answer no further questions on the ground that the answer might incriminate the witness." Because the practice of "taking the fifth" was far less common in the 1930s than it became later, Limbaugh was unsure how he should proceed, for he had never heard this constitutional right invoked in court before. However, because an attorney could not invoke the right for his client, Limbaugh overruled Dillon's objection. However, when Nelle Muench and her husband Ludwig O. Muench invoked it, Limbaugh ruled that they could not be compelled to testify.[23]

Barker next called Anna Ware to the witness stand. Again, when Barker attempted to interrogate his witness he was interrupted by a series of objections and motions by opposing counsel. This circumstance finally forced Limbaugh again to exercise his authority and stop the lawyers from continuing in this manner. Noting that the proceedings had gone very slowly to that point and that he "had been very indulgent," he warned that this must stop. He then explained that he intended to give both sides wide latitude in the offering of evidence and that he would exercise discretion later when he weighed the evidence in preparing his report. At that time, he promised to "disregard all evidence improperly admitted during the hearing," and base his decision only upon relevant testimony and evidence. After this the lawyers objected less than before, although they continued to interrupt the proceedings with objections and motions.[24]

In her testimony, given "in low tones" difficult to hear, Ware described her background, admitted to an affair with Francis Giordon, her married employer, and her decision to go to St. Louis to have her baby. Living in a suburb of Philadelphia, she undoubtedly sought to escape the ignominy then attached to a young woman having an illegitimate child. She testified that Giordon's wife arranged for her to travel by train and live with Rebecca Winner, a relative of her husband and a midwife, until the birth, and promised that the child would be placed in the home of a wealthy aunt. At the train station in St. Louis, Ware met Winner and Wilfred Jones, both of whom later became respondents in the case. Ware soon discovered that promises made to her would not be honored. She had been told that she would give birth in the hospital in a private room with a nurse, but Winner discouraged this, saying that Ware would be happier having her child at home. When Ware inquired about the wealthy aunt who was supposed to adopt her baby she was informed by Jones that he knew nothing about this. Later, Jones mentioned that he knew a couple by the name of Perkins, who "were good people" and wanted to adopt a baby. It was after this conversation that Jones took Ware in his car with another woman to Forest Park. The woman was introduced to her as Mrs. Perkins, but in court Ware identified her as Nelle Muench.[25]

Not long after these events, Ware went into labor and was attended by Dr. Chester A. Denny, a nephew of Jones, who did not give her anything for the pain during labor, or later when he sewed up a vaginal tear—an unnecessary cruelty. The boy was born at 5:45 a.m. on August 17 and remained with Ware until 11:30 that evening when Jones and a nurse arrived to take the child away. Ware testified that she had been led to believe that her child was brought to the Jewish Hospital, now Barnes-Jewish Hospital, and that as soon as she was better she could go to see him. However, a short time later at Ware's urging, Winner called the hospital to inquire if a Perkins baby was there and was told that they had no record of a baby by that name. Apparently, because Winner was helping her, Jones removed Ware to another woman's home. This strategy backfired, for the first morning of her stay with Mrs. Holliday, Ware learned from her about an impending kidnapping trial in which Nelle Muench was a defendant, and her claim to have given birth to a child in the early morning of August 18. Holliday expressed her opinion that "nobody believed" this. Later when Jones called Ware to tell her he could not visit her that day because he had a client, Holliday commented that his client was Nelle Muench.[26]

At this point, Ware testified that she feared that Jones had given her baby to the Muenches, whose lurid story was reported in the local newspapers. According to the articles, Nelle Muench was the mastermind behind a group of gangsters who had kidnapped Dr. Isaac D. Kelley, who had been held for ransom and later released through the efforts of John Rogers, a reporter on the staff of the *St. Louis Post-Dispatch*. Newspaper reports linked Muench to other criminal activities and because of the publicity, a change of venue was granted and her trial was held in Mexico, Missouri. Thirteen lawyers were employed in her defense and Sheriff E. S. Haycraft, a friend and supporter of Muench, placed only his friends in the pool from which Muench's jurors were selected. Predictably, she was acquitted on October 5, just ten days before Limbaugh began his hearings. All alone in St. Louis without money or friends, Ware wrote to her sister, Mary Whittlock, and told Jones that she wanted her baby back, regardless of who then held him. Jones, in trying to allay her fears about the Muenches, told her that her baby was with the Perkins, a wealthy couple in Memphis, Tennessee.[27]

During her cross-examination, Limbaugh allowed the respondents' attorneys wide latitude in their questioning of Ware, believing that she "should not be protected from any legitimate" questions. The Muenches' lawyer, Keating, according to one of the newspaper accounts, "fired [questions] at her for an hour and ten minutes." Instead of helping their case against her, however, Ware provided even more details which strengthened her story and damaged their case. She related how Jones would not let her see the Muench baby and tried to coach her about what to say to reporters. The next day, two reporters from the *St. Louis Star-Times* came to Holliday's home seeking to interview Ware. After their interview, she moved into the home of one of the reporters and his wife. The reporters directed her to attorney Thomas Bond, who was replaced by Barker. The newspaper also arranged a meeting for her with prosecuting attorney C. Arthur Anderson. After this, the newspapers, sensing a sensational story, ran articles every day, beginning on September 11 or 12 when the grand jury began its investigation. According to Klein, the *St. Louis Star-Times* "published seven regular editions" every day and that they often ran three or four articles about the case on some aspect of the Muenches' activities. After the trial began, the *Star-Times* devoted one to three columns, sometimes as many as ten, a day on the hearings. This coverage, he said, was in fulfillment of his promise to Ware to find her baby. The *St. Louis Globe-Democrat* and the *Post-Dispatch* also covered the case extensively—the latter expending almost $1,700 in its coverage.[28]

During the first days of the trial, Jones, one of the respondents in the case, was absent, and his lawyer, Shepard R. Evans, claimed not to know his whereabouts. Jones' absence was particularly problematic, for presumably he could tell the court where Ware's baby was and by whom he had been adopted. When questioned concerning his client's location, Evans was "evasive and indifferent," and lacking in the "kind of forthrightness" Limbaugh expected from a lawyer. However, he was willing to accord Evans the same assumption of good faith as he did to the other parties and their counsel in the case. Over the next few days this assumption became increasingly difficult to maintain, when Jones continued to avoid service of a subpoena ordering him to appear.[29]

In the meantime, testimony was taken concerning the possible whereabouts of Ware's baby. One of the witnesses was the newspaper reporter Klein, who had interviewed Jones several times and found inconsistencies in his account. According to the reporter, Jones told him that Ware's baby was then with a wealthy couple in Memphis, Tennessee. In checking various details of Jones' story, Klein found discrepancies in his account. When confronted with these, Jones admitted that he had lied to him. One of the next witnesses called was Dr. Denny, who had been employed by his uncle Jones to see to the health of Ware and deliver her baby. Denny said that he asked Jones if the Muenches had Ware's baby. His uncle denied it. When asked if he knew where Jones was, Denny said that he did not, but revealed that the day before Jones had spoken to him by telephone. He said he did not know if the call was long distance or not. At this point, Limbaugh intervened and questioned Denny himself. Learning that Denny was handling Jones' mail, over Evans' objections Limbaugh caused these letters to be opened, but no information regarding Jones' location was found in them. As the last day of the first week of hearings began, Limbaugh intended to demand that Evans produce his client, for he thought it very improbable that Jones was not also in contact with him. This confrontation became unnecessary, however, when Evans announced his intention to withdraw from the case if Jones was not in court by the beginning of next week.[30]

Ware's attorney, Barker, next called witnesses to testify regarding the question of Nelle Muench's pregnancy. The witnesses called were physicians, neighbors, a reporter, and a woman who had worked for the Muenches a couple of months in their home. The first of these was Dr. Aaron Levy, a pediatrician who had been called to the Muenches' home on July 11 to care for a sick infant. When he arrived, Dr. Muench requested that he not reveal that they had a child in their home. Levy replied that he would not be a party to any deception. The infant was taken to Jewish Hospital where he died on July 16. Levy also testified that at the time of his visit Nelle Muench did not appear to him to be pregnant. Another physician, Dr. Edgar F. Schmitz, a specialist in gynecology and obstetrics, thought it unlikely that Nelle Muench had become pregnant and had delivered a child as she claimed. He observed that a woman of forty-four years could become pregnant, but a childless woman married for twenty-three years was very unlikely to become pregnant, let alone carry the fetus to term. Pregnancies of older women were typically treated differently from those of younger women. Prenatal care and hospitalization before the child's birth was common, especially for the wife of a physician. He also testified that blood tests of mother and child could not determine "parentage," and "an examination of Mrs. Muench by physicians" more than twenty-four hours after childbirth could not conclusively determine if she had given birth to a child.[31]

In addition to the medical testimony, a number of the Muench's neighbors were called, each of them stating that they did not see any indication from her appearance that Muench was pregnant in the period before the announcement of the birth of a son on August 18. Frank Dunn, who worked for a shop located directly behind the Muenches' home, often observed her sunbathing in her backyard. Having heard that she was pregnant, he failed to see any sign that she was in the "family way." Kittie Lazaroff, who did housework and laundry in the Muench home, testified that in April and May she had noticed menstrual blood on Nelle Muench's undergarments and that she did not appear pregnant to her.[32]

The witnesses called to rebut this testimony were almost exclusively persons who worked regularly for the Muenches, or had done a variety of home improvement projects for them. These laborers cleaned house, gave facials and manicures to Nelle Muench, made her dresses, did the laundry, worked as a butler and doorman, and painted rooms. One of the women was employed as a nurse for the baby. The respondents presented only one medical professional as a witness and he was unable to provide definitive evidence of Muench's pregnancy. Dr. Maurice Thompson examined her in mid-September to determine whether she had given birth to a child recently. In his testimony, he stated that he had made his examination with Dr. Muench present and had observed that her "labia was discolored, there was a slight tear on the left side of the vaginal wall, the abdomen was soft, the uterus was larger than normal, and these conditions could have been the after effects of child birth." However, he also thought in his professional judgment that these conditions "could also have been the result of abortion, miscarriage, or instrumentation."[33]

Some of the most important testimony given early in the trial, although this was not readily apparent at the time, was that of Dr. Marsh Pitzman, described in a newspaper account as "an eminent medical research specialist." During his testimony, Limbaugh noticed that Pitzman sat facing away from the counsel's table toward the back of the courtroom. Limbaugh observed also that Nelle Muench, who was sitting directly in front of the witness stand, positioned herself more erectly than usual and that "she shifted her position frequently and appeared to . . . be making every effort possible to get the witness to look at her." In another case a year later, it would be revealed that Pitzman and Nelle Muench had been involved in an affair and that Pitzman had been led to believe that she had given birth to his child. In the spring, according to Lazaroff's testimony, Nelle Muench had dressed for a cocktail party in a manner intended to deceive a physician friend, presumably Pitzman, into believing that she was pregnant. She had even shown him an X-ray, which she claimed showed her fetus, and had Pitzman feel her abdomen, claiming that the unborn baby was moving. On August 18, he was told that she had delivered a baby and he visited that day, and observed her holding a newly born infant. At that time, he believed that the child was hers, but later he became suspicious, especially when he heard about Ware's accusation that the Muenches had taken her baby from her through Jones, whom Pitzman knew was a friend of theirs. Moreover, he testified that Nelle Muench had badgered him into signing an affidavit stating that he believed the child was hers and that he had felt the unborn baby move. After reflection, knowing that his statement was untrue, he signed a new affidavit recanting and correcting the previous. At the end of his testimony, Barker in redirect asked if he thought Nelle Muench had given birth to the child. To this question he answered unequivocally "that in his opinion Mrs. Muench did not give birth to a baby."[34]

During the first week of the hearings, Limbaugh had become accustomed to people recognizing him in public and hearing whispers about his being the judge in the Ware baby case. Each morning he encountered large crowds awaiting the beginning of the trial to whom "hawkers" sold merchandise in the lobby of the Civil Courts Building. Limbaugh had even received a phone call from a woman he had not spoken to in over twenty years requesting a seat in the courtroom. Moreover, much of his mail sought to influence his decision making, or judge his performance in court. Some letters and phone calls into the clerks' office anonymously threatened him. While Limbaugh ignored these and felt no personal peril, newspaper reporters, the judges, and the court reporter all warned him to take precautions to protect himself. Judge McCullen recommended that he carry a handgun, believing him to be "in great danger." This Limbaugh declined to do. Unknown to him, the judges had ordered two plainclothes policemen to attend the hearings and prevent any violence from occurring.[35]

Having adjourned the hearings for the weekend, Limbaugh agreed to accompany his court reporter, DaCosta, to dinner. At that time, he was unsure how he would return to Cape Girardeau. When he mentioned that he might call Bee to have her drive up to St. Louis and then return with her to Cape Girardeau, DaCosta remonstrated with him not to expose himself and his family to danger in this manner, for the Muenches were known associates of gangsters. DaCosta insisted that Limbaugh take his car, for he would be working all weekend transcribing the hearing records anyway and would not need it. This became his routine each weekend, driving home in DaCosta's automobile and returning early the following Monday morning. On these weekends, Limbaugh typically caught up on work in his own legal practice, worked on his manuscript for the Thomas Law Book Company, and attended church. He discovered that in Cape Girardeau, because the local newspaper, the *Southeast Missourian*, was not covering the trial, no one asked about the hearings and he gained a happy reprieve from thinking about it.[36]

The following Monday morning, October 21, 1935, Limbaugh briefly met with the judges before he resumed the hearings. As they began, Evans informed Limbaugh that his client Wilfred Jones was present. After hearing testimony until noon, the respondents asked Ware to be recalled to the stand to enable Jones to interrogate her. Most of Jones' questions covered the same territory as before and eventually Limbaugh sustained an objection to any further testimony on the grounds that it was repetitious. Nevertheless, after lunch, Barker recalled Ware, during which she provided details about "misrepresentations" Jones had made to her. Limbaugh believed that Jones' cross-examination of Ware was ineffective and that she had even got "the best of him" in their exchanges.[37]

Not long after Ware's testimony, her attorney, Barker, called Jones to the witness stand. Presumably through his testimony the court would learn the truth about the whereabouts of Ware's baby. From the beginning, Jones "evaded answering" many of the questions proposed to him. He also manifested animosity towards Barker and was sometimes "sarcastic and petulant" in his manner. When asked directly to reveal the names of the couple who had adopted the Ware child, Jones asserted attorney-client privilege in refusing to tell the court their names, leading to a heated exchange between the parties about the merits of this claim. This assertion of privilege not to reveal his clients' names was an issue about which Limbaugh was uncertain how to rule. Exercising caution, he did not order Jones to answer, although he expressed his suspicion that the privilege was being exercised to thwart the court's effort to locate Ware's child. His caution was wise, for if Jones had wrongly asserted the privilege he could be forced to reveal his clients' names later without doing any harm to Ware's case. Jones testified that the couple had lived in St. Louis when he first met them but had moved to Memphis. The husband, in his work as "an oil broker," traveled a good deal and was from a wealthy family. Barker also questioned Jones about the Price baby, the infant who had died after a short time in the Muench home. Apparently, Jones had been employed to find a home for this infant in the same manner as for Ware, although he claimed that the only reason he had taken the child to the Muench home was for medical treatment. After Dr. Muench was unable to help the child, Dr. Levy, whose specialty was pediatrics, was called to the Muench home. Jones never explained why he had not taken the child directly to the hospital, which was a short distance from the Muench's home.[38]

At this point court adjourned and Jones was informed that he would be required to testify the next day. In the meantime, Limbaugh began his inquiry into the question of whether Jones had the right to assert attorney-client privilege. Both sides had provided him with memoranda on the issue and he was determined to rule correctly on it. That night he spent the evening until ten o'clock in the law library on the thirteenth floor of the Civil Courts Building reading the cases cited by both sides. The next morning, Limbaugh resumed his research until it was time to start the hearing at ten. Barker continued his interrogation of Jones until it was time to break for lunch. During this time, Limbaugh prepared his decision and at the beginning of the proceedings after lunch he announced it. As he remembered this almost three decades later, he "felt . . . strangely alone." Perhaps he recognized the importance of his decision and felt the weight of the responsibility to decide correctly, which could directly influence the course of a child's entire life. Whatever the reason, he knew that the responsibility was his and that he had thoroughly researched the matter and must trust his judgment. In his statement, Limbaugh recognized the duty of Jones to protect any information justifiably considered privileged; that is anything which clients divulge to him in confidence and is of a nature that could be harmful to them if ever disclosed to others. However, he asserted that Jones had a responsibility to the court to provide it with all information pertinent to the case so long as it did not violate this privilege. As he could not conceive a reason for Jones to keep the names of his clients secret, Limbaugh ordered him to reveal them. This was necessary for the information is "the key that will unlock the mystery that now enshrouds this hearing." He also noted that Ware's agreement to give up her child was void, for she was a minor and could not legally make a contract. Thus the adoption was illegal and the court must know to whom Jones had given the child.[39]

Claiming that he had expected Limbaugh's ruling all along, Jones immediately testified that the couple was J. R. and Adele (or Adeline) Palmer. Jones had heard that they had moved to Chicago but he did not know their address. He stated that the publicity in the case had alarmed them and that despite his best efforts he had been unable to contact them. To Limbaugh this answer was unsatisfactory, and because he did not believe him, he began questioning Jones with the intention of forcing him to tell the truth. Moreover, because the adoption was not accomplished according to the law, Ware's baby must be returned and it was Jones' responsibility to effect this. Jones complained that he had tried to do this very thing, but that Ware had interrupted him in his efforts by bringing this writ of habeas corpus suit against him. Limbaugh next inquired of Jones whether or not it was true that he had been to the Muench's home recently when their counsel Keating was there as well. When he admitted that he had, Limbaugh then asked if they had discussed "how this petitioner's proceeding might be resisted." This he denied. Limbaugh also asked Jones if he had seen the infant when he was there and whether he could identify him as Ware's child. Jones claimed not to have seen the child. Although he was unable to compel Jones to answer his questions forthrightly, looking back many years later Limbaugh believed that his decision to force Jones to provide the court with the names of his clients and his other questions regarding them had provided enough information that soon their identity was discovered. Moreover, it was at this point in the proceedings that Barker indicated his intention to move that the Muenches be compelled to produce the baby in court for identification purposes.[40]

Further questioning of Jones by Barker produced nothing of importance and he was dismissed. After the day's proceedings, Limbaugh went to dinner with court reporter DaCosta, who praised his conduct in questioning Jones and admonishing the parties to be truthful. Limbaugh was not so certain that he had made the correct ruling or that he had comported himself properly as a judge, but was somewhat reassured when DaCosta disagreed with his second guessing. Much to Limbaugh's chagrin, however, the evening newspapers were filled with accounts of his forcing Jones to divulge his clients' names and his questioning of him. Reading his opinion, remarks, and questions, Limbaugh found his expressions lacking in polish and feared that in comparison to those of other lawyers and judges his statements would be considered crude and insufficient. He also spoke to his longtime friend, Commissioner Bennick, whose speaking and prose style was of the highest quality, confiding to him his feeling that he had not expressed himself well. Bennick disagreed with Limbaugh's judgment that his decisions and the manner in which they were expressed were inferior to Bennick's. He noted that it was unfair to compare his written opinions, which he had ample time to write and revise several times before being published, to Limbaugh's remarks made "in the heat of a hearing. . . . without an opportunity to correct and refine them."[41]

While he respected the opinions of DaCosta and Bennick, in retrospect many years later Limbaugh gave greater weight to those of Judge Becker, who did not agree with their praise of his handling of Jones. While Becker thought Limbaugh was correct to insist that Jones divulge the whereabouts of the Ware baby, the judge nevertheless took exception to Limbaugh's remark that "we are trifling with the law and blocking avenues of justice by not getting anything done." This statement had been prominently quoted in large bold letters beneath the front-page headline of the *St. Louis Post-Dispatch*. Judge Becker commented to Limbaugh that "you and Mr. Jones may be trifling with justice, but I hope you don't count any of the rest of us around here as participants." Reflecting upon this criticism, Limbaugh believed that Becker was correct that his behavior had been "impetuous and impulsive" rather than "calm, deliberate, judicial judgment." In the end, he had to conclude that Jones' evasions had provoked him into making poorly worded and unmeasured statements in open court.[42]

The most important information to come out of Jones' testimony was the location of James and Lucille Plummer in Minneapolis, Minnesota. Although some of the details about them were not exactly as Jones had related, such as giving their name as Palmer, it was clear that they were the couple about whom he had testified. In a very short time, the newspapers had tracked down the Plummers and persuaded Lucille Plummer to come to St. Louis. She testified that she and her husband had become acquainted with Jones when they lived in St. Louis and had agreed to board a child in need of a home temporarily. They had met him through "a Miss Matthews, matron of a School for Girls at Belt and Enright," which was full and could not accept another boarder. Although she and her husband were childless and had considered adopting a child, even discussing the matter with Jones, they had not adopted the Ware baby or any other child.[43]

After Plummer's testimony, Limbaugh believed that no reasonable doubt remained that Jones had committed perjury. During a recess, Limbaugh consulted with the judges and commissioners of the court to gain their advice about what action he should take in light of this development in the case. Believing that he should act then to insure the integrity of the process and subsequent testimony in the case, Limbaugh proposed holding Jones in contempt of court. The judges and commissioners agreed that it was imperative that he not delay taking action, but it was suggested that the best course would be for Limbaugh to announce in open court to the assistant circuit attorney, who happened to be in the courtroom, that Jones had committed perjury and should be arrested. Returning to the courtroom, Limbaugh began the proceedings by asking if Assistant Circuit Attorney James McLaughlin was present. When he replied that he was, Limbaugh informed him that he was "convinced that Mr. Jones has been guilty of perjury of the most flagrant character" and that McLaughlin should inform his superior officers to institute an investigation immediately to determine what should be done. Limbaugh promised to give the circuit attorney's office "his full cooperation as an officer of the court." To this McLaughlin replied that he would do as he was requested. During this exchange, Jones showed no emotion or surprise whatsoever. After the hearing adjourned, Jones was arrested for perjury and the newspapers were filled with stories and photographs of detectives escorting him out of the St. Louis Court of Appeals and being booked at police headquarters. Soon afterward, Plummer testified before a grand jury considering an indictment of perjury against Jones.[44]

Limbaugh's action against Jones, while praised in the newspapers—the *St. Louis Star-Times* characterizing it as "one of the most inspiring incidents in St. Louis legal history"—and supported by the judges, was questioned by others. One of these was Judge Kelly, before whom Limbaugh had often practiced as a lawyer, who asked him if he "had not exceeded [his] authority in publicly charging Wilfred Jones" with committing perjury. Limbaugh explained that he considered it his judicial duty to expose anyone who had committed perjury or any other act against the proper "administration of justice" in his presence. Kelly replied that he would never have acted in this way in his courtroom, but agreed that if Jones had committed perjury he should be prosecuted. While Kelly's restraint was more conventional judicial behavior, Limbaugh's action was actually more in accord with the direction provided to the bar in the canon of legal ethics, which made clear that it was the duty of all officers of the court to enforce the rules. Such enforcement was important, for the violation of the rules inevitably diminished the probability that the court could adjudicate a case fairly and correctly.[45]

Limbaugh's accusation against Jones led to another unusual circumstance— the filing of a motion by his lawyer "to disqualify" Limbaugh from serving any longer as special commissioner in the case. Limbaugh promised to take the matter under advisement and rule on the matter later. To save him from having to hear arguments on the motion, the next morning the judges entered the courtroom with Limbaugh, who announced that he had overruled the motion. Anticipating this, Jones' lawyer then presented to the clerk of the court an appeal of Limbaugh's decision. After promising to rule on the motion soon, the judges then left the courtroom to consider their decision. Later that same day the judges overruled the appeal. The issue then went to the Supreme Court of Missouri where Jones' lawyer charged that Limbaugh was "biased and prejudiced against this respondent and has pre-judged the rights, privileges, and immunities of this respondent." Jones' lawyer also accused him of being a tool of the *Star-Times* and the *Post-Dispatch*. The supreme court refused to remove Limbaugh from the case.[46]

As the hearings proceeded, in an era before the discovery of DNA, the testimony of medical professionals revealed that no determinative information about the child's identity could be gained through an examination of the child's and mother's eye color and blood types. Nevertheless, other characteristics such as the weight and age of the infant could possibly prove that the child was not Ware's, although these characteristics could never prove definitively that he was hers. In a very real sense, the child was evidence in the case. Therefore, the next logical step in the proceedings was to order the Muenches to bring the child into court, and allow medical professionals, other experts, and Ware to examine the child. Limbaugh, who had hoped that Jones' testimony would settle the case, then felt disappointed at the information he had gained to that point in the hearings and saw no alternative course of action. Unsurprisingly, the Muenches objected to the motion of Ware's lawyer to bring the infant into court for examination. Keating argued that the order violated the Muenches' due process rights and wrongly took from them the custody of their child before a full hearing and record could be completed. Limbaugh rejected these arguments, overruled the objection, and ordered that the Muenches have the child in the courtroom the next morning at the opening of the hearing.[47]

That night Judge Becker received a phone call from Dillon, who was representing the Muenches along with Keating, in which he requested that the court restrain its special commissioner's order. Becker indicated to Dillon that he thought it unlikely that he and the other judges would sustain his motion to quash Limbaugh's order, but that they would meet the next morning with Limbaugh and establish the record to enable the respondents to appeal to the Supreme Court of Missouri. The next morning the judges with Limbaugh again appeared in court and rejected Dillon's motion to quash the order. Through a writ of prohibition the respondents then challenged Limbaugh's authority as special commissioner to require the Muenches to produce the baby. To give the respondents time to gain a ruling from the supreme court, the judges and Limbaugh decided to postpone the deadline for producing the baby to Monday, October 28, adjourning the hearing until then.[48]

In their writ of prohibition to the supreme court, the Muench's lawyers argued that Limbaugh had not given them sufficient time to present an argument against his order to produce the child in court, that he had arbitrarily overruled their motion to quash, and that he did not have the authority to order the child into court. They claimed to have presented evidence that Nelle Muench had given birth to the child and that Ware's lawyer had not proven that the infant in the Muench's custody was hers. The Muench's lawyers also contended that bringing the child into the courtroom could harm him. In his response, Barker stated that an examination of the child's physical characteristics, age, and identifying marks was necessary in resolving the child's identity. The baby was evidence and must be produced. Moreover, the child should be held in the court's custody long enough to determine whether his hair had been dyed and to give experts time to conduct their examinations. Without this, a danger existed that the court could award the child to Ware and discover afterward that he was not her baby. The only question to be resolved by the supreme court was whether the St. Louis Court of Appeals had the authority to order the child into its custody.[49]

During the recess, Limbaugh returned home and filled his days by working on his legal practice and book manuscript, attending church, and spending time with his wife and three boys. Expecting the supreme court to rule by the time the hearing was scheduled to reconvene, Limbaugh returned to St. Louis on October 28. Arriving at his office in the Civil Courts Building, Judge Becker came by to tell him that the supreme court had not ruled yet, and appeared to be in suspense to learn its decision. It was then that the judge received a phone call from Barker and Keating informing him that they were about to be heard by the supreme court and requested that the recess be extended. This was granted and announced to those in the courtroom that morning. The delay enabled Limbaugh and the judges to finalize their plans for taking custody of the child if the supreme court upheld Limbaugh's order. As before, the judges expressed their support for Limbaugh's ruling and their belief that examination of the child was necessary. Afterwards, Limbaugh organized his notes and researched procedural matters in preparation for resumption of the hearing. The supreme court's ruling came down the following day in the afternoon by phone declining "to grant a writ of prohibition." The Muenches were notified that they must bring the infant to court the following morning of October 30.[50]

The delay in the supreme court's decision increased the public's excitement and anticipation to see the infant. That morning a large crowd gathered in the courtroom, the hallways, and the lobby to catch a glimpse of the baby. As events unfolded, those in the courtroom would not be disappointed by an absence of drama in the courtroom that day. The three judges and Limbaugh entered the packed courtroom where they observed Nelle Muench holding the child. Judge Becker, who took the lead in the proceedings, noted that he and the other judges were present because they had ordered Limbaugh "to direct that the baby be produced in court" and were there to see that the order was obeyed. Becker next directed that the baby be handed over to a nurse appointed to care for him while in court custody, who was ordered to take him into the judges' assembly room. Becker then asked Dr. Muench under oath if the baby was the same as the one held in their home since August 18. He confirmed that he was. Turning to Nelle Muench, the same question was asked. To this point, she had obeyed the court and maintained her composure, but this ended when she began to protest that the baby was hers. When Becker explained that the infant would be held in the court's custody until it decided the final outcome of the case, Nelle Muench "gave a long and continuing shriek," and rising to her feet began to scream at Becker calling him "a brute." He immediately ordered her removed from the courtroom, but when Marshal McDermott sought to escort her out she refused to go and continued her tirade against the court. Finally, a group of policemen surrounded her and "forcibly" removed her from the courtroom with her shouting and calling Becker "a tyrant" and "Nero." During her tirade, her husband attempted to calm her and apologized to Becker for his wife's behavior. The police officers were ordered to remove everyone from the room outside the courtroom and to prevent Nelle Muench from returning.

While there she referred to Ware as "that little bitch, whore" and threatened to kill a newspaper photographer if he took her picture. Concerning other incidents occurring during the hearings, a newspaper reporter testified that she had struck him and another recalled some very foul language she had used toward him.[51]

After Nelle Muench's removal from the courtroom, Becker announced that the infant would be kept in a private room at St. Louis Children's Hospital, where he would be cared for until his custody was determined. Moreover, he ordered that no one was to be allowed to visit the child except by Limbaugh's order. The hearing was recessed to enable the expert witnesses and Ware to view the child. Limbaugh was present to observe and supervise these visits. Of course, he was most curious to see Ware's reaction to the child. When she entered, Limbaugh detected "a trace of suspense and doubt" on her face, but this expression disappeared immediately when she saw the infant. In its place, he believed, was "a natural and unrestrained smile. A motherly kindness, an urge to handle and embrace the baby, a satisfying beam in her countenance and a quiet expression of contentment all combined to induce me to believe that a mother had met her child." After Ware and the other witnesses had finished viewing the baby, he was transferred by police escort to St. Louis Children's Hospital.[52]

Reconvening the hearings, Ware's attorney, Barker, called Dr. Paul J. Zentay, an instructor of pediatrics at Washington University and practicing on the staff of Jewish Hospital. In his opinion, the baby was large for his age and could not have been born prematurely as the Muenches claimed. Dr. E. F. Schmitz in his testimony agreed with Zentay that the infant could not have been born prematurely. The hair expert did not detect any evidence that the baby's hair had been dyed or tinted, but he could not be certain until later after it had grown longer. Another person testified that the infant was the same child he had observed in the Muench's home in early October. The most important testimony, however, was Anna Ware's. When asked if the child she had viewed earlier was her own, she replied "with a little hesitation" that he was. During cross-examination, Keating produced a letter she had written to Mrs. Giordan, the wife of the man with whom she had her affair, in which she described the baby as having dark hair. Ware admitted that he had blond hair and that he "did look differently . . . but that she could tell from the shape of [his] eyes" and other physical characteristics that he was her child.[53]

As the hearing drew to a close, Limbaugh questioned Dr. Schmitz, hoping that some "technical scientific knowledge or reason" might be determinative in identifying whose child was in custody of the court. Despite his efforts to discover such evidence, in the end he was forced to conclude "that medical science [in 1935] furnished no exact formula and prescribed no precise method by which the parentage of a baby could be determined." Nevertheless, when both sides rested their cases on November 6, Limbaugh was certain of his decision. In conferring with Judge Becker afterward, he explained that his clients and the Thomas Law Book Company were exerting great pressure upon him to attend to their business. Judge Becker, after checking with DaCosta, learned that the court reporter was still two or three weeks from completing the transcript of the court record and that, of course, Limbaugh could not be expected to complete his report without access to it.[54]

After spending several days in Cape Girardeau attending to the business of his clients, Limbaugh returned to St. Louis and began the laborious process of dictating his notes, summarizing the most important testimony, and outlining those legal issues he must decide. In his research, he considered the form of the reports of other special commissioners and various questions of law regarding the writ of habeas corpus, the jurisdiction of the St. Louis Court of Appeals, the attorney-client privilege, and "a number of other legal questions." In preparation for writing his report he also abstracted his and the court's action on each lawyer's motion during the hearing. All of this material was arranged to enable him to find the information quickly, make the writing of his report easier, and to insure that he did not forget to address any important issue.[55]

Limbaugh first composed a statement of facts and conclusions of law. This required a careful and often tedious checking of the record from the hearing transcript. In the report, after providing some of the details of the case, he noted that hardly any precedent of law was available to guide him in his decision. Nevertheless, Limbaugh believed that the accumulation of facts pointed very strongly to one conclusion. First, it was evident that the child in court custody was the same who had appeared in the Muench home on August 18. The age of Nelle Muench, forty-four years, and the childless condition of her marriage of twenty-three years indicated that it was highly improbable that she had become pregnant recently. If she was pregnant, Limbaugh asked, then why was Muench not placed under the care of an obstetrician? And why did she not observe the special precautions practiced by pregnant women of her age? Even the circumstances of the infant's birth seemed incredible, for Muench's labor was relatively easy for a woman of her age giving birth for the first time. Furthermore, no reason was provided to explain why she had remained at home instead of going to the hospital, especially when it is remembered that her husband was absent. The testimony of her neighbors, Dr. Levy, and others placed the Muenchs' claim under deep suspicion. Moreover, the witnesses for the Muenches were all employees and thus could hardly be considered independent and unimpeachable witnesses. Given this and other evidence, Limbaugh concluded that the Muenches were attempting to deceive the court and that Nelle Muench did not give birth to the baby as she asserted.[56]

Limbaugh found Jones' testimony, if possible, even more unbelievable than that of the Muenches. Jones had testified evasively and dishonestly and apparently intended to obscure the facts, delay the hearings, and prevent the court from determining what had really happened to Ware's child. In his report Limbaugh again accused Jones of having perjured himself when he stated that the Plummers had adopted the child. Moreover, given Jones' close association with the Muenches, it was apparent that more than coincidence explained the circumstance of Ware having her baby on the eve of the Muenchs' announcement of the birth of their child. Medical professionals also did not believe that the infant was born prematurely, for his weight was normal. These same experts believed that the facial characteristics of Ware and the infant were "strikingly similar." In concluding his report, even after sustaining all of counsels' objections, Limbaugh noted that when the remaining testimony and evidence was considered, and it was remembered that Jones had provided no information concerning the true whereabouts of the Ware baby, one could hardly come to any other conclusion than that the baby claimed by the Muenches and then in the court's custody was actually Ware's child. Thus he concluded that the child should be returned to Anna Ware.[57]

The reaction to Limbaugh's decision was almost universally favorable. The judges and commissioners of the St. Louis Court of Appeals were very pleased. The newspapers published the report proclaiming in large-lettered headlines the verdict: "Baby is Anna's, Commissioner Rules"; "Muenches' Claim to Boy Called 'Sham' in Limbaugh's Report"; and "Anna Ware Wins Baby Suit, Commissioner Finds Muenches had Her Child." The *St. Louis Star-Times* described Limbaugh's report as "one of the most forthright and outspoken documents to appear in a St. Louis court in many years. . . . [It] is blunt, straightforward, bare of legal verbiage." Both the *St. Louis Globe-Democrat* and the *St. Louis Post-Dispatch* carried lead editorials commenting on the report and case. The latter described Limbaugh's report "as the well-told story of one of the most remarkable cases in the annals of American court proceedings." During and after the hearings, friends and relatives sent articles to Limbaugh from all over the country about the case, and he received letters from strangers encouraging or denouncing his conduct and report. Perhaps the greatest tribute to his handling of the hearings and his report came from Daniel R. Fitzpatrick, the Pulitzer Prize-winning cartoonist for the *Post-Dispatch*, who drew a cartoon on the case entitled, "The Stork that Failed," which appeared on December 6. Fitzpatrick gave the original charcoal drawing to Limbaugh, inscribing it thus: "To Special Commissioner Rush H. Limbaugh who inspired this cartoon, D. R. Fitzpatrick." A few days later the St. Louis Court of Appeals adopted Limbaugh's report and this was confirmed by the Supreme Court of Missouri shortly thereafter.[58]

Later the Muenches, Jones, and Helen Berroyer, whose role in the conspiracy was peripheral, were indicted on state charges for taking custody of the Price and Ware infants without authorization from the St. Louis Juvenile Court, and were tried in 1936. The jury in the trial was dismissed after one of the jurors reported to the judge that he had been offered $100 to prevent a conviction. In the second trial, the four were convicted, but only received fines. A more serious federal indictment of mail fraud, however, was tried in the United States District Court in St. Louis against the same four defendants. The charge indicted the four conspirators with deceiving Ware in letters delivered to her through the United States mail service. Judge George H. Moore presided over the trial at which Dr. Marsh Pitzman testified that Nelle Muench had lied to him about being pregnant and having his child. Apparently, for this reason Pitzman had refused to look at Muench during his testimony in the trial before Limbaugh. In the federal trial, Pitzman, who was wealthy, testified that the Muenches had defrauded him of $18,000 to pay for Nelle Muench's defense in the Kelley kidnapping trial and other expenses. Until he had discovered her deception, Pitzman had also willed one-third of his estate to the baby and one-third to Nelle Muench. All four of the defendants were found guilty and sentenced on December 26, 1936. In a newspaper interview shortly before she was sentenced, Nelle Muench made a final dramatic statement, apologizing for having disgraced her family, ruined her husband, and admitting that she had never given birth to a child. Before Judge Moore rendered his verdict, she made a final confession and plea for mercy: "I took a baby, one that I thought no one else in the world wanted but me. I did tell Dr. Pitzman he was the father but there never was a conspiracy to defraud him of any of his property or any of his money. His purse was always open to me, as he has testified. I did it out of love, to hold him. I don't want innocent people to suffer. My husband did not know the facts until last Monday night. There never has been the slightest thought or slightest idea to violate any law in any way whatsoever. 'Please, may you and God be merciful." Even in her confession, Nelle Muench did not tell the complete truth without any misrepresentations. Perhaps for this reason and the seriousness of her crimes, Judge Moore did not heed her plea for mercy and handed down long prison terms for her and the others. Nelle Muench was ordered to serve ten years in a federal prison and fined $5,000; her husband was sentenced to eight years. Jones received ten years, and Berroyer five years.[59]

The testimony in these trials confirmed the correctness of Limbaugh's conclusions and recommendation in his report to the court. The hearing had lasted almost four weeks, eighty-seven witnesses had been heard, and Limbaugh had ruled on many legal motions. Having never presided as a judge in a courtroom, he acquitted himself well by maintaining proper judicial restraint and open-mindedness, treated the parties on both sides fairly, and concisely and accurately summarized the most important testimony and evidence found in over 1,500 transcribed pages of the record. All of this was accomplished under the scrutiny of the press, the threats of anonymous persons, and the pressure of the public, many of whom earnestly and fanatically followed the twists and turns of each day's proceedings. Moreover, even before the hearings had concluded, Limbaugh began to hear rumors that his newfound fame could open wider fields of service. Soon he faced an important and momentous decision.

Chapter Eight

The Second World War

In late 1935, while serving as special commissioner in the Muench kidnapping case, Rush H. Limbaugh was surprised to learn that he was being considered as a possible candidate for governor among some circles within Missouri's Republican leadership. As 1936 was a presidential election year and Franklin D. Roosevelt would head his party's ticket, many thought the prospects poor for Republican electoral success in Missouri and elsewhere. To overcome this difficulty, some Republicans considered Limbaugh's newfound popularity a great asset and believed that his candidacy was their only chance for victory. The first to approach him about running were reporter Hume Duval and Republican politician Walter C. Ploeser, who in 1931 had served with Limbaugh in the state House of Representatives where they had become good friends. After his speech urging the impeachment of State Treasurer Larry Brunk, Ploeser had congratulated Limbaugh on having given "the finest speech he had ever heard." Limbaugh, who later admitted to being "flattered" by Duval's and Ploeser's proposal, expressed doubt that any Republican, especially one from southeast Missouri, "which was as politically detached from the rest of the state as was Gaul from Rome," could be elected governor. He also noted that he lacked any substantial statewide political experience, a significant deficiency in his qualifications for Missouri's chief executive office.[1]

After Limbaugh's decision in the Muench case was published in the newspapers and editorial comment was almost universally favorable, the pressure to announce his gubernatorial candidacy was immediate and substantial. Both friends and "several of the active members of the state Republican committee" argued that such good publicity was rare and Limbaugh's time had come, if he would only embrace the opportunity. Among these was his friend Forrest C. Donnell, who himself would become governor in 1940. Another of these early supporters was Fred E. Kies, editor of the *Cape County Post*, who presented Limbaugh to the public as that rare Missouri politician, honest and untainted by any connections to the political machines in Kansas City and St. Louis. Despite all of this, Limbaugh was not swept away by the enthusiasm of others, having been urged to run for office several times before and still smarting from his defeat in the 1932 Cape Girardeau mayoral race. Nevertheless, he did not definitively dismiss the prospect either, perhaps in part because his wife, Bee, considered the possibility "more seriously" than he did and desired that he at least not decline running before investigating the matter further. Thus, in late 1935 he traveled with Bee to Springfield for a meeting of the Judicial Council of Missouri and afterward spoke with various Republican leaders. One of these was Mercer Arnold, then the Republican party's elder statesman and a veteran of successful runs for statewide office and a failed gubernatorial race. Limbaugh respected Arnold, who attempted to persuade him to run for governor, noting that such an opportunity came but once in a lifetime. Another acquaintance, Jesse W. Barrett, former state attorney general, however, was then openly seeking the Republican gubernatorial nomination and sought to persuade Limbaugh not to run, but promised that as a loyal Republican he would support Limbaugh's candidacy if he should gain the GOP's nomination. Limbaugh promised the same to Barrett. In the end, Limbaugh's lack of resources to conduct a statewide contest and the bleak prospect for success convinced him not to seek the nomination. His judgment proved sound when Barrett gained the nomination, and, although he conducted "a vigorous campaign," lost by a wide margin to his Democratic opponent.[2]

After deciding not to run for governor, the state Republican committee elected Limbaugh to serve as a delegate to the national convention held in Cleveland, Ohio. Having supported progressive policies in college and afterward, by 1928 Limbaugh had returned to his Republican ideological heritage of limited government and resistance to government's ever greater intrusion into American life. Along with many others, he was alarmed by the expansion of the federal government's power through the passage of New Deal legislation, especially in the creation of a great number of new bureaucracies such as the Agricultural Adjustment Administration and the National Recovery Administration. These agencies were staffed by appointed functionaries with authority over much of the country's economy. Limbaugh believed that these unelected bureaucrats had far too much power with few checks and balances upon their authority, often exercising "the functions of a legislative and executive and judicial tribunal combined. They make rules or laws, enforce their operation and pass judgment on and punish those who do not obey." These bureaucracies were harmful to the character of the American people, undermining their self-reliance and inevitably leading to a loss of freedom through expanding regulation and rules. Therefore, he judged it far better for families and communities to help their own, for they were much more likely to tender aid to those truly in need and could do so much more efficiently than the federal government. Moreover, in those instances in which governmental action was necessary, Limbaugh judged that these were usually best handled at the local and state levels. These views were held by the vast majority of the delegates at the convention and were expressed repeatedly by their presidential nominee, Alf Landon, and party leaders then and throughout the campaign. Limbaugh also shared Republicans' concern regarding Roosevelt's plan to pack the Supreme Court of the United States with liberal justices supportive of his policies. This plan was denounced by the Republican party and even a fair number of Democrats. After his landslide election, winning all but two states, Roosevelt attempted to implement this plan but failed.[3]

In the spring of 1936, the Limbaughs began the construction of a new home. The bungalow in which they had resided since 1918 was too small for their needs. After several years of looking for a house, they had found nothing satisfactory. For this reason, eventually they decided to build upon a lot located on the highest elevation in the city. After working with different architects to develop a satisfactory plan, Bee oversaw the project, ensuring that the home was constructed according to their needs and desires. The home was a two-story colonial, built with brick painted white in the style of the time. Inside the front door was a foyer and staircase. To the left was a large living room and library overlooking the rose garden with a fine view of the Mississippi River. To the right of the foyer was the dining room and kitchen. Attached to the back of their new home was a porch on the first and second floors. The house had hardwood floors throughout upon which were placed rugs partially covering them. The upstairs had four bedrooms, one of which was furnished for guests. To complete their master bedroom properly, the Limbaughs traveled to St. Louis where they purchased a bedroom set from a furniture store, which extended them credit upon the recommendation of St. Louis Court of Appeals Judge William D. Becker. Once built and furnished, the Limbaughs were greatly satisfied and looked forward to many happy years living there together.[4]

By this time, the couple's oldest son, Rush Jr., was attending the University of Missouri-Columbia, where he received his undergraduate degree and would soon begin law school. Manley, who was three years his brother's junior, wished to pursue a teaching career and decided to attend classes in Cape Girardeau at Southeast Missouri State University. Their youngest son, Stephen, was then only eight years old. During this period, Limbaugh continued to keep in touch with his siblings, exchanging visits with each. When together, the Limbaugh brothers enjoyed telling stories and jokes and often stayed up late into the night and even into the early morning conversing. Limbaugh was especially close to his brother Roscoe, who was five years his senior. Until 1922, when he purchased a farm of his own, Roscoe had remained with his wife Josie on the Limbaugh farm, where his mother Susan, brother Burette, and wife Cora remained. Every year Roscoe, who enjoyed helping and looking out for others, brought gunny sacks of corn and sausage to his urban-dwelling siblings Rush and Lillie, who lived in the nearby town of Jackson.[5]

In 1928, a house was built near Lillie's home for their mother Susan. The matriarch of the Limbaugh clan was then seventy-five years of age and was still in good health. From time to time, she visited her children for two or three weeks, and especially enjoyed returning to the old farm upon which her son Burette and his family lived, and to Roscoe's farm when it was harvest, wheat threshing, or some other time of great activity. Limbaugh loved and respected his mother and especially admired her for having raised her large family alone after the death of his father Joseph in 1898. Through her, he and his siblings had acquired a strong work ethic and an attitude of self-reliance, valuable characteristics, especially during hard economic times. Whenever he could, Limbaugh visited his mother, welcomed her to his home, took her on drives, brought her to public events—once bringing her to a local college football game—and celebrated her birthdays until her death from an intestinal obstruction on May 20, 1938. She was then eighty-five years old and was laid to rest beside her husband, who had passed away almost forty years before, in the private cemetery located on the Limbaugh farm.[6]

As noted in the previous chapter, beginning in 1933 Limbaugh had undertaken to write a series of books on the practice of law in Missouri for the Thomas Law Book Company. After various delays due to a busy law practice and his appointment as special commissioner to the St. Louis Court of Appeals, the first volume covering the municipal, justice, county, and probate courts was not finished until November 1935. This and the second volume, which was published in May 1939, were general practice books, intended to serve as reference works for lawyers explaining "the principal procedural points in all the courts" in Missouri's judicial system. The arrangement of the material enabled the practicing lawyer to understand the jurisdiction and procedure of the courts. Moreover, Limbaugh explained the purposes of an extensive number of common legal actions. In his introductory information for each of the courts, he traced their history, classifications, functions, jurisdictions, and the proper procedures a lawyer must employ when practicing before them. Although this material was necessarily concise and limited in scope, Limbaugh managed to provide the reader with interesting and little-known details and history about the courts.[7]

In these volumes, Limbaugh was determined to research his topics thoroughly and demonstrated a scholar's attention to detail and verve for research. He also exhibited a practicing lawyer's understanding of what was most relevant and important in the day-to-day work of representing clients and "the real significance of the cases" presented. The reviews of the two completed volumes in the *Missouri Law Review* were very favorable, commending Limbaugh for their organization, content, and scholarship, noting that these practice books would be useful to both the young and veteran attorney alike. It was observed that practice in each court was explained not only to serve as a guide, but also to enable attorneys to proceed intelligently by explaining the purposes of the procedures employed. The reviewer particularly praised the lucid manner in which various aspects of the common, statutory, and case law were composed, often providing the reader with their history "when necessary for an understanding of the present procedure." Moreover, the annotations were helpful, unlike those of many other law books, for the case citations were "well adapted" for directing attorneys to the information they needed. In supplying this material, Limbaugh avoided criticizing the courts but suggested where the legislature might improve Missouri's statutes, especially in probate law. In the latter, while explaining the law as it then existed, he nevertheless "paved the way for a general overhauling of the statutes in this important field of law administration." Perhaps most helpful of all, however, were the numerous legal forms provided, which served as models for lawyers in preparing written actions, affidavits, certificates, petitions, notices, and contracts, greatly reducing the time and labor normally expended in their drafting. Regarding the work as a whole, the reviewer, a law professor at the University of Missouri, observed that "no one but a practitioner of broad experience, careful scholarship, and unusual vigor could have produced the present book."[8]

Most of Limbaugh's scholarly work was accomplished in the early morning hours and in the evenings after a full day of work as a practicing lawyer. In 1937, Limbaugh wrote an article, "The Adoption of Children in Missouri," published in the *Missouri Law Review*, in which he traced the history of the practice of adoption from ancient times to the modern era, providing a detailed description of the law in Missouri. Apparently, this topic was of special interest to him for some time, for in 1914, when a student at the University of Missouri-Columbia, he had presented a talk on the subject before the Athenaean Literary Society. In 1938 the law review also began publishing his contribution to an annual series documenting the decisions of the Supreme Court of Missouri. Perhaps because he had conducted the writ of habeas corpus hearing as a special commissioner of the St. Louis Court of Appeals, the editors of the law review asked him to write about "extraordinary legal remedies," which was published each year from 1938 to 1943. In these surveys, Limbaugh considered the court's decision making regarding writs of mandamus, habeas corpus, quo warranto, and prohibition. In presenting these opinions, he explained how the court had weighed the various issues of law, fact, precedent, and constitutionality and explicated the importance, implications, and affect these decisions would have upon the practice of law.[9]

In 1940, Limbaugh became involved in litigation representing the interests of Greenville—the seat of Wayne County—and farmers whose land was condemned to make way for the Wappapello Flood Control Project. In 1936

Congress had passed legislation to cause an investigation to be made of the St. Francis River Basin to determine how best to prevent the periodic flooding of homes and farmers' fields there. In the late 1930s it was decided to dam the river near Wappapello to protect fertile land in Stoddard and Dunklin counties. This dam flooded lands north of it and created Lake Wappapello. James Franklin Paullus, presiding judge of the Wayne County Court, contacted Limbaugh, beginning a professional relationship which lasted several years. Paullus was a prosperous farmer from Coldwater and impressed Limbaugh with "his integrity, his common sense, and good judgment." Apparently, this opinion was shared by the people of Wayne County, for despite his being a Republican in a predominately Democratic region, Paullus served the county for eight years during this crucial period when sound leadership was needed.[10]

After learning that Paullus had employed him, a "large majority of" landowners whose land had been taken requested Limbaugh's representation in their suits before the federal court. Eventually, he represented more than 25 landowners holding 102 tracts of property. One of his first tasks was the investigation of different legal questions relating to the taking of property through eminent domain. Because the city of Greenville must be moved two miles to higher ground, Limbaugh considered how best to accomplish this. After researching the matter, he recommended that the town retain its government and annex the site where the new town could be built. Employing a method called shoestring annexation, Limbaugh traveled with Paullus to Shawneetown, Illinois, located on the Ohio River, where it had been removed to higher ground to escape the flooding that periodically inundated their homes. While there they spoke with town officials and others to gain advice in the hope of anticipating the practical problems they might confront.[11]

Before Limbaugh became involved in the Wappapello litigation, the federal district court in Cape Girardeau appointed a commission to establish the value of the condemned land. Limbaugh traveled to Wayne County to learn whether or not the United States Army Corps of Engineers intended to challenge any of the commission's awards. He was informed that the engineers would challenge them all. In May 1940, Limbaugh traveled to the farms of three of his clients near Greenville to walk over the land, learn about their crop production, and list the number and type of buildings and other improvements necessary for a fair valuation of their property. He then drove to Greenville to meet with businessmen there before returning home that evening. Throughout the spring and summer Limbaugh consulted with Paullus and his colleagues on the county court and his clients in preparation for the cases before the federal court.[12]

The first of the cases in which Limbaugh was involved concerned the property of Bud and Lottie Allison, who owned a farm on a very valuable tract of land just north of the dam, which by 1940 was completed. The night before the trial began, Limbaugh had met with Allison and witnesses for the trial at the local hotel where they stayed. Judge George H. Moore presided over the trial and the government's counsel was M. Walker Cooper. Wishing to start his case well, Limbaugh called his best witness, a knowledgeable and intelligent man with the facility to speak well and "fluently." It soon became clear, however, that the man was drunk, forcing Limbaugh to request a short recess. Recognizing his predicament, Judge Moore granted the delay so that he could regroup. Once the trial resumed Limbaugh questioned his next witness, who provided the court with information about land values in the area and particularly about the Allison farm. When this witness had finished, Cooper moved to strike the entire testimony "on the ground of interest," citing the fact that the witness possessed condemned land. To Limbaugh's consternation, Judge Moore agreed. Despite his strong remonstrance, the judge refused to change his decision. Because at this time it was not customary for private lawyers to employ expert witnesses, the expense being prohibitive, Limbaugh, in selecting men most knowledgeable about land values in the region, naturally chose farmers and other landowners with vast experience there. Even the testimony of Allison concerning his land was only reluctantly allowed into the trial record by Moore after Limbaugh argued that the defendant's right to testify should not be denied. From this testimony, Limbaugh provided the court with a comprehensive history of the land in question, a tract of 386.6 acres of which 187.6 acres was cleared and the rest wooded. After a tornado had damaged their "residence and other buildings," and had seriously injured Mrs. Allison, in 1924 they decided to sell their farm for $14,000. In 1926, the Allisons returned to Wayne County and were able to purchase their farm and resume farming operations there. From that time to 1940, the Allisons made a number of improvements to their property including the building of a new home, barn, smokehouse, chicken house, and side shed. Twenty to twenty-five acres of land was cleared, fencing was rebuilt, and a peach tree orchard was planted. During this period, Allison purchased eighty more acres at $75 per acre. This evidence, Limbaugh believed, demonstrated that the land was worth from $18,750 to $20,000, and was not a significant amount over the commission's recommendation that the Allisons be paid $17,500.[13]

The government, having the advantage of greater resources, employed experts who, although they were not from southeast Missouri and could hardly be considered familiar with the region's agricultural land, were well credentialed and experienced in various ways. Limbaugh vigorously cross-examined these witnesses to undermine their credibility. The difficulty of this task, however, was complicated significantly by what he considered to be Judge Moore's "antagonistic judicial attitude." One of these witnesses, Colonel O. M. Page, was head of the Department of War's Lands Division. He was familiar to Limbaugh, for he had testified as an expert in at least two previous unrelated cases against his clients' interests. In the first of these cases, Page had asserted that the flooding of the Mississippi River was very unusual and that such "a wet cycle" would not again occur in their lifetimes. Just a few years later, these words were used to undermine Page's testimony when he was reminded of his earlier testimony and was made to admit that his prognostication had been wrong. In the Allison case, Page claimed to have spoken to "a large number of people" in the region and thus was familiar with the characteristics of the land, the weather and rainfall amounts, crop productivity, and the frequency of flooding along the St. Francis River. When Limbaugh asked him to name anyone with whom he had spoken, Page could not name one, nor identify when he had spoken to them. The remaining witnesses for the government were as unfamiliar with the St. Francis River Basin as was Page, excepting one. W. C. Beaty had lived in the region for thirty years as a merchant and had traded in land. All the government witnesses placed the value of the Allisons' land from $10,000 to $12,000.[14]

Not unexpectedly, Judge Moore set aside the commission awards and ordered that a new commission be established to determine the proper compensation to the Allisons and the others. This decision proved to be very unsatisfactory, for by the time the new commission traveled to inspect the farms they were already under several feet of water. Thus, to comply with the court's order, the commissioners were forced to inspect them from a boat. From this sham investigation they recommended that the Allisons be paid $12,000. Greatly dissatisfied with this judgment and knowing that it "would doubtless influence" the amounts awarded to his other clients, Limbaugh prepared a substantial and "exhaustive brief" upon which he intended to establish a record for appeal. In it he provided a full history and description of the land, both sides' testimony, and a sampling of recent land sales in the region. Furthermore, he addressed a number of constitutional questions relating to protections of property, takings through eminent domain proceedings, and the admission of testimony in court. However, in the end the appeal was never made, for the Allisons, aged and worn down by misfortune, declined to chance further the vagaries of the United States federal courts and left Missouri, thoroughly "disheartened and disillusioned about the right of a farmer to obtain justice." In litigating the remaining cases, Limbaugh's clients fared better before Judge Charles B. Davis than did those whose trials were presided over by Judge Moore. Many of the cases were settled, ending a long period of litigation. On June 20, 1949, Limbaugh fulfilled his final duty in delivering the last payment of the United States government to the Wayne County Court for the loss of roads and other infrastructure amounting in all to $147,500.[15]

The decade of the 1940s was the busiest period of Limbaugh's legal career. During this time he was in great demand to speak at bar associations around the state and various local civic and religious organizations. Before the bar associations, he addressed topics related to his profession, including "the public duty of a lawyer"—a subject to which he would return again and again—probate reform, and the nonpartisan court reform plan. Before civic and religious organizations he spoke about Daniel Webster's life, provided more general information about the legal profession in his speech on the "law and the responsibility of citizenship," and gave his perspective on important current events such as American foreign policy at a time when world events threatened again to entangle the United States in an European conflict.[16]

In 1940 Limbaugh participated in the political campaign, speaking at different gatherings around the state supporting Republican candidates for office. During the early part of the campaign, Limbaugh spent two days with other Republican members of a committee drafting the party's state platform. To support his friend Ploeser's candidacy for Congress, Limbaugh and Bee traveled to St. Louis where he addressed a campaign rally. As already noted, having served with Ploeser in the state legislature, Limbaugh had renewed his acquaintance with him in 1935 when he had served as a special commissioner for the St. Louis Court of Appeals. At the time, Ploeser had urged him to run for governor and perhaps Limbaugh felt some obligation to support his friend's candidacy in return. Many people in St. Louis remembered Limbaugh's service on the court and his appearance undoubtedly was intended as a draw to the event. Moreover, during the campaign, Limbaugh's good friend Forrest C. Donnell, who was running for governor, and other state candidates came to Cape Girardeau for a political rally. While there Donnell and his wife stayed in the Limbaughs' home. While the Democrats retained control of the state legislature and won five statewide executive offices, Ploeser gained his seat in the United States Congress and Donnell won the governor's race.[17]

Running against the corrupt and powerful Democratic political machines in Kansas City and St. Louis, Donnell won the governor's race by less than 4,000 votes. Donnell's strategy had been effective because his opponent, Lawrence McDaniel, was part of the St. Louis political machine and had been handpicked by St. Louis Mayor Bernard F. Dickmann. The Democrats delayed Donnell's inauguration for six weeks, throwing "the state's political life . . . into unholy tumult," until the Supreme Court of Missouri intervened, ruling that the Speaker of the House must declare Donnell the winner. Thus on February 26, 1941, Donnell was inaugurated as governor. Nevertheless, this was not the end of the controversy, for McDaniel challenged the results of the election, alleging extensive election fraud and other errors favoring the Republican. Eventually, both parties agreed to a recount, which soon increased Donnell's lead to 7,000, causing McDaniel to withdraw his challenge. During this controversy some of the state's newspapers, led by the *St. Louis Post-Dispatch*, accused Mayor

Dickmann and other Democratic leaders of having engineered the attempt to steal the governorship. Apparently, these accusations resulted in Dickmann losing the mayoral race that spring to Limbaugh's good friend, St. Louis Court of Appeals Judge William D. Becker.[18]

Donnell appointed Limbaugh as one of his colonels, a largely ceremonial position, and asked him to participate in the inaugural ceremonies in Jefferson City. In preparation for this, Limbaugh purchased a military uniform for himself, and a formal gown for Bee. They and their son Stephen traveled by automobile with William J. Kies Sr., chairman of the County of Cape Girardeau Republican committee, and his wife. As part of the festivities, Limbaugh and Donnell's other colonels marched in a parade through the main streets of Jefferson City to the capitol building. After the swearing in and other ceremonies, the Limbaughs joined other dignitaries at the inaugural ball. Afterwards, Donnell sought to appoint Limbaugh to serve as the state's superintendent of insurance. The governor's advisor Barak Mattingly informed him it was the best office then available. Limbaugh, however, declined the position, stating his preference to remain in Cape Girardeau and practice law. Moreover, Limbaugh intended to make his son Rush, who was then completing his last year in law school, a partner in his firm.[19]

During this period, Limbaugh became increasingly concerned about the gathering war clouds in Europe. As a young man he had enthusiastically supported all efforts to end the Great War, and had only reluctantly supported the United States' entrance into the conflict after Germany's repeated provocations. Despite his initial hesitancy, Limbaugh fully participated in supporting the war—registering for the draft, training in a militia unit, and making speeches to rally the public and to sell war bonds. After Germany's capitulation, Limbaugh had hoped that war might be made obsolete through the establishment of the League of Nations, where countries could negotiate their disagreements. Furthermore, he had supported the founding of international courts to adjudicate legal disputes, another means for defusing disagreements between countries. Being a pragmatic man, however, after observing the ineffectiveness of these international organizations, Limbaugh, although not abandoning them altogether, no longer expected much from them either. Thus when expressing his views publicly, he sometimes noted dangerous trends in world affairs. As early as Herbert Hoover's presidency, he had noted the danger Benito Mussolini, the dictator of Italy, represented "to the peace of Europe." In a speech in 1934, Limbaugh detailed how Germany, Austria, and the Balkans had democratized temporarily after the First World War, but in just a few short years these trends had been reversed and "more than one-half of the people of the world [were] under the domination of dictatorships." In particular, the most powerful of these dictatorships were those of Germany, Italy, and the Soviet

Union, and despite the predictions of many to the contrary, Limbaugh doubted that their people would oust Mussolini, Adolph Hitler, or Josef Stalin anytime soon. "These dictators give them the promise of expansion, development, achievement, which satisfies their vanity and encourages their hope." Nevertheless, Limbaugh believed that while the international climate then favored dictatorship and military conquest, he also thought that men of goodwill must be prepared to encourage a movement toward democracy and peace when the opportunity presented itself.[20]

On May 10, 1940, however, hopes for peace were shattered when Germany crossed the Rhine, attacking the Netherlands, Belgium, and Luxembourg along the extensive fortifications of the Siegfried Line. That morning at six o'clock, Limbaugh arrived at his office, where a special edition of the *St. Louis Globe-Democrat* announced that Germany had invaded the Low Countries. Having a very full and busy day ahead of him, Limbaugh drove to Wayne County, where he attended to various matters related to the Wappapello land cases until that evening. Without a radio in his automobile, in suspense, Limbaugh returned home where he finally learned more about the events in Europe. Sadly, he concluded that another world war had begun. Recognizing that the United States might soon become entangled in the conflict, he and Bee discussed the matter for many hours before retiring that night. Later that summer their concerns increased with the beginning of the Battle of Britain— a German air assault upon London and other strategic points in preparation for an expected German invasion.[21]

Before the attack upon Pearl Harbor, many Americans, including a majority of Missourians, supported the establishment of a military draft, while still hoping that somehow the country might remain out of the conflict. In September 1940, the United States Congress passed legislation requiring all men from the ages of twenty-one to thirty-five to register for the draft. Because in just a few months Rush Jr. would be twenty-one years old and Manley eighteen, this and other preparations for war in the coming months were met somberly by Limbaugh and Bee. In a speech on May 5, 1941, before the Chamber of Commerce in Anna, Illinois, Limbaugh, who by then was convinced that the United States must soon enter the war, spoke directly to those who wished for the United States to remain neutral in the conflict. Noting the efforts of "all theorists or pacifists or isolationists or others" to avoid war, Limbaugh urged everyone to face the reality that Hitler intended to destroy "the things for which America stands" and that we had a choice "either voluntarily to become a vassal of Hitler or make war upon him." Limbaugh also reminded his audience of a long tradition of American involvement in world affairs, arguing that the country should prepare for war and create a military force so powerful "that other nations will respect us enough to listen to reason and not keep continuously starting fights." Many Americans agreed with Limbaugh, believing that England's defeat would seriously harm American interests abroad and enable Germany to prepare for the eventual conquest of North America. Thus, most Missourians supported the repeal of the Neutrality Acts, which had prohibited private or public help to warring nations in arms, war materials, and loans, and approved of the lend-lease arrangement to provide aid to England and the Soviet Union. In September 1941, Roosevelt announced his order to the United States Navy to attack German and Italian naval forces whenever necessary to defend themselves against aggression.[22]

To finish law school, Rush Jr. had obtained a deferment from the local draft board and in June 1941 was allowed two more weeks delay to take the bar examinations before entering the United States Army. Perhaps increasing everyone's anxiety, the day before Rush Jr.'s departure, the German military on June 22 invaded the Soviet Union. After his induction into the military at Jefferson Barracks in St. Louis, he was sent to Fort Warren near Cheyenne, Wyoming, where he spent the summer and fall training. Shortly after the Japanese attack on Pearl Harbor on December 7, 1941, Rush Jr. surprised the family when they received a telegram from him announcing that he had volunteered to serve in the Army Air Corps. This decision by their eldest son caused Limbaugh and Bee some concern and anxiety, for they understood that serving as a pilot was very dangerous. Nevertheless, believing as they did that the Axis powers must be defeated, they determined to support him and the war effort in any manner possible.[23]

Rush Jr.'s pilot training began at Brooks Field near San Antonio, Texas, at the Gulf Coast Air Training Center, where the Advanced Flying School prepared military pilots. A short time after he began his training, he made his first solo flight from an airfield near Cameron, Texas, a small town between San Antonio and Dallas. When Rush Jr. was sent to Perrin Field near Sherman, Texas, north of Dallas, Limbaugh and Bee traveled there by train and after a short visit returned home. To provide him with the reassurance of faith and to strengthen him spiritually for the trials ahead, Bee gave her oldest son a pocket-sized New Testament, which she admonished him to read. While in Texas, Rush Jr. crashed his plane into a cornfield after flying around bad weather and running out of fuel. This type of incident was not unusual and a number of young pilots were killed in similar incidents. Afterwards, Rush Jr. was stationed in Tullahoma, Tennessee, at Camp Forrest, where he trained pilots to fly the A-20, a twin-engine light attack bomber and fighter. This was one of the largest training facilities in operation during the war, receiving some of the first German prisoners-of-war from the Africa campaign while he was there. Telephoning beforehand, he flew over his parents' home. Limbaugh and Bee watched from their backyard with awe and joy as he flew a B-25, another twin-engine bomber, over their home (flying a little too low), creating considerable concern among some of Cape Girardeau's residents.[24]

Next, Rush Jr. was transferred to Key Field at Meridian, Mississippi, where he trained to fly the P-51 Mustang fighter, at the time the best aircraft of its kind known for its wonderful maneuverability and speed. He also instructed other pilots, although this was only a temporary duty and it was apparent that he would soon be ordered to a war zone somewhere. Just before his departure to Florida for more training, Rush Jr. received an overnight leave, flying from Mississippi to Harris Field, the new military airfield near Cape Girardeau. Limbaugh was impressed with his son's enthusiasm as he explained the wonders of the P-51 to the family. The next morning, the family accompanied Rush Jr. to Harris Field where he demonstrated his capabilities as a pilot of the Mustang fighter, buzzing the airfield, and pulling from a dive into a "corkscrew maneuver" before returning to Mississippi. While in Florida, just before going overseas, Rush Jr. underwent surgery to remove a pilonidal cyst, a common malady experienced by aviators. Bee and Stephen traveled by train to see to his needs and offer encouragement.[25]

After his recovery, Rush Jr. flew with his squadron over the Atlantic Ocean to the Azores Islands, and from there across the Mediterranean Sea and the Middle East to Karachi, India—now part of Pakistan. There a training command prepared flight crews "for combat and transport duty." Attached to the transport wing, he primarily flew the twin-engine C-46 Commando. The Commando was a workhorse capable of carrying up to 40,000 pounds of cargo and staying aloft with only one working engine unless it was overloaded, a common circumstance for most of the missions. While not flying bombing missions, the duty was still dangerous, especially those requiring flight over the Himalayas, or "the Hump," as it came to be known. Moreover, a number of unexplained midair explosions of the C-46 occurred, and the problem, leaking fuel lines, was not discovered until late in the war. When it was determined that it was no longer necessary to retain Chinese troops in Burma against Japanese forces there, Rush Jr. and other Commando crews ferried home over 25,000 Chinese soldiers and 249 American liaison personnel and their equipment, which included 1,600 horses and mules, and many trucks, artillery, and other matériel.[26]

Perhaps as compensation for the great anxiety of having their oldest son flying missions overseas, Manley and Stephen served in the military stateside. Manley became interested in naval aviation through a friend in Cape Girardeau. Before joining the Navy, Manley participated in a local club of aviation enthusiasts called the Flying Indians, and later trained at a civilian flight school in Muscatine, Iowa, for three months. He joined the Navy in June 1942 and was sent to Iowa City, Iowa, for his preflight training, but failed to complete the very rigorous training required to land aircraft upon carriers. On February

26, 1943, he married Mary Heagler. Limbaugh and Bee welcomed Mary into their family without reservation. Sometime after her marriage, Mary remembered walking with Bee and her saying that she had "always wanted a daughter and [now] I have one. And that's just the way they both treated me." Still wishing to serve his country, Manley entered the Army and attended basic training in Wichita Falls, Texas. After this, he was stationed at Harlingen Field in southern Texas, where he trained to be an aircraft gunner. He also trained to become an aircraft mechanic. Eventually, he was stationed at Davis-Monthan Field near Tucson, Arizona, working on B-29 aircraft. Newly developed, the Superfortress was the war's most sophisticated bomber. During its development, the aircraft underwent a number of modifications and it was only with great difficulty that it became available to the military by early 1944. One of its significant design problems was the tendency of its engines to overheat and catch fire under stress, often causing a catastrophic failure of the wing. For this and other reasons, Manley and the other aircraft mechanics experienced great difficulties in keeping the fifty-one B-29s based at Davis-Monthan Field flying, and generally were able to keep only about fifteen operational at a time. Fortunately, the engine problem was at least partially fixed by the installation of "banana peelers," or baffles, which directed a greater flow of air into the engine. Mary, who was able to stay with Manley in Tucson, returned to Cape Girardeau and moved into the Limbaughs' home to await the birth of their first grandchild, John Manley, who arrived on March 5, 1944. As the new mother accustomed herself to motherhood, Bee assisted her in various ways. Mary also remembered her father-in-law telling her with affectionate humor that she would never again have an uninterrupted night of sleep. For, he explained, at night newborns demand to be fed and other attentions. As they grow older into adolescence and adulthood, parents were inevitably nagged by various concerns until their offspring move away. By this time, although freed from their former concerns, parents were then at an age when uninterrupted sleep was no longer physically possible.[27]

To gain as much information about the war's progress and other events, the Limbaughs listened to radio broadcasts at noon and in the late evening hours. In particular, Limbaugh enjoyed Edward R. Murrow's broadcasts from London, along with Hans von Kaltenborn, who reported on various crises in Asia and Europe during the 1930s and the war, and William L. Shirer, who later wrote about his experiences as a correspondent in Berlin from 1934 to 1941 and penned a very important history, *The Rise and Fall of the Third Reich.* Because a housing shortage then existed, families with extra rooms in their homes were asked to rent them out. As the Limbaughs had already provided rooms to a number of nieces and nephews attending college, they naturally did their part by opening their home to others. In 1940, they boarded four college men, and in 1941 they provided a room to Miss Geneva Parmley, a college English instructor, who was a low-maintenance boarder in comparison to the college men.[28]

In 1942, the Limbaughs invited into their home Helen, the daughter of Limbaugh's brother Roscoe and his wife Josie, and Bland Seabaugh Jr., the son of Bee's brother, a superintendent of schools in Hornersville, Missouri. Helen did a variety of tasks about the house and often prepared lunch and sometimes drove to her Uncle Rush's office to bring him home for lunch and supper. This was very helpful, for during the day Bee cared for her mother, who lived three doors down the street with her sister Myrtle while she was teaching. Helen also helped with the preparation of supper, which generally consisted of meat, potatoes, and salad. She remembered meals as delightful times when everyone conversed and joked.[29]

The United States' involvement in World War Two changed the lives of all Americans. The manufacture of naval ships, aircraft, artillery, rifles, and other military supplies required the mobilization of the country's entire industrial power and resources. Thus, the Roosevelt administration requested that Americans no longer be wasteful and instituted the rationing of those materials important to the war effort. To supplement their food supply, which was rationed, many Americans, including the Limbaughs, cultivated large gardens. The restrictions upon gasoline and tires complicated Limbaugh's ability to confer with clients in the surrounding towns and counties where he practiced; especially his work on the Wappapello land litigation. Women, whose traditional role was in the home, were encouraged to work in the war factories, which sprang up all over the country. Bee, although not working in a factory, contributed in a number of ways through community organizations. After the military established Harris Field near Cape Girardeau to train pilots, Bee helped in the promotion of various social events for the young men and invited a number of them into their home for Sunday dinner. After these men completed their training and departed southeast Missouri, she carried on a correspondence with them and sent gift boxes in the same manner she did for her sons.[30]

Having turned fifty a short time before the attack on Pearl Harbor, Limbaugh recognized that he was well past the age for service as a soldier; nevertheless, he, with the help of Bee, was able to make a number of important contributions to the war effort as well. As he had done during the First World War, Limbaugh made public speeches supporting the war and in April 1943 on KFVS Radio he urged listeners to purchase war bonds. Furthermore, he served on a county legal advisory board to help men answer selective service questionnaires and, as he had done during the Great War, Limbaugh served as a prosecuting attorney for Cape Girardeau County, being appointed to the position temporarily while the regular prosecuting attorney, James A. Finch Jr., served in the military.[31]

Limbaugh's most important service to the war effort, however, was his work for the War Emergency Pipelines program. In the summer of 1942, he was asked to serve as the Missouri counsel for the government to examine titles to land through which the pipelines would be laid. This project was of the highest priority and was necessary to protect oil shipments from Texas to the East Coast, which were vulnerable to attack at sea by German U-boats. When Limbaugh was contacted, "professional right-of-way men" were already notifying landowners to gain voluntary easements, allowing the government to excavate six-foot trenches through their land into which was placed the twenty-four inch pipeline from Longview, Texas, to Norris City, Illinois—a line which was later extended to Phoenixville, Pennsylvania. Limbaugh's task included providing legal counsel concerning the easements from Little Rock, Arkansas, to Norris City, Illinois—a distance of almost 400 miles. Despite his enthusiasm for making a real contribution to the war effort, Limbaugh feared that his other professional duties might leave him with insufficient time to accomplish his task. The work was already begun in Texas and the men were laying the pipeline at a rate of five miles per day. Upon accepting the work, he "immediately began receiving arms full of easements to examine and pass upon, abstracts upon which to furnish legal opinions, and inquiries as to what could or could not be done."[32]

To gain enough time to complete this work, Limbaugh concluded that he must discontinue his work on the third volume to his Missouri Practice series, suspend teaching his young men's Sunday school class, and severely restrict leisure and social activities. To prevent any unnecessary distractions, Bee and his son Stephen, who was then in high school, helped Limbaugh by running errands and other miscellaneous tasks he normally did himself. By thus strictly budgeting his time, he accomplished the work for the War Emergency Pipelines project. It was during this period that his niece Helen remembered him working from early in the morning until late at night. In the winter months, because of wartime rationing in the evenings, the heat was turned off to the building where his law office was located. For this reason, he worked at home, placing papers and books on a card table, where he remained until late into the night. She observed that "law was the center of his life. Law came first, and second, and third, and last," as indeed it must, given the immense burden he had shouldered. After the war, the United States government sold the pipeline to the Texas Eastern Transmission Corporation with which Limbaugh established a long association, providing legal counsel and representation regarding various issues related to the pipelines.[33]

With sons serving in the military, Limbaugh found less inspiring Judge Rubey M. Hulen's appointment of him to represent a number of conscientious objectors to the war. Nevertheless, regarding it as an important part of his duty as a lawyer to ensure that everyone received vigorous representation of their interests in court, Limbaugh accepted the task of defending a number of Jehovah's Witnesses for refusing to be inducted into the United States military. In the community it was suspected that some of the young men had joined the church to avoid military service. Without a legal basis upon which to represent his clients' interests, Limbaugh argued that the defendants were only "answerable to the laws of God and not the laws of men." Judge Hulen, however, instructed the jury members, who were generally hostile to the defendants, that such a statement was no defense. Most of these cases were tried in 1944 and the defendants received sentences from Judge Hulen ranging from one year and one day to five years prison time. In five of these cases, two of the men received probation soon after their convictions, but the others were delivered to a federal penitentiary, presumably remaining there for the duration of their sentences. What is more, the negative mood of the community against conscientious objectors was shared by a majority of the members of Limbaugh's church, the Centenary United Methodist Church. A young minister, Don. E. Schooler, had served there since 1937, and while not a pacifist, "was highly opposed to any type of warfare." Although an "engaging young minister," his views were not shared by the majority of the congregation, and he voluntarily decided to return to Oklahoma. Schooler's replacement, G. C. Fain, "was a true pacifist"; a position that was tolerated until he exhibited what most of the members, including Limbaugh, considered unpatriotic behavior when Fain opposed displaying the United States flag in church. This caused a great uproar among the congregation and led to the minister's departure.[34]

As the war was coming to a close, not long after Germany surrendered, the Limbaughs' youngest son, Stephen, graduated from high school in May 1945 and joined the Navy. Seeing their last and youngest son, who was still only seventeen years old, enter the military service was very difficult. Both Limbaugh and Bee found it nearly impossible to hold back the tears when saying their goodbyes at the train station, feeling great sadness at his departure. Later after Japan's surrender, they visited Stephen at the Great Lakes training center near Chicago. Soon, the Limbaughs received the welcome news that the Army had discharged Manley from service and that he would soon be home. By the end of 1945, Rush Jr. also returned from his service overseas, leaving only Stephen in the military. After basic training, he reported to a naval aircraft station in New Orleans and remained in the service for a year and a half, although he never went to sea. With the safe return of their sons and the defeat of the Axis powers, the Limbaughs had much for which to be thankful. Nevertheless, this happiness was somewhat subdued, for many young men in the community, including their nephew Bland Seabaugh Jr., did not return home. Bland Jr., who had stayed in their home for two years, and for whom they had developed a strong affection, was killed while serving as a tanker in Patton's Third Army. His death seemed especially tragic for it occurred in April 1945, a short time before the war's end. He had received notice to report for duty while staying at their home and had left from there to be inducted. It was with sadness that they remembered this young man, then so "quick to learn, vibrant with life, dependable, truthful, conscientious, and kind." When Bee learned of her nephew's serious wounding, she and her sister Myrtle traveled to her brother and sister-in-law's home in Hornersville to offer support and await further news. On Sunday, April 15, a memorial service was held, at which Limbaugh spoke. After the war, he kept a picture of his nephew on the wall of his library to keep alive the memory and sacrifice of the young man, who had shown so much potential.[35]

On the eve of the first Memorial Day after the war's close, the municipal band and the American Legion posts of Jackson and Cape Girardeau organized a memorial service for the 112 men from Cape Girardeau County killed in the war. The service was held at Houck Field Stadium on the campus of Southeast Missouri State University. Martial and Christian music was played by the municipal band and the American Legion's drum and bugle corps—the Golden Troupers—a solo was sung, and Limbaugh gave the main address. After reviewing the long history of Cape Girardeau County's men answering the call of their country, he sadly noted the great and ultimate sacrifice each of the men had made.

> We pause now to honor those 112 brave men whose names we shall ever remember, whose courage, devotion, and sacrifice we shall always revere. They are of our flesh and blood. They have lived, seen sunset's glow and died nobly and honorably. Yesterday they were on our streets, in our schools and churches, cheering and enriching the firesides of our homes. Today they are in the eternal company of the nation's martyrs. The echo of their cheerful 'Hellos,' their reassuring 'Goodbyes' still linger on the vales of memory. They grew to maturity in the complacent environment of those who cherished the thought that the war to end war had been fought. . . . The American armies of the Second World War have disbanded. The American navies have melted away. The vast air power of the nation is still and inactive. But there will be no general order to disband this army of the dead. Their names shall ever be a benediction to their loved ones and their countrymen.

In this fitting manner, Limbaugh memorialized these young men and consoled their families. In his peroration, he noted that their sacrifice had bestowed upon the country "the blessings of American life, the stability of her character, the nobility of her faith, the hope of her Christian ideals, the realization of her democratic aims, the opportunities for her service to mankind."[36]

Chapter Nine

Limbaugh & Limbaugh

On the morning of January 1, 1946, Rush H. Limbaugh, then fifty-four years of age, walked with his oldest son downtown to his office where they drafted an agreement establishing a law partnership. Rush Jr., who before joining the military had taken and passed the bar examinations, had returned home only the day before. For the next forty years he would work with his father. To this point, Limbaugh had handled his extensive practice alone and welcomed his son's help. Like his father, Rush Jr. soon became immersed in professional and community affairs. Until his marriage almost three and a half years later, he lived at home with his parents. Limbaugh's and Bee's middle son, Manley, and his wife Mary decided to live nearby while he completed his college degree and obtained his certificate to teach high school science. Eventually they settled in Chester, Illinois. Limbaugh had carefully refrained from exerting any pressure on his sons to become lawyers. At this time the Limbaughs' youngest son, Stephen, was in the United States Navy, stationed at New Orleans, and after his discharge began his undergraduate studies during the fall of 1946 at Southeast Missouri State University in Cape Girardeau.[1]

The most important clients of Limbaugh & Limbaugh were the Erlbacher Brothers, whom Limbaugh had represented in various capacities. This association began in 1936 when Limbaugh unsuccessfully defended Eddie Erlbacher against a charge of automobile theft. Fortunately for him, coincident with his arrival to prison, the superintendent's automobile was not running properly and no one seemed to know how to fix it. Eddie offered to take a look and soon repaired it. Because of his mechanical aptitude, which would serve the Erlbachers well for many years thereafter, Eddie gained favorable treatment by maintaining the automobiles of prison personnel during his incarceration. After his release, Eddie formed a partnership with his wife and brother Robert to construct and operate diesel towboats, and also established the only dry dock between Memphis and St. Louis for barge transportation. In 1940, one of the Erlbachers' boats, *The Reese*, sank near Memphis, and Limbaugh was called to the scene to attend to the many associated problems under admiralty law, a field of the law new to him.[2]

On three different occasions, Limbaugh traveled to Washington, DC, to represent the Erlbachers' commercial interests before the Interstate Commerce Commission (ICC). After the war, Limbaugh helped the Erlbachers to negotiate with the United States Navy to purchase as military surplus eight powerful engines used in PT boats. These craft were designed to attack enemy destroyers and relied on the twelve-cylinder engines manufactured by the Packard Motor Car Corporation to attack and escape with great speed. The Erlbachers traveled to San Diego and chose diesel engines not used during the war. This purchase was a particularly good one, for the motors were powerful, reliable, and durable, the last of them not being changed out until 2007.[3]

Another aspect of the firm's business benefitting from war surplus related to Limbaugh's work on the emergency pipeline project. In 1947 the United States government sold this vast network to the Texas Eastern Transmission Corporation, a firm established to purchase the pipeline. One of the leaders of this corporation was Charles I. Francis, a member of a Houston law firm and a former college debate opponent with whom Limbaugh had competed at the University of Texas at Austin. Once it had acquired the pipeline, Texas Eastern began employing lawyers in every state through which the pipeline traversed to superintend the reexamination of titles and easements. Limbaugh completed his part of this work before Christmas but continued his association with the firm afterward as their general counsel in Missouri. Perhaps, because his practice was growing rapidly, in 1948 Limbaugh hired Florence Hyde Hines, the daughter of his good friend, Supreme Court of Missouri Judge Laurance M. Hyde. In 1950, however, because her husband obtained employment elsewhere, she resigned her position. Limbaugh then hired Joseph J. Russell, a 1949 graduate of the University of Missouri law school. Raised in Cape Girardeau, Russell was a veteran of the Second World War and had just passed the bar examination.[4]

In 1951, Limbaugh's youngest son, Stephen, graduated from law school and began the practice of law in the family firm. He believed that this was fortunate, for otherwise it would have been difficult to find a position elsewhere. The situation was ideal, for his father and brother were always available to answer questions and provide direction. The atmosphere of the office, the tone of which was set by his father, was professional and cordial, and work was conducted in a spirit of cooperation. The first work Stephen did was approving titles for the Cape Girardeau Building and Loan Association. Before a loan could be approved, titles were investigated to determine that the buyer of the property had a title unencumbered by liens or other problems. While the work was tedious, Stephen considered it "an excellent introduction to the lending and to the real estate areas" of law. This type of work kept him employed until he built up his own clientele. He gained his first clients through default; his father and brother being too busy to attend to their business themselves. Other clients, after initially consulting with his father, were assigned to him. Both he and his brother Rush also began to take over more and more work as their father became increasingly involved in his activities with the American Bar Association (ABA), the Missouri Bar, and the State Historical Society of Missouri, among other professional organizations.[5]

During his first years as a lawyer, Stephen learned much from his father, especially regarding proper business practices and legal ethics. In representing the best interests of his clients, Limbaugh believed that it was generally better to negotiate with the other party rather than to go to court, considering litigation an action of last resort. Nevertheless, when circumstances made it necessary, Stephen gained the opportunity to assist his father in trials as "second chair." In this capacity it was generally his responsibility to cross-examine the other side's witnesses. Before the trial they discussed their strategy, how to proceed, what information to elicit from witnesses, what questions to avoid, and how to handle particular witnesses. In the midst of cases they often evaluated how the trial was proceeding and sometimes modified their strategy to meet unforeseen difficulties or challenges. Generally, they sought to emphasize the strong points of their case and "gloss over" the troublesome parts. Stephen believed that his father was especially helpful in detailing to him what to expect from different lawyers. As with other people, some lawyers were reliable while others were not. Moreover, lawyers could be bad influences on their clients, causing them to do what they normally would never attempt otherwise. With the benefit of his father's experience and guidance, Stephen believed he had every opportunity to succeed. Thus, when in 1953 he handled his first case alone, a suit for damages against the driver of an automobile who had struck and injured a little girl, he credited his father's training and direction with making the victory possible. Because his father and brother thought the case a losing one, they greeted Stephen's report of winning a $2,000 judgment for his young client and her parents with great excitement and congratulations.[6]

By this period, Limbaugh's reputation as a lawyer was at its apex and it was natural for him to be tapped for important positions and tasks where his experience, expertise, and integrity contributed to the improvement of the legal profession. Thus, in 1950 the Supreme Court of Missouri appointed him a special commissioner to determine whether Armour and Company had violated Missouri's antitrust laws, against whom the state's attorney general had brought suit. Limbaugh conducted hearings in Columbia, St. Louis, Jefferson City, Kansas City, St. Joseph, and Springfield and researched extensively the Sherman Antitrust legislation "and its Missouri counterpart." For these hearings, Limbaugh recommended to the court that Herman DaCosta be employed as court reporter to keep a record of the proceedings. He had worked with Limbaugh during the Muench kidnapping trial when he had served as a special commissioner for the St. Louis Court of Appeals (see chapter seven). Finding DaCosta to be companionable and hardworking, Limbaugh wished to reward him for his diligence and many kindnesses in the former proceedings.[7]

In his discussions with State Attorney General Jonathan E. Taylor and representatives of Armour and Company, Limbaugh learned that the company did not deny that it was fixing the price of its soap. Therefore, the only substantial question remaining was whether the company's marketing practices violated Missouri's antitrust law. Discovering that no precedent existed to guide him in his decision, Limbaugh investigated the history behind the enactment of the Sherman Antitrust Act of 1890 to understand the legislative context within which Missouri's antitrust legislation was enacted. Limbaugh enjoyed historical research and had thought carefully about its proper application to the law. While he recognized that the courts were not unanimous concerning the value of examining "the legislative history of a statute," or even to what extent or limit such an investigation should proceed, Limbaugh noted that whenever a statute was "ambiguous," or its meaning was "doubtful," a consensus had developed that it was appropriate for the courts to examine the historical record. This method of determining the intent of legislators in the drafting and passing of legislation, Limbaugh noted, was fraught with potential pitfalls, even when examining "the debates and reports of a legislative body." Nevertheless, he believed that over the decades the method had proven to be useful, even necessary, to the proper determination of legislative intent in difficult cases.[8]

The premise underlying Limbaugh's desire to learn the Missouri General Assembly's intent in passing its antitrust legislation in 1891 and after was the idea that the Supreme Court of Missouri's job was to enforce the legislature's intent so long as it did not violate the state or federal constitutions. The Court's duty was *not* to determine what was best or right; ideally, however, by effecting the legislature's purpose the result would benefit society. Thus it was important, Limbaugh believed, "to construe the purpose of the legislature in giving an effective remedy for the evils in light of the conditions obtaining at the time, and honestly and faithfully, when considered historically, to put upon the language used its plain and rational meaning and promote its object and manifest purpose." Having asserted this basic jurisprudential purpose, Limbaugh also recognized the reality that legislation, once enforced and interpreted by the state authorities and the courts, could, if sufficient time transpired, be used to address "conditions unforeseen by its authors . . . to meet problems far beyond the expectation and the purposes of its authors." Thus it was necessary to apply one's interpretation of the legislation according to the drafters' intent while adapting it to the circumstances of the time. After an extensive consideration of the history of antitrust law and Missouri precedent, Limbaugh concluded in his report as special commissioner that although the legislature did not have in mind the specific type of price fixing employed by Armour and Company in this instance, the legislation was general enough that it was clear the company had violated the law. The Supreme Court of Missouri adopted his report, which included extensive findings in fact and law, and assessed "a substantial penalty" against Armour and Company.[9]

Supreme Court of Missouri Judges Laurance M. Hyde and S. P. Dalton thought enough of Limbaugh's report to express to him their approval and Hiram Lesar, a law professor at the University of Missouri, requested that he submit an article on antitrust law for the *Missouri Law Review*. In it he traced "the origin of the Sherman Anti-Trust Act and its Missouri counterpart," demonstrating a mastery of a vast array of historical and legal scholarship as well as the numerous cases consulted in his report. Considering Limbaugh's work to be authoritative on Missouri's antitrust law, in a 1955 antitrust case both John M. Dalton, attorney general of Missouri, and A. P. Stone Jr., judge of the Missouri Court of Appeals, cited Limbaugh's report. Dalton described it as "exhaustive and erudite," and his law review article as "excellent and enlightening." Judge Stone, in an opinion while sitting as a Special Judge appointed by the Supreme Court of Missouri to the Southern District, agreed with the attorney general's assessment of Limbaugh's report, noting that the court concurred with "Commissioner Limbaugh in the Armour case that there is no escape from the conclusion that vertical agreements or understandings for fixing or maintaining resale prices are within the prohibition of our Missouri anti-trust statutes."[10]

His tenure as special commissioner to the state supreme court and his extensive scholarship on probate law in Missouri probably led to Limbaugh's appointment in the fall of 1953 to serve as an advisor with Probate Judge Leslie A. Welch and Professor Lesar to assist a legislative committee in drafting a new probate code for Missouri. This area of the law had long been of particular interest to Limbaugh, who as a six-year-old boy had observed his dying father consult with a legal advisor and solemnly sign his will. As a lawyer, he had advised and drafted wills for many clients, and at the end of his long career estimated that he had written "perhaps as many as 3,000" altogether. Some of these were drafted for clients whose health was deteriorating and were not expected to live much longer. In his practice over the years, Limbaugh had observed how the needs and wishes of testators had changed and he considered reform of the probate code long overdue.[11]

Limbaugh and his fellow advisors met in Jefferson City every other weekend through much of 1954, researching and drafting their code. Because it was necessary to complete their work in time for the 1955 legislative session, the advisors and the committee felt much pressure to meet the deadline. Beginning in 1946, Limbaugh and Bee had regularly attended the ABA's annual meetings and had become friends with many top lawyers and their wives throughout the country. By the time of his appointment as an advisor to the legislative committee, Limbaugh had become particularly involved in the work of the Real Property, Probate, and Trust Law Section—a very large group promoting educational programs and the improvement of the law in these important areas. In 1948 he had served on the Probate Courts: Law and Procedure Committee, which produced a report considering problems related to the 1948 Internal Revenue Act. He was also appointed vice-chairman of the section's real property division for two years beginning in 1950. By 1954 he was vice-chairman of the section and during its meeting was elected chair. In 1955, when he began his tenure as chair, the section had 3,000 members, which grew to 3,450 under his leadership.[12]

For several decades, many involved in the probate practice had recognized the need for reform. Writing at the end of the nineteenth century, Judge John G. Woerner, commenting on the state of the probate code passed in 1825, noted that it had "been refined upon and loaded down with multitudinous and heterogeneous amendments to which every session of the legislature has diligently contributed, not always in the spirit of the original act, nor conducive to perspicuity and efficiency of its detail." In 1939, in the second volume of his work on the practice of Missouri law, Limbaugh had written extensively about probate law and had offered suggestions for its improvement. In 1950, a special committee of the Missouri Bar chaired by Judge Welch, spent three years "surveying the field of existing probate law, listing its endless imperfections, and planning its reform." In 1953, Welch presented to the legislature his proposal for the drafting of a new code leading to the formation of a Joint Probate Laws Committee, which was composed of five members from each house of the General Assembly. In their work, the committee and its advisors, of which Limbaugh was a member, considered new codes from other states, obtained advice from lawyers who had reformed the codes of their states, and inspected some of Missouri's probate records. Using the ABA's *Model Probate Code* as their starting point, the committee and advisors drafted a code, which then underwent revision after "lawyers of great skill and ability" had studied it and suggested changes. The code passed both houses of the General Assembly almost unanimously and became law on January 1, 1956. Limbaugh, exemplifying the scholar-lawyer, wrote an excellent article for the *Washington University Law Quarterly*, providing an historical account of Missouri's probate law and the need for reform.[13]

In recognition of Limbaugh's many contributions to the legal profession and his expected election to the presidency of the Missouri Bar, the University of Missouri law school requested that he present the 1955 Earl F. Nelson Memorial Lecture. Entitled "The Public Duty of the American Lawyer," Limbaugh focused on the public's contradictory opinions of the legal profession, sometimes considering lawyers to be nothing more than parasites, and on other occasions holding them in high esteem. Lawyers, Limbaugh believed, were responsible for these opinions, for they too often have acquiesced in, or even indulged the ethical lapses of their colleagues. Limbaugh, however, expressed some optimism, for through their professional organizations many lawyers were then attempting to rejuvenate the "highest traditions of honor and service" to their profession. Limbaugh believed that all lawyers, regardless of their rank or prosperity, should give back to society through public service and the maintenance of "the nation's tranquillity and sense of justice." This required lawyers always to act in the best interest of their clients and with integrity by "adher[ing] to the recognized standards of professional conduct." These standards, collected in the Canons of Professional Ethics, exhorted lawyers always to behave "as an honest man and as a patriotic and loyal citizen." Furthermore, Limbaugh asserted that a lawyer has the duty to enforce these standards whenever they are violated. Finally, he argued that it was the duty of a lawyer to shape public opinion and accept public office.[14]

To Limbaugh these standards of conduct were not simply a matter of intellectual inquiry, for over a period of almost forty years, he had practiced law ethically, had given hundreds of speeches, receiving no compensation for most of them, served as a state representative at great financial loss, accepted the calls to act as a special commissioner for both the St. Louis Court of Appeals and the Supreme Court of Missouri, and worked on several state and professional committees to improve public policy and the legal profession. In the midst of his professional duties, Limbaugh somehow had found time to serve the community as president of the Rotary Club, as a member of the Board of Trustees for the Southeast Missouri Hospital, as a member of the advisory board of the Salvation Army, and as one of the vice-presidents of the State Historical Society of Missouri. As chairman of the ABA's Real Property, Probate, and Trust Law Section, Limbaugh "began a year of endless travel, successive meetings, and grueling work" in the interest of improving the legal profession through the organized bar. In 1935, as special commissioner for the St. Louis court, Limbaugh had confronted Attorney Wilfred Jones for committing perjury and had notified the circuit attorney of this breach of legal ethics.[15]

During the 1955 annual meeting of the Missouri Bar, Limbaugh was elected president.[16] His duties included attending and often addressing regional and out-of-state bar meetings and law school functions;[17] directing the organization of meetings and seminars;[18] presiding over executive committee meetings;[19] disseminating important professional information, including the new probate code;[20] promoting reforms such as new rules of criminal procedure and the protection of neglected and abused children;[21] appointing members to various committees;[22] the coordination with other state bars on policy matters;[23]

making recommendations on the appointment of judges;[24] and improving the image of lawyers through public relations.[25] In these efforts, Limbaugh shielded the state bar association from entering partisan politics and fulfilled his responsibilities with the best interest of its members and the profession always in mind.

As president of the Missouri Bar, Limbaugh occasionally had unpleasant tasks to perform. One of these concerned the investigation of alleged lawyer misbehavior, which he handled discretely, even offering to mediate a dispute involving a lawyer in Cape Girardeau. Another was the expression of condolences to the families of lawyers and judges who had suffered serious health problems or had passed away. In addition to sending flowers, Limbaugh often attended as a representative of the bar, or arranged for another officer to attend the funeral. To promote the financial well being of the members, most of whom were self-employed, he supported an increase in fees for lawyers and salaries for judges who worked for the state and negotiated to make available healthcare insurance through a group plan. Concerning the latter he had negotiated a special policy to cover as many members as possible and received word in a letter from a member, whose voice box and vocal cords had been removed, that "the group insurance for the members of the Bar has been a wonderful thing for me." Limbaugh's final responsibility was to organize and host the annual meeting held in St. Louis. Drawing upon his extensive friendships in the ABA, Limbaugh brought from different parts of the country speakers, one of whom was a former president of that organization, to provide major addresses to the bar. When at the end of the conference he was able to hand over the duties of the presidency to his successor, Limbaugh and Bee were relieved to be "released from responsibilities that had burdened us and exhausted our energies for the last two years." Limbaugh's only regret was that during this period of service in reforming the state probate code and his year as president he had been unable "to get much professional work done in any satisfactory manner."[26]

In the fall of 1956, just as his tenure as president of the Missouri Bar was coming to a close, Limbaugh was elected to serve a three-year term as president of the State Historical Society of Missouri. In 1915, as a college student at the University of Missouri-Columbia, he and two other students had been hired by Floyd C. Shoemaker—who was then beginning a forty-five year career directing the society—to move books from Jones Hall to its new library. For their transport, Shoemaker provided Limbaugh and his fellow students with a small horse-drawn wagon. This work took several days, during which Limbaugh became well acquainted with Shoemaker. In 1931, while Limbaugh was serving in the state House of Representatives, Shoemaker visited him, and thereafter they corresponded and collaborated on various issues important to the society. This friendship led to Limbaugh's involvement in the society's work, his attendance of its annual meetings, and eventually to his election as president. This position, however, only required that he preside over meetings, leaving most of the remaining responsibilities of directing the society to Shoemaker, about whom Limbaugh once humorously stated that the society's director was "ninety-nine and ten-ninths percent" of the organization.[27]

During these years, Limbaugh became increasingly concerned about the gradual decline in Bee's health and energy. For many months in 1945 she had suffered from intermittent but chronic bouts of indigestion and abdominal pain. Gradually, this pain became more persistent, making it increasingly difficult for her to attend to her home, church, and organizational commitments. Often awakened during the night by pain, Bee sometimes found it necessary to drink warm milk to alleviate her suffering. She also restricted her diet in the hope that this would help to improve her condition. It did not. After visits to several doctors, the cause of her malady remained undiagnosed and in June 1946 she submitted to exploratory surgery. The surgeon discovered that the duct from the gall bladder to the small intestine was completely occluded. This problem was repaired, but after several weeks a persistent hoarseness afflicted Bee; a condition doctors attributed to the tubes placed down her throat during surgery. When a throat specialist discovered a tumor in her throat near her vocal cords, it was feared that she had cancer. However, after its removal the tumor was found to be benign, to the great relief of her family. When she returned home, Bee was unable to attend to her many household duties and it was necessary to hire help. By the fall, although still feeling some of the ill effects of her gall bladder surgery, Bee accompanied Limbaugh to Atlantic City for the ABA meeting and afterward traveled on to New York and Boston before returning home. Still feeling weak, she did not attend all of the meetings, nor did she visit many of the sites along the way.[28]

In the coming months, Bee slowly regained her health, although a tube bypassing the occluded duct to her small intestine irritated her side. Perhaps recognizing the need to slow down, she gave up her Sunday school work, but continued to be active in other church and community activities. One of the more important and strenuous tasks she undertook was as a member of a Girl's Town Foundation committee, later working with others to consider building a home for girls in Cape Girardeau. She also served on the foundation's board for three years beginning in 1955.[29]

As they proceeded into their sixties, despite Bee's various health difficulties, the Limbaughs considered themselves fortunate. Their three sons had reached adulthood and each had become successful in their chosen professions. Manley was the first to marry, wedding Mary during the war. Their eldest, Rush Jr., remained a bachelor until May 21, 1949, when he wedded Millie Armstrong in her hometown of Kennett, Missouri. That night, while they were absent from home, a tornado cut a swath "as wide as 352 yards" through Cape Girardeau, destroying property and injuring and killing a number of people. One of the neighborhoods damaged was that of North Henderson Avenue, where the Limbaughs' home stood. In all, twenty-two people were killed, 202 homes were destroyed with another 231 damaged, leaving approximately 1,000 people homeless. The storm also leveled nineteen businesses and damaged fourteen others.[30]

Returning home after the wedding reception, the Limbaughs were completely unaware of the calamity which had befallen them and their neighbors in their absence. Arriving in town, the police, who were directing traffic around the destruction, informed the Limbaughs and directed them to take a circuitous route to their neighborhood. Along the way they saw debris and an unusually large number of people on the sidewalks, streets, and near their cars. Despite driving very slowly, debris eventually prevented them from proceeding by car. The storm had passed through only three hours before. The roof and attic of their home was gone, including many personal items, and much of their property on the second floor was damaged. That night many friends came to offer their condolences and aid, including Limbaugh's brother Roscoe, who, after the wedding had heard about the storm and made his way to them with great difficulty.[31]

Fortunately, that night they were able to sleep at the home of Bee's mother and sister, who lived only three doors down from them but whose home had been left undamaged. Early the next morning Limbaugh went back to survey the destruction. He and Bee were fortunate to receive the aid of many volunteers and friends who helped remove the salvageable property still exposed to the elements. That night they stayed with Limbaugh's sister Lillie in Jackson and afterward lived for a short time in the apartment of their son Rush and new daughter-in-law Millie, who were then absent on their honeymoon. Despite many kind offers of assistance from others, they returned to the home of Bee's mother and sister until their home was rebuilt by the end of the summer. While insurance enabled them to restore their home and replace furnishings and other items, it could not replace various personal items, including keepsakes dear to them. Among these was the framed and signed original of the political cartoon, "The Stork that Failed," given to Limbaugh by Daniel R. Fitzpatrick, the Pulitzer Prize-winning artist for the *St. Louis Post-Dispatch,* in appreciation for the manner in which he had conducted the hearings of the Muench kidnapping case as special commissioner of the St. Louis Court of Appeals.[32]

During this period, the family continued to grow. Born in January 1946, Mary, Manley, and their eldest John welcomed Daniel to their family. In February 1950, Patricia was born and in June 1953 Robert joined them. Almost a year later, Millie bore her first child, Rush III. To distinguish him from his father and grandfather, the family typically referred to him by his nickname: Rusty. On December 27, 1950, the Limbaughs' youngest son Stephen married Anne Mesplay, whom he had met at the University of Missouri-Columbia. In January 1952, their first son Stephen Jr. was born. Later that year his cousin David was born to Rush Jr. and Millie. Stephen Sr. and Anne soon added James to their family. And finally, the last two grandchildren, numbers nine and ten, arrived in 1960. Andrew was born to Stephen and Anne. Mary Bee, named for her mother and grandmother, was their last grandchild, joining Mary and Manley, her three brothers, and a sister. The Limbaughs delighted in their grandchildren, upon whom they bestowed love and interest in their development and accomplishments.[33]

In August 1958, during the annual meeting of the ABA in Los Angeles, Limbaugh and Bee had conversed with a number of the organization's former presidents and their wives at one of the receptions. Limbaugh believed that these conversations had led someone with ties to the State Department to recommend him for service "as a United States specialist" to India. He and Bee with his good friend Harold Reeve and his wife were selected "to spend two months in India lecturing [on] American culture and particularly in law and government in America."[34]

At the time of their trip, relations between the United States and India were good, although Prime Minister Jawaharlal Nehru maintained a posture of neutrality between the United States and the Soviet Union. Eisenhower judged his Indian counterpart's attitude toward "the Communists" to be somewhat naive, but because they shared many of the same values, Eisenhower was confident that he could work with Nehru. In December 1956, India's prime minister traveled to the United States where he met with the president for several hours discussing problems in the Middle East, the recent Hungarian uprising, socialism and communism, and a wide range of other international topics. Throughout, Eisenhower sought to work with him wherever India's and the United States' interests intersected. To foster understanding and cooperation between them, United States specialists were sent to India to exchange ideas about the two countries' cultural, economic, political, legal, and constitutional institutions.[35]

In preparation for their trip of more than two months, Limbaugh arranged for his sons Rush and Stephen and Joseph Russell to handle his pending law business. Limbaugh also began to study various topics in preparation for the many lectures—twenty-seven in all—he would present during his travels through India. To meet this challenge, Limbaugh studied Indian history and made a fresh study of American institutions. Although very familiar with the constitutional and legal system of the United States, Limbaugh wished to present the information in an unbiased and neutral manner to prevent any offense to his hearers who would naturally be sensitive to Western expressions of superiority or criticism. Bee shared her husband's concerns and after reading Philip Wylie's story, *The Last Ambassadors* (1957), and Eugene Burdick's and William Lederer's novel, *The Ugly American* (1958), vowed that she and her husband would not behave in the arrogant manner of the Americans portrayed in these novels. Instead, she sought to be sensitive to the viewpoints, traditions, and cultural sensibilities of the Indian people.[36]

When they left their home on November 2, 1958, the Limbaughs were both sixty-seven years old. Remembering their humble origins, they could not help but think that some kind of a mistake had been made and how that their "old friends at Sedgewickville" would be astonished at "what Rush Limbaugh and Bee Seabaugh [are] up to now." From St. Louis they flew to Washington, DC. When he learned that Harold and Ilena Reeve were not there yet, Bee noted that her husband was "all upset . . . [for] he never has believed that we are going to India." Nevertheless, the Reeves arrived the following day, and Limbaugh and Harold went to the State Department for briefings on India and their mission. On November 4, the Limbaughs and the Reeves flew to New York City and departed the following day on the Greek ship, the SS *Queen Fredericka*. During the twelve-day-long voyage, Limbaugh and Harold spent a good part of their time preparing lectures and attending various social events and meals on board.[37]

After being at sea for a week, the ship traveled within sight of Portugal's shores and docked near the Rock of Gibraltar. The Limbaughs went ashore here for a brief time. The next day they stopped at Barcelona, Spain, and arrived at Naples, Italy, on November 16. Finally, after docking at Salerno and Messina, Sicily, they arrived in Athens, Greece, on November 18. While there, the Limbaughs toured Athens, visiting the Temple of Zeus and the Parthenon. From there they descended to Mars' Hill, where the Apostle Paul had preached to the Athenians about "the Unknown God" almost 2,000 years before. Late that night they began a ten-hour flight, stopping at Beirut, Lebanon, from where they connected to Karachi, Pakistan. While there they stayed with James and Lucille Mesplay, the parents of their daughter-in-law Anne, who was married to their youngest son, Stephen. On the afternoon of November 20 they departed by airplane for New Delhi, their first stop in India.[38]

On their first full day in India, Limbaugh and Harold Reeve received a briefing at the United States embassy on their finances, transportation, and schedule. Having the weekend free, the Limbaughs shopped and visited the Red Fort in Old Delhi, and the tomb of Gandhi. Later they visited the site of his assassination. On Monday, Limbaugh and Harold returned to the United States embassy and were briefed on United States policy and were warned about various health hazards, receiving quinine in case they contracted malaria.[39] Because the next two days were an Indian national holiday and the embassy was closed, the Limbaughs and Reeves hired a car and driver and went to Agra, a distance of over 120 miles south of Delhi. Along the way they observed the poverty of the people and the primitive methods of agriculture then employed to make a living upon the soil, which to Limbaugh appeared "poor and rocky." He also noted that the roads were packed with human and animal travelers, including "caravans of camels and herds of livestock." Arriving at Agra, they checked into a hotel and visited the Taj Mahal. Limbaugh considered the palace "majestic and magnificent."[40]

On November 28, a Friday, the Limbaughs and Reeves were driven to the Indian Parliament to observe a session of the House and later to the Supreme Court building where they visited with the Solicitor General. Saturday was occupied with shopping and preparations to fly the following day to Madras. On December 1, they learned that they still were not scheduled to speak to an Indian audience, despite it having been a month since they had left home and ten days since arriving in India. Limbaugh had not traveled halfway around the world to sightsee and was "extremely anxious" to begin giving the lectures he had prepared. In the meantime, on December 2 the Limbaughs and the Reeves visited the home of Basheer Ahmed Sayeed, a justice of the High Court of Madras, who had founded a school for girls. The following day, December 3, Limbaugh, Reeve, and Arthur Funk visited the home of another justice of the High Court, P. N. Ramaswanie, with whom they discussed Indian, English, and American law. They later attended a session of the Magistrates' Court meeting of prosecuting and defense attorneys.[41]

On December 4, Limbaugh and Reeve were finally scheduled to give their first speeches in India. Both men developed lectures on the theme of "freedom under the law." That evening they traveled to the Hall of the Parliamentary Association, where Reeve spoke first before an audience of approximately 200 people. His topic and Limbaugh's was on the constitutional principle of the separation of powers. Each man spoke for twenty minutes. In his talk, Limbaugh explained that while "our doctrine of separation was accepted generally with checks and balances . . . in the overlapping of functions of the different departments there was not strict adherence to the doctrine in actual practice." Afterward, they answered several questions.[42]

After lunch on December 5, the Limbaughs and the Reeves took a car to the High Court Building to a meeting of the Association of Advocates where some 300 or 400 judges had gathered. Reeve spoke first paying "a fine tribute to the bar of India and the progress of India under her new constitution." Limbaugh spoke on the purposes of cross-examination, which he illustrated through the historical examples of "[Patrick] Henry's cross-examination in the Randolph trial . . . [and] [Abraham] Lincoln's use of the almanac in the murder trial." From there they proceeded to a meeting of the Bar Council where apprentice lawyers awaited their presentations. Limbaugh explained the American system of legal education, which unlike the Indian system, did not include an apprenticeship under the tutelage of an experienced lawyer. He also noted that some of the United States' greatest lawyers—including Patrick Henry, Thomas Jefferson, John Marshall, and Daniel Webster had received no, or very little, formal instruction in a law school. After their presentations, Limbaugh and Reeve were taken to observe the Chief Justice and another judge holding court. They next visited a trial at the Sessions Court where a defendant was on trial for fraud. Afterward, the Limbaughs and the Reeves attended a reception given for them at which a number of lawyers were present.[43]

With no events scheduled on December 6 and 7, the Limbaughs and the Reeves hired a driver to take them to a nearby village where they viewed the architecture and interacted with the villagers, some of whom were very poor and begged for food. After returning to their hotel, most of the remainder of the day was spent in preparing lectures and packing for their departure by plane to Hyderabad. On December 8, Limbaugh prepared a lecture for the following day at a seminar for law school professors, judges, law students, and others, some of whom came from as far as 500 miles away. A flyer with pictures and short biographies of Limbaugh and Reeve advertised the seminar and provided a schedule of their talks. In his first talk, Limbaugh spoke for fifty minutes on "parallel legal developments in India and America," and answered questions for an hour afterward. That day he and Reeve had also participated in a seminar discussion of the United States' judicial system. On December 10, having considered their parallels the day before, Limbaugh, Reeve, and the Indian participants considered the differences of the Indian and American legal systems. At a later session of the seminar series, Limbaugh presented a sketch of the history of the Supreme Court of the United States to 1900, and Reeve spoke on the Little Rock crisis, explaining how that Arkansas Governor Orval Faubus had attempted to prevent the integration of Central High School there. To uphold the federal court's decision ordering the admission of black students, President Eisenhower deployed the 101st Airborne to Little Rock.[44]

On December 11, although Bee had been ill, they went sightseeing around Hyderabad and then returned to their hotel where Limbaugh prepared for his talk that night at the Law College. The meeting place was packed with faculty and students, some of whom "were jamming the windows and doors," and a large group assembled outside. After Reeve had spoken on the United States judiciary, Limbaugh addressed his remarks primarily to the students on their responsibilities as lawyers, concluding his remarks "by reading a young lawyer's pledge when admitted to practice in Missouri." Apparently, the students were impressed with the passion and sincerity with which Limbaugh spoke, for during his remarks "there was a solemn stillness in an attentive audience and a hearty applause at the close." Afterward, Limbaugh found himself surrounded by students asking him for his autograph and shaking his hand. Moved by their reaction, he assured them of the United States' goodwill for India.[45]

The following day, Limbaugh met with a university political science department to which he spoke about "the progress of democracy." Later, before some 300 lawyers and judges at a meeting of the Bar Council at the High Court Building, Limbaugh lectured on "humility as one of the disregarded qualifications of a successful lawyer." His example, a very apt one, related Abraham Lincoln's association with Edwin M. Stanton, who in working on a case with the future president had snubbed and treated him badly. Despite this, Lincoln did not harbor a grudge and later chose Stanton to serve as his Secretary of War—a selection which proved to be a very good one for the country in the midst of civil war.[46]

Taking a flight to Bombay where they would spend the next few days, Limbaugh and Reeve were very busy speaking before university and law school audiences primarily. On December 15, both men addressed the faculty and students of the political science department at Ruparel College, where they spoke about the drafting of the Constitution of the United States. Limbaugh's talk considered certain "extra-constitutional instrumentalities," such as the development of political parties, which were necessary to make the Constitution function properly. Later that day at the University of Bombay, Limbaugh spoke on the courts' role in the American constitutional system. On December 16, he addressed the faculty of a law school about the concept of eminent domain, using examples from his private practice. Later that night, he spoke to the political science department of the University of Bombay on the decisions of some of the most important justices of the Supreme Court of the United States. Questions afterward led to Limbaugh giving an impromptu "talk on the Little Rock and segregation issues."[47]

On December 17, Limbaugh and Reeve spoke at the Government Law College on the development of constitutional law to a large group of faculty and students. In the evening they also spoke before the political science department at the University of Bombay on individual rights. After the talk Limbaugh noted that "a South African student of the rabblerousing kind tried to press a question to us on race discrimination," but was not allowed to pursue it by the faculty. This question was apparently uppermost in the minds of many, some of whom honestly wished to understand the constitutional issues related to the *Brown v. Board of Education* decisions, while others hostile to the United States considered this an opportunity to attack its representatives. Such attacks were misdirected, for both Limbaugh and Reeve were opposed to segregation and the treatment of African Americans as second-class citizens. For years, Limbaugh had encouraged the participation of African Americans in politics in southeast Missouri and later would work diligently to support civil rights in Missouri and the United States.[48]

At this time, the United States presented itself to the rest of the world as a model of freedom and an antidote to the tyranny of communist nations, foremost of which were the Soviet Union and China. However, because the United States had failed to protect the individual rights of nonwhites under the Constitution, the country's reputation was tarnished and its message to the rest of the world undermined. "The mouthpieces of Soviet propaganda," Eisenhower noted later, "in Russia and Europe were blaring out that 'anti-Negro violence' in Little Rock was being 'committed with the clear connivance of the United States government.'" While this was untrue, for from the beginning Eisenhower and his administration had sought to uphold the *Brown* decisions and encourage school districts to comply, nevertheless Soviet propaganda was credible because of the long history of discrimination against nonwhites in the United States. During the 1950s and 1960s, critics of the United States, including those in India, pointed to Jim Crow laws and other discriminatory practices to undermine the American message to the rest of the world. While the Eisenhower administration endeavored to enforce the *Brown* decisions, many Southern schools refused to desegregate, a circumstance that was not easy to explain to foreign audiences unfamiliar with our system of divided authority between the state and federal governments.[49]

On the morning of December 18, Limbaugh spoke to law students and faculty at the Ruparel College of Law on "Liberty and the Rule of Law." After lunch he visited the High Courts and met the Advocate General of Bombay. In the evening, Limbaugh spoke to members of the Synthetic Jurisprudence Society on the responsibilities of citizenship. Afterward, with the Reeves and Bee, he attended a dinner held at the residence of Daniel P. Oleksiw, director of the United States Information Services (USIS) in Bombay, where they met a number of prominent members of the local legal and educational establishment. The following day Limbaugh and Reeve again addressed students at the Government Law College. At both events, they answered a number of questions. Also, at the request of India Radio, Limbaugh taped a ten-minute "farewell address to the people of India," which was broadcast repeatedly throughout India. On December 20, Limbaugh and Reeve spoke to a group of law professors on legal education in the United States.[50]

On December 21, the Limbaughs, the Reeves, and Milton Leavitt, who worked for the USIS, traveled by car to Poona, attending a cricket match, and the following day toured the grounds of Ferguson College and some of the government buildings there. That evening Limbaugh spoke on the judiciary to lawyers, judges, professors, and other prominent people at the Cultural Club. The next day Limbaugh spoke on legal and constitutional interpretation, noting that in the United States, unlike India, it was customary to comment upon and criticize court decisions. On Christmas Eve, they returned to Bombay, where they exchanged gifts with the Reeves and Limbaugh read aloud to Bee from chapters one and two of the Gospel of Luke in which the fullest account of Christ's birth is found.[51]

On Christmas Day the Limbaughs and Reeves attended a party at the consular office and afterward attended a dinner where Sidney Hook and his wife were present as well. Hook, a professor of philosophy at New York University, whom Limbaugh described as "quite talkative [and] sure of himself," was then on a lecture tour of Asia. While still considering himself a socialist, Hook was an ardent anti-communist, especially anti-Soviet, and was well known among New York City intellectuals as a controversialist accustomed to the rough and tumble of bare-knuckled political debate. During his tour, which was about to end, the outspoken Hook had criticized "the double standard of Nehru's foreign policy" at a press conference in Bombay, a statement which had infuriated local journalists. Here Hook may have had in mind Nehru's readiness to condemn the West for transgressions, while often rationalizing much worse breaches by China and the Soviet Union, which two years before had brutally crushed an uprising in Hungary. When Indians confronted him with the United States' race problems, Hook agreed, but he also called the Indian people's attention to the great injustice of their own caste system and their "degrading treatment of Indian women." Such candor did not make him many friends. During their dinner together, Limbaugh was apparently amused when "Oleksiw called [Hook] on the error of some of his impressions."[52]

The day after Christmas, the Limbaughs and Reeves departed for Calcutta. Over the next few days Limbaugh and Reeve attended the conference of the All-Indian Law Teachers Association at a law college and were voted honorary members of their organization. On December 29, Limbaugh gave his last address in India to this organization speaking on "Some Essentials of a Legal Education from the Standpoint of a Practicing Lawyer." After attending other social functions, including a Rotary Club meeting, the Limbaughs and Reeves began their long journey home on December 31, arriving in Bangkok, Thailand, just before midnight. After spending two days in Thailand, they departed for Hong Kong, staying there until January 5, 1959. From there they proceeded on to Tokyo and to Honolulu, Hawaii, the following day. Spending three days there, Limbaugh and Bee took a boat tour of Pearl Harbor and did some sightseeing before saying goodbye to the Reeves and leaving for Los Angeles. Arriving in St. Louis on January 10, it was with great relief that they were met by their son Rush and their grandson David, who drove them the last miles home ending a complete circuit of the globe. Exhausted, but glad to be home, they "had the thrill of seeing again the old familiar and satisfying homestead, a quiet refuge from the days of adventure, travel, toil, anxiety, and duty [they] had known since [they had] left."[53]

Chapter Ten

Civil Libertarian

As a representative of the United States government in India, Rush H. Limbaugh had learned firsthand how others perceived the US in light of discrimination against nonwhite persons. The Cold War arms race and propaganda war between the East and West was then fully engaged and the United States presented itself to the rest of the world as a bulwark against the tyranny of communism. The United States undermined this message by failing to provide equal protection to the rights and liberties of all its citizens. Throughout the United States' history, many of its greatest statesmen have recognized that to the extent the nation failed to attain its ideals, it was vulnerable to just criticism and attack. Thus during the 1858 United States senatorial campaign, Abraham Lincoln observed that slavery "deprives our republican example of its just influence in the world–enables the enemies of free institutions, with plausibility, to taunt us as hypocrites–causes the real friends of freedom to doubt our sincerity, and especially because it forces so many really good men amongst ourselves into an open war with the very fundamental principles of civil liberty–criticising [sic] the Declaration of Independence, and insisting that there is no right principle of action but self-interest." In the same way, during the 1950s and 1960s, critics of the United States, especially its Cold War antagonists, pointed to Jim Crow laws and other discriminatory practices to undermine its message to the rest of the world.[1]

Living in southeast Missouri where "there was absolute segregation in . . . [the] public schools and use of municipal facilities," these issues had concerned Limbaugh for some time. While serving as chairman of the Cape Girardeau County Republicans in the 1920s and 1930s, despite the prevailing prejudices of the time, he had encouraged the participation of African Americans in the Republican Party and the political process. To facilitate this, Limbaugh helped blacks form a Lincoln Club in Cape Girardeau, even writing the organization's constitution. As a candidate for the office of mayor, he had spoken at African American churches, actively seeking votes. Outside of politics, during a Billy Sunday revival of the mid-1920s in Cape Girardeau, Limbaugh helped organize a special evangelical service for African Americans at which he expressed his belief that their participation in the community was important. Moreover, Limbaugh and Bee were horrified by the senseless acts of violence occasionally committed against African Americans, such as the 1942 lynching of Cleo Wright in the nearby town of Sikeston. Thus later, when Cape Girardeau's school board voted to integrate the public schools a short time before the Supreme Court of the United States handed down its historic decision in *Brown v. Board of Education*, Limbaugh rejoiced that one of the principal props of discrimination in his community had been removed. This decision also meant that his son Stephen, then a young lawyer beginning his professional and public career, had the distinction of being the last commencement speaker at John S. Cobb High School, Cape Girardeau's all-black high school.[2]

After the Brown decision in 1954, Limbaugh supported the prompt integration of schools, although he believed the Court should have based its decision upon the privileges or immunities and the equal protection clauses of the Fourteenth Amendment as expressed in Justice John Marshall Harlan's dissent in *Plessy v. Ferguson* (1896). By the fall of 1956, only 723 of 10,000 southern school districts had complied with the Court's ruling, and resistance to integration was well organized and determined. The most notable of these efforts was led by Arkansas Democratic Governor Orval Faubus, who intervened to prevent the integration of a public high school in Little Rock. Without Faubus' intervention, the high school would have been integrated according to a plan proposed by the Little Rock school board and accepted by a federal district court. In an effort to derail the planned integration of the high schools, a group petitioned the Arkansas State Chancery Court. Faubus appeared and argued "that desegregation in Little Rock might lead to violence." The court issued a restraining order. "The next day, however, on the petition of the Little Rock school board, the United States District Court issued an order to prevent anyone's interfering" with the planned integration. At that time, District Judge Ronald N. Davies from North Dakota was on assigned temporary duty in Arkansas when this matter came before the federal court. Davies firmly ordered the integration of the Little Rock high school to proceed as planned. After the federal judge's ruling, Faubus ordered the Arkansas National Guard to Little Rock to prevent black students from entering Central High School, again claiming that integration would cause violence. Actually, the governor's action rallied those opposed to integration, who until then had acquiesced in the school board's plan. Eventually, after attempting to gain the governor's voluntary compliance with the federal district court order, Republican President Dwight D. Eisenhower nationalized the Arkansas National Guard, thus placing them under his command, and ordered in the 101st Airborne Division to prevent any further violence and to protect the black students.[3]

Before this, Democratic President Harry S. Truman had sought the passage of civil rights legislation and also ordered the integration of the United States military. The civil rights legislation never passed, for Southern Democratic senators refused to budge, making progress on civil rights very difficult during the Truman years and after. Furthermore, despite his executive order to integrate the military, again no real progress occurred. As historian David A. Nichols noted in his seminal work on Eisenhower's civil rights record, much misinformation remains on both presidents' roles in ending segregation in the military. "The assertion that President Truman desegregated the armed forces in 1948 has been a staple in American history textbooks for decades." Nevertheless, Truman failed to follow up and enforce obedience to his order, and thus the military remained largely segregated during his presidency. However, from the beginning of his administration, President Eisenhower promoted civil liberties, and was especially effective where he could act independently using the powers of his office. He was the first president to appoint an African American, E. Frederic Morrow, to the position of administrative assistant in the White House and ordered desegregation in the federal government and in housing, employment, and public accommodations in Washington, DC. Adam Clayton Powell Jr., then the only African American member of Congress, later emotionally recalled what it was like for blacks in the nation's capitol before the president was inaugurated. "Four years ago in Washington, I couldn't eat in any place except a Jim Crow restaurant. I couldn't get a room in a hotel. I couldn't get into any theater except a Negro one. But Dwight D. Eisenhower overnight made Washington D.C. better for all people than New York City." Moreover, by Eisenhower's order "segregation came to an end in schools on military posts, among civilian employees at naval bases, throughout the armed forces, and in Veterans Administration hospitals." He also "established a committee, with Vice President [Richard M.] Nixon as chairman, to combat racial discrimination in employment in work performed under government contract."[4]

Immediately after the Brown decision, Eisenhower brought the commissioners of the District of Columbia into the Oval Office, urging them to take the lead in integrating the Washington, DC public schools, to serve "as an example to the entire country." That fall, just a few months after the Court's opinion had been published, the public schools in the nation's capitol were integrated. Nevertheless, in March 1956 approximately one hundred Southern congressmen, most of them Democrats, published a manifesto "committ[ing] themselves to use every legal means to overturn" Brown. Earlier that year in his State of the Union Address, Eisenhower had proposed that Congress establish a bipartisan commission to investigate why only one in four African Americans legally eligible to vote were registered in the South. After discussions with his cabinet and FBI director, J. Edgar Hoover, who reported violence and intimidation against African Americans, Eisenhower proposed "a four-point program, calling for a new bipartisan civil rights commission, a civil rights division under a new Assistant Attorney General in the Department of Justice, new laws to aid in enforcing voting rights, and amendments to existing laws to permit the federal government to seek in civil courts preventive relief in civil rights cases." As Eisenhower remembered later, "at the time, these proposals were little less than revolutionary." Noting the turmoil sure to follow, Attorney General Herbert Brownell supported the president, observing "that to do less would not be in keeping with Republican tradition."[5]

In July 1956, eighty-three representatives from the South, all but four being Democrats, signed a manifesto against Eisenhower's civil rights legislation. In the House, the bill passed with 168 Republican and 111 Democratic votes for, and 102 Democratic and 24 Republican votes against it. In the Senate, in what had become a pattern for civil rights legislation, the bill was sent to the judiciary committee where its chair, Senator James O. Eastland (D-Mississippi), killed it. After winning reelection, in his 1957 State of the Union Address Eisenhower again pressed Congress to pass his civil rights agenda, leading once more to the House passing the measure in much the same proportion of Republicans and Democrats in favor and in opposition as the previous year. After its passage in the House, Senator William F. Knowland (R-California), objected to the legislation again being sent to the Senate judiciary committee, winning a crucial vote to send it directly to the floor for consideration in a vote of 45 to 39. Of those voting to prevent Eastland from killing the bill in committee were 34 Republicans and 11 Democrats. The opposition was composed of 34 Democrats and 5 Republicans. Of those voting to stop the bill, Eisenhower thought it ironic that among them were senators who had often promoted themselves to the public as liberals and champions of the "little people." Among these senators were William Fulbright, Albert Gore Sr., Lyndon B. Johnson, and John F. Kennedy. Of the Republicans, the most prominent opponent was Barry Goldwater.[6]

A key part of the Civil Rights Act of 1957 was Title III, which provided the attorney general with the power "to seek injunctions against violations of any civil right, voting or nonvoting." The opponents to the bill argued that this would give the attorney general and federal government too much power and lead to abuses such as coercing "a co-mingling of white and Negro children" in Southern public schools. Seeking to undermine the legislation's effectiveness, senators opposed to the bill offered an amendment giving to anyone cited for contempt in federal court the right to trial by jury. In effect, the measure removed from federal judges the power to imprison persons refusing to testify in court. It was understood by everyone that all-white juries in the South would never convict anyone cited for violating the civil rights of a black person, or refusing to testify in court or before a newly created Civil Rights

Commission. Attorney General Brownell and many supporters of Eisenhower's bill, including Jackie Robinson, the first African American baseball player in the major leagues during the modern era, believed that unless this amendment was somehow overturned it would be better not to pass any bill at all. Among those voting for this amendment were Johnson, Gore, Kennedy, and Goldwater. Eventually, the Senate worked out a compromise in which a judge retained the option of imposing a lesser penalty for contempt, or sending the cause to a jury to obtain a harsher punishment. After this, additional obstacles to the passage of an effective civil rights bill were easily overcome. The Eisenhower administration used these new powers vigorously, investigating over 4,000 reports of civil rights violations, most of which were settled, and trying more than one hundred cases in federal court. Additionally, Eisenhower appointed federal judges he believed would support the civil rights of blacks and uphold Brown. These appointments were made despite strong opposition from Southern Democratic senators, who lobbied the president for judges supporting segregation. Later, Kennedy, who as president was anything but a "profile in courage," undid much of the good accomplished by his predecessor by appointing "a slew of die-hard segregationists to the federal bench in the South." Attorney General Herbert Brownell, who had been involved in recommending federal judges to Eisenhower, remembered a conversation he had with Democratic Senator Eastland of Mississippi, "an archsegregationist." With Kennedy in charge, Brownell asked Eastland how "the appointment of federal judges" was going. Eastland "replied with a twinkle in his eye, 'it's much better than when you were here!'"[7]

During this period, the issue of civil rights was also debated among the membership of the American Bar Association (ABA). Limbaugh became involved personally in this matter when ABA president Whitney North Seymour appointed him to serve as chairman of the Standing Committee of the Bill of Rights in 1960. This committee, under the leadership of Joseph Harrison, a lawyer from Newark, New Jersey, had submitted a report at the 1959 annual meeting of the ABA's session of the House of Delegates, which "turned out to be the most controversial report presented" at the meeting. Many members objected to its support of twenty-four opinions of the Supreme Court of the United States in which it restricted some of the methods employed in the investigation of communist subversion upon the grounds that they violated certain rights guaranteed by the Constitution. A few months earlier the House of Delegates had accepted a report from the Communist Tactics Committee, which had criticized these decisions by the Court and had recommended that Congress pass legislation shoring up gaps in the security of the country. This controversy may have led to Harrison's replacement with one of the report's critics, Alfred J. Schweppe, a lawyer from Seattle, Washington, and a critic of the Brown decision. Seymour, a Republican lawyer from New York and a member of the state's civil rights commission, was probably anxious to replace Schweppe, who opposed the Brown decision and President Eisenhower's action enforcing the federal district court's injunction to integrate the schools in Little Rock.[8]

Limbaugh was surprised when president-elect Seymour offered him the chairmanship of the Committee on the Bill of Rights, for other members of the committee had served much longer than him "and were much more familiar with [its] work." The committee's main tasks were to educate lawyers and the public concerning the history and meaning of the Bill of Rights—including the Thirteenth through the Fifteenth Amendments—and to expose violations of their principles. Of course, one's interpretation of the Bill of Rights was important in determining the manner and scope of the committee's work. As to be expected, any group of knowledgeable persons, especially lawyers, disagreed on many matters. In particular, Limbaugh recognized that some members of the committee were unsympathetic to the Brown decisions, while others "favored a highly activist policy" in its enforcement. A third group, with which he aligned himself, "advocated an activist program pursued with moderation and restraint."[9]

To promote greater public awareness of the Bill of Rights, Limbaugh sent a letter to state governors, ministers, and the editors of major newspapers and radio and television outlets, asking them to announce that December 15 is "Bill of Rights Day." He also wrote to "prominent members of the bar" around the country requesting information regarding civil rights violations. Limbaugh summarized these replies in a letter to members of the committee in which it was clear that some lawyers, among whom were some of the ABA's leadership, were hostile to such an inquiry. One of these leaders was Loyd Wright, a former president of the ABA. In his reply, instead of seriously addressing the problem of civil rights in California (where he resided), Wright cited as an egregious violation of civil rights the kidnapping of Adolf Eichmann by Israeli agents to bring him to justice for his complicity in the murder of Jews during the Holocaust. Fortunately, many of Limbaugh's correspondents were more serious and offered real examples of civil rights violations, or at least types of cases into which the committee might inquire. Some of these were concerns about First and Fifth Amendment protections to free speech and against coerced self-incrimination, strong support for the integration of the public schools, and the suggestion of Jefferson B. Fordham, dean of law at the University of Pennsylvania, that perhaps the ABA should establish a new human rights section. One of the replies interjected a measure of humor when a correspondent claimed that since his marriage he had no civil liberties, but he promised to inform the committee if his situation changed.[10]

During this period, feeling a deficiency in his own knowledge of the Bill of Rights, Limbaugh began a period of study, widely reading primary sources, such as the Journal of the Continental Congress, and a number of secondary scholarly works as well. In light of "the stress of world tensions and the impudence of [the] Soviet challenge," he believed that it was important to reexamine "the origins and history of our institutions and . . . their stability and promise for the exigencies of our times." Such an examination was important—and should not be feared—in light of the recent controversies concerning "whether an American citizen should claim the protection of the Fifth Amendment when challenged to tell whether he had ever belonged to the Communist Party," and the equally important issue of school integration involving "the enforcement of the equal protection provision of the Fourteenth Amendment." Limbaugh also hoped to promote through the ABA a primer on the Bill of Rights for both lawyers and laymen.[11]

As chair, Limbaugh traveled to where Bill of Rights protections were ignored and held hearings, afterward reporting the abuses and making recommendations. Many years later, he remembered that "we had a number of meetings where we discussed the unrest that was taking place . . . particularly in the South, like in the state of Mississippi and in other states in the South where the Bill of Rights was frequently disregarded." Another of Limbaugh's responsibilities as chair was to set an agenda for the committee during the 1961 annual meeting of the ABA. To facilitate the committee's work, Limbaugh assigned different tasks to members and prepared for the meeting held in St. Louis. While there, Limbaugh privately consulted with various persons about aspects of the committee's agenda and its written report to be distributed to the House of Delegates. The thirty-five-page report covered the committee's promotion of the Bill of Rights Day, a summary of the investigation regarding the violation of civil rights around the country, and decisions of federal courts on civil rights controversies. One of the major concerns expressed by a number of lawyers regarded the denial of "the basic right of counsel . . . . in juvenile and domestic cases." Another problem concerned the refusal of lawyers to represent unpopular defendants, such as African Americans charged with raping a white woman, and "freedom riders"—persons demonstrating against discrimination in the South, often forcing judges to change the venue of the case. It was also noted that in the past the committee had filed amicus curiae (friend of the court) briefs in civil rights cases, but that for several years the committee had not so acted after determining that their intervention was unnecessary, discovering that defendants were already "adequately represented," often by lawyers working for civil rights organizations.[12]

The most controversial part of the report analyzed the Supreme Court of the United States' decisions in civil rights cases. Under the heading, "Constitutional Rights and Criminal Procedure," the committee observed that in *Mapp v. Ohio* (1961) the Court had incorporated the Fourth Amendment to the states, applying federal court rules to state cases. This decision thereafter excluded from trial any evidence illegally acquired by law enforcement. The committee supported this and added that while its members supported the police and recognized "the great difficulties of criminal law enforcement," it nevertheless thought that "unconstitutional conduct by public officers is an intolerable remedy." The committee also supported the overturning of convictions based upon coerced confessions. Concerning "the Cold War and the Constitution," three important cases "involving communism" were reported. In the first of these cases, *Communist Party of the United States* v. *Subversive Activities Control Board*, the Court ruled that the government could require the Communist Party of the United States "to register as a Communist-action organization under the Subversive Activities Control Act of 1950." Moreover, in Scales v. United States, "the Court upheld the 'membership clause' of the Smith Act of 1940," criminalizing a person's membership in "any society, group, or assembly of persons" seeking the overthrow of the United States government through "force or violence." However, it should also be noted that the Court ruled that the Communist Party of the United States did not qualify as this type of association as defined by the Smith Act. In a final case, the Court held that the United States government had the discretion to withhold employment from persons who might pose a risk to national security "without a hearing or further explanation."[13]

Finally, the report noted that for some time the Court had been moving away from the Plessy decision, which had declared racial segregation constitutional so long as separate but equal facilities were provided for blacks. Many of the Court's earlier decisions, such as *McLaurin v. Oklahoma State Regents* (1950) and *Sweatt v. Painter* (1950), had ruled that the states of Texas and Oklahoma had treated African Americans unequally in their dispositions to provide them with a legal education. In a 1938 case brought against the University of Missouri's law school, *Missouri ex rel. Gaines v. Canada, Registrar*, the Court had ruled that a state could not discharge its responsibility to provide legal education to African Americans by sending them elsewhere free of charge. In light of these opinions and others, the Court's ruling in Brown "was by no means surprising to one who evaluated the preceding series of adjudications." Moreover, given the fact that since Brown the Court had upheld it in a number of other cases, one must finally conclude that "as a constitutional issue, racial differentiation in public treatment by this time had been solidly settled; such separation offends the Constitution." The committee called for the states to respect the Fourteenth and Fifteenth Amendment rights of their citizens and cease resistance to the Court's rulings and end segregation. The committee also noted the detrimental affect the reports of these violations against nonwhites had upon the reputation of the United States abroad. "Constitutional freedom is all of one piece. People cannot be encouraged to disregard constitutional rights in some areas without jeopardizing them in all." To those state and federal officers who disagree with a decision of the Court, the committee advised them to direct their opposition through the proper channels of constitutional "amendment or judicial reconsideration. Attitudes other than this denigrate the entire structure of orderly government which is essential to all freedom." Having strongly supported the Court's decisions overturning segregation and explaining their importance, the committee concluded its report in a conciliatory manner to those members of the ABA, especially its southern members, who disagreed. While the conclusion's authorship cannot be known with any certainty, its style and tone reflects exactly Limbaugh's beliefs and character.

> The First Article of the Constitution of our Association states that one of our objects is to "encourage cordial intercourse among the members of the American bar" and to this endeavor our committee gives hearty concurrence. When we speak with regret of the actions of some states and some of their officials, including some of our professional brethren, we speak without any intention of rancorous criticism. But other objects are recited in that same article. Our association is "to uphold the honor of the profession of law; to apply its knowledge and experience in the field of law to the promotion of the public good"; of these things, too, we are conscientiously mindful. And predominantly this report is motivated by the first objective recited in our first article,—"to uphold and defend the Constitution of the United States and maintain representative government."[14]

A member of the committee, former chair Alfred J. Schweppe, strongly disagreed with parts of the report and asserted that until 1954 Congress and state governments had upheld the Fourteenth Amendment rights of all citizens through the passage of legislation providing separate but equal accommodations for African Americans in accord with the Plessy decision. To support his position, Schweppe pointed to congressional legislation, passed a short time after the Fourteenth Amendment's ratification, establishing segregated schools, which he believed proved that the amendment's framers did not consider segregation unconstitutional. He also argued that the Warren Court in Brown had not addressed this matter of congressional intent—an omission admitted even by the decision's proponents, and that the Court had overreached in overturning precedent "so long settled." More recent scholarship, however, demonstrates conclusively that while Schweppe and others were correct in criticizing the Court's adoption of "a nonhistorical interpretive methodology," which had "seriously weakened [its] decision," nevertheless, the historical record shows "that a very substantial portion of the Congress, including leading framers of the amendment, subscribed to the view that school segregation violates the Fourteenth Amendment." These framers in the 1870s, all of whom were Republicans, while able for the first time to establish schools for black children—a significant advance for the time—were unable to overcome the objection of predominately Democratic congressional opposition, and presumably white public opinion in both the North and South, to integration. Thus, despite their intention to outlaw segregation, the framers could not overcome the strong prejudice of whites at that time. This prejudice remained in 1954 and accounts for the backlash which erupted when, in the opinion of many, the justices of the Warren Court, instead of faithfully interpreting the text of the Constitution, "willfully misinterpreted [it] . . . in the service of social engineering." Thus, these justices exposed themselves to this charge by using social science research to support their decision instead of consulting the historical record, a much more authoritative and persuasive type of evidence to lawyers, legal scholars, and the public.[15]

Unfortunately, some members of the House of Delegates shared Schweppe's opposition to the Brown decision and to the committee's report. As chair of the committee, Limbaugh was scheduled to appear and summarize the report before the House of Delegates in which, as he remembered it, there was "a seething opposition to certain parts of" it. As he waited to make his presentation, former ABA president Ross Malone approached and whispered his concern, and that of president Seymour, about the opposition arrayed against the committee's report in the hall. Fearing that some of the members might disrupt the meeting or turn it into a forum on segregation, both Malone and Seymour thought it best that Limbaugh not speak and instead "permit the chairman of the House of Delegates to refer" the members to the committee's report. Malone was too late, though, for before Limbaugh had any time to act on their advice, he was called to the speaker's rostrum. Thus, he made a brief presentation for approximately five minutes, and upon concluding was immediately confronted by members challenging some of his remarks. One of his interrogators was Ben R. Miller from Baton Rouge, Louisiana, who had worked with the committee as a liaison from his state. As he challenged some of Limbaugh's statements, it was clear that Miller was very angry and strongly disagreed with the committee's conclusions concerning the South's response to the Supreme Court's decisions on segregation. When answering Miller, Limbaugh spoke respectfully, but firmly, pointing out that until then they had never had a harsh word between them, and expressed surprise "at his antagonistic attitude." Nevertheless, Limbaugh stated his belief in free speech and observed that he was aware that many others in the hall agreed with Miller. With that a delegate moved to adjourn for lunch—as it was then noon—bringing to an end the assault on the report and Limbaugh's leadership.[16]

After the 1961 annual meeting, John C. Satterfield, the new president of the ABA, appointed Schweppe to replace Limbaugh as chair of the Committee on the Bill of Rights, although he remained a member of the committee. Both Malone and Seymour were very unhappy with this appointment, as were many members of the committee, for Schweppe had taken a firm stand opposing the federal courts' and the government's efforts to enforce Brown. Because of Limbaugh's stand on human rights, Schweppe developed "an intense dislike" for him. Satterfield, a lawyer from Yazoo City, near Jackson, Mississippi, was an ardent supporter of segregation and the South's racist and discriminatory Jim Crow laws, which were especially harsh in the Magnolia State.[17] Since the Brown decision, Satterfield had fought against integration and the civil rights movement at the local, state, and national levels. In 1958, Satterfield, "a prominent Methodist layman and lawyer," spoke to students at Millsaps College, a private Methodist institution near Jackson, after a local Citizens' Council—a vigilante group organized to enforce Jim Crow laws—badgered the college's administration into inviting him. The Citizens' Council objected to Millsaps College having invited Professor Ernest Borinski from Tougaloo College, an African American institution, to speak about and criticize discrimination in Mississippi. In his speech, Borinski "explained blacks' dissatisfaction with the un-Christian segregation." To counter this, Satterfield assured Millsaps College students that "it was 'possible to have a Christian attitude and believe in segregation.'" In 1962 as ABA president, he became the most prominent lawyer in the fight against integration in Mississippi and was Democratic Governor Ross Barnett's main legal advisor serving "as a special assistant attorney general" during the state executive's efforts to prevent the admission of James Meredith into the University of Mississippi. Indeed, the obstructionism of segregationists had been so successful in Mississippi that in 1964 not a single black student had been integrated into white public schools throughout the state. As late as 1970, less than one hundred black children had integrated into white schools in Satterfield's hometown, where 3,500 children were enrolled. When the federal court ordered the local school district to be integrated without further delay, Satterfield and other local segregationists played a final unseemly trick upon the federal courts and African Americans by integrating Yazoo City's high school, but segregating the classrooms within it. Other white parents would not even countenance this, and, like in many other school districts, enrolled their children in private schools rather than allow them to be instructed alongside black children.[18]

Because Satterfield was president of the ABA during part of the Meredith controversy, the issue of segregation and the Kennedy administration's response of ordering troops and US Marshals to Oxford, Mississippi, led to debate among the ABA's members concerning the organization's proper position on the matter. In October 1962, Satterfield's successor, Sylvester C. Smith Jr., released a statement to the press supporting the federal government's action.

Satterfield protested Smith's communication as a "personal discourtesy," without authority from the House of Delegates. Unmoved, Smith responded that Satterfield's actions in this matter had "embarrassed the American Bar Association," and that he as president believed it was important to disavow any attempt to thwart the enforcement of Brown. While admitting that he had published his press release without first gaining an official resolution supporting it, Smith noted that "many members of the House have urged that a statement be made." Furthermore, he believed his position was the same as that of a majority in the House of Delegates and expected them to confirm this later. This expectation was fulfilled when the Board of Governors unanimously endorsed Smith's statement before the end of the year.[19]

The Meredith controversy was the beginning of a particularly tumultuous time in American race relations. Despite promising during the 1960 presidential campaign to end school segregation immediately and to ensure the voting rights of African Americans, President Kennedy and his brother, Attorney General Robert F. Kennedy, proved to be reluctant civil rights warriors. To be fair, administration leaders and personnel in the Civil Rights Division experienced the usual difficulties in familiarizing themselves with their new responsibilities. Another important factor hindering their efforts was the need to exercise caution in not undertaking too many causes at the same time, especially when it was clear that a good many, if not most, were destined to fail because of white jury nullification. Moreover, at that time the federal courts had not defined the limits of the division's "enforcement authority"; prudence thus required that care be taken not to exceed its statutory power. One of the deficiencies of the Civil Rights Act of 1957, which established the Civil Rights Division, was its omission of power to the attorney general to intervene on behalf of citizens in cases not involving voting rights. This omission, it has been correctly observed, explains why the Department of Justice did not intervene in school segregation cases, although like the Eisenhower administration, the division filed amicus curiae briefs on behalf of integration and expanded this role to include oral arguments and even the questioning of witnesses. As the Little Rock crisis had led to President Eisenhower's intervention with federal troops and the decision to seek passage of a civil rights bill, so also violent opposition to the admission of James Meredith into the University of Mississippi led to President Kennedy's decision to send federal troops and to seek the passage of a civil rights bill in 1963. This turn of events was ironic given Kennedy's criticism of his predecessor for sending troops to Little Rock some five years before and Eisenhower's attempt to close the Title III loophole of the Civil Rights Act of 1957, a loophole which Kennedy had supported as a United States senator.[20]

The period from the University of Mississippi controversy to the summer of 1963 had been marked by increasing frustration among African Americans and their leadership. The final straw for many black civil rights leaders came during a meeting on December 17, 1962, with Kennedy at the White House, where the president refused most of their requests, including the promotion of a new civil rights bill. By the following summer, even Martin Luther King Jr.—long an advocate of nonviolent resistance—observed that the situation was very dire and that African Americans were on the verge of violent revolt. Thus, he "warned the White House of an impending national calamity because of the 'snail-like pace of desegregation.'" His own personal impatience was amplified when he stated to a crowd in Chicago that "we're through with tokenism and gradualism and see-how-far-you've-comeism." Additionally, in gauging the prevailing racial tensions, Attorney General Kennedy was shaken by the realization that unlike before, when only whites committed violence against blacks, the situation had changed, and blacks were now threatening and assaulting whites, forcing the administration to address their demands more fully and forcefully. Responding to this circumstance, President Kennedy, recognizing that he would gain little support from southern Democrats, initiated a meeting with the Republican congressional leadership about a new civil rights bill. Fortunately, he found willing allies in Illinois Senator Everett M. Dirksen and Indiana Representative Charles Halleck, who, urged by former President Eisenhower to do so, quickly offered the president a proposal he could support. In it, they agreed to accept as "prima facie evidence" the completion of the sixth grade as proof of literacy to vote, to authorize the attorney general to sue school boards refusing to integrate their districts, to create "a Community Relations Service" to negotiate desegregation at the local level, to renew the Civil Rights Commission, to empower the administration to refuse federal funds to "programs or public works" where discrimination in hiring was practiced, and the establishment of a Commission on Equal Employment Opportunity. On June 19, Kennedy announced this civil rights bill to the American people.[21]

Just two days later, at the White House, Kennedy met with over 240 lawyers from around the country "urg[ing them] to join with other community leaders in seeking voluntary solutions to Negro grievances." Presenting an "eight point program for lawyers," the president sought local cooperation with African Americans to create "biracial committees" to end discrimination in bar associations and activities, "to urge respect for the judiciary and the legal process," and to use the media to speak out in favor of equal rights and the fair treatment of all nonwhite persons. In reply, ABA president Smith promised to pursue "solutions consistent with the rights of all individuals within the framework of the rule of law." Demonstrating his determination to promote civil rights, Smith then established a new Special Committee on Civil Rights and Racial Unrest, appointing some of the lawyers who had attended the White House conference and others not invited, including Limbaugh.[22]

Shortly after the White House meeting, the committee met on July 12 in Washington, DC, where the members first discussed the great number of organized demonstrations for civil rights and the "proper treatment to Negro Troops." They next considered the administration's suggestion of establishing local "biracial committees" as a forum for whites and blacks to foster understanding and hammer out agreements. Most of the southern members opposed this suggestion because they were unwilling to compromise, while others like Sherwood W. Wise from Jackson, Mississippi, who favored compliance with Brown and an end to Jim Crow, thought that local opposition to biracial committees made them impossible. In explaining the strong opposition to any progress in Mississippi, Wise, who had refused to join the Jackson Citizens' Council, mentioned a recent incident in which he had been involved. During the so-called "kneel ins"—an organized effort by African Americans to gain admission to white churches—as senior warden of St. Andrew's Episcopal Church, Wise and junior warden Robert Warren admitted blacks into their services, being the only white church to do so. Unfortunately, because of this, Wise did "not know whether his friends are still his friends," and he also feared that he had exposed himself to retaliation professionally. Other southerners on the committee, however, minimized the seriousness of race problems, including a lawyer from Birmingham, Alabama—where Martin Luther King Jr. had recently been jailed—while others expressed their support for Mississippi's action. William B. Spann Jr. from Atlanta, Georgia, and a supporter of Satterfield's efforts to prevent integration of the schools, blamed the protestors and the federal government for the racial turmoil then prevalent in the country. The committee next heard from Satterfield, who was not a member of the committee, but who had requested an opportunity to speak before it. In addition to his testimony, he provided a paper in which he warned against the oppressive and expanding power of the federal government and argued that the legislation proposed by the administration went much further than Brown. Instead of enforcing it, Satterfield asserted that the administration sought to give the federal government the power "to go into any place it decides there is a 'racial imbalance!'" At the end of the meeting, the members established subcommittees and composed a report for the ABA's annual meeting the next month. Although he was unable to attend this first meeting of the committee, Limbaugh was assigned to chair a subcommittee dealing with the issue of the legal representation of clients in unpopular causes.[23]

In preparation for the meeting on August 10 in Chicago, Limbaugh wrote to different leaders of the legal profession in Missouri and elsewhere to better understand the circumstances of African American lawyers, especially in relation to their membership in bar organizations; their participation in these organizations' activities; whether they were accorded "equal treatment"; and their appointment to important positions, including judgeships. Apparently, he sought this information after learning that the National Association for the Advancement of Colored People (NAACP) had strongly criticized the failure of ABA president Smith to appoint any black lawyers to the Special Committee on Civil Rights and Racial Unrest. Limbaugh learned that until the early 1950s black lawyers had not been admitted into the Bar Association of St. Louis, but that these exclusions ended after a black Harvard Law School graduate was rejected and some of the organization's most prominent white members protested. Unfortunately, after this few black lawyers had applied to the organization, although a large number of African Americans were then members of the Lawyers Association of St. Louis, an organization which routinely admitted any licensed lawyer in good standing without regard to race. Limbaugh's correspondent in Kansas City was unaware of any black members of the local professional organizations and thought that an effort should be made to recruit them. Limbaugh also identified the problem of bar associations booking accommodations for its members with hotels and restaurants where blacks were not served. To ensure that African Americans felt welcome and could act in every capacity as full-fledged and active members, bar organizations should refuse to patronize any company which discriminated against their members. Moreover, while African Americans were admitted into the Missouri Bar, Limbaugh learned that only one or two blacks had been appointed to executive committees and that during annual meetings and other functions, unlike their white counterparts, they were not invited to some of the more important and exclusive social events. These problems convinced Limbaugh that it was very important that strong efforts be made to include African Americans at every level of the legal and political spectra. This conclusion explains Limbaugh's later insistence that the Missouri Commission on Human Rights replace its black vice-chairman, who had resigned, with a nonwhite member of the commission.[24]

Unfortunately, chairman Schweppe did not share Limbaugh's concerns about greater African American representation in bar organizations, and he certainly did not desire to integrate the committee. Apparently strengthened in this resolve by the committee's southern members, Schweppe refused to include "Negro lawyers," even as consultants at the committee's first meeting. He also rejected president Smith's suggestion to include black members of the ABA or the National Bar Association—a professional organization for African Americans—on the committee, or even as liaisons at the August 10, 1963, meeting. This concession, Schweppe argued, "would look like recognizing the validity of the NAACP resolution in Chicago lambasting you and the association" for not appointing blacks to the special committee. Instead, he suggested that committee members anxious to learn the perspective of African American lawyers could gain this on their own before the meeting. Furthermore, he thought it inadvisable for the committee to make a recommendation concerning the Civil Rights Act of 1963, noting that "the pending legislation is so hotly political–more political than legal–that we should not deal with the problem in our report at all." If the committee decided to offer a recommendation, Schweppe warned that it would be rendered at the cost of "a divided committee, a divided Board of Governors, and a divided House of Delegates; moreover, it will put the association in the middle of the political fire for at least the ensuing year." Finally, reflecting his own opposition to the civil rights movement, he advised Smith to remove civil rights considerations from the Committee on the Bill of Rights to another, such as the Committee on American Citizenship, for, he argued, "this national problem is never going to be solved on a legal Bill of Rights basis."[25]

Despite Schweppe's desire not to include any testimony from prominent African Americans at the committee meeting, a majority of the committee apparently disagreed, for representatives from the American Civil Liberties Union and Roy Wilkins, president of the NAACP, were provided time to present their views to the committee. Limbaugh believed that most of the committee members agreed with him and were in favor of extending equal rights to African Americans, although some of the southern members were adamantly opposed and insulted Wilkins and the other African Americans there to testify. In their presence, one of the southern lawyers used very inflammatory and provocative language, stating that "there [were] three things you could always tell about a nigger. He lies, he steals, he stinks." Others made clear their belief that blacks were "inferior" and thus should not be accorded the same rights as whites. Remembering this committee meeting many years later, Limbaugh thought that Wilkins demonstrated extraordinary self-composure in not replying in kind to these lawyers and remarked that he "had a very fine impression of Mr. Wilkins, [who] was very patient with opposition."[26]

Apparently, a stalemate developed between Schweppe and his supporters and Limbaugh and those in favor of civil rights reforms, for in its August 1963 report the Special Committee on Civil Rights and Racial Unrest offered no recommendations on the pending civil rights legislation. Instead, the committee urged lawyers to find "voluntary solutions of racial unrest" in their communities, to show "due respect for the law," and, in a swipe at civil rights protestors, to discourage civil disobedience, warning that to do otherwise would lead to more "chaos and anarchy." As an alternative, the committee argued that "the settlement of the critical racial problems at hand must be made around the conference table and cannot be made on the streets." Of course, for this approach to work southern whites must act in good faith promptly to end segregation and Jim Crow. Nothing in the recent or remote past provided any basis for optimism that such an approach would work. Much of the South's history had demonstrated the intransigence of white southerners, even in the face of numerous federal court rulings, in their determination to deny civil rights to African Americans. Indeed, in much the same spirit most of the committee members from the South and their sympathizers, including Schweppe, had conspired successfully to prevent the committee from taking a position on the Kennedy administration's civil rights bill. This type of obstructionism had been effective since the 1954 Brown decision, and had led to more forceful and militant action among the African American community, which finally, after many broken promises, had forced the Kennedy administration to act. Limbaugh left behind no record of his thoughts concerning Schweppe's leadership of the committee and its report, but when one considers his previous and later actions it is highly probable that he favored forceful support of Kennedy's civil rights bill, the participation of African Americans on the committee, and an aggressive effort to recruit black lawyers into the ABA.[27]

In 1966, Limbaugh entered a new field of action in the civil rights arena when Democratic Governor Warren E. Hearnes appointed him to serve on the Missouri Commission on Human Rights. After the resignation of Reverend Arthur Fullbright, initially Hearnes had narrowed his selection of a replacement to four clergymen from southeast Missouri, all of whom could not, or would not, serve on the commission. Unable to find a suitable Democrat from the region to serve, the governor apparently received the suggestion of Limbaugh's name with some enthusiasm, for he moved quickly to appoint him. He would reappoint him to this post in 1968 and 1971. In the mid-1950s, Limbaugh and Hearnes had worked together on a committee reforming Missouri's probate law, when the governor was a young state representative and Limbaugh was acting as a legal advisor to the committee. Meeting biweekly for more than a year, both men had ample time to become well acquainted. Presumably, during this time Limbaugh had impressed Hearnes as a conscientious, hardworking, and congenial member of the committee, or otherwise the governor, who was committed to ending racial discrimination in Missouri, would not have appointed him. Moreover, he had learned from Forrest P. "Flip" Carson, chairman of the commission, and executive director Peter C. Robertson that Limbaugh had served on an ABA committee involved in promoting civil rights, although they were unclear about the details. An added benefit, the governor undoubtedly considered, was that Limbaugh was very well respected throughout the state, even among many Democrats, and that his reputation would add luster to the commission, which was then viewed with some suspicion in the General Assembly and throughout the state.[28]

The Missouri Commission on Human Rights was established in 1957, but was originally intended to be in operation for only two years to gather information about discrimination and to publish a report with recommendations. The commission focused particularly upon complaints of alleged "discrimination in places of public accommodation, in employment, in schools, [and] in housing." In 1960, the commission reported to the governor and the legislature that discrimination against African Americans was embedded "in all aspects of Missouri life," leading to the decision to provide the agency with expanded authority to investigate accusations of discrimination, to hold public hearings, and to make policy. In 1961, Missouri's General Assembly passed fair housing legislation, and in 1963 increased the commission's funding. After Congress passed the Civil Rights Act of 1964, imposing regulations to prevent discrimination against African Americans and measures to punish noncompliant states, the commission undertook an educational program to inform Missouri's citizens about their rights and responsibilities under the new law. The commission informed the public accommodations industry—which included hotels, motels, restaurants, and resorts—of the law and negotiated an agreement with "ten leading hotel, motel, restaurant, and resort associations, many of which had previously opposed" compliance with the new federal law. The commission also held regional conferences "to discuss the law and practical problems related to its implementation." In attempting to meet its responsibilities, it became clear that the commission was inadequately staffed, and so just prior to Limbaugh's appointment the legislature approved funding to increase the full-time staff from two to fourteen persons.[29]

Limbaugh attended his first commission meeting on September 13, 1966, just days before his seventy-fifth birthday. Very much a team player, he worked diligently to support the commission's efforts to ensure that all Missourians enjoyed the full measure of their civil and political rights. As the representative from southeast Missouri, which was the most problematic region of the state, he proposed that the commission establish "a branch office" there, for he believed that "a great deal of educational work needs to be done." This comment led some to suggest sending speakers to address service groups such as local Lions and Rotary clubs. Limbaugh, however, urged the commission to do more by holding a regular meeting in southeast Missouri, and he thought it would be helpful to have Governor Hearnes attend. Limbaugh also proposed that an educational component be included and suggested that "an open forum" be held either before or after their meeting. Wishing to get right to work, he also requested the case file on the Caruthersville schools, which were then under investigation for remaining segregated.[30]

The major difficulty in implementing Limbaugh's suggestions for southeast Missouri was that the commission's staff members, despite the new hires, were overwhelmed by their duties. In addition to investigating and handling a large number of civil rights complaints, the commission's responsibilities included educating the public and industries concerning federal fair housing, public accommodations, school segregation, and fair employment laws. To gain more help, Robertson and Carson met with Governor Hearnes, who agreed to an "increase in staff and staff salaries," and to improving and enlarging the commission's central office in Jefferson City. However, the governor declined to seek funding for new branch offices around the state, although he thought it would not hurt to establish "skeleton" offices where necessary. Reflecting the special need for extra effort in the Bootheel region, the commissioners decided to establish its first branch office in Sikeston and to seek private funding to support it. Before this, Lewis A. (Pete) Akenhead had worked alone, operating out of his home in Kennett. Soon the need for more personnel was recognized and in September 1968 the commission hired Rita Cook, who worked first as a secretary and later as a field representative.[31]

Akenhead had grown up in small-town Arkansas—much the same background as the people of southeast Missouri. Prior to his employment by the commission in July 1965, he had been offered a temporary federal position to interview superintendents of school districts in Mississippi to seek the integration of their schools. He was told that once they refused, for it was a foregone conclusion that they would, Akenhead would then write a report and repeat the process at the next school district until presumably he had visited them all. He declined this position, regarding it to be an exercise in futility and folly. Shortly thereafter, he gained employment with the commission and was sent to southeast Missouri, where he hoped he could work to end all forms of racial discrimination. At first, he found progress slow, and working with Fullbright sometimes frustrating. Once Limbaugh was appointed, Akenhead's circumstances improved, for the new commissioner permitted him to work without interference, only insisting that he keep him informed. Akenhead also learned that Limbaugh was unwavering in his support of civil rights despite strong opposition from many whites, some of whom sent anonymous threats warning the septuagenarian to stop interfering in their affairs. In particular, Akenhead heard from members of the NAACP in the region, especially from the chapter in Cape Girardeau, who stated that Limbaugh was relentless in his advocacy for an end to Jim Crow policies.[32]

When Limbaugh first began his work on the commission, its primary priority was to end discrimination against hiring African Americans. At a meeting in late 1966, the commissioners decided to work more closely with federal agencies on employment matters and upon Limbaugh's motion voted to allow the commission's staff to record the race of applicants for the Labor Department. Occasionally, when their procedures proved ineffective, the staff consulted with the commissioners about possible changes, or even recommendations, to the legislature to modify the existing law. Thus, believing that too many firms were excluded, the staff proposed to amend the Missouri Fair Employment Practices Act to include companies with four or more employees under the statute's jurisdiction, rather than just those with twenty-five or more as it then applied. In fulfilling its educational role, the commission also distributed 10,000 fair employment posters "to all covered employers, labor unions, employment agencies, government agencies, and school boards." Furthermore, after gaining approval from the commissioners, the staff began preparations to undertake "an up-to-date study of employment patterns and practices insofar as they relate to race among Missouri state agencies and other governmentally supported agencies in the state of Missouri." Conducted in 1968, they reported that "the State of Missouri cannot take pride in the data presented in this report." While the proportion of African Americans and women employed by the state were proportionate to the population, the report also concluded "that both groups are disproportionately confined to the bottom end of the pay scale. The discrepancy is greatest when statistics for Negro males and for non-Negro males are compared." The commission believed that the statistics show "that some agencies are in all probability not complying with the requirements of the Missouri Fair Employment Practices Act. The Highway Department and the Highway Patrol are particularly suspect."[33]

During his first year as a field representative, Akenhead received very few complaints, in part because blacks feared retaliation from whites, and in part because Robertson had directed him never to go to businesses and request that they hire blacks. Instead, he was to wait for the complaints to come in, to document them, and only then "to work the cases." Robertson adopted this cautious policy, for to do otherwise would have almost certainly led to a severe cut in the commission's budget by State Senator J. F. (Pat) Patterson, who lived in southeast Missouri and was the chair of the appropriations committee. In early 1966, while testifying before Patterson's committee, Robertson had angered him when he had asserted that the senator's hometown of Caruthersville, as well as McCarty, were not in compliance with civil rights law. During the hearing, Patterson accused Robertson "of trying to arouse racial tension rather than to eliminate it." The powerful senator also accused Robertson of "being dictatorial" at a local meeting on unemployment and claimed that the Missouri Commission on Human Rights, instead of solving problems and bringing peace, wanted "more tension and racial strife." Senator Patterson's wrath, however, was misdirected, for Robertson was only citing the recent report of the United States Commission on Civil Rights to Congress and the president in which it singled out for criticism the Caruthersville public schools and others in southeast Missouri for remaining segregated.[34]

At first, Akenhead dutifully followed Robertson's instructions and did not intervene with any business concerning employment matters. His frustration grew, however, when he learned during the summer of 1966 that the newly established Caruthersville Shipyard, which would soon begin the construction of barges in southeast Missouri, had hired 150 welders, laborers, and layout men, but that not one African American was among them. Driving over to the shipyard to meet with the plant manager, Akenhead first handed to him a copy of the fair employment law, "which" he admitted many years later, "I was not supposed to do." Not wishing to be confrontational and fearing that the manager might call Robertson to complain, Akenhead asked what types of skills were required by the shipyard. The manager admitted that the skills necessary were not high. Really, all that was necessary was that a person weld strong joints, adding that "they didn't have to be pretty." The manager, sensing a problem, forthrightly asked if he had to hire blacks. As diplomatically as possible, Akenhead replied that he wanted to be certain he understood the manager's question correctly. If he wanted to know what would happen if the shipyard only hired whites, Akenhead observed that much would depend upon circumstances. But he warned that if later a black applicant filed a formal complaint with the commission and it was discovered that the shipyard had hired less-qualified whites than the black applicant, then the commission would have no choice but to rule that the black applicant had been discriminated against. Once this determination was made the company would be forced to hire and pay the black applicant back pay from the date of his application to the time he was hired. This surprised the plant manager and to his credit he immediately asked where he could find qualified blacks to hire. Akenhead promised to help and called a friend at the Tri-County Trade School, where eighty percent of the students were black and classes in welding were taught. Eventually, the shipyard employed approximately 150 blacks there. Akenhead considered this meeting to be a great success, even though it had occupied perhaps twenty minutes of his time.[35]

Akenhead's success with the Caruthersville Shipyard, however, was not his last, although most of his later accomplishments came only slowly and after much struggle, for white resistance to civil rights reforms remained formidable in southeast Missouri. Only after careful investigation demonstrated that illegal discrimination had occurred and the appropriate remedy was applied to redress the situation could a permanent and widespread change in the circumstances of African Americans be effected. Fortunately, Akenhead received timely help from the United States Commission on Civil Rights, which had just published a report exposing many problems of discrimination in the region. Following up on this report, the Missouri Advisory Committee scheduled a public meeting in April 1966 at the Portageville High School to gather information concerning conditions relating to black employment, the problem of poverty, progress in desegregating the schools, and "on the conditions of negroes and their relations with the total community." At this meeting, probably to no one's surprise, the committee uncovered "problems in employment, housing, and public accommodations."[36]

Newspaper accounts of this investigation noted the Missouri Commission on Human Rights' role as a civil rights enforcement agency. Different factors tended to prevent African Americans from challenging white dominance at that time, but the most important of these was the caution conditioned by living for many decades under the oppression of segregation and the lack of organization among blacks to challenge Jim Crow in southeast Missouri. Because of this caution, few complaints were brought against the discriminatory practices which permeated almost every aspect of life there. Occasionally the commissioners instituted complaints themselves, though, especially whenever a situation seemed likely to disturb "the public peace." In late 1966, such a case originated in Howardsville, where a restaurant refused service to two African American men, who, fearing retaliation, carried weapons with them when they returned to demand service again. Their action led to an accusation that they had drawn their weapons upon the owner, although in his investigation Akenhead determined this to be untrue. When serving the charges, the restaurant owner was outraged at being told that he could not refuse service to whomever he wished and called the town's deputy sheriff, demanding that he arrest the young field representative. When the deputy sheriff arrived, Akenhead simply presented to him his state identification card. Recognizing his authority, the deputy sheriff explained to the owner that he could not arrest Akenhead, and turning to him said, "I wouldn't have your job, son."[37]

Following up on its work, in March 1967 the Missouri Advisory Committee held an eight-hour, closed hearing in Caruthersville. At the meeting were Jacques E. Wilmore, director of the southern field office of the United States Commission on Civil Rights, along with Jerry Belenker and Akenhead from the Missouri Commission on Human Rights, who all attended as observers. "Numerous witnesses from throughout southeast Missouri" testified concerning discrimination in the implementation of the anti-poverty program and in the hiring of African Americans. As a result, a number of complaints were made to the Missouri Commission on Human Rights. Even more important was the NAACP's decision to institute "a summer project" in the area. In May, the organization announced that it would begin a six week-long effort on July 30, and that it would be headquartered in Charleston, Governor Hearnes' hometown. The project began with a rally in Kennett at which Roy Wilkins, executive director of the NAACP, spoke to more than 1,000 whites and blacks. He urged his listeners to eschew violence and promised southeast Missouri's residents that he and the others were not there to stir up trouble, but instead "to develop local leadership in the Negro community, as well as to delve into the problems of housing, unemployment, school desegregation, and voter registration." What they were not there for was to create "any type of civil disturbances." Wilkins also touted cooperation between whites and blacks as important to resolving these problems. This message was especially important at this time, for some within the African American community were then advocating violence and separatism through the Black Power movement. A week later, Kivie Kaplan, the president of the NAACP, presented much the same message to an audience in Caruthersville.[38]

Part of the group traveling to Kennett for the rally was commissioner John B. Ervin, who was the first African American dean at Washington University in St. Louis. He and others had taken a Greyhound Bus charter, which stopped at a restaurant in Sikeston, some seventy miles northeast of Kennett. As it turned out, the establishment was segregated, and the driver directed the African American passengers to enter a room in the back where they would be served. As was almost always true of segregated accommodations, the facilities were very inferior to those provided to whites, and blacks were charged more for items on the menu of equal or worse quality than those served in the front room to whites. Ervin, who was probably the most aggressive of the commissioners, out of frustration at the slow progress in civil rights, once exclaimed that "maybe we need more revolution and street fighting." During the meeting in Kennett, he sat with Akenhead, and, because the young field representative was white, Ervin earnestly explained why segregated public accommodations were such a great trouble and injustice to black people. Later, this lesson was reinforced when Akenhead drove black commissioner Lucile Bluford, a veteran journalist and publisher of the *Kansas City Call*, from Kansas City to St. Louis. During the trip, he asked Bluford more than once if she did not want to stop for lunch. When he stopped for fuel, she refused even to go in for a cup of coffee or to use the restroom. Her excuse was that she wasn't really hungry and would prefer to wait until they were in St. Louis. However, when the trip was almost over, she confided to Akenhead that between Kansas City and St. Louis there was no restaurant or restroom available to blacks. Concerning this, Bluford, who was then in her midfifties, "was embarrassed" and humiliated.[39]

As a result of the NAACP's summer project, for the first time African Americans in southeast Missouri were armed with the training and knowledge necessary to challenge segregation and discrimination effectively. Soon, the number of complaints to the commission originating from the region increased dramatically. One of the first was made by the NAACP against the restaurant in Sikeston and Greyhound Bus. Akenhead went to the owner of the restaurant, but he refused to cooperate. Because Greyhound had a contract with the establishment, Akenhead next traveled to Memphis, Tennessee, where he spoke with a representative of the company about the problem. At first, he "was very intractable," and contended that the discrimination was not Greyhound's responsibility. However, when Akenhead pointed out that their driver had directed blacks to go to the rear of the establishment, the representative could not deny at least some culpability in the matter. When Akenhead made clear the commission's intention of suing Greyhound if they did not sign a decree promising to comply with the law, he became nervous and recognized that a court case would generate a lot of bad publicity. He then promised to take up the matter with executives of the company, and in the end Greyhound severed its contract with the restaurant. At a different location, it built a new bus station where blacks and whites were served together, and equally. Later, the Sikeston restaurant closed its backdoor room and made its front room accessible to everyone.[40]

Despite this and other successes, several months after the NAACP's summer project, the commission learned that some complainants were dissatisfied at the delay in the commission's handling of their cases. These delays were not the result of a lack of zeal on the part of Akenhead and Limbaugh to process the complaints, but instead stemmed from the commission's lack of the resources and personnel necessary to investigate and close the flood of cases then coming from there. The field representative's job was to investigate complaints and send the case file to Jefferson City, where the conciliator, usually one of the staff lawyers, then sought to gain voluntary compliance with the law. The vast majority of the cases were conciliated, but the most difficult were forwarded to Limbaugh, who then held hearings on the matter and ultimately decided them. These decisions had the force of law. While only fragmentary evidence is extant, Limbaugh adjudicated employment cases in which African American employees alleged that they were being "paid less than white employees," along with various public accommodation cases, such as those brought by the NAACP against Harold's Tavern and the Southern Kitchen in Kennett, discrimination in hiring cases, and a complaint against a county sheriff for maintaining segregated facilities and unsatisfactory jail conditions.[41]

The dissatisfaction with the commission because of the delays in processing complaints led to representatives of the NAACP coming to Jefferson City on February 2 and 3, 1968, to meet with Limbaugh, African American commissioner Ervin, and the commission staff about the situation in southeast Missouri. Althea Simmons, a member of the NAACP Legal Defense Fund, and Julius Williams, regional director of the NAACP in Kansas City, expressed concern about the delays, which had "disenchanted" many of the complainants, and sought better coordination with the commission "to help alleviate the many inequalities." During their meeting, they discussed a number of problems, including enforcement of the fair employment law, discrimination in the state welfare program, school segregation, and the need for the commission to keep complainants informed about the status of their cases. Perhaps to reassure Simmons and Williams concerning their good faith, the staff presented statistics demonstrating that they were handling a large number of cases as expeditiously as possible. Of the 140 public accommodation cases then before the commission, fifty of these originated in southeast Missouri, of which twenty-seven were then pending. Moreover, the commission was handling forty-six employment cases. Simmons and Williams were promised to keep complainants better informed about their cases. Another matter discussed was the commission's decision during its December 1967 meeting to conduct "a compliance review" of schools throughout the state beginning in the Bootheel region, where the problem was greatest. Moreover, the commission informed Simmons and Williams of their intention to work on increasing the hiring of blacks in the "shoe and garment industry in southeast Missouri," to work to improve the state's record of promoting and paying equally African American employees, and to "give high priority" to conciliating the two cases brought against Pepsi-Cola in Malden. At the end of their meeting, Simmons and Williams left reassured and satisfied that the commission was working diligently to enforce Missouri's civil rights laws.[42]

The results of the special meeting on southeast Missouri was reported at the March 1968 commission meeting. The commission also discussed a report on school desegregation in which the staff proposed that the commission "initiate complaints" against those school districts where "the racial breakdown" of the schools strongly indicated that they were segregated. From Akenhead's and Grant Stauffer's survey of schools in southeast Missouri, it was clear that the problem was still acute in the Bootheel, and it was proposed to begin there. Their results showed little change from the findings of the United States Commission on Civil Rights report from two years before, observing that the vast majority of the remaining segregated schools in Missouri were in southeast Missouri. Moreover, the NAACP's report on its summer 1967 project confirmed these findings, observing "only token integration in [the] bootheel elementary schools." The NAACP also noted that in many schools only a small percentage of black students attended, and that some schools remained 100 percent black. The conclusion could not be avoided that resistance to integration in a number of schools continued there. While most whites understood that "sooner or later" their schools would be desegregated, "they just didn't want it to be sooner." Thus, presented with overwhelming evidence of segregated schools, commissioner Bluford moved that the commission adopt the staff's plan for integration, and Limbaugh seconded it, the motion being carried unanimously.[43]

In particular, this decision pleased Akenhead very much, for he had long wished to pursue the issue of school desegregation more aggressively. As already noted, in 1966 the United States Commission on Civil Rights had charged the Caruthersville public schools "with failing to comply with their pledge to desegregate." Under the Office of Education's supervision, the Caruthersville schools and others in Pemiscot County had adopted a "freedom-of-choice plan for desegregation," in which students were allowed to choose the school they wished to attend. Despite this program, the Caruthersville schools remained largely segregated. Of the three elementary schools, one was all white, another all black, and the third was 97.3 percent white. Of the two junior high schools, one was 97.8 percent white and the other was all black. Concerning the high schools there, the United States Commission on Civil Rights Report noted that "administratively there [was] only one high school but actually there [were] two buildings and in effect two schools. One, 97 percent white, [was] known as Caruthersville High School." The other was all black and was "known as the Eighteenth Street Center." The curricula of these schools were very different, for the black school focused on "vocational education," while the white high school provided a much fuller educational experience, including college preparatory courses. This treatment of black students reflected the attitude of most whites in a community where blacks were relegated to living "in a cotton patch area outside of town." The meanness of the community toward its black residents extended even to the petty refusal of providing water and sewage services to them.[44]

After receiving a complaint in 1966 about the Caruthersville schools, Robertson allowed Akenhead to investigate the matter discreetly. This was necessary after State Senator Patterson's dressing down of Robertson before the appropriations committee and because Patterson's property was adjacent to the high school grounds. Another consideration was their desire not to embarrass Governor Hearnes, who was a strong supporter of the commission's efforts and was from the region. Despite Akenhead's care, the *Caruthersville Journal* apparently got wind of some type of an investigation being conducted, but was unsure if it was by a state or federal agency. In the expectation of bringing a Class A lawsuit, to gather useful evidence of segregation, Akenhead questioned new black families about the circumstances regarding the enrollment of their children in school. In particular, Robertson wanted to know if the school authorities had directed their children to a black school. Akenhead also gathered evidence showing that white students were sent to white schools. The same information was collected regarding the assignment of black and white teachers. When Akenhead asked a black school principal if the Caruthersville schools were segregated, "he laughed for three minutes." However, in the end "Robertson decided not to file . . . suit," despite the considerable evidence Akenhead had amassed, recognizing that Patterson could reduce the commission's funding, and thus the case could potentially do more harm than good to civil rights in Missouri.[45]

Fortunately, this circumstance did not continue much longer. Apparently, because of the United States Commission on Civil Rights' harsh assessment of continued segregation of the Caruthersville Schools, in April 1967 officials from the Office of Education held closed meetings with members of the Caruthersville school board to gain their "compliance with the Civil Rights Act of 1964." Without an acceptable plan, the schools were warned that they would lose federal funding and "be liable to court action" like many schools in the South. This threat, which the local newspaper complained was using their federal tax dollars to coerce them, convinced the school board to craft a plan acceptable to the Office of Education. In it, for the fall term of 1967, the school board agreed to assign four black teachers to the white elementary and junior high schools and three white teachers to the black elementary and junior high schools. The integration of elementary and junior high schools would be voluntary. The faculty and students at the high school level would be fully integrated. By the fall of 1969, the school board promised to integrate the schools fully. The plan was published in the local newspapers and information was sent to parents explaining the agreement. During this process, Limbaugh was in contact with the school district's lawyers, and in his capacity as commissioner explained to them their legal responsibilities. Afterward, however, concerned that he and his fellow commissioners act fairly and properly, at a commission meeting Limbaugh requested that a policy be established to guide commissioners in their interactions with the parties in a case, especially when the possibility remained that a commissioner might be called upon to act as a judge over the matter later.[46]

Despite the Office of Education's success with the Caruthersville schools, several school systems in southeast Missouri remained segregated. To address this problem, the Missouri Commission on Human Rights reviewed the results of the school compliance survey that Akenhead and Stauffer had conducted and also set aside time at a commission meeting to hear from Akenhead. Prior to the meeting, he had spoken with eighteen school superintendents about desegregating their schools. From most of them he gained admissions that their schools were segregated. After presenting this information to the commissioners, Akenhead argued that it was time to take forceful action, and recommended that they authorize the staff to initiate complaints to begin the process of finally ending school segregation in Missouri once and for all. Although some of the commissioners did not like a field representative telling them what to do, the commissioners all agreed to move forward according to Akenhead's advice. Limbaugh supported his young colleague in all his efforts, and let him know that he "was doing a good job." After the meeting, the commission filed charges against "the largest school districts in southeast Missouri." To expedite these cases, the entire staff dropped everything else they were doing, traveled to southeast Missouri, and in pairs investigated these seven school districts. After finding probable cause of violation of the law, Harold Whitfield, a lawyer on the staff, Sandra Neese, and executive director Richard E. Risk completed the work by gaining desegregation settlements from all of the school districts, except one. During these proceedings Limbaugh provided valuable help, for lawyers representing the schools knew and trusted him to explain frankly and honestly the schools' legal obligations and the consequences of noncompliance. These conciliation agreements effectively ended most of the remaining resistance to integration of the schools, for the smaller districts, observing the capitulation of the larger districts, quickly complied with the law. Thus by September 1969, integration of the schools in southeast Missouri was largely completed, although one school district held out for a time longer.[47]

During this period, Akenhead remembered that Limbaugh "certainly was right in the center of the [school desegregation] controversy." Akenhead heard from various contacts, including his NAACP friends, that Limbaugh made frequent public appeals for integration, stating his desire "to see the segregated way of life ended and to bring about a thing where we're no longer separate but equal, but just equal." In private, however, Limbaugh expressed to Akenhead some concern that integration might lead to new unanticipated problems as young white and black children were thrown together for the first time. This concern, however, never deterred him from supporting integration without reservation. At the time, Akenhead dismissed these concerns, but many years later concluded that Limbaugh was "probably right" to worry about the unintended consequences of integration.[48]

Over the next year and a half, Akenhead and Limbaugh worked together to enforce the civil rights laws in southeast Missouri. John R. Rencher, then a recent graduate of Lincoln University and a native of the Bootheel region—he was from Oran—temporarily worked at the Sikeston office as a field representative, providing Akenhead with some much-needed help. In 1969, the commission received in total thirty-two cases from the Bootheel region, nineteen of which were employment cases, the rest being public accommodation matters. This represented a dramatic increase in the number of cases that the commission had received from the area during the previous three and a half years. In the almost five years since Akenhead began his work in southeast Missouri, the commission had closed 103 cases. Soon fewer cases were filed and both Akenhead and Rencher no longer conducted investigations exclusively in southeast Missouri. Eventually, because of the progress in southeast Missouri, the Sikeston office was closed. Nevertheless, despite these many accomplishments, in the commission's March 1970 newsletter Limbaugh argued that more must be done, for

we cannot overlook the fact that problems of discrimination, poverty and prejudice remain, but it appears that the people in this area are aware of these problems and are patiently and persistently seeking properly to cope with them. In order to achieve equality and the purposes of civil rights legislation, it is necessary that we keep constantly before us a public purpose of effective enforcement of the laws prohibiting discrimination because of race, creed, color, religion, sex or national origin. In achieving this purpose, the commission seeks the cooperation and a will to comply on the part of all the people who hold any positions of responsibility in education, business, industry, and agencies serving the public interest.[49]

In 1971, Governor Warren E. Hearnes requested that Limbaugh, who was then approaching eighty years of age—"four score years" as he expressed it—consent to reappointment for another two-year term upon the Missouri Commission on Human Rights. Fortunately, by this time the civil rights work in southeast Missouri had lessened considerably from the flood of cases he and the commission's staff had handled during the peak period from 1968 to 1970. Because of his age, Limbaugh's family had become increasingly concerned about his frequent journeys back and forth between Cape Girardeau and Jefferson City to attend commission meetings. Nevertheless, he accepted the appointment, a reaffirmation of his strong belief in a citizen's and lawyer's duty to give back to one's community. Whenever possible, Limbaugh took a flight to Jefferson City or traveled by Greyhound bus. Occasionally, his fellow commissioner Larry Carp, who was much younger than himself, drove him from Jefferson City to the bus station in St. Louis. From their conversations, Carp gained a deep appreciation of Limbaugh's character, his "vision" for accomplishing good, and his commitment to the work of the commission. Although a proud liberal and Democrat, Carp admired his Republican friend and believed him to be oblivious to distinctions of party and race. Very active in party politics and current events, as a young man Carp had worked as an assistant to United States Senator Paul Douglas (D-Illinois), and had gained a wide acquaintance with many state and national leaders of his party. Many years later, out of recognition for his long and faithful service to the Democratic Party, President Bill Clinton appointed Carp to serve as a public delegate to the United Nations. In reflecting back over his career and the many important people he had known, Carp concluded that "of all the persons I have known from government and politics, Rush was outstanding."[50]

Chapter Eleven

Twilight Years

Despite his age, from all appearances, Rush H. Limbaugh's health remained good despite earlier setbacks. In 1965, the year before his appointment to the Missouri Commission on Human Rights, Limbaugh's personal doctor had warned him that he was in danger of becoming diabetic and advised him to lose weight and reduce his consumption of sugar. This diagnosis seemed particularly ominous to him, for his oldest brother, Arthur, and other family members had developed diabetes and he was aware of the danger the malady posed to his health. Following his doctor's orders, Limbaugh reduced his daily diet to 1,200 calories and stopped eating sweets. Within a few months, he lost five inches around his waist and felt better. Despite his advancing years, he continued his professional work, which, coupled with his duties on the commission, occupied most of his time. In 1966, he occasionally experienced abdominal pains, which were at first infrequent, but soon increased in frequency and intensity. In late March 1967, one of these attacks incapacitated him and led to hospitalization and the removal of his gall bladder. While in the hospital, the doctors also discovered "a prostate condition" requiring surgery, but they considered it unwise to operate until after he had completely recovered from his gall bladder surgery. This decision proved to be a wise precaution, for after returning home an infection developed, requiring another stay in the hospital. His second surgery that year occurred on the last day of August. For a number of years after this, Limbaugh's health was very good, although he suffered from the occasional cold, and in 1973 developed pneumonia, for which he was briefly hospitalized.[1]

Unfortunately, Bee's health was not as strong as her husband's, and had been deteriorating progressively for some time. After the Second World War, she had suffered from a recurring gall bladder problem for which she had undergone surgery. Later, her vocal cords were operated upon to remove a benign tumor. During this period, Limbaugh had noted with alarm her general decline, but he also admired her resilience and toughness when she made slow progress in regaining at least part of her former strength. Soon, she resumed most of her duties at home, church, and in the community, although, in a concession to her health, she cut back on some activities. Determinedly, however, Bee continued to aid her husband in his various responsibilities. Perhaps the most taxing of these, when both of them were then in their late sixties, was their trip to India as goodwill ambassadors representing the United States.[2]

In 1961, Bee fell and broke her arm, and because it did not mend properly, she suffered from pain for several months thereafter. Through the years, she also suffered from a recurring abdominal problem, a malady that became increasingly painful, forcing a return to the hospital in July 1964. As before, the doctors were unsure about the source of her troubles and decided to do exploratory surgery. Limbaugh and the rest of the family were fearful that she had cancer. The surgeon quickly discovered, however, that her gall bladder was not functioning properly and removed it. This procedure ended most of her abdominal problems so long as she watched her diet carefully. On December 5, 1964, delayed a few months by Bee's surgery, the Limbaughs celebrated their fiftieth wedding anniversary. To mark this happy occasion, Dr. Ivan Lee Holt, who had conducted the marriage ceremony on August 29, 1914, returned to Cape Girardeau to join them, their family, and friends in the celebration.[3]

During this period, Limbaugh received a number of awards in recognition of his devoted labors to his church and community. In 1965, American Bar Association (ABA) president Edward W. Kuhn reappointed him as chair of the Committee on the Bill of Rights and to serve on the Special Committee on Civil Rights and Racial Unrest. The following year, Limbaugh became a member of the ABA's new Section of Individual Rights and Responsibilities, which took over the responsibilities of three committees dealing with civil rights issues. That same year, the local Chamber of Commerce awarded him the Golden Deeds Award, and the Cape County Bar Association, in recognition of his fifty years as a practicing lawyer, presented to him a resolution signed by the entire Missouri Senate. Ten years later the local bar association would again honor his continued practice of the law.[4]

As the 1960s came to a close, Limbaugh felt great concern about the direction in which the country was heading and about his, and especially Bee's, future. In particular, he was troubled by the turmoil on college campuses across the country, where students staged protests against the Vietnam War, took over campus buildings, and generally defied authority. While he initially opposed the war, Limbaugh also believed that once the nation had entered the conflict, it should be fought to win. His concerns about the war only increased after his grandson Daniel, who had graduated from West Point, was sent to Vietnam, where he led troops in battle. Moreover, Limbaugh's unease was further reinforced by the violence and assassinations that increasingly became a part of the political arena, especially as the civil rights controversy came to a head. Another development which greatly disturbed him was the rejection of traditional values by the younger generation, many of whom embraced a new permissiveness regarding the use of illegal drugs and sex outside of marriage. Even Attorney General Ramsay Clark, the country's top law-enforcement official under President Lyndon B. Johnson, seemed more concerned with devising new schemes for the rehabilitation of criminals than he was with protecting law-abiding citizens. While all of this was very disturbing, Limbaugh "tried to roll with the times," never becoming a scold or issuing jeremiads, but instead he maintained an optimism founded in his belief in the inherent goodness of the people of America and its constitutional system. While their faith sustained them, both he and Bee could not ignore that the vast majority of their life together was then behind them, especially with the recent passing of so many relatives and friends of their generation. Among those who had died by the end of the decade were his brothers Arthur and Roscoe and their wives, his brother-in-law Dr. Dayton L. Seabaugh, and his neighbors Dr. Frank Hall and Robert Erlbacher, to name only a few.[5]

During this time, making concessions to his age, Limbaugh decided to cease trying cases before juries, although he occasionally appeared in court "for hearings and other proceedings." The focus of his work thereafter was on providing legal counsel to individuals and corporations, negotiating agreements, and drafting various types of legal documents—in effect becoming "a desk lawyer." He also disengaged himself from all leadership positions in the ABA by 1968, opting to focus upon his work with the Missouri Commission on Human Rights. Despite his desire to slow down and spend more time at home with Bee, he found this difficult, for firms and individuals still depended upon him and he felt a responsibility not to abandon them completely. Still, in 1969 and 1970, he and Bee took extended vacations to Alaska and England. At this time, Limbaugh also turned over to others the responsibilities of managing the law firm, and as a board member of the Cape Girardeau Federal Savings and Loan Association.[6]

As the years passed, Bee became increasingly dependent upon others. Eventually, someone was hired to do the housework and complete other chores. Despite her many setbacks, she carried on with her usual aplomb, or "austere stoicism," as her husband admiringly referred to her fortitude in persevering without complaint. Fortunately, the Limbaughs' daughters-in-law, Mary, Millie, and Anne, and their grandchildren helped with various tasks and errands. In 1972 Bee developed sinus problems, which her physicians suspected might be caused by allergies, but were unable to provide her with much relief. Despite all of this, in July 1973 Bee was determined to accompany the rest of the family to Texas for the wedding of their grandson Stephen Jr. to Marsha D. Moore, whom he had met while attending Southern Methodist University. On their return home, traveling with their son Stephen, his wife Anne, and grandson Andy, the group traveled to the Alamo in San Antonio before returning to Cape Girardeau. In 1975, Limbaugh and Bee traveled to Tacoma, Washington, to visit their grandson Daniel and his family. Unfortunately, Bee's poor health forced them to return home early.[7]

During her final years, Bee's health continued to worsen. Suffering from dizzy spells, she was no longer stable on her feet, eventually forcing her to use a walker and later a wheelchair. After a series of eye surgeries, she was no longer able to read. Knowing the disappointment of this setback to Bee, Limbaugh began reading to her books about the lives of the American founders and other important leaders, classic books and novels, and Shakespeare's plays. During the day, in an effort to spend more time with his ailing wife, Limbaugh often came home to eat lunch with her. In 1977, it was necessary to provide a personal nurse to attend to her around the clock. Limbaugh, increasingly concerned for her welfare, spent more and more time with her and sought to bring her comfort. On July 4, 1977, their son Stephen, wishing to see how his parents were doing, went over to their home in the morning and walked back to their bedroom, where he found them holding hands and singing "America the Beautiful." By this time, the bad days far outstripped the good ones, but whenever possible Limbaugh took his wife out on drives and to visit the family. These jaunts out of the house were brief and became more infrequent as the summer progressed.[8]

On August 14, the family gathered to help the Limbaughs celebrate their sixty-third wedding anniversary. The celebration was held fifteen days early to enable as many members of the family as possible to attend. For many of them, this was their final farewell to Bee. On the day of their anniversary, Limbaugh asked her if she remembered what had happened in August 1914. She replied that it "was the beginning of the war." Limbaugh then asked her if she recalled what had happened on August 29, 1914. With "an impish smile she said sweetly, 'Yes, that was the beginning of our war, wasn't it?'" After this, Bee's condition deteriorated rapidly. On August 31, sensing that her death was imminent, she expressed to her husband of more than six decades regret that she could not remain to care for him. On September 3, after experiencing heart troubles, at the age of eighty-six, the matriarch of the Limbaugh clan died peacefully in her sleep, leaving behind a large and prosperous family of children, grandchildren, great-grandchildren, and her greatly distressed and bereaved husband.[9]

The evening of Bee's death, Limbaugh and his daughter-in-law Mary had spent time with her and returned home only to receive a phone call summoning them back to the hospital. Upon arriving, the hospital personnel told them of her passing, and they "went into the room just to sit with her for awhile." Sensing that he wanted to be alone with her, Mary left the room, a gesture for which Limbaugh was deeply grateful, for then he had the opportunity to "sit there by himself," as he expressed it, "with the girl he always loved." Grappling with the meaning of Bee's death, Limbaugh realized that "for the first time in 63 years I was utterly alone except for memories of the greatest soul I ever knew." His main support during this difficult time was his faith and family, who rallied around him and were always present to offer their sympathy and encouragement when sadness overtook him. Some years later, in a speech to a group of high school seniors, Limbaugh recommended that they find their "eternal" love—a partner with whom to share life's struggles and joys—a relationship, although he left this unsaid, like his with Bee. Despite his grief, Limbaugh tried to carry on as before, turning to his professional and community work to fill the void of his loss. Apparently, resuming his routine was therapeutic, for he soon immersed himself in his legal work and was again speaking publicly and participating in public affairs.[10]

Just months before Bee's death, the first of Limbaugh's grandsons finished law school and passed the bar examination. Daniel, after his service in Vietnam, completed his education and prepared to pursue the legal profession in the military. Nevertheless, perhaps leaving open the possibility of joining his grandfather's firm later, he applied for acceptance into Missouri's bar. For this reason, the family traveled to Jefferson City to witness Daniel's swearing in before the Supreme Court of Missouri. As it turned out, Limbaugh arrived late to the ceremony, and while attempting to slip in unnoticed, he took a seat in the back row of the gallery. However, one of the judges of the court spotted him, and in a spontaneous show of respect, the ceremony was interrupted as all seven judges stood as a sign of their respect and announced "that Rush Limbaugh had just entered the courtroom." Daniel was the first of a number of grandsons whose swearing in Limbaugh had the pleasure of celebrating, for on the same day as Bee's death, his grandson Stephen received word that he had passed the Missouri bar examinations. Because he had already passed the bar in Texas, where he had attended law school at Southern Methodist University, he was allowed to practice at the Limbaugh firm temporarily so long as he passed the Missouri portion of the bar examinations in a timely manner. The following summer, Limbaugh's grandson David, Rush Jr.'s son, joined the firm, and a short time later Manley's son John, began his legal career there as well.[11]

Despite his age, throughout the 1980s, Limbaugh continued to be very active in his profession and showed no signs of diminished physical or mental capacity. During this time, he became acquainted with the district's congressman, Bill Emerson, and his aide Lloyd Smith. Limbaugh probably first became acquainted with Emerson and Smith in consultation over some matter for a client. Limbaugh, Emerson, and Smith soon became good friends because of their mutual interests in the community, politics, history, and Abraham Lincoln. Smith remembered many interesting discussions between Limbaugh and

Emerson about their hero Lincoln, whom both seemed to know almost intimately, and about the American Civil War. Of particular interest was Limbaugh's stories about men he remembered who had participated in the war; men who had lived in the age of Lincoln![12]

Sometime in the early 1980s, Limbaugh consulted with Congressman Emerson on a matter for a client, Missouri Electric Works. Apparently, the Environmental Protection Agency (EPA) was concerned about a lubricant used in transformers, which had leaked into the soil. This lubricant contained PCBs, an artificial chemical that remains in the environment for a very long time and was considered potentially detrimental to both animal and human health. Limbaugh came to the congressman with a plan to remove and transport the contaminated soil. Together, they presented this plan to EPA bureaucrats. What astonished Smith was the ability of this man, then in his nineties, who spoke without notes and with ease remembering "all the details . . . down to the minutiae," including how many transformers Missouri Electric Works had replaced or rehabilitated and when the work was accomplished. Eventually, Emerson and Smith looked forward to these meetings with the local EPA officials, normally not the sort of consultations one anticipated with pleasure, for they found entertaining the spectacle of this elderly man deftly negotiating with the bureaucrats. Always maintaining the character of a gentleman, Smith recalled, Limbaugh "had a way of putting bureaucracy in its place."[13]

Later in the 1980s, the city council of St. Mary, Missouri, a town some fifty miles north of Cape Girardeau, hired Limbaugh and his grandson Stephen to represent it in a dispute with a contractor, who had constructed a new sewer system for St. Mary and had placed a mechanic's lien upon the property of the entire town, both public and private. In preparation for the pending litigation, he and Stephen made several trips to St. Mary to consult with and advise the city council on the complicated case. Again, Limbaugh demonstrated his ability to handle difficult and important legal suits in spite of his age, for eventually St. Mary won its suit. Stephen cherished this experience, for through it he learned a great deal and gained the opportunity of spending time with his grandfather.[14]

Wishing to commemorate his many decades of public service, different organizations and institutions honored Limbaugh with awards recognizing his many achievements over the course of his long career. In 1983, Southeast Missouri State University presented to him the Friend of the University Award. The following year, the Missouri Bar awarded him the Spurgeon-Smithson Award for his "singular contributions in the administration of justice." On a notable occasion in May 1985, the Cape Girardeau Rotary Club honored him, recruiting a number of prominent persons to tell the story of his life and accomplishments, including Chief Justice James A. Finch Jr. of the Missouri

Supreme Court; Howard C. Tooke, mayor of Cape Girardeau; United States Congressman Bill Emerson; and John Arnold, president of the Missouri Bar. Among those who could not attend but sent videotaped messages or letters were Governor John Ashcroft; President Ronald Reagan; John Shepard, president of the ABA; and Justice Lewis F. Powell Jr. Mayor Tooke, who referred to Limbaugh as his "boyhood hero," presented to him a resolution of the Cape Girardeau city council and Governor Ashcroft proclaimed May 17, 1985, as Rush H. Limbaugh Sr. Day. The highlight of the evening, however, was Limbaugh's short response to the speakers, which combined wit, humor, and humility in a manner that demonstrated better than the speakers' efforts why he had so many admirers and friends. In this response, or "rebuttal," as Rotary Club president John Blue characterized it, Limbaugh observed humorously that "if anybody ever did amount to anything, after an occasion like this he would never be fit for it again." He quoted Mark Twain on the need for humility, noted that his parents and siblings, having made it possible for him to attend college were largely responsible for his achievements, and thanked everyone for their kindness.[15]

The 1980s was marked by other important milestones. In July 1983, President Reagan appointed Limbaugh's son Stephen to the federal bench. On June 18, 1984, his last surviving sibling, Lillie Lucretia Seabaugh, died just two months before her 100th birthday. In 1987, his grandson Stephen was appointed a state circuit court judge, a happy event, although it also meant that he must leave his grandfather's firm. Another interesting milestone was the beginning of the meteoric rise of Limbaugh's namesake, Rush Limbaugh III, whose career in radio was just then gathering momentum after many years of struggle and frustration.[16]

In 1990, Limbaugh's oldest son, Rush Jr., who was suffering from diabetes and had been in ill health for some time, went into the hospital to remove a toe, which had turned gangrenous due to the loss of circulation—a common problem for diabetics. A series of setbacks related to the disease and his weakened condition made his recovery impossible, and he died on December 8. His son David remembered that his grandfather "was very sad, but as always very strong," and offered comfort to his grandson and the rest of the family in their time of bereavement.[17]

Approaching his centennial year, Limbaugh continued to work at the profession he enjoyed so much. One of his clients had been George Thurm, president of a bank in Winona, a small town located in south-central Missouri. A tornado had recently destroyed much of the town and the community needed to rebuild its school. Because of the community's small tax revenue base, alternative forms of funding were sought. Fortunately, Thurm had left "a substantial portion of his estate to the local school district," and Congressman Emerson found federal funds as well. Emerson, his aide Lloyd Smith, and Limbaugh traveled to Winona for the school's groundbreaking ceremony. Held in January or February, Smith remembered that the day was cold, making their time in the open air uncomfortable. A flatbed trailer was used as a makeshift platform upon which Emerson and Limbaugh addressed the crowd. Emerson spoke first for approximately twenty-five minutes from prepared remarks that he and his aide, Smith, had drafted. After him, Limbaugh spoke without notes for perhaps five minutes in which, according to Smith, "he went from the Northwest Ordinance . . . and got us to the flatbed trailer in Winona." In his remarks, Limbaugh quoted from the third article of the Northwest Ordinance of 1787, which the Confederation Congress had passed to provide public funding for schools, in which the drafters had noted that without education in "religion, morality and knowledge" there could be no "good government and the happiness of mankind." The main theme of Limbaugh's brief talk was that "an educated public was the cornerstone of democracy and the cornerstone of the freedoms of the United States." As the elderly lawyer made his remarks, Emerson was so struck by his eloquence and wisdom that he leaned over to Smith and self-deprecatingly observed that he was Edward Everett to Limbaugh's Lincoln—a reference to the dedicatory speeches given at Gettysburg in 1863. Everett, who was at the end of a long political and diplomatic career, was celebrated for his elaborately prepared orations. His specialty was speeches commemorating Americans' battlefield heroics, and so it seemed natural for him to make the primary speech and Lincoln to follow with only a few remarks. Everett had carefully researched the events of the three-day battle at Gettysburg and had memorized his carefully crafted text, which took two hours to present. In contrast, Lincoln's address occupied only three minutes, but today is known as the Gettysburg Address, while Everett's effort is largely, although undeservedly, forgotten today.[18]

One of the unfortunate byproducts of a long life is that inevitably one outlives many friends and loved ones. Nevertheless, Limbaugh's intellectual curiosity and ability to make friends, stemming primarily from his genuine interest in others and his youthful spirit, helped him to cope and kept him mentally alert. At the office, he enjoyed discussing legal questions and offering advice to the young lawyers, who profited a great deal from his knowledge and experience. In particular, he reveled in the camaraderie and was never one to expect special treatment or deference from others. Instead, he was happy simply to be one of the group, having lunch at a fast-food restaurant or being involved in some other activity. It should also be remembered that he continued to be a top producer for the firm, although some of the lawyers believed that he charged too little for his services. According to his secretary Glenda Wunderlich, who worked for him for over forty years, Limbaugh's main concern was charging a fair fee, even going so far as dropping the minimum charge if he thought it was too much for the work accomplished. On the other hand, he was also very proud still to be earning a living.[19]

In September 1991, Limbaugh traveled to Kansas City to attend the annual meeting of the Missouri Bar. The meeting happened to be held on the weekend of his birthday and the profession celebrated the life and accomplishments of the state's oldest practicing lawyer. On Wednesday, his son Stephen and daughter-in-law Anne had driven him from St. Louis to Kansas City, and on Thursday he took several continuing education classes provided by the Missouri Bar. That evening he and Stephen attended a Missouri Council of Trial Lawyers dinner at which he was recognized. The following day, September 27, was his 100th birthday. From the Hyatt Regency Crown Center, where he attended more continuing education classes, Limbaugh and several family members traveled in a limousine provided by KMVZ Radio to the station where his famous namesake awaited to interview him on his syndicated radio show. After speaking extemporaneously on the air for an hour and a half about nineteenth- and twentieth-century history and about his long life, Limbaugh humbly accepted his grandson's on-air congratulations for having lived such a remarkable and long life. Rush—who afterwards marveled at the fluidity of his grandfather's speech and mastery of the details of American, legal, and constitutional history—remembered the great impression the interview left upon his listeners. This impact is still felt today, for, Rush noted, not a week goes by that someone does not request that he replay his grandfather's interview.[20]

After the celebration of his centennial year, Limbaugh returned to the routine of his law practice, working on an EPA case and other legal matters. Still strong physically, he was able to walk vigorously and take care of himself, although someone was employed to cook his meals and clean his house. Nevertheless, certain concessions to his age were made, for he found it necessary to give up driving and to use a cane to steady himself. In December 1991, he contracted pneumonia and afterward never regained his former vigor. Yet, Limbaugh at age 101 continued going to his law office five days a week and working eight hours a day. In 1994, at the age of 102, he began taking a two-hour "lunch followed by a short nap" before resuming his work in the afternoon. By this time, he was taking medication for his heart and the family employed "sitter[s]" to monitor his health at home and to be there in case of an emergency.[21]

While his intellect remained keen throughout his life, Limbaugh became increasingly frail and his poor health eventually confined him to his home. During this period, needing someone with him around the clock, the family employed persons to stay with him, and his daughters-in-law Anne, Millie, and Mary were especially involved in seeing after his needs. Despite his poor health, he remained interested in what was happening at the firm and did not fail to ask his secretary Glenda Wunderlich, who visited him once a week, about the work she and the others were doing. As his condition worsened, Limbaugh apparently recognized that his time was short, for he began to express his feelings to friends and family, making a point to tell them of their importance to him. At the end of one of her visits, he took Wunderlich's hand and said, "You are so precious to me." In a similar fashion, as his son Manley and daughter-in-law Mary prepared to leave after a visit, Limbaugh, who was by then confined to his bed much of the time, sat up and told them, "Remember, I love you." To his famous namesake, shortly before his death, in the first and only instance Rush could ever recall, his grandfather uncharacteristically communicated concern for himself by asking, "What's going to happen to me?" As his condition worsened, he slipped in and out of consciousness and final farewells were made. Nearing the end, he asked his daughter-in-law Mary to read the Bible to him. Limbaugh died on April 8, 1996, without a struggle or murmur, at the great age of 104.[22]

Three days later, some 400 people gathered for Limbaugh's funeral at Centenary United Methodist Church in Cape Girardeau, where he had been a faithful and active member for over eighty years. In the eulogy, Reverend Neil Stein spoke of his life and faith. The service was free from pomp or ostentation, reflecting the values of the deceased, who embodied the simple republican virtues and Christian values of a bygone era. After the service, Limbaugh's grandsons served as pallbearers and carried his body on its final journey to Lorimier Cemetery in Cape Girardeau, where he was returned to the side of his beloved wife, Bee.[23]

Less than three months after Limbaugh's death, his friend and fellow history and Lincoln enthusiast, Congressman Bill Emerson, died from lung cancer on June 22. Since the late 1980s, he had been working on obtaining federal funding for building a new bridge across the Mississippi River at Cape Girardeau and a new federal courthouse with a sitting judge. Such projects require a great deal of planning and much preparation before construction can begin. In a conversation with his aide and friend Lloyd Smith, as they were driving to the old bridge, Emerson expressed his desire that "if something happens to me," to have the new bridge named after him and the new federal courthouse "after Rush Limbaugh Sr." This was long before construction had begun on either project. In 2003, the bridge was completed and named after Emerson, but the federal courthouse project continued several years longer.[24]

After various delays, including the decision to scrap the original architectural design of the building in 2001 and to expand the plans to accommodate three courtrooms, everything was finally ready on October 6, 2008, for the dedication ceremony of the Rush Hudson Limbaugh Sr. United States Courthouse in Cape Girardeau. Without the preparatory work of Congressman Emerson and, after his death, the efforts of his wife, Congresswoman Jo Ann Emerson, and those of United States Senator Christopher "Kit" Bond, the courthouse could not have been built. In their remarks, some of the speakers mentioned the great need in southeast Missouri for a federal courthouse and for a "resident United States District Judge in Cape Girardeau." This appointment went to Limbaugh's grandson Stephen N. Limbaugh Jr., who became the first United States District Judge to be seated "in a United States courthouse named after his grandfather." In their speeches, Congresswoman Emerson, Senator Bond, and Limbaugh's son and grandson, Stephen N. Limbaugh Sr. and Stephen Jr., told the story of Limbaugh's rise from humble origins to become a well-respected lawyer and citizen committed to making a positive and lasting imprint upon his community, state, and country. Despite having numerous opportunities to operate in wider fields of endeavor and to gain greater prominence and fame, Limbaugh remained in Cape Girardeau, where he committed himself to public and professional service. Perhaps, this decision was made in much the same spirit as that of the ancient historian Plutarch, who, when explaining why he remained in his tiny hometown, commented that he did not wish to make it smaller by his absence. But Limbaugh's decision went beyond his love for southeast Missouri and went to the heart of his faith and philosophy of life, which was best summarized by the words of the Apostle Paul in Romans 12—one of his favorite chapters of the Bible—and begins with these words:

> I beseech you therefore, brethren, by the mercies of God, that ye present your bodies a living sacrifice, holy, acceptable unto God, which is your reasonable service. And be not conformed to this world; but be ye transformed by the renewing of your mind, that ye may prove what is that good and acceptable and perfect will of God. For I say through the grace given unto me, to every man who is among you not to think of himself more highly than he ought to think; but to think soberly according as God hath dealt to every man the measure of faith.[25]

Notes

Preface

1. Doreen Dodson, in discussion with the author, January 18, 2009; Rush H. Limbaugh III, in discussion with the author, April 14, 2009. See chapter six for the account of Rush H. Limbaugh Sr.'s handling of the Ware-Muench case.

2. Rush H. Limbaugh III, in discussion with the author, April 14, 2009; Rush H. Limbaugh Sr., interview by Rush H. Limbaugh III, KMVZ Radio, September 27, 1991.

3. Rush H. Limbaugh Sr., interview by Rush H. Limbaugh III, KMVZ Radio, September 27, 1991.

4. Rush H. Limbaugh III, in discussion with the author, April 14, 2009.

5. Stephen N. Limbaugh Sr., in discussion with the author, December 13, 2008; Doreen Dodson, in discussion with the author, January 18, 2009.

6. Stephen N. Limbaugh Sr., in discussion with the author, December 31, 2008; Rush H. Limbaugh III, in discussion with the author, April 14, 2009; E. A. Richter, "A Conversation with Rush H. Limbaugh Sr.," *The Missouri Supreme Court Historical Journal* 5, no. 3 (December 1994): 14; James M. Altman, "Review: Modern Litigators and Lawyer-Statesmen," *The Yale Law Journal* 103, no. 4 (January 1994): 1031–33. According to Stephen N. Limbaugh Jr., his grandfather especially dedicated himself to serve others according to Paul's direction in Romans 12.

Chapter 1

1. Rush H. Limbaugh Sr.'s birth certificate; Rush H. Limbaugh Sr. to Malcolm H. Hudson, February 3, 1978, papers in the possession of Stephen N. Limbaugh Jr. (hereafter cited as Limbaugh Papers).

2. Limbaugh Land, Inc., 1980 report, 16–25; Rush H. Limbaugh Sr. to De-lores L. Hudson and Lou Hudson Pellican, February 3, 1978; Noble W. Lim-baugh, "Missouri Limbaughs," (unpublished manuscript); Rush H. Limbaugh Sr., "Reminiscences on November 3, 1984 while standing at almost the exact spot of my birth and viewing the surrounding scenes in which I spent my child-hood and youth," (unpublished manuscript), 20 (hereafter cited as Limbaugh, "Reminiscences of the Farm"), Limbaugh Papers; Rush H. Limbaugh Sr., inter-view by Rush H. Limbaugh III, KMVZ Radio, September 27, 1991.

3. Limbaugh Land, Inc., 1980 report, 16–25; Rush H. Limbaugh Sr. to Delo-res L. Hudson and Lou Hudson Pellican, February 3, 1978; Noble W. Limbaugh, "Missouri Limbaughs," Limbaugh Papers; online Family Search Pedigree Re-source of the Church of Jesus Christ of Latter-Day Saints, October 29, 2008.

4. Rush H. Limbaugh Sr. to Delores L. Hudson and Lou Hudson Pellican, Feb-ruary 3, 1978, Limbaugh Papers; James Lal Penick Jr., *The New Madrid Earth-quakes, Revised Edition* (Columbia: University of Missouri Press, 1981), viii.

5. Penick, *The New Madrid Earthquakes*, 67—73, 83, 89, 140—41.

6. Limbaugh Land, Inc., 1980 report, 16—25; Limbaugh, "Reminiscences of the Farm," 11—14; Rush H. Limbaugh Sr. to Delores L. Hudson and Lou Hudson Pellican, February 3, 1978, Limbaugh Papers; Manley and Daniel Lim-baugh, in discussion with the author, November 24, 2008.

7. Limbaugh, "Reminiscences of the Farm," 4—6, 19, 66—68, Limbaugh Pa-pers.

8. Ibid.," 6—11, 24—26; Rush H. Limbaugh Sr., "Memories of My Father," August 2, 1990 (unpublished transcript), 15—16, Limbaugh Papers (hereafter cited as Limbaugh, "Father").

9. Limbaugh, "Reminiscences of the Farm," 13—15; Rush H. Limbaugh Sr., "My Experience as a Special Commissioner of the St. Louis Court of Ap-peals," (unpublished manuscript), 22—25 (hereafter cited as Limbaugh, "Spe-cial Commissioner"); Rush H. Limbaugh Sr.'s eulogy of his sister Lillie Lucretia Limbaugh Seabaugh, Limbaugh Papers.

10. Limbaugh, "Father," 11—15; Limbaugh, "Reminiscences of the Farm," 14—16, 19, 23, 37—38, 67—68, Limbaugh Papers.

11. Limbaugh, "Reminiscences of the Farm," 38—40, Limbaugh Papers.

12. Ibid., 40—41.

13. Ibid., 64—65, 69—70.

14. Limbaugh, "Father," 2—5, Limbaugh Papers; George C. Suggs Jr., ed., *Rush Hudson Limbaugh and his Times: Reflections on a Life Well Lived* (Cape Girardeau: Southeast Missouri State University Press, 2003), 166—67.

15. Bruce Palmer, *"Man over Money": The Southern Populist Critique of American Capitalism* (Chapel Hill: University of North Carolina Press, 1980), 199—221; Adrienne Koch and William Peden, eds., *The Life and Selected Writ-ings of Thomas Jefferson* (New York: The Modern Library, 1972), 279—81.

16. Paul Kennedy, *The Rise and Fall of Great Powers: Economic Change and Military Conflict from 1500 to 2000* (New York: Random House, 1987), 194—248; Peter H. Argersinger, *The Limits of Agrarian Radicalism: Western Populism and American Politics* (Lawrence: University Press of Kansas, 1995), 37—39; Douglas Steeples and David O. Whitten, *Democracy in Desperation: The Depression of 1893* (Westport, CT: Greenwood Press, 1998), 42, 52—53; Charles Hoffman, "The Depression of the Nineties," *The Journal of Economic History* 16, no. 2 (June 1956): 138.

17. Rush H. Limbaugh Sr., "Boyhood in the 90's," (unpublished transcript); Limbaugh, "Father," 1—2, 5, Limbaugh Papers; Argersinger, *Agrarian Radicalism*, 39; Steeples and Whitten, *Depression of 1893*, 58.

18. Limbaugh, "Reminiscences of the Farm," 34; Rush H. Limbaugh Sr., memorandum on visits made to Sedgewickville primarily between 1900 and 1907 (hereafter cited as Limbaugh, Sedgewickville), Limbaugh Papers.

19. Rush H. Limbaugh Sr., "The Old School Road," (unpublished manuscript), Limbaugh Papers.

20. Ibid.

21. Limbaugh, "Father," 1; Rush H. Limbaugh Sr., "Address before the Bollinger County Teachers Association at Will Mayfield College, Marble Hill, Missouri on October 9, 1908 on the subject 'Qualifications of a Teacher'" (hereafter cited as Limbaugh, "Qualifications of a Teacher"), Limbaugh Papers.

22. Limbaugh, "Reminiscences of the Farm," 42—44, Limbaugh Papers.

23. Limbaugh, "Father," 12—14.

24. Ibid.

25. Limbaugh, "Reminiscences of the Farm," 17; Limbaugh, "Father," 14—15; Last will and testament of Joseph H. Limbaugh, July 5, 1898; Rush H. Limbaugh Sr., "Nature and character of legal work performed by Rush H. Limbaugh prior to and since the formation of this firm as he remembers it," (unpublished manuscript), 183—84 (hereafter cited as Limbaugh, "Legal Work"), Limbaugh Papers.

26. Limbaugh, "Reminiscences of the Farm," 16—18, 48; Limbaugh, "Special Commissioner," 23; Limbaugh, "Father," 16—18, Limbaugh Papers.

27. Limbaugh, "Reminiscences of the Farm," 29—35, 44, 51—54, 59—60.

28. Ibid., 59—64.

29. Ibid., 35—36, 53, 59—64; Thomas Gray, "Elegy Written in a Country Church-Yard."

Chapter 2

1. Rush H. Limbaugh Sr., "Reminiscences on November 3, 1984 while standing at almost the exact spot of my birth and viewing the surrounding scenes in which I spent my childhood and youth," (unpublished manuscript), 19–23;

the Rush Hudson Limbaugh Sr. papers in the possession of Stephen N. Limbaugh Jr. (hereafter cited as Limbaugh, "Reminiscences of the Farm"); "The Family of Joseph Headley Limbaugh and Susan Frances Presnell Limbaugh," (unpublished manuscript), the Rush Hudson Limbaugh Sr. papers in the possession of Stephen N. Limbaugh Jr. Rush H. Limbaugh Sr., "eulogy of his sister Lillie Lucretia Seabaugh;," (unpublished manuscript), papers in the possession of Stephen N. Limbaugh Jr.; hereinafter cited as Limbaugh Papers; Stephen N. Limbaugh Sr., in discussion with the author, August 13, 2007.

2. Limbaugh, "Reminiscences of the Farm," 47—51, Limbaugh Papers.

3. Limbaugh, "Reminiscences of the Farm," 49—51, 65; Rush H. Limbaugh Sr., "Reminiscences of Boyhood: Thanksgiving Day," (unpublished manuscript), Limbaugh Papers; Ulysses S. Grant, *Memoirs and Selected Letters, Personal Memoirs of U. S. Grant: Selected letters 1839–1865* (New York: Viking Press, 1990), 22.

4. Rush H. Limbaugh Sr., "Address before the Bollinger County Teachers Association at Will Mayfield College, Marble Hill, Missouri on October 9, 1908 on the subject 'Qualifications of a Teacher,'" the Rush Hudson Limbaugh Sr. papers in the possession of Stephen N. Limbaugh Jr. (hereafter cited as Limbaugh, "Qualifications of a Teacher)," Limbaugh Papers.

5. Rush H. Limbaugh Sr., "The St. Louis World's Fair," (unpublished manuscript); "Limbaugh remembers fair of 1904," undated newspaper clipping, Limbaugh Papers.

6. Ibid.

7. Rush H. Limbaugh Sr., "He Praiseth Her or My Life with My Wife," (unpublished manuscript), 7, 14 (hereafter cited as Limbaugh, "Life with My Wife"); Rush H. Limbaugh Sr., "Going Away to School," (unpublished manuscript); Limbaugh, "Fifteen," Limbaugh Papers; Stephen N. Limbaugh Sr., in discussion with the author, August 13, 2007; George C. Suggs Jr., ed., *Rush Hudson Limbaugh and his Times: Reflections on a Life Well Lived* (Cape Girardeau: Southeast Missouri State University Press, 2003), 64, 80.

8. Limbaugh, "Life with My Wife," 15; Limbaugh, "Fifteen"; Suggs, ed., *Reflections*, 64, 80–84, 87–90; Rush H. Limbaugh Sr., "October's Resolve," (unpublished manuscript), Limbaugh Papers (hereafter cited as Limbaugh, "October's Resolve").

9. Limbaugh, "Reminiscences of the Farm," 27–28; Suggs, ed., *Reflections*, 88–89; Limbaugh, "Life with My Wife," 15.

10. Rush H. Limbaugh Sr., "Notes on the Lone Grove School," (unpublished manuscript), Limbaugh Papers (hereafter cited as Limbaugh, "Notes"); Rush H. Limbaugh Sr., "The Lone Grove School as I Remember it," (unpublished manuscript), Limbaugh Papers (hereafter cited as Limbaugh, "Lone Grove School reminiscences").

11. Limbaugh, "Notes"; Limbaugh, "Lone Grove School reminiscences"; Limbaugh, "October's Resolve," Limbaugh Papers.

12. Limbaugh, "Notes"; Limbaugh, "Lone Grove School reminiscences"; Limbaugh, "Qualifications of a Teacher," Limbaugh Papers. Contrast the experience of Rush's students to that of Sidney Hook, who described the rigid, strict, and unimaginative pedagogy of his teachers. See Sidney Hook, *Out of Step: An Unquiet Life in the 20th Century* (New York: Harper & Row, 1987), 11–18.

13. Limbaugh, "Life with My Wife," 1–10.

14. Limbaugh, "October's Resolve"; Limbaugh, "Life with My Wife," 16–18.

15. Limbaugh, "Life with My Wife," 18–27; Limbaugh, "October's Resolve."

16. Limbaugh, "Life with My Wife," 27–28; *New York Times*, October 2, 1901.

17. Limbaugh, "Life with My Wife," 28–31.

18. Ibid., 31–34, 53; Limbaugh, "Reminiscences of the Farm," 74, Limbaugh Papers.

19. Limbaugh, "Life with My Wife," 35–36.

20. Ibid., 36–37.

21. Ibid., 34–40.

22. Rush H. Limbaugh Sr., "Birthdays," September 27, 1910; "American Democracy," September 28, 1910; and "How Cannonism was Revealed," September 30, 1910, Limbaugh Papers. Recent scholarship into the congressional revolt against Speaker Cannon has demonstrated that the traditional understanding of it is too simplistic, both in its portrayal of Cannon as corrupt and of the Republican congressmen who opposed him as principled, progressive politicians. See John D. Baker, "The Character of the Congressional Revolution of 1910," *The Journal of American History* 60, no. 3, (December 1973): 679–91; Eric D. Lawrence, Forrest Maltzman, and Paul J. Wahlbeck, "The Politics of Speaker Cannon's Committee Assignments," *American Journal of Political Science* 45, no. 3 (July 2001): 551–62.

23. Limbaugh, "Life with My Wife," 40–42; Rush H. Limbaugh Sr. to Bee Seabaugh, December 31, 1910, Limbaugh Papers.

24. Limbaugh, "Life with My Wife," 42–43; Suggs, ed., *Reflections*, 25–29; R. H. Garner to Rush H. Limbaugh, October 11, November 17, and December 15, 1910, Limbaugh Papers.

25. Limbaugh, "Life with My Wife," 43–44, 53–54; *Cape Girardeau* (MO) *Capaha Arrow*, February 1 and March 1, 1911.

26. *Cape Girardeau* (MO) *Capaha Arrow*, February 1, 1911; Rush H. Limbaugh, "The Peril of American Politics," Cape Girardeau, Missouri State Normal School, 1911.

27. *Cape Girardeau* (MO) *Capaha Arrow*, February 1 and March 29, 1911.

28. *Cape Girardeau* (MO) *Capaha Arrow*, April 12 and 26, 1911; Limbaugh, "Life with My Wife," 44.

29. *Cape Girardeau* (MO) *Capaha Arrow*, April 12, 1911; Limbaugh, "Life with My Wife," 44, 56.

30. Limbaugh, "Life with My Wife," 44–52.

31. Ibid., 52–60.

32. Limbaugh, "Life with My Wife," 64–66; *Cape Girardeau* (MO) *Capaha Arrow*, September 27, 1911.

33. Limbaugh, "Life with My Wife," 64; *Cape Girardeau* (MO) *Capaha Arrow*, September 27, 1911.

34. *Cape Girardeau* (MO) *Capaha Arrow*, September 27 and October 11, 1911.

35. Limbaugh, "Life with My Wife, 68–69; Bee Seabaugh to Rush H. Limbaugh Sr., January 28 and March 6, 1912, Limbaugh Papers.

36. New Year's resolution, January 1, 1912, Limbaugh Papers; Limbaugh, "Life with My Wife," 67–68.

37. *Cape Girardeau* (MO) *Capaha Arrow*, January 24, February 7 and 21, 1912; Bee Seabaugh to Rush H. Limbaugh Sr., January 14 and 22 and February 2, 4, and 11, 1912, Limbaugh Papers.

38. Rush H. Limbaugh Sr., "Political Ideals and Industrial Progress," Cape Girardeau, Missouri, State Normal School, 1912.

39. *Cape Girardeau* (MO) *Capaha Arrow*, March 6 and 20, 1912; Limbaugh, "Reminiscences of the Farm," 74, Limbaugh Papers.

40. Bee Seabaugh to Rush H. Limbaugh Sr., April 14, 21, and 28, 1912, Limbaugh Papers; *Cape Girardeau* (MO) *Capaha Arrow*, March 6 and May 1 and 15, 1912; Limbaugh, "Reminiscences," 68–69, Limbaugh Papers.

41. *State Normal Bulletin* (Emporia, KS), April 30 and May 7, 1912.

42. Limbaugh, "Reminiscences of the Farm," 68–70; Rush H. Limbaugh Sr. to Roscoe Limbaugh, March 26, 1912, Limbaugh Papers; Bee Seabaugh to Rush H. Limbaugh Sr., May 2 and 20, 1912, Limbaugh Papers.

43. *Cape Girardeau* (MO) *Capaha Arrow*, May 29 and September 26, 1912; Limbaugh, "Life with My Wife," 70.

Chapter3

1. Rush H. Limbaugh Sr., "He Praiseth Her or My Life with My Wife," (unpublished manuscript), 69–70 (hereafter cited as Limbaugh, "Life with My Wife"), 69–70; John S. Moore to Arthur W. Vaughan, April 25, 1912; Vaughan to Moore, April 30, 1912; Moore to Rush H. Limbaugh Sr., May 29, 1912, the Rush Hudson Limbaugh Sr. papers in the possession of Stephen N. Limbaugh Jr. (hereafter cited as the Limbaugh Papers).

2. Limbaugh, "Life with My Wife," 77; B. P. Taylor to Rush H. Limbaugh Sr., September 14, 1912; Bee Seabaugh to Rush H. Limbaugh Sr., November 9, 1912, Limbaugh Papers.

3. Rush H. Limbaugh Sr., "Quarterly Report of the Secretary for Method-ist Students in the University of Missouri," November 30, 1912; "Work for Methodist Students," undated, Limbaugh Papers; Limbaugh, "Life with My Wife," 86.

4. Athenaean Literary Society, "Record from 1903 to 1913," vol. 9: 341–54, Records of the Athenaean Literary Society, 1842–1925, Western Historical Manuscript Collections, State Historical Society of Missouri, Columbia (here-after cited as Records, Athenaean Literary Society).

5. James Chace, *1912: Wilson, Roosevelt, Taft & Debs–the Election that Changed the Country* (New York: Simon & Schuster, 2004), 118, 200–7; Charles Henry Davis, *Party Platforms: Progressive, Democratic, Republican in Deadly Parallel* (New York: Stoddard-Sutherland Press, 1912); Theodore Roosevelt, *Theodore Roosevelt's Confession of Faith before the Progressive National Con-vention, August 6, 1912* (New York: Stoddard-Sutherland Press, 1912); Albert J. Beveridge, *"Pass Prosperity Around": Speech of Albert J. Beveridge, Temporary Chairman of Progressive National Convention* (New York: Stoddard-Sutherland Press, 1912).

6. Bee Seabaugh to Rush H. Limbaugh Sr., May 2 and 20, November 10, 1912, Limbaugh Papers; B. F. Beazell to Rush H. Limbaugh Sr., October 23, 1912; campaign flyer of 1912; Rush H. Limbaugh Sr., "Sedgewickville," (un-dated and unpublished manuscript); and 1928 campaign speech for Herbert Hoover, Limbaugh Papers.

7. Limbaugh, "Life with My Wife," 70, 77–78; Rush H. Limbaugh Sr., "Quar-terly Report of the Secretary for Methodist Students in the University of Mis-souri," February 27, April 10, and May 31, 1913; and J. C. Jones to Rush H. Limbaugh Sr., September 5, 1913, Limbaugh Papers; Bee Seabaugh to Rush H. Limbaugh Sr., May 14, 1913, Limbaugh Papers.

8. Records, Athenaean Literary Society, vol. 10: 19, 22, 24–25, 27, 34, 42, 52, 60–62; Rush H. Limbaugh Sr., "My Experience as a Special Commissioner of the St. Louis Court of Appeals," (unpublished manuscript), 360; Rush H. Lim-baugh Sr., "For a Literacy Test for Immigrants," (unpublished manuscript, De-cember 1913); Arthur W. Vaughan to Rush H. Limbaugh, April 23, 1914; Rush H. Limbaugh Sr., "The World Movement," (unpublished manuscript, February 1914); and Arthur W. Vaughan, February 14, 1914; and "Daniel Webster, the Orator," (unpublished manuscript, June 1914), Limbaugh Papers; *Daily Texan* (Austin, TX), April 18, 1914; *Columbia Tribune*, May 9, 1914; Limbaugh, "Life with My Wife," 89–90.

9. Bee Seabaugh to Rush H. Limbaugh Sr., May 14, 17, 18, 22, 27, 1913, Lim-baugh Papers; Ivan Lee Holt to Rush H. Limbaugh Sr., August 25, 1914, Lim-baugh Papers; Limbaugh, "Life with My Wife," 71–80.

10. Limbaugh, "Life with My Wife," 80–85.

11. Ibid., 85–87.

12. George C. Suggs Jr., ed., *Rush Hudson Limbaugh and his Times, Reflections on a Life Well Lived* (Cape Girardeau: Southeast Missouri State University Press, 2003), 108; William F. Fratcher, *The Law Barn: A Brief History of the School of Law, University of Missouri-Columbia* (Columbia: School of Law, University of Missouri-Columbia, 1978), 33–34, 95–97.

13. Fratcher, *Law Barn*, 91–92, 95–97.

14. Suggs, ed., *Reflections*, 98–100, 104–5; Julius Stone, "Manley Hudson: Campaigner and Teacher of International Law," *Harvard Law Review* 74, no. 2 (December 1960): 215–25.

15. Records, Athenaean Literary Society, vol. 10: 66, 71–72, 74; Rush H. Limbaugh Sr., "The Decline of State Legislatures," (unpublished manuscript, November 1914), Limbaugh Papers; "Debating Time is Here," *University of Missouri Alumni Magazine*, November 1914, 48.

16. Limbaugh, "Life with My Wife," 91–92.

17. J. G. Babb to Rush H. Limbaugh Sr., October 15, 1914; and Rush H. Limbaugh Sr., "Is there a Substitute for Force in International Relations?," (unpublished manuscript, June 1915), Limbaugh Papers; Limbaugh, "Life with My Wife," 92; Records, Athenaean Literary Society, vol. 10: 90; Program for the "Fourth Annual Missouri State Peace Oratorical Contest," April 21, 1915, Liberty, Missouri.

18. Limbaugh, "Life with My Wife," 92–93; Secretary of the Missouri Debating Board to A. A. Paddock, May 28, 1915; Rush H. Limbaugh Sr., "Account of Athenaen Literary Society Banquet," Limbaugh Papers; *Boulder* (CO) *Morning News*, April 17, 1915; "Won and Lost in Debate," *University of Missouri Alumni Magazine*, April 1915, 211; "Athenaean Column," *University of Missouri Alumni Magazine*, June 1915, 273; Records, Athenaean Literary Society, vol. 10: 109–12; Ulysses S. Grant confirms Catron's story in his account of the surrender of Vicksburg. See Ulysses S. Grant, *Memoirs and Selected Letters, Personal Memoirs of U. S. Grant: Selected letters 1839–1865* (New York: Viking Press, 1990), 379–83.

19. *University of Missouri Alumni Magazine*, June 1915, 285; *Harvard Crimson*, February 19, 1915; Limbaugh, "Life with My Wife," 96; Rush H. Limbaugh Sr., "Diary of American Bar Association Meeting, 1923," (unpublished manuscript, 1923), 16–17, Limbaugh Papers.

20. Limbaugh, "Life with My Wife," 94; William Leighton Grane, *The Passing of War: A Study in Things that Make for Peace* (London: Macmillan and Co., Ltd., 1914), xxxiv, 237–38, 247. This book was inscribed to Limbaugh on July 6, 1915, and can be found at the Jane Stephens Honors Program at Southeast Missouri State University.

21. Limbaugh, "Life with My Wife," 87–88, 93–94.

22. Ibid., 95.

23. Records, Athenaean Literary Society, vol. 10: 134; Harry K. Poindexter to Rush H. Limbaugh Sr., September 14 and 20, 1915, Limbaugh Papers.

24. Limbaugh, "Life with My Wife," 96–98.

25. A. L. Campbell to Rush H. Limbaugh Sr., December 13, 1915; P. C. Stepp to Limbaugh, December 26, 1915; Will C. Borland to Limbaugh, January 13, 1916; J. C. Young to Limbaugh, January 24, 1916; Ray Lucas to Limbaugh, February 12, 1916; R. S. Douglass to Limbaugh, February 18, 1916; Ralph L. Brown to Limbaugh, February 19, 1916; and J. Hall to Limbaugh, February 26, 1916, Limbaugh Papers; Limbaugh, "Life with My Wife," 100–101.

26. Rush H. Limbaugh Sr. to Benson C. Hardesty, December 1915; Hardesty to Limbaugh, December 23, 1915, April 7 and 14, 1916; and Limbaugh to Robert S. Douglass, February 18, 1916, Limbaugh Papers; Limbaugh, "Life with My Wife," 43, 102.

27. Limbaugh, "Life with My Wife," 99–100, 102–4.

28. Limbaugh, "Life with My Wife," 104–6; Rush H. Limbaugh to Manley O. Hudson, February 15, 1917, Manley O. Hudson Papers, Harvard Law Library; *Kansas City Star*, November 26, 1994; Rush H. Limbaugh Sr., "Nature and Character of Legal Work Performed by Rush H. Limbaugh Prior to and Since the Formation of This Firm as He Remembers It," (unpublished and undated manuscript), 1–3; E. A. Richter, "A Conversation with Rush H. Limbaugh Sr.," *The Missouri Supreme Court Historical Journal* 5, no. 3 (December 1994), 3–4.

29. Limbaugh, "Life with My Wife," 105.

Chapter Four

1. Rush H. Limbaugh Sr. to the American Association for International Conciliation, February 8, 1917; F. P. Keppel to Limbaugh, February 14, 1917; and Limbaugh to Manley O. Hudson, March 31, 1917, Manley O. Hudson Papers, Harvard Law Library; *New York Times*, March 1 and 2, 1917.

2. Rush H. Limbaugh Sr., "An Impression of Mr. Bryan," (unpublished and undated manuscript), Limbaugh Papers; Rush H. Limbaugh Sr., "He Praiseth Her or My Life with My Wife," (unpublished manuscript), 175–76 (hereafter cited as Limbaugh, "Life with My Wife"), 175–76; Stephen N. Limbaugh Sr., in discussion with the author, February 17, 2009; Hew Strachan, *The First World War* (New York: Penguin Books, 2003), 227–28.

3. Rush H. Limbaugh Sr., "The War and the Red Cross," June 19, 1917; speech at Morehouse, Missouri, March 30, 1918; and addresses in August and September 1918 in Cape Girardeau listed in his "Occasional Addresses of a Country Lawyer," (hereafter cited as Limbaugh, "Occasional Addresses"), Limbaugh Papers.

4. Limbaugh, "Life with My Wife," 108–12; *Southeast Missourian*, March 16 and 18, 1918.

5. Limbaugh, "Life with My Wife," 110–12.

6. Limbaugh, "Life with My Wife," 106–8, 114–15; *Southeast Missourian*, March 2 and 15, 1918; Limbaugh, "Occasional Addresses."

7. *Southeast Missourian*, March 15 and 18, 1918.

8. *Southeast Missourian*, March 20 and 22, 1918; Rush H. Limbaugh Sr. to Manley O. Hudson, February 15, 1917, Manley O. Hudson Papers, Harvard Law Library.

9. *Southeast Missourian*, March 20, 1918.

10. *Southeast Missourian*, March 21, 23, 25, 26, and April 3 and 9, 1918; Limbaugh, "Life with My Wife," 108. For an excellent account of the mood of the country against dissenters and a prosecution of three persons whose case was adjudicated before the Supreme Court of the United States see Richard Polenberg, *Fighting Faiths: The Abrams Case, the Supreme Court, and Free Speech* (Ithaca, NY: Cornell University Press, 1987).

11. Rush H. Limbaugh Sr., "Firm of Hardesty & Limbaugh" (unpublished and undated manuscript), 1–3, Limbaugh Papers, (hereafter cited as Limbaugh, "Firm of Hardesty & Limbaugh"); *Southeast Missourian*, March 2, 1918.

12. Limbaugh, "Life with My Wife," 106, 112. Stephen N. Limbaugh Sr., in discussion with the author, February 17, 2009.

13. *Southeast Missourian*, December 16 and 17, 1919.

14. *Southeast Missourian*, December 17 and 18, 1919.

15. *Southeast Missourian*, December 19, 1919.

16. William M. Morgan, Rush H. Limbaugh, and Charles G. Revelle, "Statement, brief, and argument for plaintiff in *Oscar Fuller, Respondent v. Charles R. Presnell, Appellant*," an appeal from the Circuit Court of Bollinger County, Springfield Court of Common Pleas, March 1920 term (St. Louis, MO: St. Louis Law Printing Co., nd), 1–8, vol. 7 of bound briefs in Limbaugh Law Firm, Cape Girardeau, Missouri (hereafter cited as Morgan, Limbaugh, and Revelle, "Brief in *Fuller v. Presnell*"); Rush H. Limbaugh Sr., "Memoir on Legal Work," (unpublished and undated manuscript), 66–68 (hereafter cited as Limbaugh, "Legal Work").

17. Morgan, Limbaugh, and Revelle, "Brief in *Fuller v. Presnell*," 1–2; Limbaugh, "Legal Work," 68.

18. Morgan, Limbaugh, and Revelle, "Brief in *Fuller v. Presnell*," 9–14; William M. Morgan, Rush H. Limbaugh, and Charles G. Revelle, "Abstract of record, statement, and brief in *Charles R. Presnell v. Argus Cox, John S. Farrington, John H. Bradley, Judges of the Springfield Court of Appeals*," Supreme Court of Missouri, October 1921 term (St. Louis, MO: St. Louis Law Printing Co., nd), 1–8, 17–27.

19. Limbaugh, "Life with My Wife," 114–15; Limbaugh, "Legal Work," 4–6; George C. Suggs Jr., ed., *Rush Hudson Limbaugh and his Times, Reflections on a Life Well Lived* (Cape Girardeau: Southeast Missouri State University Press, 2003), 102–3; Benson C. Hardesty and Rush H. Limbaugh Sr., "Respondent's statement, brief, and argument in *Dewey Robison, by next friend v. Floesch Construction Company, a corporation*," Supreme Court of Missouri, April 1921 term (Cape Girardeau, MO: Missourian Print, nd), 10–13, volume 8 of bound briefs in Limbaugh Law Firm, Cape Girardeau, Missouri (hereafter cited as Hardesty and Limbaugh, "Respondent's statement in *Robison v. Floesch Construction*").

20. Limbaugh, "Life with My Wife," 116; Limbaugh, "Legal Work," 5–8; Limbaugh, "Respondent's statement in *Robison v. Floesch Construction*," 14.

21. Limbaugh, "Life with My Wife," 116–17; Limbaugh, "Legal Work," 4, 8–10.

22. Ibid; *Southeast Missourian*, December 5 and 6, 1919.

23. Arthur L. Oliver and Allen L. Oliver, "Appellant's reply brief in *Dewey Robison, by next friend v. Floesch Construction Company, a corporation*," Supreme Court of Missouri, April 1921 term (Cape Girardeau, MO: Missourian Print, nd), 7–12, 17–19, 21, volume 8 of bound briefs in Limbaugh Law Firm, Cape Girardeau, Missouri (hereafter cited as Oliver and Oliver, "Appellants reply in *Robison v. Floesch Construction*").

24. Hardesty and Limbaugh, "Respondent's statement in *Robison v. Floesch Construction*," 14–21, 36. For a discussion of *Missouri Pacific Railway Co. v. Lasca*, see *Southeastern Reporter*, April 2–May 28, 1921, 910–12.

25. Oliver and Oliver, "Appellants reply in *Robison v. Floesch Construction*," 17–19. Arthur L. Oliver and Allen L. Oliver, "Abstract of the record on behalf of the appellant in *Dewey Robison, by next friend v. Floesch Construction Company, a corporation*," Supreme Court of Missouri, April 1921 term (Cape Girardeau, MO: Missourian Print, nd), 2–15.

26. Hardesty and Limbaugh, "Respondent's statement in *Robison v. Floesch Construction*," 1–5, 40–45.

27. Rush H. Limbaugh Sr. to Manley O. Hudson, 26 March and 22 December 1921. Manley O. Hudson Papers, Harvard Law Library; Burdett A. Rich and M. Blair Wailes, eds., *American Law Reports Annotated*, vol. 20 (Rochester and Northport, New York and San Francisco, California, The Lawyers Co-operative Publishing Company; Edward Thompson Company; and Bancroft-Whitney Company, 1922), 1239, 1247; Limbaugh, "Life with My Wife," 117. The case for the parents was *J. C. Robison v. Floesch Construction Company*; Limbaugh, "Legal Work," 4, 10–11.

28. Limbaugh, "Legal Work," 152–57; Limbaugh, "Life with My Wife," 118; Manley O. Hudson to Rush H. Limbaugh Sr., 29 May 1921. Manley O. Hudson Papers, Harvard Law Library.

29. Limbaugh, "Firm of Hardesty & Limbaugh," 4–5, Limbaugh Papers.

30. *Southeast Missourian*, March 13 and 14, 1923; Limbaugh, "Life with My Wife," 118; Limbaugh, "Legal Work," 11–13; James A. Finch, James A. Barks, Rush H. Limbaugh, "Respondent's statement, brief, and argument in *City of Cape Girardeau v. Herminia Hunze et al.*," Supreme Court of Missouri, October 1925 term (Cape Girardeau, MO: Missourian Printing Company, undated), 1–2, 9–10, volume 3 of bound briefs in Limbaugh Law Firm, Cape Girardeau, Missouri (hereafter cited as Finch, Barks, and Limbaugh, "Respondent's statement in *Cape Girardeau v. Hunze*"). Finch and Barks were only nominally involved with the case.

31. Limbaugh, "Legal Work," 12–13; Finch, Barks, and Limbaugh, "Respondent's statement in *Cape Girardeau v. Hunze*," 3, 11.

32. Finch, Barks, and Limbaugh, "Respondent's statement in *Cape Girardeau v. Hunze*," 6–8.

33. Ibid., 8–12, 18.

34. Ibid., 16–17.

35. Ibid., 18–23.

36. Rush H. Limbaugh Sr. to the *New Republic*, July 24, 1923; Limbaugh to John Junnell, July 24 and August 4, 1923; Limbaugh to A. C. Paul, July 24, 1923; and John Junnell to Limbaugh, July 26 and August 10, 1923, Limbaugh Papers; Rush H. Limbaugh Sr., "A record of events in connection with our trip to Minneapolis to attend the American Bar Association meeting in August 1924 [1923] as made from day to day during our journey" (unpublished typed transcript of diary), 1 (hereafter cited as Limbaugh, "1923 Diary").

37. Limbaugh, "1923 Diary," 1–4.

38. Ibid., 4–10. "Expenses on Trip to Minneapolis," 1–3, Limbaugh Papers.

39. Limbaugh, "1923 Diary," 12–13.

40. Ibid., 13–16.

41. Limbaugh, "1923 Diary," 16–30; "Expenses on Trip to Minneapolis," 5.

42. Limbaugh, "Life with My Wife," 108–9; Stephen N. Limbaugh Sr., "Application for Rush H. Limbaugh Sr. to receive the 1987 American Bar Association's Fellows Award," 15–16; Limbaugh, "Occasional Addresses," 1–2. Also included are a series of public addresses given by Rush H. Limbaugh Sr.: "Political Parties"; an untitled speech on the commission form of city government; "The New Responsibilities of American Citizenship," May 31, 1920, commencement speech at New Madrid, Missouri; "The Legal Status of Women"; "The Boy Scouts of America"; "Christianity and Bolshevism"; "Washington," address at Southeast Missouri State Teachers' College, February 21, 1921; commencement address at high school in St. Genevieve, Missouri, May 18, 1922; "Some of the Tasks of Present Day Youth"; untitled speech at Whitewater, Missouri, October 26, 1922; "Christ and Lincoln," address at college YMCA, February 14, 1922; "The Permanent Court of International Justice, Its Origin, History

and Status"; "America and the World Court"; untitled commencement address at Jackson High School, May 16, 1924; address made at Centenary Methodist Church, February 14, 1926; Fourth of July addresses at Marble Hill and Jackson, Missouri, July 4, 1926; "Application for Charter for Local Council," July 1, 1930, Boy Scouts of America, Greater St. Louis Area Council, Cape Girardeau, Missouri.

43. Rush H. Limbaugh, "America and the World Courts"; untitled commencement address at Jackson High School, May 16, 1924.

44. Limbaugh, "Life with My Wife," 125–26. Death certificate of Daniel F. Limbaugh, website of the Secretary of State of Missouri.

45. Limbaugh, "Life with My Wife," 127–28; Rush H. Limbaugh Sr. to Roscoe Limbaugh, 15 March 1926. Limbaugh Papers; Limbaugh, "Speech for Mayor Jos. A. Barks before Colored Congregation in Wm. A. Sunday Tabernacle at Cape Girardeau during Sunday Campaign, March 1926".

46. Limbaugh, "Life with My Wife," 128–31. Undated obituaries, Limbaugh Papers. Death certificate of Marguerite V. Limbaugh, website of the Secretary of State of Missouri.

47. Limbaugh, "Life with My Wife," 131–33; Bee Limbaugh to Rush H. Limbaugh Sr., July 9, 11, and 13, 1926. Limbaugh Papers.

Chapter Five

1. Rush H. Limbaugh Sr. to Helen Cowles LeCron, February 12, 1927; Limbaugh to *Better Homes and Gardens*, undated, the Rush Hudson Limbaugh Sr. papers in the possession of Stephen N. Limbaugh Jr. (hereafter cited as Limbaugh Papers); Rush H. Limbaugh Sr., "He Praiseth Her or My Life with My Wife," (unpublished manuscript), (hereafter cited as Limbaugh, "Life with My Wife"), 139–45.

2. Limbaugh, "Life with My Wife," 133–34.

3. Limbaugh, "Life with My Wife," 159–60; Rush H. Limbaugh to Roena Shaner, January 14, 1930; Shaner to Limbaugh, January 16, 1930; and Limbaugh to Attorney General William D. Mitchell, June 19, 1931; Limbaugh, Two speeches for Herbert Hoover's candidacy for president, 1928, Limbaugh Papers.

4. Ibid.

5. Rush H. Limbaugh Sr., "Memoir on Legal Work," (unpublished and undated manuscript), (hereafter cited as Limbaugh, "Legal Work"), 159–64.

6. Limbaugh, "Legal Work," 164–68.

7. Ibid., 168–70.

8. Ibid., 169–73, 175.

9. Limbaugh, "Legal Work," 173–78; Rush H. Limbaugh Sr., "Firm of Hardesty & Limbaugh" (unpublished and undated manuscript), 9–10,(hereafter cited as Limbaugh, "Firm of Hardesty & Limbaugh"), Limbaugh Papers.

10. Limbaugh, "Life with My Wife," 135–36; Frederick Lewis Allen, *Only Yesterday: An Informal History of the 1920s* (New York: Harper and Row, 1964), 132–40, 271, 280; Richard S. Kirkendall, *A History of Missouri*, vol. 5 (Columbia: University of Missouri Press, 1986), 38, 54; Amity Shlaes, *The Forgotten Man: A New History of the Great Depression* (New York: HarperCollins, 2007), 103–4.

11. Limbaugh, "Life With My Wife," 158–59; George C. Suggs Jr., ed., *Rush Hudson Limbaugh and his Times: Reflections on a Life Well Lived* (Cape Girardeau: Southeast Missouri State University Press, 2003), 183, 207; John B. Heagler to Limbaugh, 7 September 1930; Limbaugh to Heagler, 11 September 1930; flyer for "The Thirteenth Annual Commencement of Gideon Consolidated District, Thursday, May 16th, 1929"; flyer for "Eighteenth Annual Commencement, May 1929, Central High School, Cape Girardeau," 30 May 1929; "Material used in commencement address, Central High School, Cape Girardeau, Missouri, 30 May 1929"; "The Constitution of the United States," undated; "The Meaning of Washington to the American of Today"; and "Theodore Roosevelt: An Address Delivered Before Rotary Club, Cape Girardeau, Missouri, October 13, 1930", Limbaugh Papers.

12. Suggs, ed., *Reflections*, 167–68; Limbaugh, "Life with My Wife," 136, 159.

13. Rush H. Limbaugh Sr., "Memoranda Diary (Political)," unpublished manuscript, 5 January 1931 entry; (hereafter cited as Limbaugh, "Diary"); Limbaugh, "Life with My Wife," 136–37.

14. Limbaugh, "Diary," January 6 and 15, 1931. *Jefferson City Capitol News*, January 6, 1931; *St. Louis Post-Dispatch*, January 14, 1931; *State Ex inf. Stratton Shartel, Attorney General, Petitioner v. Larry Brunk*, State Treasurer, 326 *Missouri Reports* (1930), 1181–89; Limbaugh, "Legal Work," 128.

15. Limbaugh, "Diary," January 6 and 7, 1931.

16. Limbaugh, "Diary," January 7, 8, 15, 29, and February 19, 1931; Kirkendall, *History of Missouri*, 54. *Southeast Missourian*, February 15, 1932.

17. *Kansas City Star*, January 12, 1931; *Jefferson City Capital News*, January 13 and 14, 1931.

18. Limbaugh, "Diary," January 13, 1931; "Races: Lynching No. 1," *Time*, January 19, 1931; *Jefferson City Capital News*, January 15, 16, 18, 20, February 8, and March 10, 1931; Lorenzo Johnston Greene, Gary R. Kremer, and Antonio Frederick Holland, *Missouri's Black Heritage* (Columbia: University of Missouri Press, 1993), 148–49; Kirkendall, *History of Missouri*, 54, 154; Dorothy Penn and Floyd C. Shoemaker, eds., *The Messages and Proclamations of the Governors of the State of Missouri*, vol. 13 (Columbia: The State Historical Society of Missouri, 1947), 132–33.

19. *St. Louis Globe-Democrat*, February 20, 22, and 25, 1931; *St. Louis Star*, February 21, 1931; *St. Louis Post-Dispatch*, February 22, 23, and 25, 1931; *St.*

Louis Times, February 23, 1931; Statement of the St. Louis High School Teachers' Association, February 24, 1931; statement of the St. Louis Grade Teachers' Association, February 24, 1931; and undated news clipping, Limbaugh Papers.

20. Henry S. Caulfield to W. C. Bahn, 26 January 1931. Henry S. Caulfield Papers, Western Historical Manuscripts Collection, State Historical Society of Missouri; Joseph A. Serena to Limbaugh, January 5, February 13, 18, and March 3, 10, 23, 1931; Serena to Willis H. Meredith, February 13, 1931; Limbaugh to Serena, March 4, 1931, Limbaugh Papers. Limbaugh, "Diary," March 2 and 4, 1931.

21. Henry S. Caulfield to W. C. Bahn, 26 January 1931. Henry S. Caulfield Papers, Western Historical Manuscripts Collection, State Historical Society of Missouri; Joseph A. Serena to Limbaugh, March 3 and 10, 1931; Fred Naeter to Limbaugh, March 3, 1931; Fred E. Kies to Limbaugh, March 23, 1931; and Limbaugh to Kies, March 25, 1931, Limbaugh Papers; Limbaugh, "Diary," February 13, 18, and March 2, 7, 13, and 24, 1931; *Jackson Cash-Book*, March 20, 1931.

22. Limbaugh, "Diary," February 25 and March 2, 1931. *Jefferson City Capital News*, March 1, 1931; G. V. B. Levings to E. W. Kiethly, March 4, 1931, Limbaugh Papers.

23. Fannie D. Robb to Limbaugh, February 26, 1931; Limbaugh to F. R. Long, March 10, 1931; Limbaugh to Reverend M. H. Markley, March 10, 1931; Limbaugh to J. S. Calfee, March 10, 1931; and Arthur H. Armstrong to Limbaugh, March 16, 1931, Limbaugh Papers; Limbaugh, "Diary," March 11, 1931; *Jefferson City Capital News*, March 12, 1931.

24. Limbaugh, "Diary," January 7, and 3 and March 3 and 5, 1931; Charles Starzinger to Limbaugh, February 17, 1931; Theodore W. Meyer to Limbaugh, March 5, 1931; Irvin E. Deer to Limbaugh, March 5, 1931; Limbaugh to Nell G. Burger, March 10, 1931; and Limbaugh to Charles Starzinger, March 10, 1931, Limbaugh Papers; *Jefferson City Capital News*, January 23, and March 11, 1931; *St. Louis Post-Dispatch*, March 5, 1931.

25. Suggs, ed., *Reflections*, 169. *Jefferson City Capital News*, January 22, 1931; *St. Louis Globe-Democrat*, February 26 and 27, 1931; *Kansas City Star*, April 11, 1931; *St. Louis Post-Dispatch*, March 16, 1931; Limbaugh, "Diary," January 5, March 20 and 26, 1931; H. I. Himmelberger to Limbaugh, February 23, 1931; Railway Employees Association to members of the Missouri legislature, February 25, 1931; petition to Russell Dearmont and Limbaugh from the citizens of Whitewater, Missouri, February 26, 1931; J. A. Kinder to Limbaugh, February 26, 1931; R. B. Oliver to Limbaugh, February 29, 1931; William H. Vedder to Limbaugh, March 5, 1931; G. O. Walthers to Limbaugh, March 5, 1931; Limbaugh to Walthers, March 10, 1931; Limbaugh to J. T. Hulehan, March 10, 1931; Limbaugh to Vedder, March 10, 1931; Limbaugh to John W. Burns, March 21, 1931; C. L. Harrison to Limbaugh, February 24, 1931;

and the Automobile Club of Missouri to Limbaugh, February 25, 1931, Limbaugh Papers.

26. Limbaugh, "Diary," February 26 and 27, 1931; *Jefferson City Capital News*, February 11 and 26–28, 1931; *Kansas City Star*, February 26, 1931; *St. Louis Globe-Democrat*, February 26, 1931; David Falcone, "The Missouri State Highway Patrol as a Representative Model," *Policing: An International Journal of Police Strategies and Management* 24, no. 4, (2001): 587–88.

27. Suggs, ed., *Reflections*, 169; Limbaugh to Lee W. Kaizer, March 4, 1931; and Limbaugh to W. F. D. Batjer, March 10, 1931, Limbaugh Papers; Limbaugh, "Diary," April 17 and 20, 1931; *St. Louis Post-Dispatch*, March 16, 1931.

28. Limbaugh, "Diary," January 8 and 15, 1931; Limbaugh, "Is our system of taxation in the state antiquated, unjust, and inadequate?" February 18, 1931, Limbaugh Papers. Edwin R. A. Seligman, *Essays in Taxation*, (New York and London: MacMillan Company, 1897); Ajay K. Mehrotra, "Envisioning the Modern American Fiscal State: Progressive-Era Economists and the Intellectual Foundations of the U.S. Income Tax," *UCLA Law Review* 52 (2005): 1793–1865; Suggs, ed., *Reflections*, 166; Kirkendall, *History of Missouri*, 56.

29. Limbaugh, "Diary," January 22, February 11 and 18, 1931; *Jefferson City Capital News*, February 18, 1931.

30. *Jefferson City Capital News*, March 20, 21, and 26, 1931; *St. Louis Post-Dispatch*, March 16, 1931; *St. Louis Globe-Democrat*, February 27, and March 15, 1931; Kirkendall, *History of Missouri*, 153.

31. Limbaugh, "Diary," January 16, and April 23, 1931.

32. Limbaugh, "Diary," April 22, 1931.

Chapter Six

1. Rush H. Limbaugh Sr., "Memoranda Diary (Political)," unpublished manuscript, January 15 and 16, 1931 (hereafter cited as Limbaugh, "Diary").

2. Limbaugh, "Diary," January 15, March 10, 12, 18, 20–24, 26, April 2, 20, and 21, 1931; George C. Suggs Jr., ed., *Rush Hudson Limbaugh and his Times: Reflections on a Life Well Lived*, (Cape Girardeau: Southeast Missouri State University Press, 2003), 170–72.

3. Limbaugh, "Diary," January 20, 1931.

4. Limbaugh, "Diary," January 20 and 22, 1931; *Jefferson City Capital News*, January 17 and 22–24, February 17, 1931; *St. Louis Post-Dispatch*, February 24, 1931; "Report and Recommendations of the Special Investigating Committee Relative to Larry Brunk, State Treasurer Made to the House of Representatives of the State of Missouri, Fifty-sixth General Assembly, Submitted Tuesday, February 17, 1931" in *Appendix to the House and Senate Journals of the Fifty-sixth General Assembly, State of Missouri*, vol. 3 (Jefferson City, MO: n.p., 1931), 5–6 (hereafter cited as "Report of the Brunk Investigative Committee").

5. Limbaugh, "Diary," January 14–16, 22, and 29, 1931; *St. Louis Post Dispatch*, January 15, 1931; *Jefferson City Capital News*, January 16, 1931.

6. Limbaugh, "Diary," January 22, 27, 28, 29, 30, and March 24, 1931; "Report of the Brunk Investigative Committee," 11–14.

7. Limbaugh, "Diary," January 26, 27, and 31, 1931; *Jefferson City Capital News*, January 27, 1931.

8. Limbaugh, "Diary," January 27, 1931; *Jefferson City Capital News*, January 27, 1931; *St. Louis Post-Dispatch*, February 24, 1931.

9. *Jefferson City Capital News*, February 1 and 4, 1931; Limbaugh, "Diary," February 9–14, 1931.

10. Limbaugh, "Diary," February 16 and 17, 1931; *Jefferson City Capital News*, February 17 and 18, 1931; "Report of the Brunk Investigative Committee."

11. Limbaugh, "Diary," February 24, 1931; *Jefferson City Capital News*, February 24, 1931.

12. Limbaugh, "Diary," February 24, 1931; *Jefferson City Capital News*, February 24, 1931; *St. Louis Post-Dispatch*, February 24 and 25, 1931; *St. Louis Globe-Democrat*, February 25, 1931; *Kansas City Star*, February 24, 1931.

13. Limbaugh, "Diary," February 24 and 28, 1931; *Jefferson City Capital News*, February 24, 1931; *St. Louis Post-Dispatch*, February 24 and 25, 1931; *St. Louis Globe-Democrat*, February 25, 1931; *Kansas City Star*, February 24 and 26, 1931.

14. Limbaugh, "Diary," February 25, March 2 and 10, 1931; Limbaugh to H. R. Stevenson, March 10, 1931, Limbaugh Papers; *Jefferson City Capital News*, February 25 and March 18, 1931; *St. Louis Post-Dispatch*, February 25, 1931; *St. Louis Globe-Democrat*, February 25, 1931; Rush H. Limbaugh Sr., "He Praiseth Her or My Life with My Wife," (unpublished manuscript), 378.

15. Limbaugh, "Diary," March 4, 6, 9, 10, and 11, 1931.

16. Limbaugh, "Diary," January 15, March 10, 12, 16, and 17, 1931.

17. Limbaugh, "Diary," March 17, 1931; *Jefferson City Capital News*, March 18, 1931; Rush H. Limbaugh Sr., "Memoir on Legal Work," (unpublished and undated manuscript), (hereafter cited as Limbaugh, "Legal Work"), 129.

18. Limbaugh, "Diary," March 17, 1931; *Jefferson City Capital News*, March 18, 1931; Limbaugh, "Legal Work," 132.

19. Limbaugh, "Diary," March 10, 13, 17, 18, 23, 25, and 26, 1931.

20. Limbaugh, "Diary," February 26, March 7, 9, 11, 18, and 20, 1931; *St. Louis Post-Dispatch*, February 25, 1931; *Jefferson City Capital News*, February 26 and 27, 1931.

21. Limbaugh, "Diary," March 19, April 1, 3, 21, and 22, 1931; *Jefferson City Capital News*, March 25, 1931; *St. Louis Post-Dispatch*, April 3, 1931; *Kansas City Star*, May 22, 1931.

22. Limbaugh, "Diary," March 23, 24, 26, and 27, 1931; *Jefferson City Capital News*, March 21 and 26, 1931; *Articles of Impeachment Relative to Larry Brunk*,

prepared and presented by the select committee of the House of Representatives of the State of Missouri (Jefferson City, MO: Botz Printing and Stationery Company, 1931).

23. Limbaugh, "Diary," April 2, 1931; John G. Madden, *Before the Senate of the State of Missouri In Re: The Matter of the Articles of Impeachment Relative to Larry Brunk, Treasurer of the State of Missouri–Plea and Motion of Respondent Larry Brunk* (filed April 2, 1931).

24. Limbaugh, "Diary," March 18, 20, 21, 22, 23, 24, 25, 26, 27, 28, 30, and 31, April 2, 10, 20, and 21, 1931; Limbaugh, "Legal Work," 132, 134–35.

25. Limbaugh, "Diary," February 2 and 5, April 21, 1931; John G. Madden, *Before the Senate of the State of Missouri In Re: The Matter of the Articles of Impeachment Relative to Larry Brunk, Treasurer of the State of Missouri–Motion of Respondent, Larry Brunk, to Quash and Dismiss the Articles of Impeachment Aforesaid* (filed May 2, 1931).

26. *St. Louis Globe-Democrat*, May 18 and 19, 1931; *St. Louis Post-Dispatch*, May 18, 1931; *Jefferson City Capital News*, May 19, 1931; *Kansas City Star*, May 20, 1931.

27. Limbaugh, "Legal Work," 135–36; *St. Louis Globe-Democrat*, May 19, 1931; *Jefferson City Capital News*, May 20, 1931; *St. Louis Post-Dispatch*, May 18, 1931; *Kansas City Star* May 19, 1931; "Before the Senate of the State of Missouri In Re: The Matter of the Articles of Impeachment Relative to Larry Brunk, Treasurer of the State of Missouri," a transcript for the impeachment trial from Monday, May 18, 1931, to June 12, 1931, in *Appendix, House and Senate Journals, 56th General Assembly*, vol. 4, Impeachment Proceedings (Jefferson City, MO: n.p. 1931), 76–81 (hereafter cited as "Transcript of Impeachment Trial of Larry Brunk"); Raoul Berger, *Impeachment: the Constitutional Problems* (Cambridge, MA: Harvard University Press, 1973), 53–102; *Constitution of Missouri, 1820*, article 3, sections 29 and 30, article 4, sections 6, 16, and 21, and article 5, section 16.

28. "Transcript of Impeachment Trial of Larry Brunk," 82–92; *Kansas City Star*, May 19, 1931.

29. "Transcript of Impeachment Trial of Larry Brunk," 93, 96–97, 101, 109; *Kansas City Star*, May 19, 1931; *Jefferson City Capital News*, May 20, 1931.

30. "Transcript of Impeachment Trial of Larry Brunk," 142, 144–219, 221–23, 270, 281–83, 287–94, 1463–64, 1468, 1470–72; *St. Louis Post-Dispatch*, May 20 and 22, June 9, 1931; *Jefferson City Capital News*, May 21, 1931; *St. Louis Globe-Democrat*, May 21, 1931.

31. "Transcript of Impeachment Trial of Larry Brunk," 275–76; *St. Louis Post-Dispatch*, May 22, 1931; *Jefferson City Capital News*, May 22, 1931; *St. Louis Globe-Democrat*, May 22, 1931; *Kansas City Star*, May 27, 1931.

32. *St. Louis Globe-Democrat*, May 22, 23, and 26, 1931; *Kansas City Star*, May 21 and 25, 1931; *St. Louis Post-Dispatch*, May 25 and 27, 1931; *Jefferson City Capital News*, May 26–28, 1931.

33. "Transcript of Impeachment Trial of Larry Brunk," 531–62; Limbaugh, "Diary," January 27, 1931; *St. Louis Post-Dispatch*, May 26 and June 9, 1931; *Jefferson City Capital News*, May 26, 1931; *St. Louis Globe-Democrat*, May 26, 1931.

34. *Kansas City Star*, May 26, 1931; *St. Louis Post-Dispatch*, May 26 and 27, 1931; *Jefferson City Capital News*, May 26 and 27, 1931; *St. Louis Globe-Democrat*, May 26 and 27, 1931; "Report of the Brunk Investigative Committee," 13.

35. "Transcript of Impeachment Trial of Larry Brunk," 790–820; *Kansas City Star*, May 28, 1931; *St. Louis Globe-Democrat*, May 28 and June 6, 1931; *St. Louis Post-Dispatch*, May 25, 27, and 28, 1931; Limbaugh, "Diary," January 22, 1931; *Jefferson City Capital News*, May 28 and June 11, 1931.

36. *Kansas City Star*, May 25 and 29, 1931; *St. Louis Post-Dispatch*, May 28 and 29, 1931; *Jefferson City Capital News*, May 28 and 29, 1931.

37. "Transcript of Impeachment Trial of Larry Brunk," 270, 976–86; *St. Louis Globe-Democrat*, June 2 and 3, 1931; *Kansas City Star*, May 29, 1931; *Jefferson City Capital News*, May 30 and June 3, 1931.

38. *St. Louis Post-Dispatch*, June 3, 1931; *Jefferson City Capital News*, June 4, 1931; *St. Louis Globe-Democrat*, June 6, 1931.

39. *Jefferson City Capital News*, June 5, 1931; *St. Louis Post-Dispatch*, June 5, 1931.

40. Ibid.

41. *Kansas City Star*, June 9, 1931; *St. Louis Post-Dispatch*, June 9, 1931; *St. Louis Globe-Democrat*, June 10, 1931; *Jefferson City Capital News*, June 10 and 11, 1931.

42. "Transcript of Impeachment Trial of Larry Brunk," 1437–42, 1444–52, 1476–78; *St. Louis Post-Dispatch*, June 10, 1931; *St. Louis Globe-Democrat*, June 10, 1931; *Kansas City Star*, June 12, 1931.

43. "Transcript of Impeachment Trial of Larry Brunk," 275–76, 1444–51, 1453, 1456, 1458, 1463–66, 1468–69, 1470–72, 1473–76, 1486, 1490, 1522–27; *St. Louis Post-Dispatch*, June 10, 1931; *St. Louis Globe-Democrat*, June 10, 1931.

44. "Transcript of Impeachment Trial of Larry Brunk," 1479–82, 1492–1502; *St. Louis Post-Dispatch*, June 10, 1931; *St. Louis Globe-Democrat*, June 10, 1931.

45. "Transcript of Impeachment Trial of Larry Brunk," 1500–17, 1521–22; *St. Louis Post-Dispatch*, June 10, 1931; *St. Louis Globe-Democrat*, June 10, 1931.

46. *St. Louis Post-Dispatch*, June 11, 1931; *St. Louis Globe-Democrat*, June 12, 1931; *Jefferson City Capital News*, June 12, 1931.

47. *Jefferson City Capital News*, June 12 and 13, 1931; *St. Louis Post-Dispatch*, June 12, 1931; *Kansas City Star*, June 12, 1931.

48. *St. Louis Post-Dispatch*, June 12, 1931; *St. Louis Globe-Democrat*, June 13, 1931; *Jefferson City Capital News*, June 13, 1931.

49. *Kansas City Star*, October 2, 1994; Suggs, ed., *Reflections*, 170–72.

50. *St. Louis Globe-Democrat*, May 21, 22, 26 and June 2, 3, 6, 9, and 13, 1931.

51. *St. Louis Post-Dispatch*, June 14, 1931. Although no byline was given for the *Post-Dispatch* articles, the likelihood is that Boyd Carroll wrote them. As previously noted, Carroll did not protest the House investigators' decision to hold secret meetings and apparently was able to view this from the perspective of what was best for the public good—a view of the matter that Hutson seemed unwilling to consider.

52. Rush H. Limbaugh Sr., "Impeachment," *Missouri Bar Journal* 2, no. 7 (July 1931): 5–7.

53. Joseph Fred Benson, "A Brief Legal History of Impeachment in Missouri," *University of Missouri at Kansas City Law Review* 75 (Winter 2006): 354–61; In the Matter of the Impeachment of Judith K. Moriarty, Supreme Court of Missouri, 902, S.W. 2d 273 (hereafter cited as Impeachment of Moriarty).

54. *Kansas City Star*, October 2, 7, and 12, 1994; *St. Louis Post-Dispatch*, September 16, October 6, 7, and 11, and December 13, 1994.

55. Stephen N. Limbaugh Jr., in discussion with the author, May 26, 2009; Impeachment of Moriarty.

Chapter Seven

1. Rush H. Limbaugh Sr., "Firm of Hardesty & Limbaugh" (unpublished and undated manuscript), 10–11 (Rush H. Limbaugh papers in the possession of Stephen N. Limbaugh Jr. (hereafter cited as Limbaugh, "Firm of Hardesty & Limbaugh"), Limbaugh Papers. Rush H. Limbaugh Sr., "He Praiseth Her or My Life with My Wife," (unpublished manuscript), 136–37 (hereafter cited as Limbaugh, "Life with My Wife"), 136–37; George C. Suggs Jr., ed., *Rush Hudson Limbaugh and his Times: Reflections on a Life Well Lived* (Cape Girardeau: Southeast Missouri State University Press, 2003), 170–72. For the daily details of his legal practice and other activities see Rush H. Limbaugh Sr., "Year Book 1934," (unpublished diary), Limbaugh Papers, (hereafter cited as Limbaugh, "Year Book 1934").

2. Limbaugh, "Life with My Wife," 136–39. In matter of Sturdivant Bank, Cape Girardeau, Missouri, Clyde A. Vandivort, Receiver for Cape Girardeau Bridge Company v. Sturdivant Bank, a corporation, Cape Girardeau, Missouri, St. Louis Court of Appeals, October 1933 term.

3. Limbaugh, "Life with My Wife," 139, 148–49.

4. Ibid., 145–48.

5. Limbaugh, "Year Book 1934," January 10 and 17, February 26, 27, and 28, March 4, April 1, 21, 27, and 28, May 6, 12, 24, 25, 27,30, and 31, June 3 and 4, August 12 and 26, September 9, October 28, November 4, 11, 14, 15, 18, 23, 25, 29, and 30, December 16, 17, 19, and 23, 1934; Limbaugh, "Life with My Wife," 169.

6. Limbaugh, "Year Book 1934," January 3–13, 20, 22, February 14, and July 30, 1934; Limbaugh, "Life with My Wife," 166–69.

7. Limbaugh, "Year Book 1934," April 27, May 16, 18, 21, 22, 24, 28, and 29, June 1, 4, 5, 8, 9 14, 22, and 29, July 3, 7, 9, 13, 16, 20, 25, and 31, August 5, 6, 7, 14, 18, 21, 22, 23, 27, 28, and 29, September 1, 3, 4, 5, 10, 11, 13, 15, 16, 17, and 18, October 26–31, November 1, 2, 3, 5, 6, 7, 10, 13, 14, 22, and 24, and December 10 and 29, 1934; Limbaugh, "Life with My Wife," 159.

8. Rush H. Limbaugh Sr., "Memoranda Diary (Political)," unpublished manuscript, April 13, 1931 entry (hereafter cited as Limbaugh, "Diary"); *Southeast Missourian*, February 12, 13, 15, March 11 and 16, 1932; Rush H. Limbaugh, *Pleading, Practice, Procedure, and Forms in Missouri: A Treatise on the Law Prevailing in Missouri and a Helpful Guide in the Application of the Law Through the Processes of Pleading, Practice, and Procedure in all Branches of the Judiciary and Before all Agencies of the State Government in all Kinds of Actions and Proceedings*, volume 1 (St. Louis, MO: Thomas Law Book Company, December 1935), dedication page.

9. *Southeast Missourian*, March 2, 5, and 21, 1932.

10. *Southeast Missourian*, February 16, March 15–18, and 21–23, 1932.

11. *Southeast Missourian*, March 28, 29, and 30, 1932.

12. *Southeast Missourian*, March 29 and 30, April 2, 1932; Limbaugh, "Diary," 7 January 1931 entry.

13. *Southeast Missourian*, March 31 and April 1–6, 1932; Limbaugh, "Life with My Wife," 138, 159.

14. Limbaugh, "Life with My Wife," 164–66; Limbaugh, "Year Book 1934," February 19 and 20, March 9 and 30, April 5, 23, 24, 26, and 30, June 13, August 24, and December 5 and 7, 1934. According to his notes for much of 1934 (326 recorded days in all), Limbaugh spent over 950 hours working on his book, averaging just under three hours a day.

15. Rush H. Limbaugh Sr., "My Experience as a Special Commissioner of the St. Louis Court of Appeals," (unpublished manuscript), 1–4 (hereafter cited as Limbaugh, "Special Commissioner").

16. "In the matter of Anna Ware," September 25, 1935, 50–51, Limbaugh Papers; Limbaugh, "Special Commissioner," 28, 410.

17. Limbaugh, "Special Commissioner," 4–8, 119; *St. Louis Star-Times*, October 8, 1935.

18. Limbaugh, "Special Commissioner," 7–16.

19. Ibid., 17–22.

20. Ibid., 22–25.

21. Ibid., 30–33; *St. Louis Star-Times*, October 18, 1935.

22. Limbaugh, "Special Commissioner," 35–39.

23. Ibid., 40–46; *St. Louis Post-Dispatch*, October 15, 1935; *St. Louis Star-Times*, October 15, 1935.

24. Limbaugh, "Special Commissioner," 48–56, 59–61.

25. Limbaugh, "Special Commissioner," 66–71, 78, 139. Jones later claimed that the woman in the car with him that night was a woman by the name of Madge Hill, *St. Louis Post-Dispatch*, October 15, 1935; *St. Louis Star-Times*, October 15, 1935.

26. Limbaugh, "Special Commissioner," 71–75, 289–90, 292.

27. Ibid., 74–75; Ernest Kirschten, *Catfish and Crystal* (Garden City, NY: Doubleday, 1960, St. Louis: Patrice Press, 1989), 379–84; *St. Louis Star-Times*, October 16, 1935; *St. Louis Post-Dispatch*, October 16, 1935; *St. Louis Globe-Democrat*, October 16, 1935.

28. Limbaugh, "Special Commissioner," 78–80, 112–13, 289, 306–10; *St. Louis Star-Times*, October 16, 1935; *St. Louis Post-Dispatch*, October 16, 1935; *St. Louis Globe-Democrat*, October 18, 1935.

29. Limbaugh, "Special Commissioner," 54, 86, 94, 97–99.

30. Ibid., 91–93, 97–98, 104–5; *St. Louis Star-Times*, October 18, 1935; *St. Louis Post-Dispatch*, October 16, 1935.

31. Limbaugh, "Special Commissioner," 88–89, 187–88; *St. Louis Star-Times*, October 17, 1935; *St. Louis Post-Dispatch*, October 24, 1935.

32. Limbaugh, "Special Commissioner," 107, 168–70; *St. Louis Star-Times*, October 18, 1935; *St. Louis Post-Dispatch*, October 18, 1935.

33. Limbaugh, "Special Commissioner," 172–74, 246–53, 259–63, 282, 298–99, 304–5.

34. Ibid., 107, 120–26; Kirschten, *Catfish and Crystal*, 386–87; *St. Louis Star-Times*, October 18 and 21, 1935; *St. Louis Post-Dispatch*, October 18 and 21, 1935; *St. Louis Globe-Democrat*, October 22, 1935.

35. Limbaugh, "Special Commissioner," 30–32, 46–48, 60, 87, 101–3, 113–16; *St. Louis Post-Dispatch*, October 22, 1935.

36. Limbaugh, "Special Commissioner," 114, 116–18.

37. Ibid., 119–20, 126–27; *St. Louis Star-Times*, October 21, 1935.

38. Limbaugh, "Special Commissioner," 127–35; *St. Louis Globe-Democrat*, October 22, 1935; *St. Louis Star-Times*, October 21 and 22, 1935; *St. Louis Post-Dispatch*, October 21 and 22, 1935.

39. Limbaugh, "Special Commissioner," 136–43; *St. Louis Globe-Democrat*, October 23, 1935; *St. Louis Star-Times*, October 23, 1935; *St. Louis Post-Dispatch*, October 22 and 23, 1935.

40. Limbaugh, "Special Commissioner," 145–56; *St. Louis Globe-Democrat*, October 23, 1935; *St. Louis Star-Times*, October 23, 1935; *St. Louis Post-Dispatch*, October 22 and 23, 1935.

41. Limbaugh, "Special Commissioner," 160–64.

42. Ibid., 175; *St. Louis Post-Dispatch*, October 22, 1935.

43. Limbaugh, "Special Commissioner," 177–79; *St. Louis Star-Times*, October 24, 1935; *St. Louis Post-Dispatch*, October 24, 1935; *Southeast Missourian*,

October 24, 1935; *St. Louis Globe-Democrat*, October 25, 1935.

44. Limbaugh, "Special Commissioner," 180–82, 202; *St. Louis Post-Dispatch*, October 24 and 25, 1935; *St. Louis Globe-Democrat*, October 25 and 29, 1935; *St. Louis Star-Times*, October 24 and 25, 1935.

45. Limbaugh, "Special Commissioner," 330–31; Limbaugh to O. L. Williams, May 25, 1936, Limbaugh Papers; *St. Louis Star-Times*, December 14, 1935.

46. Limbaugh, "Special Commissioner," 180–82, 222, 231, 233. Motion of Wilfred Jones, October 30, 1935, to the judges of the St. Louis Court of Appeals, Limbaugh Papers; *St. Louis Globe-Democrat*, October 29, 1935.

47. Limbaugh, "Special Commissioner," 166–67, 175–76, 190; *St. Louis Star-Times*, October 25, 1935; *St. Louis Post-Dispatch*, October 25, 1935.

48. Limbaugh, "Special Commissioner," 192–99; Rush H. Limbaugh, "Order to Ludwig O. and Nelle Tipton Muench to produce the child," October 24, 1935; "Motion to quash Limbaugh's order, October 25, 1935," Limbaugh Papers; *St. Louis Star-Times*, October 25, 1935; *St. Louis Post-Dispatch*, October 25, 1935; *Southeast Missourian*, October 26, 1935; *St. Louis Globe-Democrat*, October 26, 1935.

49. "Writ of prohibition," October 25, 1935; petitioner's response to the writ of prohibition, undated; and respondents' motion "in support of petition for writ of prohibition, undated, Limbaugh Papers.

50. Limbaugh, "Special Commissioner," 199, 203–11; *St. Louis Star-Times*, October 25–29, 1935; *Southeast Missourian*, October 26, 28, and 29, 1935; *St. Louis Globe-Democrat*, October 25–29, 1935; *St. Louis Post-Dispatch*, October 25–29, 1935.

51. Limbaugh, "Special Commissioner," 211–18, 228–30, 311, 313–17; *St. Louis Post-Dispatch*, October 30, 1935; *St. Louis Globe-Democrat*, October 31, 1935; *St. Louis Star-Times*, October 30, 1935; *Southeast Missourian*, October 30, 1935.

52. Limbaugh, "Special Commissioner," 218–21; *St. Louis Post-Dispatch*, October 30, 1935; *St. Louis Globe-Democrat*, October 31, 1935; *St. Louis Star-Times*, October 30, 1935.

53. Limbaugh, "Special Commissioner," 222–26, 231–38; *St. Louis Star-Times*, October 30, 1935.

54. Limbaugh, "Special Commissioner," 236–37, 321–25, 327–31.

55. Ibid., 331, 334–40.

56. Ibid., 336–42; Rush H. Limbaugh Sr., Anna Ware, an Infant, by Mary Ware, Her Next Friend, Petitioner v. Ludwig O. Muench and Nelle Tipton Muench, His Wife, Wilfred Jones, Helen Berroyer, Rebecca Winner, and Carl M. Dubinsky, Respondents, 232 Mo. App. 41 (hereafter cited as Limbaugh, *Ware v. Muench, Muench, and Jones*).

57. Limbaugh, *Ware v. Muench, Muench, and Jones*; Stephen N. Limbaugh Sr., in discussion with the author, August 21, 2007.

58. Limbaugh, "Special Commissioner," 347, 353–57, 362–63; *St. Louis Star-Times*, December 5–6, 14, and 19, 1935; *St. Louis Post-Dispatch*, December 5–6, 15, and 19, 1935; *St. Louis Globe-Democrat*, December 5–6, 1935; *Time*, December 16, 1935, and January 4, 1937; *New York Times*, December 6, 1935; *Chicago Daily Tribune*, October 25, December 6 and 14, 1935; *Salina Journal* (Salina, KS), December 5, 1935; Braymer, *Missouri Bee*, December 18, 1935. Unfortunately, Fitzpatrick's original drawing was lost when a tornado struck the Limbaugh home on May 21, 1949.

59. Limbaugh, "Special Commissioner," 378–84; Kirschten, *Catfish and Crystal*, 386–89; *Time*, January 4, 1936; *St. Louis Post-Dispatch*, October 22, 1935.

Chapter Eight

1. Rush H. Limbaugh Sr., "My Experience as a Special Commissioner of the St. Louis Court of Appeals," (unpublished manuscript), 300–3 (hereafter cited as Limbaugh, "Special Commissioner").

2. Rush H. Limbaugh Sr., "He Praiseth Her or My Life with My Wife," (unpublished manuscript), 162–64 (hereafter cited as Limbaugh, "Life with My Wife"); Limbaugh, "Special Commissioner," 332–33, 357–58, 363–66, 369–70; Stephen N. Limbaugh Sr., in discussion with the author, August 13, 2007.

3. Limbaugh, "Life with My Wife," 159–60; Stephen N. Limbaugh Sr., in discussion with the author, August 13 and 21, 2007; Rush H. Limbaugh Sr. to Charles Evans Hughes, February 18, 1937, Limbaugh Papers; *Alameda* (CA) *Times-Star*, July 28, 1934; William E. Leuchtenburg, "When the People Spoke, What did they say?: the Election of 1936 and the Ackerman Thesis," *Yale Law Journal* 108, no. 8 (1999): 2090–92.

4. Limbaugh, "Life with My Wife," 108, 151–57, 199–202; Helen Gillespie, in discussion with the author, September 4, 2009.

5. Helen Gillespie, in discussion with the author, September 4, 2009; Limbaugh, "Life with My Wife," 151.

6. Helen Gillespie, in discussion with the author, September 4, 2009; Stephen N. Limbaugh Sr., in discussion with the author, August 13, 2007; Rush H. Limbaugh Sr., "Year Book 1934," (unpublished diary), January 17, 26, February 28, March 4, May 6, 25, 27, June, November 3, 4, 18, 23, December 17 and 19, 1934, Limbaugh Papers. Death certificate of Susan Francis Presnell Limbaugh, website of the Secretary of State, Missouri.

7. Limbaugh, "Life with My Wife," 164–66; Limbaugh, "Special Commissioner," 2, 17–18, 200–1, 230, 345–46. Limbaugh to Lillian Wright, December 5, 1935, Limbaugh Papers; Rush H. Limbaugh Sr., *Pleading, Practice, Procedure, and Forms in Missouri: A Treatise on the Law Prevailing in Missouri and a Helpful Guide in the Application of the Law Through the Processes of Pleading, Practice, and Procedure in all Branches of the Judiciary and Before*

All Agencies of the State Government in All Kinds of Actions and Proceedings Together with Useful Forms Designed for the Ordinary Needs of a Practicing Lawyer, vol. 1 (St. Louis: Thomas Law Book Company, December 1935), v–vi, 66–72.

8. Limbaugh, "Life with My Wife," 165; Thomas E. Atkinson, review of *Pleading, Practice, Procedure, and Forms in Missouri,* volume 1, *Missouri Law Review* 2 (January 1937): 121–23; Thomas E. Atkinson, review of *Pleading, Practice, Procedure, and Forms in Missouri,* volume 2, *Missouri Law Review* 4 (November 1939): 475–77.

9. Rush H. Limbaugh Sr., "The Adoption of Children in Missouri," *Missouri Law Review* 2 (June 1937): 300–12; Rush H. Limbaugh Sr., "The Work of the Missouri Supreme Court for 1937 [through 1942] (Extraordinary Legal Remedies)," *Missouri Law Review* 3 (November 1938): 383–92; 4 (November 1939): 389–406; 5 (November 1940): 433–45; 6 (November 1941): 432–47; 7 (November 1942): 377–95; and 8 (November 1943): 247–61.

10. Limbaugh, "Life with My Wife," 183–85; Rush H. Limbaugh Sr., "Memoir on Legal Work," (unpublished and undated manuscript), 89–92 (hereafter cited as Limbaugh, "Legal Work"); *Daily Dunklin Democrat* (Dunklin, MO), November 7, 2008; Stephen N. Limbaugh Sr., email message to the author, October 5, 2009.

11. Limbaugh, "Life with My Wife," 186–90; Limbaugh, "Legal Work," 92–93, 106.

12. Limbaugh, "Legal Work," 92–97.

13. Limbaugh, "Legal Work," 97–101; Rush H. Limbaugh Sr., "Memorandum submitted by landowners in support of their exceptions," in United States of America v. Certain Lands situate in the County of Wayne in the state of Missouri known as tract no. 184, Wappapello Reservoir, St. Francis River Project, and Lottie M. Allison, et al., Limbaugh Papers (hereafter cited as Limbaugh, "Landowners' Memorandum").

14. Limbaugh, "Legal Work," 19, 23–24, 100–2; Limbaugh, "Landowners' Memorandum."

15. Limbaugh, "Legal Work," 102–8; Limbaugh, "Landowners' Memorandum"; *Greenville* (MO) *Sun,* June 23, 1949.

16. Limbaugh, "Life with My Wife," 192–94; Rush H. Limbaugh Sr., "Daniel Webster," address before the Rotary Club in Cape Girardeau, January 22, 1940; and notes for an address before the St. Joseph Bar Institute, October 12, 1940, Limbaugh Papers.

17. Limbaugh, "Life with My Wife," 194–95.

18. Richard S. Kirkendall, *A History of Missouri, 1919 to 1953,* volume five (Columbia: University of Missouri Press, 1986), 219–21; Gerald T. Dunne, *The Missouri Supreme Court: from Dred Scott to Nancy Cruzan* (Columbia: University of Missouri Press, 1993), 148–49; *Time,* "Missouri: *Ex Machina,*" April 14,

1941; State ex rel. Donnell v. Searcy and State ex rel. Donnell v. Osborn, 347 Mo. 469 and 1052.

19. Limbaugh, "Life with My Wife," 202–5; James T. Altman, "Review: Modern Litigators and Lawyer-Statesmen" *Yale Law Journal* 103, no. 4 (January 1994): 1033.

20. Limbaugh, "Life with My Wife," 174–77; Rush H. Limbaugh Sr., "Companionship with Personalities of the Present," (undated); and "The Decline of Democracy and the Rise of dictatorship Since the War," April 12, 1934, Limbaugh Papers.

21. Limbaugh, "Life with My Wife," 190–91, 196–97.

22. Kirkendall, *History of Missouri*, 242–44; Limbaugh, "Life with My Wife," 197–98; Rush H. Limbaugh Sr., "Address at Anna," May 5, 1941, Limbaugh Papers; *Anna* (IL) *Gazette-Democrat*, May 8, 1941.

23. Limbaugh, "Life with My Wife," 205–6, 213–15; Stephen N. Limbaugh Sr., in discussion with the author, August 13, 2007; Stephen N. Limbaugh Sr., email message to the author, September 10, 2009.

24. Limbaugh, "Life with My Wife," 218–20, 223–25; Stephen N. Limbaugh Sr., email message to the author, September 10, 2009; Thomas E. Alexander, *The Wings of Change: The Army Air Force Experience in Texas During World War II*, Military History of Texas Series (Abilene, TX: McWhiney Foundation Press, McMurry University, 2003), 32–33.

25. Limbaugh, "Life with My Wife," 228–29; Stephen N. Limbaugh Sr., email message to the author, November 5, 2009.

26. Limbaugh, "Life with My Wife," 234; A. Russell Buchanan, *The United States and World War II*, vol. 2 (New York: Harper & Row, 1964), 480–86.

27. Limbaugh, "Life with My Wife," 218, 226–27, 229–30; Manley and Mary Limbaugh, in discussion with the author, October 27, 2009; Mary Limbaugh, in discussion with the author, March 8, 2010.

28. Limbaugh, "Life with My Wife," 208–9; Helen Gilespie in discussion with the author, September 4, 2009; Stephen N. Limbaugh Sr., in discussion with the author, August 13, 2007.

29. Limbaugh, "Life with My Wife," 236–37; Helen Gilespie, in discussion with the author, September 4, 2009.

30. Limbaugh, "Life with My Wife," 217–19, 226–27, 230. Stephen N. Limbaugh Sr., email message to the author, November 5, 2009.

31. Unidentified to Rush H. Limbaugh Sr., undated, on "Copy fact sheet originally prepared by Office of War Information, Domestic Radio Bureau," Limbaugh Papers; *Southeast Missourian*, January 28, 1941, September 2, 1942, and July 1, 1943.

32. Limbaugh, "Life with My Wife," 221–23; Suggs, ed., *Rush Hudson Limbaugh and his Times*, 124–26, 199; *Life*, "Biggest Pipeline," October 26, 1944.

33. Limbaugh, "Legal Work," 178; Limbaugh, "Life with My Wife," 223; Helen Gilespie, in discussion with the author, September 4, 2009.

34. Limbaugh, "Legal Work," 51–52; Suggs, ed., *Reflections*, 44, 52–54; Stephen N. Limbaugh Sr., in discussion with the author, August 13, 2007; Stephen N. Limbaugh Sr., email message to the author, November 5, 2009; *United States v. Henry Chisem, United States v. Elgie Morris, United States v. Isaac Taylor Quinn, United States v. Vernon Lemons,* and *United States v. Richard Leonard Riley,* tried in the Eastern District of Missouri, Southeastern Division. National Archives and Records Administration, Central Plains Region, Kansas City, Missouri.

35. Limbaugh, "Life with My Wife," 232–34, 236, 246–47; Stephen N. Limbaugh Sr., in discussion with the author, August 13, 2007; Stephen N. Limbaugh Sr., email message to the author, November 5, 2009; Suggs, ed., *Reflections*, 105.

36. Rush H. Limbaugh Sr., "Memorial Address," May 29, 1946, Limbaugh Papers; *Southeast Missourian*, May 30, 1946.

Chapter Nine

1. Rush H. Limbaugh Sr., "He Praiseth Her or My Life with My Wife," (unpublished manuscript), 238–39, 255, 276, 277, 300–2 (hereafter cited as Limbaugh, "Life with My Wife"); Stephen N. Limbaugh Sr., in discussion with the author, August 21, 2007.

2. Limbaugh, "Life with My Wife," 198; Stephen N. Limbaugh Sr., in discussion with the author, August 13, 2007.

3. Limbaugh, "Life with My Wife," 230–31; Rush H. Limbaugh Sr. to Bee Limbaugh, October 1, 1941, and Limbaugh to "Dearest Loved Ones," April 9, 1944, Limbaugh Papers; Rush H. Limbaugh Sr., "Memoir on Legal Work," (unpublished and undated manuscript), 116–19, 122–25 (hereafter cited as Limbaugh, "Legal Work"); Application of Erlbacher Brothers and Eddie Erlbacher for Permits to Operate as Contract Carriers by Water. Reply of Protestants to Applicants' Exceptions to the Proposed Report of Examiner Carl A. Schlager, American Barge Line Company, De Bardeleben Coal Corporation, d/b/a Coyle Lines, River Terminals Corporation, Union Barge Line Corporation, Mississippi Barge Line Company, Protestants, February 6, 1942; Application of Erlbacher Brothers and Eddie Erlbacher for Permits to Operate as Contract Carriers by Water. Brief on Behalf of Protestants, June 5, 1942; Application of Erlbacher Brothers, Reply of Protestants to Applicants' Exceptions to the Proposed Report of Examiner Carl A. Schlager, July 18, 1942; Stephen N. Limbaugh Sr., in discussion with the author, August 13, 2007.

4. Limbaugh, "Life with My Wife," 278–80, 283–85, 310, 314; Stephen N. Limbaugh Sr., in discussion with the author, August 21, 2007; *Southeast Missourian,*

September 9, 2006; Stephen N. Limbaugh Sr., email message to the author, November 30, 2009.

5. Limbaugh, "Life with My Wife," 314, 323; Stephen N. Limbaugh Sr., in discussion with the author, August 21, 2007. See also Rush H. Limbaugh Sr., "Diary of Rush H. Limbaugh of Trip to India on Mission for State Department, November 1958-January 1959," (hereafter cited as Limbaugh, "Diary of Trip to India"), November 11, 1958, Limbaugh Papers;

6. Stephen N. Limbaugh Sr., in discussion with the author, August 13 and 21, 2007; Dianne Sue DeLay, by James Delay and Marjorie Delay, Her Next Friends (Plaintiff) Respondent v. Jase M. Ward, (Defendant) Appellant, appeal from the Circuit Court of Stoddard County, Bloomfield, Springfield Court of Appeals, April 1953 session.

7. Limbaugh, "Life with My Wife," 313, 324, 343–44, 348–49; Rush H. Limbaugh Sr., "My Experience as a Special Commissioner of the St. Louis Court of Appeals," (unpublished manuscript), 412; Rush H. Limbaugh Sr., "Report of Rush H. Limbaugh, Special Commissioner," 3, in State of Missouri, On the Information of J. E. Taylor, Attorney General v. Armour & Company, in the Supreme Court of Missouri, Missouri State Archives, Jefferson City, Missouri (hereafter cited as Limbaugh, "Report of Special Commissioner").

8. Limbaugh, "Life with My Wife," 343–44; Limbaugh, "Legal Work," 144–49; Rush H. Limbaugh Sr., "Historic Origins of Anti-Trust Legislation," *Missouri Law Review* 18, no. 3 (June 1953): 215–18 (hereafter cited as Limbaugh, "Anti-Trust Legislation").

9. Limbaugh, "Anti-Trust Legislation," 223–24, 227–28; Limbaugh, "Life with My Wife," 343; Limbaugh, "Legal Work," 144–49; Limbaugh, "Report of Special Commissioner," 31–33.

10. Limbaugh, "Life with My Wife," 244; Limbaugh, "Legal Work," 149; State e rel. Dalton v. Miles Laboratories, Inc., 282 S.W. 2d, 564.

11. Limbaugh, "Life with My Wife," 254; Limbaugh, "Legal Work," 183–93. For a fuller account of Limbaugh's volumes on the Missouri practice, see chapter eight.

12. Limbaugh, "Life with My Wife," 293, 325–28, 333, 345–47, 351, 355; *American Bar Association, Section of Real Property, Probate and Trust Law, Proceedings* 3 (1948): vii, 89; 4 (1950): 3, 118–31; 7 (1952): v–vi; 8 (1953): v; and 9 (1954): v; *American Bar Association Journal* 40 (1954): 1004–5.

13. Limbaugh, "Life with My Wife," 355; Rush H. Limbaugh Sr., "The Sources and Development of Probate Law," *Washington University Law Quarterly* 4 (December 1956): 419–47.

14. Rush H. Limbaugh Sr., "The Public Duty of the American Lawyer," *Missouri Law Review* 20, no. 3 (June 1955): 223–55; Limbaugh, "Life with My Wife," 356. Limbaugh spent two days "working in seclusion" on this address, which is his most mature and fullest statement on this topic.

15. Limbaugh, "Life with My Wife," 238–39, 300, 312–14, 324, 352, 357–59, 367; Stephen N. Limbaugh Sr., in discussion with the author, August 13 and 21, 2007.

16. Limbaugh, "Life with My Wife, 357–58; Limbaugh to the American Bar Association, October 12, 1955, Limbaugh Papers.

17. Limbaugh, "Life with My Wife," 363–66; "Addresses Made by Rush H. Limbaugh as President of the Missouri Bar," undated; William Johnson to Limbaugh, March 13, 1956; Limbaugh to Harry Gershenson, April 16, 1956; and "Minutes of Annual Meeting, Board of Governors, Missouri Bar," October 4–6, 1956, Limbaugh Papers.

18. Limbaugh, "Life with My Wife," 360, 362; Missouri Bar organizational chart, October 21, 1955; and Roberts P. Elam to Limbaugh, May 21, 1956, Limbaugh Papers.

19. Minutes of executive committee and administrative chairmen, December 17, 1955, Limbaugh Papers.

20. Limbaugh, "Life with My Wife," 360.

21. Mrs. B. B. Lloyd to Limbaugh, November 27, December 28, 1955, March 21, and April 13, 1956; Limbaugh to Lloyd, December 6, 1955, January 13 and April 18, 1956; Limbaugh to Robert L. Spurrier, January 11, 1956; Frank P. Aschemeyer, vice president of the General American Life Insurance Company, to Limbaugh, March 28, 1956; Limbaugh's statement, April 3, 1956; Robert L. Spurrier to Limbaugh, January 5, 1955 [probably 1956], May 25, 1956; and an undated Missouri Bar resolution to Governor Phil M. Donnelly to create a commission "to study the present laws and facilities of Missouri relating to children and youth," Limbaugh Papers.

22. Limbaugh to Norman Carlton, December 12, 1955, Limbaugh Papers.

23. Wade F. Baker to Limbaugh, March 6, 1956; Limbaugh to Baker, March 7, 1956; and Limbaugh to Fred B. Hulse, March 7, 1956, Limbaugh Papers.

24. "Minutes of Meeting of Executive Committee and Administrative Chairmen held at Mayfair Hotel, St. Louis, Missouri," December 17, 1955; James O. Eastland to Limbaugh, May 15, June 19, 1956; Limbaugh to Eastland, May 21, June 25, 1956; Limbaugh to Harry Gershenson, June 7, 1956; Gershenson to Limbaugh, June 8, 1956; Allan F. Wherritt to Limbaugh, June 22, 1956; Clarence O. Woolsey to Limbaugh, June 22, 1956; Limbaugh to Wherritt, June 25, 1956; Limbaugh to Woolsey, June 25, 1956; Limbaugh to Harry Rooks, June 25, 1956; Limbaugh to Horace F. Blackwell, July 13, 1956, Limbaugh Papers.

25. John D. Hasler to Fred B. Hulse, chairman of Advisory Committee, December 20, 1955; Hasler to Limbaugh, December 23, 1955; C. L. Thomas, vice president of KXOK, to Limbaugh, June 4, 1956; and Limbaugh to Thomas, June 7, 1956; Limbaugh to C. A. Leedy Jr., July 5, 1956, Limbaugh Papers.

26. Limbaugh, "Life with My Wife," 363–65; Limbaugh to Rufus Burrus, August 26, 1955; Burrus to Limbaugh, October 12, 1955; Limbaugh to Lynn F.

Ewing, November 4 and 14, 1955; Ewing to Limbaugh, November 9, 1955; Horace F. Blackwell to Limbaugh, December 5, 1955; Harry Rooks to Horace F. Blackwell, December 6, 1955; Limbaugh to Blackwell, December 8, 1955; Limbaugh to William A. Collet, December 8, 1955; Jack L. Oliver to Limbaugh, February 28, 1956; Limbaugh to Russell Doerner and Harry Gershenson, March 5, 1956; Gershenson to Limbaugh, March 6, 1956; Charles E. Cates, Industrial Commission of Missouri, to William D. Cosgrove, March 14, 1956; Cosgrove to Limbaugh, March 19, 1956; Limbaugh to Cosgrove, March 26, 1956; Cates to Limbaugh, March 27, 1956; Limbaugh to Cates, April 5, 1956; Paul D. Hess Jr. to Harry Rooks, April 25, 1956; Limbaugh to Hess, May 17 and June 18, 1956; Limbaugh to Richard M. Duncan, July 9, 1956; Limbaugh to John A. Shaw, September 18, 1956; and Limbaugh to Judge Marshall Craig, October 31, 1956, Limbaugh Papers.

27. Limbaugh, "Life with My Wife," 369; Suggs., ed., *Rush Hudson Limbaugh and his Times*, 162–66; Alan R. Havig, *A Centennial History of the State Historical Society of Missouri, 1898–1998* (Columbia: University of Missouri Press, 1998), 4, 51, 104–6.

28. Limbaugh, "Life with My Wife, 250–53, 256–77, 290.

29. Ibid., 244–46, 277, 323, 333–36, 370–71.

30. Limbaugh, "Life with My Wife," 300–302; *Southeast Missourian*, May 21, 2009.

31. Limbaugh, "Life with My Wife," 302–5.

32. Limbaugh, "Life with My Wife," 305–8, 310–12; Rush H. Limbaugh Sr., "My Experience as a Special Commissioner of the St. Louis Court of Appeals," (unpublished manuscript), 357; Limbaugh to Laurance M. Hyde, 25 May 1949. Laurance M. Hyde Papers, Western Historical Manuscript Collection, Columbia, Missouri.

33. Limbaugh, "Life with My Wife," 256, 308–10, 314, 321, 324, 345; Stephen N. Limbaugh Jr., email message to the author, November 24, 2009.

34. Limbaugh, "Life with My Wife," 441–43; Stephen N. Limbaugh Sr., in discussion with the author, August 13, 2007; Rush H. Limbaugh Sr., "Report of Rush H. Limbaugh of his Itinerary and Activities Serving as a United States Specialist, from his home in Cape Girardeau, Missouri, beginning November 2, 1958, to India and Return to Washington D. C., January 16, 1959 under United States government Grant Authorization No. 381–9, Obligation No. 787, dated October 21, 1958, issued by Martha G. Geesa, Acting Chief, American Specialists Branch, Leaders in Specialists Division, Activity No. 1878, Appropriation Symbol 1991128, Allotment No. 9M-1069," cover page, Limbaugh Papers (hereafter cited as Limbaugh, "Report on Trip to India").

35. Dwight D. Eisenhower, *Waging Peace, 1956–1961* (Garden City, NY: Doubleday & Company, Inc., 1965), 6, 106–14, 494–95, 499–504.

36. Limbaugh, "Life with My Wife," 443–45, 449–52, 457.

37. Limbaugh, "Life with My Wife," 445–47; Limbaugh, "Diary of Trip to India," November 2–11, 1958; Bee Limbaugh, "Diary," November 3, 1958.

38. Limbaugh, "Life with My Wife," 446–47, 451; Limbaugh, "Diary of Trip to India," November 12–20, 1958.

39. Limbaugh, "Diary of Trip to India," November 21–24, 1958; Limbaugh, "Report on Trip to India," 2; Limbaugh, "Life with My Wife," 453–54.

40. Limbaugh, "Diary of Trip to India," November 25–27, 1958; Limbaugh, "Report on Trip to India," 3; Limbaugh, "Life with My Wife," 454.

41. Limbaugh, "Diary of Trip to India," November 28–December 3, 1958; Limbaugh, "Report on Trip to India," 4–5; Limbaugh, "Life with My Wife," 448.

42. Limbaugh, "Diary of Trip to India," December 4, 1958; Limbaugh, "Report on Trip to India," 5; Limbaugh, "Life with My Wife," 456–57.

43. Limbaugh, "Diary of Trip to India," December 5, 1958; Limbaugh, "Report on Trip to India," 5–6.

44. Limbaugh, "Diary of Trip to India," December 6–10, 1958; Limbaugh, "Report on Trip to India," 6–8, 16–17; David A. Nichols, *A Matter of Justice: Eisenhower and the Beginning of the Civil Rights Revolution* (New York: Simon & Schuster, 2007), 169–213.

45. Limbaugh, "Diary of Trip to India," December 10–11, 1958; Limbaugh, "Report on Trip to India," 7–8; *Deccan Chronicle* (Secunderabad, India), December 12, 1958.

46. Limbaugh, "Diary of Trip to India," December 12, 1958; Limbaugh, "Report on Trip to India," 8–9; Limbaugh, "Life with My Wife," 448, 454–55.

47. Limbaugh, "Diary of Trip to India," December 14–16, 1958; Limbaugh, "Report on Trip to India," 9–10.

48. Limbaugh, "Diary of Trip to India," December 18, 1958; Limbaugh, "Report on Trip to India," 10, 17; Rush H. Limbaugh Sr., "Year Book 1934," November 14, 1934, (unpublished diary), Limbaugh Papers; Eisenhower, *Waging Peace*, 107–10.

49. Eisenhower, *Waging Peace*, 148–76; for the quotation see 168. For perhaps the seminal article on the effect of foreign policy concerns on civil rights issues see Mary L. Dudziak, "Desegregation as a Cold War Imperative," *Stanford Law Review* 41, no. 1 (November 1988): 61–120; David A. Nichols, *A Matter of Justice*, 178, 198, 204.

50. Limbaugh, "Diary of Trip to India," December 18–19, 1958; Limbaugh, "Report on Trip to India," 11–12.

51. Limbaugh, "Diary of Trip to India," December 21–24, 1958; Limbaugh, "Report on Trip to India," 12–13.

52. Limbaugh, "Diary of Trip to India," December 25, 1958; Limbaugh, "Report on Trip to India," 14; Sidney Hook, *Out of Step: An Unquiet Life in the 20th Century* (New York: Harper & Row, 1987), 587–88; Eisenhower, *Waging Peace*, 107–10. For Hook's polemics see his dispute with Hannah Arendt over the

Little Rock episode in Norman Podhoretz, *Ex-Friends: Falling out with Allen Ginsberg, Lionel and Diana Trilling, Lillian Hellman, Hannah Arendt, and Norman Mailer* (San Francisco: Encounter Books, 2000), 149–51.

53. Limbaugh, "Diary of Trip to India," December 26, 1958–January 10, 1959; Limbaugh, "Report on Trip to India," 15.

Chapter Ten

1. Abraham Lincoln, *The Collected Works of Abraham Lincoln*, Roy P Basler, ed., vol. 3 (New Brunswick, NJ: Rutgers University Press, 1959), 14; Dwight D. Eisenhower, *Waging Peace: The White House Years, 1956–1961* (Garden City, New York: Doubleday & Company, 1965), 152–53, 168, 171.

2. Stephen N. Limbaugh Sr., email message to the author, December 4, 2009; and Stephen N. Limbaugh Jr., email message to the author,, February 1, 2010.

3. Stephen N. Limbaugh Sr., email message to the author, December 4, 2009; Eisenhower, *Waging Peace*, 162–71; Nicholas A. Bryant, *The Bystander: John F. Kennedy and the Struggle for Black Equality* (New York: Basic Books, 2006), 53.

4. Eisenhower, *Waging Peace*, 149–50; Bryant, *Bystander*, 43; David A. Nichols, *A Matter of Justice: Eisenhower and the Beginning of the Civil Rights Revolution* (New York: Simon & Schuster, 2007), 21–50, 136. During the presidential campaign of 1952, President Harry S. Truman scoffed at the idea that Eisenhower could use his authority as president to end segregation in Washington, DC. Truman was wrong. Herbert Brownell, with John P. Burke, *Advising Ike: The Memoirs of Attorney General Herbert Brownell* (Lawrence: University Press of Kansas, 1993), 186–87.

5. Nichols, *A Matter of Justice*, 151, 153–54.

6. Ibid., 154–55.

7. Eisenhower, *Waging Peace*, 156–62; Bryant, *Bystander*, 61–79, 286–88; Nichols, *A Matter of Justice*, 75–90, 146–47, 266–67; Brownell, *Advising Ike*, 182–84; Anne S. Emanuel, *Elbert Parr Tuttle: Chief Jurist of the Civil Rights Revolution* (Athens: University of Georgia Press, 2011).

8. Alfred J. Schweppe, "Enforcement of Federal Decrees: A 'Recurrence to Fundamental Principles,'" *American Bar Association Journal* 44, no. 2 (February 1958): 113–16; *American Bar Association Journal* 45, no. 10 (October 1959): 363–64, 1102–3.

9. Rush H. Limbaugh Sr., "He Praiseth Her or My Life with My Wife," (unpublished manuscript), 463–64 (hereafter cited as Limbaugh, "Life with My Wife").

10. Limbaugh to Governor John Patterson of Alabama, November 30, 1960; Limbaugh to Fred H. Brand, December 9, 1960; Limbaugh to the editor of the

Atlanta Constitution, December 13, 1960; and Limbaugh to committee, February 14, 1960, Limbaugh Papers.

11. Notes on the Bill of Rights, undated, Limbaugh Papers.

12. Report of the Standing Committee on Bill of Rights, August 1961, Limbaugh Papers; Suggs, ed., *Rush Hudson Limbaugh and his Times*, 155–59.

13. Ibid. For a balanced view of the appropriateness of anti-Communist measures see Sidney Hook, *Out of Step: An Unquiet Life in the 20ᵗʰ Century* (New York: Harper & Row, 1987), 498–508.

14. Ibid.

15. Report of the Standing Committee on Bill of Rights, August 1961, Limbaugh Papers. For the traditional analysis of the *Brown* decision leading to a (in my opinion) flawed consensus regarding the historical record of the intent of the framers of the Fourteenth Amendment see Alexander M. Bickel, "The Original Understanding and the Segregation Decision," *Harvard Law Review* 69, no. 1 (November 1955): 1–65. For a rebuttal to this consensus view see Michael W. McConnell, "Originalism and the Desegregation Decisions," *Virginia Law Review* 81, no. 4 (May 1995): 947–1140, especially 950–53, 1093–98, and 1132–40.

16. Limbaugh, "Life with My Wife," 466–68; *American Bar Association Journal* 47, no. 10 (October 1961): 1040.

17. Mississippi was notorious among African Americans throughout the South for its particularly mean-spirited and harsh system of discrimination and segregation. See John Howard Griffin, *Black Like Me* (New York: Signet, 1962), 53–80.

18. Stephen N. Limbaugh Sr., email message to the author, July 22, 2009; Willie Morris, "Yazoo . . . Notes on Survival," *Harper's*, June 1970, 46–49, 52, 54, 61–62; James W. Silver, "Mississippi: the Closed Society," *The Journal of Southern History* 30, no. 1 (February 1964): 25–26; Charles W. Eagles, "The Closing of Mississippi Society: Will Campbell, 'The $64,000 Question,' and Religious Emphasis Week at the University of Mississippi," *The Journal of Southern History* 67, no. 2 (May 2001): 371; John C. Satterfield to Sylvester C. Smith Jr., 7 October, 1962. John C. Satterfield/American Bar Association Collection, University of Mississippi (hereafter cited as Satterfield Papers).

19. Sylvester C. Smith Jr. to John C. Satterfield, October 5, 1962; John C. Satterfield to Sylvester C. Smith Jr., October 7, 1962; Alfred J. Schweppe to David Lawrence, October 10, 2, November 2 and 9, 1962; Gibson C. Witherspoon to William B. Spann Jr., October 12, 1962; Meade Whitaker to John C. Satterfield, October 12, 1962; John C. Satterfield to Sylvester C. Smith Jr., October 17 and 19, 1962; Richard E. Wilbourn II to the Board of Governors, December 5 and 17, 1962; and Sylvester C. Smith Jr. to Richard E. Wilbourn II, December 14, 1962, Satterfield Papers, University of Mississippi.

20. Brian Landsberg, "The Kennedy Justice Department's Enforcement of Civil Rights: A View from the Trenches" in *John F. Kennedy, History, Memory, Legacy: An Interdisciplinary Inquiry*, John Delane Williams, Roger G. Waite, and Gregory S. Gordon, eds. (online book, 2010), 1–14; Richard Reeves, *President Kennedy, Profile of Power* (New York: Simon & Schuster, 1993), 356; Bryant, *Bystander*, 111–17, 145, 331–33.

21. Bryant, *Bystander*, 1–4, 361–63, 391–93, 399–407. Reeves, *Kennedy*, 527–28. Nichols, *A Matter of Justice*, 269.

22. *American Bar News, a news bulletin of the American Bar Association* 8, no. 7 (July 15, 1963): 4–5; ABA News Release, July 2, 1963; and Department of Justice, "Statement of Attorney General Robert F. Kennedy before the House Committee on the Judiciary regarding H.R. 7152, The proposed Civil Rights Act of 1963, June 26, 1963," Limbaugh Papers.

23. "Memorandum of meeting of special committee on race relations" July 12, 1963, Washington, DC; and John C. Satterfield, "Shall we Legislate out of fear now and hereafter?" July 9, 1963, Limbaugh Papers; Sherwood Willing Wise, *The Way I See It* (Jackson, MS: self-published, 1996), 79–84; Sherwood W. Wise Jr., email message to the author, July 8, 2009; Joseph Wise, email message to the author, July 9, 2009; Robert P. Wise, email message to the author, July 9, 2009; Stephen N. Limbaugh, email message to the author, July 22, 2009. Apparently, Wise was not liked by the other southern members of the committee. Perhaps these members and Satterfield were responsible for his losing support from Senator James O. Eastland and others for a nomination as judge to the United States Court of Appeals for the Fifth Circuit because of his support for civil rights in Mississippi.

24. Wade F. Baker to Limbaugh, July 22, 1963; Orville Richardson to Limbaugh, July 23, 1963; Roy P. Swanson to Limbaugh, July 26, 1963; Alfred J. Schweppe to committee, July 29, 1963; and Karl C. Williams to Limbaugh, July 31, 1963, Limbaugh Papers; Minutes of the commission meeting held on August 14 and 15, 1970, papers of the Missouri Commission on Human Rights, Missouri State Archives, Jefferson City, Missouri (hereafter cited as Records, Missouri Commission on Human Rights).

25. Alfred J. Schweppe to Sylvester C. Smith Jr., July 31, 1963, Limbaugh Papers.

26. Suggs, *Reflections*, 155–59.

27. "The Final Report of the Committee as Approved by the House of Delegates August 13th, 1963 with but one dissenting vote," Limbaugh Papers; *American Bar Association Journal* 49 (1963): 990.

28. Memorandum of Peter C. Robertson and Forrest P. Carson to Governor Warren E. Hearnes, June 15, 1966; Peter C. Robertson to Hearnes, July 12, 1966; Limbaugh to Hearnes, July 20, 1966, January 6 and 14, 1971, and March 8, 1971; Hearnes to the Secretary of State, July 25, 1966 and March 4, 1971;

Hearnes to Limbaugh, January 8 and 12, 1971; Nancy Dinwiddie to Hearnes, March 2 and 3, 1971; and Richard J. Chamier to Hearnes, February 11, 1970. Governor Warren E. Hearnes Papers, Missouri State Archives, Jefferson City, Missouri; Larry Carp, in discussion with the author, January 19, 2010; Stephen N. Limbaugh Sr., in discussion with the author, August 13, 2007.

29. "Report on the Missouri Commission on Human Rights activities from 1 January 1964 to 30 June 1966." Records, Missouri Commission on Human Rights, Missouri State Archives; Gary R. Kremer, "Presentation [on] the 50th Anniversary of the Missouri Commission on Human Rights, delivered in Jefferson City, Truman Conference Center, January 21, 2009," 12 (hereafter cited as Kremer, "50th Anniversary").

30. Minutes of commission meeting held on September 13, 1966 and memorandum of Margaret Meadows to Peter C. Robertson, September 14, 1966, Records, Missouri Commission on Human Rights, Missouri State Archives; Stephen N. Limbaugh Sr., in discussion with the author, August 13, 2007; Larry Carp, in discussion with the author, January 19, 2010; Harold Whitfield, in discussion with the author, January 29, 2010.

31. Minutes of commission meeting held on 4 November 1966 and *Progress*, March 1970, 1; Records, Missouri Commission on Human Rights, Missouri State Archives; Lewis A. Akenhead, in discussion with the author, February 5, 2010.

32. Lewis A. Akenhead, in discussion with the author, February 5, 2010; Stephen N. Limbaugh Sr., in discussion with the author, February 10, 2010.

33. Minutes of commission meetings held on November 4, 1966 and January 4, 1967; and "Report to the Honorable Warren E. Hearnes Governor State of Missouri: A Survey of Employees of the State of Missouri, 1968," Records, Missouri Commission on Human Rights, Missouri State Archives; Lewis A. Akenhead, in discussion with the author, February 5, 2010.

34. Lewis A. Akenhead, in discussion with the author, February 5, 2010; *Caruthersville Journal*, February 24 and March 3, 1966.

35. Lewis A. Akenhead, in discussion with the author, February 5, 2010; *Caruthersville Journal*, May 5, 1966.

36. *Caruthersville Journal*, April 21, 1966; *Progress*, March 1970, 1; Records, Missouri Commission on Human Rights, Missouri State Archives.

37. *Caruthersville Journal*, April 21, 1966; Lewis A. Akenhead, in discussion with the author, February 5, 2010; Minutes of commission meeting held on 4 November 1966, Records, Missouri Commission on Human Rights, Missouri State Archives.

38. *Caruthersville Journal*, March 14, May 9, and August 1 and 8, 1967; Roy Wilkins, with Tom Mathews, *Standing Fast: The Autobiography of Roy Wilkins* (New York: Da Capo Press, 1994), 318–22.

39. Lewis A. Akenhead, in discussion with the author, February 5, 2010.

40. Ibid.

41. List of cases docketed, December 1967 and January 1969, and minutes of commission meeting held on March 15 and 16, 1968, Records, Missouri Commission on Human Rights, Missouri State Archives; Lewis A. Akenhead, in discussion with the author, February 5, 2010.

42. Memorandum on meeting on southeast Missouri on February 3, 1968 and minutes of commission meeting held on March 15 and 16, 1968, Records, Missouri Commission on Human Rights, Missouri State Archives.

43. Memorandum on meeting on southeast Missouri on February 3, 1968, "Staff Recommendation to Missouri Commission on Human Rights Recommendation for Commission Action to eliminate School Segregation," "Project Report of NAACP Summer Project, 1967," Richard E. Risk to Carl Hutchison, superintendent of Caruthersville schools, December 13, 1967; and minutes of commission meeting held on March 15 and 16, 1968, Records, Missouri Commission on Human Rights, Missouri State Archives; *Caruthersville Journal*, March 17, 1966.

44. Lewis A. Akenhead, in discussion with the author, February 5, 2010; *Caruthersville Journal*, February 24, 1966.

45. Lewis A. Akenhead, in discussion with the author, February 5, 2010; *Caruthersville Journal*, July 28, 1966.

46. *Caruthersville Journal*, April 11 and 25, 1967; Limbaugh to Richard E. Risk, July 25, 1966, Records, Missouri Commission on Human Rights, Missouri State Archives.

47. Lewis A. Akenhead, in discussion with the author, February 5, 2010; Minutes of commission meeting held on May 10 and 11, 1968, Limbaugh to Richard E. Risk, July 25, 1966; "Staff Recommendation to Missouri Commission on Human Rights Recommendation for Commission Action to eliminate School Segregation," and *Progress*, March 1970, 1, 2, 5, Records, Missouri Commission on Human Rights, Missouri State Archives.

48. Lewis A. Akenhead, in discussion with the author, February 5, 2010.

49. Ibid.; *Progress*, March 1970, 1, 2, 5, Records, Missouri Commission on Human Rights, Missouri State Archives.

50. Larry Carp, in discussion with the author, January 19, 2010; *Southeast Missourian*, March 4, 1971.

Chapter Eleven

1. Rush H. Limbaugh Sr., "He Praiseth Her or My Life with My Wife," (unpublished manuscript), 494–98, 555 (hereafter cited as Limbaugh, "Life with My Wife"); *Southeast Missourian*, April 4, 1967.

2. See chapter nine.

3. Limbaugh, "Life with My Wife," 482–84, 490–91; *Southeast Missourian*, December 7, 1964.

4. *Southeast Missourian*, April 22, 1964, September 25, 1965, July 9 and October 4, 1966, and July 4, 1976; Limbaugh, "Life with My Wife," 491–93.

5. Limbaugh, "Life with My Wife," 471–72, 505–6; Stephen N. Limbaugh Sr., in discussion with the author, August 13 and 21, 2007.

6. Stephen N. Limbaugh Sr., in discussion with the author, August 21, 2007; Limbaugh, "Life with My Wife," 472–81, 508–40, 558; Stephen N. Limbaugh Jr., in discussion with the author, March 3, 2010; E. A. Richter, "A Conversation with Rush H. Limbaugh Sr.," *The Missouri Supreme Court Historical Journal*, vol. 5, no. 3 (December 1994), 12 (hereafter cited as Richter, "Conversation with Limbaugh").

7. Limbaugh, "Life with My Wife," 481, 484–85, 487–90, 540, and 545–53; Daniel Limbaugh, email message to the author, May 3, 2010.

8. Limbaugh, "Life with My Wife," 540, 553–69, 570–80; Stephen N. Limbaugh Sr., in discussion with the author, August 21, 2007 and January 9, 2009; Stephen N. Limbaugh Sr., email message to the author, March 2, 2010.

9. Limbaugh, "Life with My Wife," 580–83.

10. Ibid., 583; Mary Limbaugh, in discussion with the author, March 8, 2010; Rush H. Limbaugh III, in discussion with the author, April 14, 2009; Videotape of Rush H. Limbaugh Sr., Rotary Club Speech, May 4, 1987.

11. Daniel B. Limbaugh, email message to the author, April 23, 2009; David Limbaugh, email message to the author, March 3, 2010; Stephen N. Limbaugh Jr., in discussion with the author, March 3, 2010.

12. Lloyd Smith, in discussion with the author, March 1, 2010.

13. Ibid.

14. Stephen N. Limbaugh Jr., in discussion with the author, January 9, 2009, and March 3, 2010.

15. Videotape of Rotary Club Meeting, May 17, 1985; *Southeast Missourian*, October 30, 1983, October 14, 1984, May 19 and 21, 1985, April 22, 1988, and October 4, 1990; Stephen N. Limbaugh Sr., email message to the author, March 2, 2010.

16. Patricia A. Hill, "Recent Additions to the Bench," *St. Louis Bar Journal* 30, no. 2 (Fall 1983): 58; Rush H. Limbaugh Sr., untitled eulogy of Lillie Lucretia Seabaugh, July 22, 1984; Rush H. Limbaugh Sr. to Daniel, Paulette, Nathan, Emily, and Julie Limbaugh, January 13, 1987, Limbaugh Papers; Stephen N. Limbaugh Jr., in discussion with the author, March 3, 2010.

17. David Limbaugh, email message to the author, March 3, 2010.

18. Lloyd Smith, in discussion with the author, March 1, 2010; Stephen N. Limbaugh, email message to the author, March 5, 2010; Garry Wills, *Lincoln at Gettysburg: The Words that Remade America* (New York: Simon & Schuster, 1992), 24, 32–36.

19. Stephen N. Limbaugh Sr., in discussion with the author, August 13, 2007; Stephen N. Limbaugh Jr., in discussion with the author, January 9, 2009; David

Limbaugh, in discussion with the author, January 9, 2009; Glenda Wunderlich, in discussion with the author, April 14, 2009; Rush H. Limbaugh III, in discussion with the author, April 14, 2009; Larry Carp, in discussion with the author, January 13, 2010.

20. Stephen N. Limbaugh Sr., in discussion with the author, December 31, 2008; Rush H. Limbaugh III, in discussion with the author, April 14, 2009; Stephen N. Limbaugh Jr., in discussion with the author, January 9, 2009.

21. Richter, "Conversation with Limbaugh," 1, 9, 13.

22. Videotaped comments presented as part of the annual Joseph H. Low Jr. Lecture from the Department of Communication Studies at Southeast Missouri State University, January 19, 1996; Glenda Wunderlich, in discussion with the author, April 14, 2009; Mary Limbaugh, in discussion with the author, March 8, 2010; Rush H. Limbaugh III, in discussion with the author, April 14, 2009; Stephen N. Limbaugh Sr., in discussion with the author, March 17, 2010.

23. "A Service of Death and Resurrection for Rush Hudson Limbaugh Sr.," April 11, 1996; *Southeast Missourian*, April 12, 1996; Larry Carp, in discussion with the author, January 13, 2010.

24. *New York Times*, June 24, 1996; *Washington Post*, June 24, 1996; Lloyd Smith, in discussion with the author, March 1, 2010.

25. *Washington Post*, November 27, 1996; Congresswoman Jo Ann Emerson, in discussion with the author, February 4, 2010; Transcript of "Rush Hudson Limbaugh Sr., United States Courthouse, Cape Girardeau, Missouri Dedication Ceremony," October 6, 2008, 7, 24–55; *Southeast Missourian*, February 5, 1989; Stephen N. Limbaugh Jr., in discussion with the author, January 9, 2009; Ian Scott-Kilvert, trans., *The Age of Alexander: Nine Greek Lives by Plutarch* (New York: Penguin Books, 1977), 189; Romans12:1–3 (King James Version).

Bibliography

Primary Sources

American Bar Association News Release, July 2, 1963; and Department of Justice, "Statement of Attorney General Robert F. Kennedy before the House Committee on the Judiciary regarding H.R. 7152, The proposed Civil Rights Act of 1963, June 26, 1963."

Alameda (CA) *Times-Star*, 1934.

Anna (IL) *Gazette-Democrat*, 1941.

Articles of Impeachment Relative to Larry Brunk, prepared and presented by the select committee of the House of Representatives of the State of Missouri. Jefferson City, MO: Botz Printing and Stationery Company, 1931.

Athenaean Literary Society Records, 1842–1925. Western Historical Manuscript Collections, State Historical Society of Missouri, Columbia.

Atlanta Constitution, 1960.

Boulder (CO) *Morning News*, April 1915.

Capaha Arrow (Cape Girardeau, MO), 1911–1912.

Caruthersville (MO) *Journal*, 1966.

Chicago Daily Tribune, 1935.

Columbia (MO) *Tribune*, May 1914.

Daily Texan (Austin, TX), April 18, 1914.

Death certificate of Marguerite V. Limbaugh, website of the Secretary of State of Missouri, www.sos.mo.gov/archives/resources/deathcertificates/.

Death certificate of Susan Francis Presnell Limbaugh, website of the Secretary of State, Missouri, www.sos.mo.gov/archives/resources/deathcertificates/.

Deccan Chronicle (Secunderabad, India), 1958.

Governor Warren E. Hearnes Papers. Missouri State Archives, Jefferson City.

Greenville (MO) *Sun*, 1949.

Harvard Crimson, February 1915.

Henry S. Caulfield Papers. Western Historical Manuscripts Collection, State Historical Society of Missouri, Columbia.

Jackson (MO) *Cash-Book*, 1931.

Jefferson City (MO) *Capitol News*, 1931.

John C. Satterfield/American Bar Association Collection. University of Mississippi, Oxford.

Kansas City Star, 1931, 1994.

Laurance M. Hyde Papers. Western Historical Manuscripts Collection, State Historical Society of Missouri, Columbia.

Limbaugh, Rush H., Sr. "Diary of Rush H. Limbaugh of Trip to India on Mission for State Department, November 1958–January 1959," November 11, 1958, unpublished manuscript.

———. "Memoranda Diary Political," unpublished manuscript.

———. "A record of events in connection with our trip to Minneapolis to attend the American Bar Association meeting in August 1924 [1923] as made from day to day during our journey," unpublished typed transcript of diary.

———. "Report of Rush H. Limbaugh of his Itinerary and Activities Serving as a United States Specialist, from his home in Cape Girardeau, Missouri, beginning November 2, 1958, to India and Return to Washington D. C., January 16, 1959 under United States government Grant Authorization No. 381–9, Obligation No. 787, dated October 21, 1958, issued by Martha G. Geesa, Acting Chief, American Specialists Branch, Leaders in Specialists Division, Activity No. 1878, Appropriation Symbol 1991128, Allotment No. 9M-1069."

———."Report of Rush H. Limbaugh, Special Commissioner," 3, in State of Missouri, *On the Information of J. E. Taylor, Attorney General v. Armour & Company*, in the Supreme Court of Missouri, Missouri State Archives, Jefferson City.

———. "Year Book 1934," unpublished diary.

Manley O. Hudson Papers. Harvard Law Library, Cambridge, MA.

New York Times, 1996.

Records, Missouri Commission on Human Rights, Missouri State Archives, Jefferson City.

"Report and Recommendations of the Special Investigating Committee Relative to Larry Brunk, State Treasurer Made to the House of Representatives of the State of Missouri, Fifty-sixth General Assembly, Submitted Tuesday, February 17, 1931" in *Appendix to the House and Senate Journals of the Fifty-sixth General Assembly, State of Missouri*, vol. 3. Jefferson City: n.p., 1931.

Rush H. Limbaugh Sr. Papers. In the possession of Stephen N. Limbaugh Jr., Cape Girardeau, Missouri.

St. Louis Globe-Democrat, 1931.

St. Louis Post-Dispatch, 1931, 1935, 1994.

St. Louis Star, 1931, 1935.

St. Louis Times, 1931.

Salina (KS) *Journal*, 1935.

Southeast Missourian (Cape Girardeau, MO), 1918–1919, 1923, 1932, 1935, 1941, 1942, 1943, 1946, 1964, 1965, 1966, 1967, 1976, 1983, 1984, 1985, 1988, 1989, 1990, 1996, 2006, and 2009.

State Normal Bulletin (Emporia, KS), 1912.

Time, 1935, 1937, and 1941.

Transcript of "Rush Hudson Limbaugh Sr., United States Courthouse, Cape Girardeau, Missouri Dedication Ceremony," October 6, 2008.

Videotaped comments presented as part of the annual Joseph H. Low Jr. Lecture from the Department of Communication Studies at Southeast Missouri State University, January 19, 1996. In the possession of Stephen N. Limbaugh Jr., Cape Girardeau, Missouri.

Videotape of Rush H. Limbaugh Sr., Rotary Club Speech, May 4, 1987. In the possession of Stephen N. Limbaugh Jr., Cape Girardeau, Missouri.

Washington Post, 1996.

Legal Briefs and Summaries

Dianne Sue DeLay, by James Delay and Marjorie Delay, Her Next Friends Plaintiff Respondent v. Jase M. Ward, Defendant Appellant, appeal from the Circuit Court of Stoddard County, Bloomfield, Springfield Court of Appeals, April 1953 session.

In the Matter of the Impeachment of Judith K. Moriarty, Supreme Court of Missouri, 902, S.W. 2d 273.

In matter of Sturdivant Bank, Cape Girardeau, Missouri, Clyde A. Vandivort, Receiver for Cape Girardeau Bridge Company v. Sturdivant Bank, a corporation, Cape Girardeau, Missouri, St. Louis Court of Appeals, October 1933 Term.

Limbaugh, Rush H., Sr., *Anna Ware, an Infant, by Mary Ware, Her Next Friend, Petitioner v. Ludwig O. Muench and Nelle Tipton Muench, His Wife, Wilfred Jones, Helen Berroyer, Rebecca Winner, and Carl M. Dubinsky, Respondents*, 232 Mo. App. 41.

Limbaugh, Rush H., Sr., James A. Finch, and James A. Barks, "Respondent's statement, brief, and argument in *City of Cape Girardeau v. Herminia Hunze et al.*," Supreme Court of Missouri, October 1925 term. Cape Girardeau: Missourian Printing Company, nd.

Limbaugh, Rush H., Sr., William M. Morgan, and Charles G. Revelle, "Statement, brief, and argument for plaintiff in *Oscar Fuller, Respondent v. Charles R. Presnell, Appellant,*" an appeal from the Circuit Court of Bollinger County, Springfield Court of Common Pleas, March 1920 term. St. Louis: St. Louis Law Printing Co., nd.

——. "Abstract of record, statement, and brief in *Charles R. Presnell v. Argus Cox, John S. Farrington, John H. Bradley, Judges of the Springfield Court of Appeals,*" Supreme Court of Missouri, October 1921 term. St. Louis: St. Louis Law Printing Co., nd.

Limbaugh, Rush H., Sr. and Benson C. Hardesty, "Respondent's statement, brief, and argument in *Dewey Robison, by next friend v. Floesch Construction Company, a corporation,*" Supreme Court of Missouri, April 1921 term. Cape Girardeau: Missourian Print, nd.

Madden, John G. *Before the Senate of the State of Missouri In Re: The Matter of the Articles of Impeachment Relative to Larry Brunk, Treasurer of the State of Missouri–Plea and Motion of Respondent Larry Brunk,* filed April 2, 1931.

——. *Before the Senate of the State of Missouri In Re: The Matter of the Articles of Impeachment Relative to Larry Brunk, Treasurer of the State of Missouri–Motion of Respondent, Larry Brunk, to Quash and Dismiss the Articles of Impeachment Aforesaid,* filed May 2, 1931.

Missouri Pacific Railway Co. v. Lasca, see *Southeastern Reporter, April 2–May 28, 1921,* vol. 106. St. Paul, MN: West Publishing Company, 1921, 910–12.

Oliver, Arthur L., and Allen L. Oliver, "Abstract of the record on behalf of the appellant in *Dewey Robison, by next friend v. Floesch Construction Company, a corporation,*" Supreme Court of Missouri, April 1921 term. Cape Girardeau: Missourian Print, nd.

——. "Appellant's reply brief in *Dewey Robison, by next friend v. Floesch Construction Company, a corporation,*" Supreme Court of Missouri, April 1921 term. Cape Girardeau: Missourian Print, nd.

Rich, Burdett A., and M. Blair Wailes, eds. *American Law Reports Annotated,* vol. 20. Rochester and Northport, New York and San Francisco, California, The Lawyers Co-operative Publishing Company; Edward Thompson Company; and Bancroft-Whitney Company, 1922.

State e rel. Dalton v. Miles Laboratories, Inc., 282 S.W. 2d, 564.

State ex inf. Stratton Shartel, Attorney-General, Petitioner v. Larry Brunk, State Treasurer, 326 *Missouri Reports* 1930, 1181–89.

State ex rel. Donnell v. Searcy and State ex rel. Donnell v. Osborn, 347 Mo. 469 and 1052.

United States v. Henry Chisem, United States v. Elgie Morris, United States v. Isaac Taylor Quinn, United States v. Vernon Lemons, and United States v.

Richard Leonard Riley, tried in the Eastern District of Missouri, Southeastern Division. National Archives and Records Administration, Central Plains Region, Kansas City, Missouri.

Secondary Sources

Books and Manuscripts

Alexander, Thomas E. *The Wings of Change: The Army Air Force Experience in Texas During World War II*. Abilene, TX: McWhiney Foundation Press, McMurry University, 2003.

Allen, Frederick Allen. *Only Yesterday: An Informal History of the 1920s*. New York: Harper & Row, 1964.

Argersinger, Peter H. *The Limits of Agrarian Radicalism: Western Populism and American Politics*. Lawrence: University Press of Kansas, 1995.

"Before the Senate of the State of Missouri In Re: The Matter of the Articles of Impeachment Relative to Larry Brunk, Treasurer of the State of Missouri," a transcript for the impeachment trial from Monday, May 18, 1931 to June 12, 1931, in *Appendix, House and Senate Journals, 56th General Assembly*, vol. 4, Impeachment Proceedings. Jefferson City, MO: n.p. 1931.

Berger, Raoul. *Impeachment: the Constitutional Problems*. Cambridge, MA: Harvard University Press, 1973.

Beveridge, Albert J. *"Pass Prosperity Around": Speech of Albert J. Beveridge, Temporary Chairman of Progressive National Convention*. New York: Stoddard-Sutherland Press, 1912.

Brownell, Herbert with John P. Burke. *Advising Ike: The Memoirs of Attorney General Herbert Brownell*. Lawrence: University Press of Kansas, 1993.

Bryant, Nicholas A. *The Bystander: John F. Kennedy and the Struggle for Black Equality*. New York: Basic Books, 2006.

Buchanan, A. Russell. *The United States and World War II*, vol. 2. New York: Harper & Row, 1964.

Chace, James. *1912: Wilson, Roosevelt, Taft & Debs–the Election that Changed the Country*. New York: Simon & Schuster, 2004.

Davis, Charles Henry. *Party Platforms: Progressive, Democratic, Republican in Deadly Parallel*. New York: Stoddard-Sutherland Press, 1912.

Dunne, Gerald T. *The Missouri Supreme Court: from Dred Scott to Nancy Cruzan*. Columbia: University of Missouri Press, 1993.

Eisenhower, Dwight D. *Waging Peace, 1956–1961*. Garden City, NY: Doubleday, 1965.

Emanuel, Anne S. *Elbert Parr Tuttle: Chief Jurist of the Civil Rights Revolution*. Athens: University of Georgia Press, 2011.

Fratcher, William F. *The Law Barn: A Brief History of the School of Law, University of Missouri-Columbia*. Columbia: School of Law, University of Missouri-Columbia, 1978.

Grane, William Leighton. *The Passing of War: A Study in Things that Make for Peace*. London: Macmillan and Co., Ltd., 1914.

Grant, Ulysses S. *Memoirs and Selected Letters, Personal Memoirs of U. S. Grant: Selected letters 1839–1865*. New York: Viking Press, 1990.

Greene, Lorenzo Johnston, Gary R. Kremer, and Antonio Frederick Holland. *Missouri's Black Heritage*. Columbia: University of Missouri Press, 1993.

Griffin, John Howard. *Black Like Me*. New York: Signet, 1962.

Havig, Alan R. *A Centennial History of the State Historical Society of Missouri, 1898–1998*. Columbia: University of Missouri Press, 1998.

Hook, Sidney. *Out of Step: An Unquiet Life in the 20ᵗʰ Century* New York: Harper & Row, 1987.

Kennedy, Paul. *The Rise and Fall of Great Powers: Economic Change and Military Conflict from 1500 to 2000*. New York: Random House, 1987.

Kirkendall, Richard S. *A History of Missouri*, vol. 5. Columbia: University of Missouri Press, 1986.

Kirschten, Ernest. *Catfish and Crystal*, foreword by Glen E. Holt. Garden City, New York: Doubleday, 1960; St. Louis: Patrice Press, 1989.

Koch, Adrienne, and William Peden, eds. *The Life and Selected Writings of Thomas Jefferson*. New York: Random House, 1944; reprint 1972.

Limbaugh, Rush H. Sr. "Firm of Hardesty & Limbaugh," unpublished and undated manuscript.

——. "He Praiseth Her or My Life with My Wife," unpublished manuscript.

——."My Experience as a Special Commissioner of the St. Louis Court of Appeals," unpublished manuscript.

——. *The Peril of American Politics*. Cape Girardeau: Missouri State Normal School, 1911.

——. *Pleading, Practice, Procedure, and Forms in Missouri: A Treatise on the Law Prevailing in Missouri and a Helpful Guide in the Application of the Law Through the Processes of Pleading, Practice, and Procedure in all Branches of the Judiciary and Before all Agencies of the State Government in all Kinds of Actions and Proceedings*, vol. 1. St. Louis: Thomas Law Book Company, December 1935.

——. *Political Ideals and Industrial Progress*. Cape Girardeau: Missouri State Normal School, 1912.

Lincoln, Abraham. *The Collected Works of Abraham Lincoln*, vol. 3, Roy P Basler, ed. New Brunswick, NJ: Rutgers University Press, 1959.

Nichols, David A. *A Matter of Justice: Eisenhower and the Beginning of the Civil Rights Revolution*. New York: Simon & Schuster, 2007.

Online Family Search Pedigree Resource of the Church of Jesus Christ of Latter-Day Saints, October 29, 2008.

Palmer, Bruce. *"Man over Money": The Southern Populist Critique of American Capitalism.* Chapel Hill: University of North Carolina Press, 1980.

Penick, James Lal, Jr. *The New Madrid Earthquakes, Revised Edition.* Columbia: University of Missouri Press, 1981.

Penn, Dorothy and Floyd C. Shoemaker, eds. *The Messages and Proclamations of the Governors of the State of Missouri,* vol. 13. Columbia: The State Historical Society of Missouri, 1947.

Podhoretz, Norman. *Ex-Friends: Falling out with Allen Ginsberg, Lionel and Diana Trilling, Lillian Hellman, Hannah Arendt, and Norman Mailer.* San Francisco: Encounter Books, 2000.

Polenberg, Richard. *Fighting Faiths: The Abrams Case, the Supreme Court, and Free Speech.* Ithaca, NY: Cornell University Press, 1987.

Reeves, Richard. *President Kennedy, Profile of Power.* New York: Simon & Schuster, 1993.

Roosevelt, Theodore. *Theodore Roosevelt's Confession of Faith before the Progressive National Convention, August 6, 1912.* New York: Stoddard-Sutherland Press, 1912.

Scott-Kilvert, Ian, trans. *The Age of Alexander: Nine Greek Lives by Plutarch.* New York: Penguin Books, 1977

Seligman, Edwin R. A. *Essays in Taxation.* New York and London: Macmillan Company, 1897.

Shlaes, Amity. *The Forgotten Man: A New History of the Great Depression.* New York: HarperCollins, 2007.

Steeples, Douglas, and David O., Whitten, *Democracy in Desperation: The Depression of 1893.* Westport, CT: Greenwood Press, 1998.

Strachan, Hew. *The First World War.* New York: Penguin Books, 2003.

Suggs, George C., Jr., ed., *Rush Hudson Limbaugh and his Times: Reflections on a Life Well Lived.* Cape Girardeau: Southeast Missouri State University Press, 2003.

Wilkins, Roy, with Tom Mathews. *Standing Fast: The Autobiography of Roy Wilkins.* New York: Da Capo Press, 1994.

Wills, Garry. *Lincoln at Gettysburg: The Words that Remade America.* New York: Simon & Schuster, 1992.

Wise, Sherwood Willing. *The Way I See It.* Jackson, MS: self-published, 1996.

Articles

Altman, James M. "Review: Modern Litigators and Lawyer-Statesmen," *Yale Law Journal* 103, no. 4 (January 1994): 1031–71.

American Bar Association, Section of Real Property, Probate and Trust Law, Pro-
    ceedings 3 (1948): vii, 89; 4 (1950): 3, 118–31; 7 (1952): v–vi; 8 (1953): v;
    and 9 (1954): v.
American Bar News, a news bulletin of the American Bar Association 8, no. 7
    (July 15, 1963): 4–5.
American Bar Association Journal 40 (1954): 1004–5.
———. 45, no. 10 (October 1959): 363–64, 1102–3.
———. 47, no. 10 (October 1961): 1040.
———. 49 (1963): 990.
"Athenaean Column," *University of Missouri Alumni Magazine*, June 1915, 273.
Atkinson, Thomas E. Review of *Pleading, Practice, Procedure, and Forms in
    Missouri*, volume 1, *Missouri Law Review* 2 (January 1937): 121–23.
———. Review of *Pleading, Practice, Procedure, and Forms in Missouri*, volume
    2, *Missouri Law Review* 4 (November 1939): 475–77.
Baker, John D. "The Character of the Congressional Revolution of 1910," *Jour-
    nal of American History* 60, no. 3, (December 1973): 679–91.
Benson, Joseph Fred. "A Brief Legal History of Impeachment in Missouri," *Uni-
    versity of Missouri at Kansas City Law Review* 75 (Winter 2006): 354–61.
Bickel, Alexander M. "The Original Understanding and the Segregation Deci-
    sion" *Harvard Law Review* 69, no. 1 (November 1955): 1–65.
Dudziak, Mary L. "Desegregation as a Cold War Imperative," *Stanford Law Re-
    view* 41, no. 1 (November 1988): 61–120.
Eagles, Charles W. "The Closing of Mississippi Society: Will Campbell, 'The
    $64,000 Question,' and Religious Emphasis Week at the University of
    Mississippi" *Journal of Southern History* 67, no. 2 (May 2001): 331–72.
Falcone, David. "The Missouri State Highway Patrol as a Representative Mod-
    el," *Policing: An International Journal of Police Strategies and Management*
    24, no. 4, (2001): 587–88.
Hill, Patricia A. "Recent Additions to the Bench," *St. Louis Bar Journal* 30, no.
    2, (Fall 1983): 58.
Hoffman, Charles. "The Depression of the Nineties," *Journal of Economic His-
    tory* 16, no. 2 (June 1956): 137–64.
Landsberg, Brian. "The Kennedy Justice Department's Enforcement of Civil
    Rights: A View from the Trenches" in *John F. Kennedy, History, Memo-
    ry, Legacy: An Interdisciplinary Inquiry*, John Delane Williams, Roger G.
    Waite, and Gregory S. Gordon, eds. Online book (2010): 1–14.
Lawrence, Eric D., Forrest Maltzman, and Paul J. Wahlbeck, "The Politics of
    Speaker Cannon's Committee Assignments," *American Journal of Political
    Science* 45, no. 3 (July 2001): 551–62.
Leuchtenburg, William E. "When the People Spoke, What did they say?: the
    Election of 1936 and the Ackerman Thesis," *Yale Law Journal* 108, no. 8
    (1999): 2077–2114.

Limbaugh, Rush H., Sr. "The Adoption of Children in Missouri," *Missouri Law Review* 2 (June 1937): 300–12.

———. "Historic Origins of Anti-Trust Legislation," *Missouri Law Review* 18, no. 3 (June 1953): 215–18.

———. "Impeachment," *Missouri Bar Journal* 2, no. 7 (July 1931): 5–7.

———. "The Public Duty of the American Lawyer," *Missouri Law Review* 20, no. 3 (June 1955): 223–55.

———. "The Sources and Development of Probate Law," *Washington University Law Quarterly* 4 (December 1956): 419–47.

———."The Work of the Missouri Supreme Court for 1937 [through 1942] Extraordinary Legal Remedies," *Missouri Law Review* 3 (November 1938): 383–92; 4 (November 1939): 389–406; 5 (November 1940): 433–45; 6 (November 1941): 432–47; 7 (November 1942): 377–95; and 8 (November 1943): 247–61.

McConnell, Michael W. "Originalism and the Desegregation Decisions" *Virginia Law Review* 81, no. 4 (May 1995): 947–1140.

Mehrotra, Ajay K. "Envisioning the Modern American Fiscal State: Progressive-Era Economists and the Intellectual Foundations of the U.S. Income Tax," *UCLA Law Review* 52 (2005): 1793–1865.

Morris, Willie. "Yazoo . . . Notes on Survival" *Harper's*, June 1970, 43–64.

Richter, E. A. "A Conversation with Rush H. Limbaugh, Sr." *Missouri Supreme Court Historical Journal* 5, no. 3 (December 1994): 1–14.

Schweppe, Alfred J. "Enforcement of Federal Decrees: A 'Recurrence to Fundamental Principles,'" *American Bar Association Journal* 44, no. 2 (February 1958): 113–16.

Silver, James W. "Mississippi: the Closed Society" *Journal of Southern History* 30, no. 1 (February 1964): 3–34.

Stone, Julius. "Manley Hudson: Campaigner and Teacher of International Law," *Harvard Law Review* 74, no. 2 (December 1960): 215–25.

"Won and Lost in Debate," *University of Missouri Alumni Magazine*, April 1915, 211.

Index

Memphis, Tennessee, 69, 139, 140, 143, 173, 212
Meredith, James, 200-201
Meredith, Willis H., 98, 104, 105, 121-22
Meridian, Mississippi, 167
Messina, Sicily, 184
Mesplay, Anne. *See* Anne Limbaugh
Mesplay, James, 184
Mesplay, Lucille, 184
Mexico, 42
Middle East, 167, 183
Miller, Ben R., 199
Millersville High School, 16-17
Millsaps College, 200
Minneapolis, Minnesota, 58, 59, 62, 77, 146
Mississippi, 167, 193, 194, 196, 200, 203, 208
Mississippi River, 2, 3, 15, 56, 57, 157, 162, 228
Missouri Advisory Committee, 210-11
Missouri Bar (state lawyer association), ix, xi, xiv, 69, 175, 178, 179, 180, 204, 223, 224, 225, 227
Missouri Bar Journal, 124
Missouri Board of Health, 131
Missouri Commission on Human Rights, xiv, 204, 206, 209, 211, 216, 218, 219, 221
Missouri Council of Trial Lawyers, 227
Missouri Court of Appeals, 177
Missouri Department of Health, 128
Missouri Electric Works, 224
Missouri ex rel. Gaines v. Canada, Registrar, 197
Missouri Fair Employment Practices Act, 208-9
Missouri Highway Department, 209
Missouri Hotel (Jefferson City), 70
Missouri Labor Department, 208
Missouri Law Review, 158, 159, 177
Missouri legislature, 69-81, 98-126, 127, 128, 129, 130, 159, 163, 176, 178, 180, 207, 208, 220

Missouri National Guard, 43, 72
Missouri Pacific Railroad Company v. Lasca, 52
Missouri counties: **Bollinger,** 32; **Cape Girardeau,** 70, 169, 172; **Dunklin**, 160; **Johnson**, 73, 102; **Nodaway**, 72-73; **Pemiscot**, 215; **Stoddard**, 160; **Wayne**, 159, 160, 161, 162, 165
Missouri towns and cities: **Aurora**, 117, 118, 119; **Cape Girardeau**, ix, 2, 17, 19, 20, 21, 22, 23, 25, 28, 29, 30-34, 40-47, 52-53, 55-57, 59, 61-62, 65-66, 69, 71, 74-75, 79, 82, 105, 110, 127-35, 142-43, 151, 155, 157, 160, 163-64, 167-69, 172-74, 180-82, 190-91, 208, 218, 220-22, 224-25, 228-29; **Caruthersville**, 209, 210, 211, 212; **Charleston**, 46, 211; **Coldwater**, 160; **Columbia**, 29, 30, 32, 33, 34, 36, 40, 43, 75, 105, 157, 159, 175, 180, 183; **Greenbrier**, 52; **Greenville**, 159, 160; **Hornersville**, 169, 172; **Howardsville**, 211; **Ironton**, 128; **Jackson**, 6-7, 20, 44, 70, 74, 157, 172, 182; **Jefferson City**, 40, 70, 78, 79, 100, 102, 105, 107, 113, 120, 164, 175, 177, 208, 213, 218, 223; **Kansas City**, ix, 31, 71, 72, 79, 80, 113, 123, 155, 163, 175, 204, 212, 213, 227; **Kennett**, 181, 208, 211-13; **McCarty**, 209; **Malden**, 214; **Marble Hill**, 14, 49, 50; **Marquand**, 15; **Maryville**, 72; **Mexico**, 139; **Millersville**, 12, 16, 17, 20, 52; **Morehouse**, 43; **New Madrid**, 3; **Perryville**, 34; **St. Joseph**, 72, 175; **St. Louis**, ix, 10, 15, 16, 20, 31, 32, 56, 57, 59, 70, 73, 79, 80, 81, 101, 114, 120, 128, 133-40, 142-43, 146, 149-53, 155, 157-59, 163-64, 166, 173, 175-76, 180, 182, 184, 189, 196, 218, 227; **St. Mary**, 224; **Sedgewickville**, 8, 15, 18-22, 27, 32-34, 39-40, 184; **Sikeston**, 25, 69, 191, 208, 212, 213, 217; **Smelterville**, 130; **Springfield**, 28, 50, 75, 104, 156, 175;